THE PROBLEMS OF SOUTH SUDAN

*Did Independence
Come to South Sudan
A Bit Too Prematurely?*

PETER ADWOK NYABA

The publisher wishes to acknowledge and thank Dr. Douglas H. Johnson for his invaluable help and support for Africa World Books and its mission of preserving and promoting African cultural and literary traditions and history. Dr. Johnson and fellow historians have been instrumental in ensuring that African people remain connected to their past and their identity. Africa World Books is proud to carry on this mission.

Copyright © 2024 Peter Adwok Nyaba

All rights reserved. It is illegal to reproduce, duplicate or transmit any part of this book in either electronic means or printed format. Recording of this publication is strictly prohibited. No part of this publication may be reproduced, stored in a retrieval system, or transmitted, in any form, or by any means, electronic, mechanical, photocopying, recording or otherwise, without the prior permission of the publishers.

ISBN: 9780975630426

This book is sold subject to the conditions that it shall not, by way of trade or otherwise, be lent, re-sold, hired out or otherwise circulated without the publisher's prior consent in any form of binding or cover other than in which it is published and without a similar condition including the condition being imposed on the subsequent purchaser.

Cover design: Moses Orlando
Typesetting and layout: Africa World Books
Unit 3, 57 Frobisher St, Osborne Park, WA 6017
P.O. Box 1106 Osborne Park, WA 6916

To the eternal Memory
of
Dong Samuel Luak

CONTENTS

Preface vii

Introduction xvii

1: The Republic of the Sudan:
Before and After Partition 1

2: The Southern Region [1972-1983]
Southern Sundanese's First Ever Experience
with Power 95

3. The Sudan People's Liberation Movement /Army:
The Revolution that Inspired Fear and Despair 175

4. International Humanitarian Intervention
in Southern Sudan 283

5: The Republic of South Sudan:
A Shadow State in the Hands of Business Cartels
and Community Elders 319

6: The IGAD Peace Process on South Sudan
The 'Imposed' Agreement on Resolution of
the Conflict in South Sudan (ARCISS)
The Revitalized Agreement on the Resolution
of the Conflict in South Sudan (R-ARCSS)   371
7: Living Among the Giants in a Weak State   423
8: Did Independence Come to South Sudan
a Bit Too Prematurely?   447

Appendix: List of South Sudan Nationalities   *481*
References   *483*
Index   *487*

PREFACE

The people of South Sudan were recently treated to an ecumenical pilgrimage that entailed the Holy Father, Pope Francis, the Archbishop of Canterbury, and the Moderator of the General Assembly of the Church of Scotland. This was an experience, first of its kind, and many ordinary people hooked their hopes for peace in the country on this ecumenical pilgrimage. They had spent ten out of twelve years of independence in great tribulations and immense trepidation as a result of the communal conflicts, civil wars, floods, droughts, and economic hardships. South Sudanese are highly spiritual; they believe in miracles and therefore. they viewed the papal visit as a form of divine intervention. They walked all the way from Rumbek, Bor, Yambio and Torit to Juba to be witness of the interdenominational prayers at Dr. John Garang Memorial Grounds.

The Ecumenical visit and the interdenominational prayers 2023 were a follow up of similar interdenominational prayers for peace in South Sudan conducted in the Vatican in April 2019 in which the Pope invited the leaders, signatories to the September 2018 revitalized agreement on the resolution of the conflict in South Sudan (R-ARCSS). Pope Francis performed a rare feet-kissing exercise of the four leaders: President Salva Kiir Mayardit, Dr. Riek Machar Teny-Dhurgon, then first vice president Gen. Taban Deng Gai and Mama Rebecca Nyandeng de Mabior. Many South Sudanese people believed, and wrongly so, that the feet-kissing would prick on the leaders' conscience to enable the implementation of R-ARCSS precede without a hitch. The events in the Vatican and the papal feet-kissing seemed not to have profound impact on the leaders; only President Salva Kiir and Gen. Taban Deng returned to Juba, while Dr. Riek Machar and Rebecca Nyandeng each took different flight to Khartoum and Nairobi respectively, to the chagrin of the masses who were expecting immediate and unhindered start of the implementation of the peace agreement.

This apparent dispersal of the leaders put on-hold the implementation processes of the peace agreement. There were no political consultation between the political leaders hence it was impossible for them to build consensus on some of intricate issues in the implementation process. Only President Kiir had all the threads in his hands, and therefore, the one to determine when and what process in the peace agreement implementation could occur. Then, ten months later, on 20th February 2020, President Salva Kiir appointed Riek Machar the first vice president, and the wheels of R-ARCSS implementation then started to move albeit slowly and selectively.

THE PROBLEMS OF SOUTH SUDAN

A casual spectator of the South Sudan political landscape would ask why the leaders remained hesitant to implement the agreement they voluntarily signed; what could be the sticking point. It is not difficult to discern and delineate the sticking point. The difficulties afflicting the country stem from a power struggle between President Salva Kiir Mayardit and his deputy Dr. Riek Machar Teny-Dhurgon; a power struggle whose parameters are personal rather than ideological, but which IGAD Mediator's introduction of the power-sharing formula exacerbated and rendered more complex. Moreover, the peace agreement had no stringent outside enforcing mechanism; it depended on the good will of the same leaders. For instance, President Salva Kiir could have rejected the peace agreement (2015) that imposed Riek Machar as his first vice president, and no power in the region could override his sovereign decision. I wished he had done that, for this could have perhaps forced a rethinking of the power-sharing modality the IGAD mediators adopted as the resolution to the conflict. President Kiir only refused to sign alongside the other parties leaders to underscore his disdain for the imposition of Riek Machar. It's a truism that IGAD Special Envoys had erred in their prognosis of the conflict, its triggers and drivers otherwise they could have borrowed a leaf from other experiences. The problem of President Salva Kiir was not about power-sharing *per se*; in Kiir's perception of power in South Sudan, it is neither an institution that is impersonal nor is it shared. However, it could only be delegated to a loyal colleague like James Wai Igga, and not to a hostile competitor like Dr. Riek Machar, Pagan Amum

Okiech or Rebecca Nyandeng de Mabior. Kiir's problem, therefore, was that he resented Dr. Riek Machar and therefore didn't want IGAD to impose on him leaders he did not want.

However, on rejecting the IGAD imposed agreement, President Salva Kiir didn't have a better alternative to the negotiated agreement (BATNA). Thus, the twenty-six reservation points he presented on signing the peace document a week later did not address the cardinal problems in the conflict and therefore the IGAD imposed (ARCISS) stuck. This placed South Sudan in a dilemma. President Salva Kiir signed the IGAD imposed ARCISS fully aware that he would sabotage the implementation of its provisions save that on the formation of the transitional government of national unity (TGONU); this was one horn of the dilemma. The other horn was Dr. Riek Machar's acceptance of the ARCISS just to become Kiir's first vice president. He knew very well that the two of them couldn't form a stable working team; With Riek Machar as first vice president, it was obvious that President Salva Kiir could return the country to war. IGAD's imposition of Riek Machar is at the root of Kiir's reluctance to implement ARCISS, its eventual collapse in July 2016 and his current procrastination in the implementation of the R-ARCSS.

President Salva Kiir has grown paranoid about his presidency that he could easily return the country to war than lose the presidency never mind whether South Sudan and its people dither and waste away. This is the gist of the problem; and that exactly was what the IGAD mediators and international interlocuters in their rush to resolve the conflict in South Sudan failed to realize;

they went for the quick fix in form of power-sharing, this led to the intensification of the war and its escalation to hitherto peaceful areas in Equatoria and western Bahr el Ghazal. It also led to the proliferation of political and armed opposition to the regime creating new political actors and split the old ones setting in fractal politics – the true picture of chaos. The power-sharing formula inadvertently created a dysfunctional South Sudan state; fragmented the institutions to accommodate political actors never mind their suitability in terms of qualification and experience; heightened political patronage and erosion of the state legitimacy because of the divided loyalty and allegiance. And at the end of all this South Sudan is governed on the basis of a perpetual transitional arrangements the leaders now find appropriate to keep themselves in power, while nothing functions.

The people of South Sudan are in a state of profound fear, despair and uncertainty about the future given the inability of the state to meet its obligations; as a result, they are organizing as communities and arming themselves. In fact, some communities are armed better the South Sudan Defence Force (SSDP), which itself is paralyzed by ethnic fragmentation within its ranks and file. The failure or deliberate refusal to depoliticize, de-ethnicize, professionalize and transform the SPLA into a professional national armed forces has paid back negatively. In the recent Nuer white army attack on the Chollo Kingdom, the Nuer SSPDF commanding officer in Oweci, Malakal, Wau and Kodok refused to counter the attackers on account of not having received orders from the SSPDF GH/QS in Juba. Similarly, the Dinka Bor officers refused to face their kith and kins, the pastoralist, who massacred innocent farmers in Kajo-Keji; the Governor of Jonglei State, Mr. Denay Chagour, welcomed and fêted the Nuer Lou white army returning from the incursion from Pibor Independent Administrative Area where they massacred Murle women, children and the elderly. This was an expression of divided loyalty.

South Sudan is bubbling everywhere with insecurity, community resource-based conflicts, acute economic and food insecurity, natural disasters of floods, droughts and diseases. The weakness and paralysis of the armed forces and other security organs has encouraged lawlessness almost everywhere in the country. Thousands of heavily armed Dinka Bor pastoralist invaded sedentary agrarian communities' lands in Central and Eastern Equatoria States destroying farms and killing innocent people; it peaked in Kajo-Keji in which twenty-seven Kuku youths working for international organizations were captured and massacred provoking lukewarm response of the government. The Lou Nuer white army supported by elements of Dinka Bor armed youths invade Murle land ostensibly in vengeance of earlier raids. The Fangak-Ayod Nuer and Dinka white army led by their spiritual leader Makuac Tut Khor invade the Chollo Kingdom with the intention to capture and behead the King. The youths of Twic in Warrap have been battling it out with the youths of Abyei, assumed to be part of South Sudan, over the land south of Kiir river. And recently, the Toposa youths battled it out with the elements of Kenyan Army ignoring the international borders to encroach on South Sudan lands. All these insecurities obtain because the political elite has deliberately weakened the state to enable the extraction and plunder of the natural resources in collaboration with regional and international comprador capitalism.

The ecumenical pilgrimage and the well-attended interdenominational prayers at Dr. John Garang Memorial Grounds and the Mausoleum were both a moral boost for the people of South Sudan. However, the state and the political establishment have not digested the messages the Holy Father, the Archbishop of Canterbury and the Moderator of the General Assembly of the Church of Scotland jointly delivered, and therefore, President Kiir's inappropriate reference to the 'Hold-out Groups', as though they were the only obstacle to peace depressingly became the anti-climax of this ecumenical pilgrimage. It was an arrogant expression of remorselessness and lack of care for the people. There is nothing in the R-ARCSS for the 'Hold-Out Groups' to endorse or to improve simply because even the R-TGONU did not in good faith implement the R-ARCSS.

The South Sudan political leaders, whether in or out of government, should on the contrary be reflecting deeply on a paradigm shift towards crafting a political philosophy that could place the masses of the people in the centre of their political engineering. President Salva Kiir, Riek Machar, James Wani Igga, Pagan Amum Okiech and others, including those who have decamped from the SPLM, cannot deny that they had mobilized and organized the people of South Sudan in an armed struggle to transform the centuries-old condition of poverty, ignorance and cultural backwardness. The ideological shifts from the revolution and national liberation these leaders beat towards liberal political pluralism and free market economic policies dictated by the Bretton Institutions that ignored the masses in the provision of social services and economic development are at the core of the current social, economic and political crises that afflict South Sudan.

The southern provinces of the Sudan have never had any kind of social and economic development; its people were submerged in abject poverty, ignorance, superstition and cultural backwardness. But the land was potentially rich in natural resources; it only required development of the people's productive forces to change the situation. The essence of war of national liberation therefore was to free the people of South Sudan from all kinds of foreign domination and control, and to development these natural resources in a manner that served the national economy. Instead of launching the national democratic revolution to construct a national democratic developmental state in South Sudan, the SPLM/A political and military elite opted for political pluralism and liberal free market economy transforming themselves into an elitist class competing along ethnic and regional lines for the control of state and its resources until it imploded into the civil war.

Therefore, the political conversation and consultation amongst the leaders shouldn't be about absorbing into the system the 'Hold-Out Groups' but instead should revolve around lifting the South Sudan people out of poverty, ignorance and cultural backwardness that submerge their consciousness preventing them to correctly perceive reality vide which they are oppressed.

The two-year extension of the transition period inspires no hope for peace as long as the political leaders are only concerned about being in government. It is a spirit that has made meaningless the independence people struggle and sacrificed for so long; as long as there is meaningful contact between the politicians and the civil society groups, or as long as the people are fragmented along ethnic and regional contour lines there is no hope that South Sudan could sustain and evolved into a viable modern state. Lack of unity among the people prevents the emergence and evolution of a critical mass capable of leading the struggle for change. And indeed, it is difficult, if not impossible, to speak of regime change in South Sudan even though it is the only way out of this condition as along as no credible alternative socio-political has sprouted onto the political stage to lead the struggle. The regime has instilled in the people apathy, despair, fear, indifference and lack of empathy. No matter how difficult the situation may become no divine intervention would help the people liberate themselves from this totalitarian dictatorship; they will have to do it by themselves albeit through patient cultivation of social awareness and building political consciousness. This will help regenerate the social capital that bonded the people throughout their past struggles against foreign invaders, and would create conditions for unity for renewed struggle for social change. This social capital that enabled them to struggle for national liberation, but, which power politics and competition among the elites eroded is possible to regenerate through common struggle for social and economic development since long denied the people.

The only hope for the people of South Sudan is the growing inequality across ethnic and regional lines perpetuated by the parasitic capitalist class that catapulted to citadel of the state political and economic power. This social development, in the manner the economy of the country is organized, could sooner than later lead to social stratification of citizens along the 'haves' and the 'haves not'- two antagonistic classes with the 'haves not' being the vast majority of the deprived masses, while the 'haves' would comprise the parasitic capitalist class, which through the agencies of the kleptocratic totalitarian regime they constructed in a space of ten years, have pillaged the country's natural resources leaving impoverished the vast majority of the population. This social configuration would render division along ethnicity and ethnic lines something of the past. The dynamics of the emerging situation will definitely create a social-political force for social change. It's always preferable that the struggle for social change emerged along class lines, it creates conditions for unity of the masses.

Peter Adwok Nyaba
Juba, February 2023

INTRODUCTION

In Memoria, Dr. John Garang de Mabior

The greatest conspiracy ever hatched against the national interest of the people of South Sudan since the colonial occupation in the eighteenth century was the assassination of Dr. John Garang de Mabior on 30th July 2005. Whoever committed this evil act had condemned the country and the people in perpetuity to confusion and political disorientation, and therefore, must be seen as a crime against humanity. Not that Garang wasn't destined to die; as a mortal, Garang was bound to die someday. But coming just twenty-one days into his presidency of the government of South Sudan, Garang's tragic death not only obscured, but also postponed to a later date the resolution of the SPLM internal premonitions. These exploded much later in a civil war that completely shattered the hope for a civilized modern state in South Sudan.

In the many official and unofficial discussions of the matter

I always argued against the notion that the NCP leaders, even though some of them were reported to have celebrated the tragedy. could have been responsible for Garang's demise. They couldn't have done so; in fact, many of these NCP leaders wanted Dr. Garang alive in order to wade them out of the murky situation they had plunged themselves in their relationship with the United States of America and the rest of the international community. In the same vein, I dismissed the narrative that some South Sudan politicians, Dr. Garang's personal enemies who openly celebrated his demise, were behind the plot to eliminate him; they were in no material position to undertake such a task. I strongly still believe the person who killed Dr. Garang had the means to successfully undertake it, but most importantly must have vested interests in South Sudan without Dr. John Garang. Garang's absence could permit management of the nascent South Sudan affairs from behind the fence. Dr. Garang was an astute politician; he precisely wouldn't have permitted the extraction, plunder and pillage of South Sudan vast natural resources in the manner that occurred under the leadership of his successor, and that has left the nascent state in such a pathetic situation. This criminal must have exploited the lapse in Garang's security protection. I believe, had he travelled to Uganda in his official capacity as the first vice president of the republic of the Sudan, and not as a casual private visitor, Garang would still be alive today. Perhaps, Garang overplayed his self-confidence.

The death of Dr. John Garang was not natural or expected as in situations of serious ailments. No, his death was linked to his leadership of the SPLM/A, South Sudan, and its geopolitical location in the Horn and Great Lakes Regions of Africa. The Republic of South Sudan is an integral part of the two regions and both African regions were characterized by conflicts, wars and competition for resources and markets. Dr. Garang, in this respect was also a competitor in the regional and African political marketplace, and therefore had enemies outside the Sudan. In view of South Sudan's poor showings and ratings in the regional, African, and international arena, Garang's death in that tragic helicopter crash, explained only as a 'human error', couldn't have been anything but a conspiracy not only to deprive South Sudan of leadership roles in the Horn of Africa and Great Lakes regions, but also to render its natural resource potential amenable to underhand pillage. This lends credibility to the theory that people interested in extraction and plunder of South Sudan vast natural resource potentials plotted the death of Dr. John Garang de Mabior. It advertently plunged the people of South Sudan into disorientation, civil war, and confusion.

On another note, Garang's tragic death was what people would sometimes categorize as a blessing in disguise. Garang's arrival in Khartoum on 8th July, and his constitutional oath of office as the first vice president of the republic of the Sudan as well as president of the subnational entity, Government of Southern Sudan on 9th July stirred up lots of political dusts in the SPLM/A and in southern Sudan. His tragic death, therefore, averted two equally treacherous political situations, no one could have predicted what would have transpired in South Sudan had any of them had exploded. The first was simmering discontent within the SPLM/A. I believe it was an extension of what transpired and popularly known as Yei crisis on the eve of the CPA in 2004 exacerbated by Garang's decisions to transform both the SPLM and the SPLA. This entailed dissolution of the SPLM/A Leadership Council, decommission of senior SPLA officers to pave way for its professionalization. These generated premonitions on an impending implosion in the SPLM/A along regional contour lines. Most of the officers affected by Garang's decision, including Cdr. Salva Kiir Mayardit himself, hailed from Bahr el Ghazal subregion. Therefore, the fault lines of the implosion ran parallel to Bahr el Ghazal – Upper Nile borderline. The second crisis was triggered by Gen. Paulino Matip Nhial, the leader of Nuer tribal militia allied to NIF regime against the SPLM/A during the war of national liberation. Gen. Paulino Matip had threatened war if the SPLA set foot or raised its flag in Bentiu, the capital of Unity state. These were threatening scenarios that if Garang has not died on that fateful day, the first few months of the CPA implementation would have been spent in multi-dimensional conflicts many of them of course instigated by the NCP. The history of South Sudan could have perhaps been changed in an unpredictable fashion. Dr. John Garang de Mabior died but South Sudan and its people survived; the whole nation mourned him and rests in the memory of many.

The ascension to the helm of the SPLM/A of Cdr. Salva Kiir Mayardit helped ward off the anger of Bahr el Ghazal officers, and the threats of Gen. Paulino Matip Nhial suggesting that Dr.

THE PROBLEMS OF SOUTH SUDAN

John Garang had trodden on a path not to the liking of many Southern Sudanese in or outside the SPLM/A. The twenty-one years of Garang's leadership had created divisions and sufficient blood had been spilt among southerners fighting themselves. But most importantly, what from the very beginning of the struggle in 1983 had divided the political leadership of southern Sudan resulting in the loss of many important leaders eventually became the same secession and independence of South Sudan. The people of South Sudan still suffer from the relics and legacies of the war of national liberation prosecuted outside its political and ideological content and has created fragmentation of the people on ethnic or regional fault lines. **The Problems of South Sudan**

This book is about the political history of South Sudan, which for lack of a better name, has been entitled 'the problems of South Sudan' of which most of its problems include whether or not its independence couldn't have come a little too prematurely. The idea of writing this book came to me as an afterthought when my original plan flopped. I had wanted to publish a third edition of 'The Politics of Liberation in South Sudan: An Insider's View' to mark the twenty-five years since its publication in 1997. In the second edition published in 2000 to celebrate the Noma Award for publishing in Africa 1998, I did ask the questions; what and where was the SPLM? These two questions remained unanswered to date. In my planning I had wanted, therefore, to revisit my hypothesis then that the SPLM did not exist but only the SPLA existed. Of course, it was always said that the SPLM and the SPLA were one thing, or each was the flip side of the other. But that was exactly the confusion some of us in the liberation movement wanted to avoid and make things straight.

Although I had plans to write a book, I only had vague notion of what to write about. It was after the publication of my autobiography (Nyaba, 2022) that ideas, that could constitute a valuable contribution to the political history of South Sudan, started to concretised in my mind. I had time and sufficient intellectual energy to marshal towards the project. A wide gap remained uncovered in the political history of South Sudan particularly from the narratives of authentic native writers. I thought I should write something analytical of the SPLM/A and the current context of South Sudan: a stunted state, politically fragile, fragmented citizenry, and unending vicious cycle of peace, transition, and war.

The demise of Dr. John Garang de Mabior and the ascension to the helm of Salva Kiir Mayardit have had profound impact on the political evolution of South Sudan. Dr. Garang did not live to witness how his ideas that made up the SPLM/A and the political and diplomatic dynamics of the war of national liberation policies. President Salva Kiir introduced a leadership style that although similar to Garang's leadership in its lack of institutionality, nevertheless contributed in a larger measure to the mess in the country and exacerbated the political contradictions and standoffs in the SPLM. Most of my thoughts on the political developments in South Sudan have been carried in my previous publications namely, 'South Sudan: The State We Aspire to' (2010), 'South Sudan: The crisis of Infancy (2014), and 'South

Sudan: Elites, Ethnicity, Endless Wars and the Stunted State' (2019). This book, in my opinion, should be a qualitative shift from descriptive generalities of the problem that has plagued the SPLM/A and the people of South Sudan to locating and pinning the problem where they belong.

The biggest problem that has dogged South Sudanese intellectuals in general and the SPLM/A leaders in particular, remains the solace they find in avoiding critical and in-depth discussion of their differences and/or their conflicting political interpretations on specific or general ideas in the development and evolution of South Sudanese political thought. In fact, many falsely believe that ideological and political differences could disappear by just ignoring or procrastinating on discussing them. Had they been courageous enough to discuss those differences the cancer in the form of civil strife that now threatens to erase the two decades of common struggle, could have been located and treated. This's the kind of situation that usually stalks people who work together for a cause but don't possess a common conviction in what they are doing; or have different perceptions of what they are doing together but are afraid of each other because they are in a competitive mode owing to divergent social, economic or political objectives. Under such circumstances trust and confidence would be in deficit.

The 'problems of South Sudan' are many, intrinsic and have been accentuated by its leaders' ignorance, arrogance, lack of political experience and refusal to learn from the experience of others. These problems are rooted in history of South Sudan but have been exacerbated by political elites' blind belief that contradiction will dissolve, or applying the same formula to the growing number of complex issues in the hope to obtain different results but in the cause of time commit the same mistakes.

The fundamental problems of Southern Sudan remain the centuries old condition of poverty, ignorance, and cultural backwardness of its people. These are the primary contradictions but over the years and due to misdiagnosis and wrong policies they generated secondary and, in some cases, tertiary contradictions. These secondary and tertiary contradictions became triggers and drivers of the current complex situation. As an illustration, misdiagnosis of the nature of the fundamental contradictions propelled the Southern Sudanese in the fifties into demanding secession instead of forging unity with northern Sudanese living under the same socioeconomic and political conditions of neglect, marginalization, and exclusion. In fact, old school southern politicians exaggerated and advanced the sociocultural and religious difference to build a wedge between the southerners and the Africans: in Dar Fur, Kordofan, Blue Nile, Northern Province and Eastern parts of the Sudan.

Unlike the old school politicians, the SPLM/A leadership came closer a correct and democratic articulation of the contradictions that underpinned the conflict in the Sudan. Unfortunately, this articulation was not supported by a correct understanding and knowledge of the national liberation process in terms political organization and ideological orientation of the combatants, cadres and leaders. As a result, after twenty-one years of struggle the war ended in the partition of the Sudan.

In fact, militarism and subversion of political enlightenment and organization in the movement were not appropriate tools for liberation. They were tools for domestication and were utilized to dampen people's consciousness. It was easy for southerners unlike the Nuba or Funj to identify themselves separately and people struggling for a separate course. In its current context, South Sudan presents the picture of a post-colonial African state, product of Lancaster House negotiations, rather than a product of twenty-one-year war of national liberation. It is still pregnant with relics and legacies of political oppression, social discrimination, and marginalization against which the people fought the war of national liberation.

The book is a personal initiative driven by the desire to contribute to the correct understanding of South Sudan, the struggle of its people to be freedom. The idea was to generate knowledge that may help the people of South Sudan extricate themselves out of the terrible situation the political elite have plunged them. In the spirit of revolutionary honesty, as part of this political elite I count myself as contributor to this situation either by commission or omission. For the last five years, have relinquished all political relationship with the SPLM (2014), the SPLM/A (IO) in 2017 nevertheless I consider myself and my political efforts in writing as part of the struggle for freedom, justice, fraternity and social change.

The problems of South Sudan apart from poverty, ignorance, cultural backwardness, and superstition, also includes poor leadership, ethnic nationalism, nepotism and tribalism, regionalism, corruption, extraction and plunder of natural resources, environmental degradation, pollution, diseases, cattle rustling, women and child abduction, land grabbing, insecurity, community conflicts over land and resources, inequality in the distribution of power and wealth, primitive accumulation of wealth. Many of these problems are peculiar to South Sudan, which has been transformed into a shadow by its sons and daughters. It is a hunting ground for many of its sons and daughters in the Diaspora.

The book divides into eight chapters; each chapter deals with specific features of the problems, but all have relevance to each other as part of the same theme of the book. The subtitle 'did independence come a bit too prematurely' is one aspect of the many problems but chosen to give the title shouting colours. It was invoked by the crude and raw nature of the South Sudan intellectuals; political and military leaders and the assumption was that a long waiting period would have afforded them time to learn the etiquette of managing a state.

In **Chapter one,** we discussed the Sudan before and after partition in 2011. As a colonial construct, North and South Sudan were not necessarily antithetical or incompatible binary that they were bound to separate at one point in time. The partition that occurred only in 2011 was part of the political engineering od the Sudanese state that went awfully astray. Bad politics could lob countries like Somalia or Yemen, predominantly made up of the same people professing same religion in such straits and penchant for war and conflict compared to multicultural US or Canada because of the political system they constructed. The failure to manage sociocultural diversity in order to construct a genuine national unity is a shared responsibility between the Sudanese political class both from northern and southern Sudan. However, there's no need shedding tears over spilt milk so they say; the current challenges facing the two neighbouring states, parts of a once united country, should force a paradigm shift in the political thinking of their leaders towards a political philosophy of democratic governance to rescue them from further trending to failure and total collapse.

The glaring benchmarks of this period before partition were insurrection in southern Sudan (1955) followed by declaration of the independence in the Parliament (1956), the military coup (1958), the October popular uprising (1964), the May revolution (1969), the Addis Ababa Agreement (1972), the mutiny in Bor and formation of SPLM/A (1983), the National Islamic Front military coup (1989), the comprehensive peace agreement (2005), the referendum and secession of South Sudan (2011). The NIF usurpation of state power was a radical departure from the political drudgery of the liberal multiparty democracy that characterized the political context punctuated by military intervention in politics since independence in 1956.

The NIF rule however, transformed Sudan's political landscape negatively resulting in partition of South Sudan. It contrasts with the leftist coup of 25th May 1969, which provided for national unity based on recognition and promotion of democratic rights to socioeconomic and cultural development of Southern Sudan. This did not last long as the revolution beat a retreat due to influence of the pan-Arab forces in and outside the Sudan. However, the discourse on the Sudan and South Sudan kicks off from an important discovery that partition produced two instead of one failed state. This is food for thought and in my opinion the contexts presented by the two neighbours warrants serious rethinking; whether or not this failure was consequential to partition.

In **chapter two**, the Southern Region is discussed in the context that it was an achievement the people of southern Sudan won through armed rather than social and political struggle in the towns and villages in southern Sudan. The Southern Region marked the crystallization of Southern Sudanese nationalism, if it could be so categorized, as it was when southerners started to feel they were an entity; nevertheless, at the same time, the Southern Region became the source of failure to attain the unity of the different sociocultural groups in southern Sudan. It was a product of a political settlement perceived as a gift from the strongest party – the Government of the Sudan, and for that matter, Field Marshall Gaafar Mohammed Numeiri to the weak side - people of Southern Sudan. This was the greatest weakness of the Addis Ababa Agreement and that underpinned Numeiri's ultimate action abrogating and declaring the agreement was 'neither a Bible nor a Quran', to return the Sudan to war that swept him away from power. Ethnicity and ethnic nationalism remain strong and destructive forces in South Sudan and could be its unmaking as a modern state.

The Sudan People's Liberation Movement and the Sudan

People's Liberation Army (SPLM/SPLA) was discussed in **chapter three**. Note the deliberate use of the verb 'was' rather than 'were' to connote the two were essentially one in one; the army (A) was the movement (M), which itself was the army. The return to war in Southern Sudan was not accidental although it was easy to discover that there was no pre-planning or political preparation for its eruption. The return to war was spontaneous; people reacted to variegated political developments and numerous contradictions the May regime generated throughout the country. However, I would add that everything linked to SPLM/A leadership in terms of political and military support from the friends fell into place by mere chance.

The SPLM/A's initial political objective to build socialism in the Sudan was a bit farfetched and could have been peddled only to solicit political and military support from the socialist camp fronted in the region of the Horn of Africa by Socialist Ethiopia. The Communist Party of the Sudan (CPS) considered this socialist sloganeering as a bluff nevertheless it offered moral support in the context of a common struggle against Numeiri's totalitarian regime. Many of the revolutionary democrats who joined the ranks of the SPLM/A did not take long to discover the populist nature of its leadership; indeed, this leadership did not need the revolutionary democrats nor their revolutionary ideology. In hindsight, the SPLM/A could have been South Sudanese right wing's Trajan horse smuggled into the internationalists stockade for the purposes mentioned above. The defeat of the Derg in Ethiopia and the collapse of the Soviet Union exposed the true colours of the SPLM/A leadership. The populist character of its leadership was exposed. This leadership utilize a political and organizational methodology akin to the process of domestication and robotization of the combatants in order to promote the leader's cult of personality. In this respect, militarization, militarism, and intense indoctrination to the leader's cult of personality demonstrated that the SPLM/A was something different from other liberation movements in the region of the Horn of Africa.

This was clear from the relations it built internally with the civil population and externally with the reactionary forces in Africa and beyond. Internally the SPLM/A produced an elitist class of political and military leaders whose social, economic, and political interests did not align with the masses of the people. The SPLM-led Government of Southern Sudan (GOSS) in cohorts with the Bretton Institutions established the Joint Multi-Donor Trust Fund, which placed Southern Sudan on liberal economic policies and a free market. Something that Amilcar Cabral in the weapon of theory (Cabral, 1966) said, that the petty bourgeoisie must first commit suicide as a class to be reborn as a revolutionary worker and peasant, completely identified with the deepest aspiration of the people to which they belong, in order to a lead a national liberation movement. The revolutionary and Marxist slogan the SPLM/A leaders chanted were mere lip service; they had no inner connections with the aspirations of the masses.

In **chapter four**, we discussed the international humanitarian intervention in Southern Sudan and how it distorted not only the concept of national liberation but the lives of the masses involved in the support of the struggle. The SPLM/A leadership in the prosecution of the war of national liberation deliberately made the movement of rely heavily on external resources. This was a complete departure from the ethos revolutionary guerrilla warfare. Though considered an act of solidarity, resources from political and ideological friends, SPLM/A's complete dependence on them in the conduct of a people's war contradicted the principles of self-reliance that underly the concept and practices in a people's war. There was nothing to warrant or justify locating SPLA rear bases in western Ethiopia save to create logistical nightmare for the Ethiopian benefactors. The creation of refugee camps to support the SPLA in the fronts lines forced and pushed the massive civil population movement away from their villages into refugee camps to become food coupons for the army.

Pushed by the need to solicit sufficient logistic support for the Army, the SPLM/A leadership negotiated and signed the tripartite agreement between the SPLM/A, the Government of the Sudan and the United Nations Children's Fund to establish the United Nations Operations Lifeline Sudan (UN/OLS). The unintended negative consequences of the international humanitarian and relief intervention in Southern Sudan are still living with the people in many parts of South Sudan. In this way, the SPLM/A forfeited the opportunity to build rear bases inside South Sudan and to transformed itself in a guerrilla army prosecuting a war of national liberation. In this respect, these rear bases could have performed political, social, economic, and cultural functions of the national liberation movement. As a result of this and many other factors, the SPLM/A did not shoot itself into power as the Eritrean People's Liberation Front (EPLF) or the Ethiopian People's Revolutionary Democratic Front (EPRDF) did in Asmara and Addis Ababa respectively. It beat a retreat from revolution to liberalism to enable it seal a political compromise – the comprehensive peace agreement (CPA), with the government of Sudan. This ideological shift coincided with the political shift from the concept and vision of the 'new' Sudan to Southern Sudan and the right of the people therein to self-determination resulting in the partition of the Sudan and the independence of South Sudan than the realization of the New Sudan. This left in the political cold the Nuba, the Funj, and the other Sudanese who joined the ranks and file of the SPLM/A genuinely believing in democratic transformation of the Sudan; it bordered on betrayal and the fate of the Ngok Dinka of Abyei hangs on the precipice unclear whether or not they will become part of South Sudan. The government of South Sudan cold footed the Abyei referendum it conducted in October 2012.

The discussion of the republic of South Sudan follows in **chapter five**. Although it was a product of a protracted struggle nevertheless South Sudan appears as though it became independent by mistake serving the political, economic and security interests of a foreign power. It's possible that had southern Sudan been part of a country friendly to USA and not of a pariah state called the Sudan with an ICC indicted president called Omer Hassan Ahmed Al-Bashir, it wouldn't have won the right to exercise self-determination. Salva Kiir's presidency of South

Sudan has turned it into a cauldron of political violence, civil wars, humanitarian disasters in which millions of South Sudanese elected with their feet to become refugees in the neighbouring countries that most of the friends that supported the SPLM/A bit for self-determination now look the other way. A parasitic capitalist class sprouted on to the helm of state political and economic power but due to its primitive nature, lack of sophistication, correct understanding that a modern state functions only through accountable institution, this class has turned South Sudan into a shadow state serving its interests and those of the regional compradors.

The mismanagement of the nascent state triggered serious internal SPLM contradictions. These contradictions driven by personal rivalry for power and competition for primitive accumulation of wealth, exploded into a civil war in December 2013 prompting the Inter-Governmental Authority on Development (IGAD) to intervene. **Chapter Six** discusses the IGAD-initiated peace processes to resolve the conflict in South Sudan. It was based on a peace-making modality predicated on power-sharing between the parties in order to effect reforms in the system. The IGAD mediators' perception of this peace-making modality was outside the context of the fundamental contradictions in the conflict; these could never be resolved through power-sharing. Thus, the imposed agreement on the resolution of the conflict in South Sudan (ARCISS) of August 2015 proved ineffective in addressing the fundamental contradiction underlying the conflict and collapsed just three months into its implementation in July

2016. The IGAD High-Level Revitalization Forum (HLRF) negotiated and sealed the revitalized agreement on the resolution of the conflict in South Sudan (R-ARCSS) on 18th September 2018 again based on the ARCISS modality. It took President Salva Kiir eighteen months to start R-ARCSS' implementation and the formation of the revitalized transitional government of national unity (R-TGONU) on 20th February 2020.

This delay affected the implementation of the transitional processes leading to the elections and establishment of an elected government. The extension of the transition to February 2025 doesn't inspire hope as the dominant parties namely the incumbent transitional government of national unity (ITGONU) formed after the collapse of ARCISS in 2016 and the SPLM/A (IO) continue to undermine each other. The renewed conflict in Western Equatoria and in the Chollo Kingdom in Upper Nile State are part of this toxic relations between the parties to R-ARCSS.

The republic of South Sudan is home to more than sixty-four nationalities at different levels of social and cultural development and differential demographic weights. The weakening of the state in South Sudan and the collapse of its security institutions has serious ramification for the smaller nationalities, which could be registered as existential threat to the 'small tribes' in South Sudan. This is discussed in **chapter seven** in the context of ethnic demographic weight being the determinant of each nationality's physical and cultural existence or political visibility at either local, state or national level of government. The weakness of the state, represented by not being the sole controller of means of force and coercion means that the 'smaller tribes' would sooner than later find themselves squeezed between the demographically larger ones. As South Sudan returns to the Hobbes state of nature, whereby life is described as solitary, poor, nasty, brutish and short, this could be a pointer to physical and/or cultural extinction of some of very small ethnic communities. It would be difficult for them to survive in the absence of government.

The many and variegated social, economic, and political ailments afflicting the people of South Sudan make one to think aloud that the independence of South Sudan could have come a bit to prematurely. This is discussed in **chapter eight**. This notion of South Sudan's premature independence may be supported by the political immaturity demonstrated by the leaders, state institutions, and instruments of public authority. It's clear, the political class has recoiled back into their respective sociocultural formations that the notion of a modern state in South Sudan is quickly receding.

The primary objective of this work, like my other books, is to provoke debate among the intellectuals, politicians and political activists on the unsavoury realities afflicting the people of South Sudan, and to build a consensus on how to bail the country out. There is a growing tendency to erode the concept of the state as something belonging to all the citizens therein. This initially was driven by false idiosyncrasies generated in the context of war of national liberation, whereby demographical preponderance of ethnicity triggered the surge of ethnic nationalism.

After the war ended, ethnic nationalism in turn stimulated the notion of community as a basic unit of political organization and supplanted the SPLM, which had strong roots in society. These false idiosyncrasies triggered the current acute social, economic, and political crises exacerbated by the growing inequality in the distribution of power and wealth likely to sculpt into an explosive amalgam, which could sooner than later detonate and shatter the country into pieces or render it completely ungovernable. The insecurity that had simmered and exploded in Upper Nile especially the Nuer-Chollo war is an aspect of ungovernability. The present context is alienating large sections of South Sudan society particularly the youth, who find it easier to pick the gun at the behest of the politicians. It is high time they ceased being tools for their own exploitation.

CHAPTER ONE

THE REPUBLIC OF THE SUDAN: BEFORE AND AFTER PARTITION

1. Preliminary Remarks

A young South Sudanese, who had spent his childhood and early adolescence in the refugee camp in Uganda, coming back to South Sudan only in 2014 a few months into the civil war, spent the difficult years of the war dodging bullets in Juba. Then, sometimes in 2020, for the first time since coming back to the country, he had the opportunity to be part of Southern Sudan team travelling to Khartoum to mediate the Sudanese conflict. It was his first ever visit to the city and to see Khartoum city. The configuration: streets, high rise building, gardens and public squares was fascinating. Nevertheless, he wanted to compare life in the two capitals of the divided Sudan and so he requested to sightsee and spent close to twelve hours crisscrossing the streets of Khartoum, Khartoum North, and Omdurman.

On coming back to the hotel late in the evening from his day-long excursion, Lado, an avid observer, had this to say to his colleagues; "Why did they have to separate the Sudan; they shouldn't have done it, because instead of two we would have only one failed state". On hearing what the young man said, people were taken aback. "But just as in Juba," he continued, "here in Khartoum I found people crowding under trees, on the street corners or in the shops' veranda drinking tea, coffee or smoking shisha and happily whiling away time. People have nothing to do but seemed happy although despair and depression can be read on every seven out of ten faces I met and spoke to. There seems nothing to inspire hope; how couldn't this country not fail?"

One instead of two failed countries! Speaks to the episodes that was the Sudan: the futility of southern Sudanese secessionist movement on the one hand and the vanity of maintaining an exclusive, discriminatory, repressive one united Sudan on the other hand. The two divergent movements produced the same result - state failure. Sudan didn't fare well as one country because the political class was fragmented. What was taken to be the national centre only represented the social, economic and political interests of the jellaba. It excluded all the other Sudanese people in the central, western, eastern, northern and southern Sudan. The two Sudans (Sudan and South Sudan) also as separate countries following the partition in 2011 couldn't fare any better. They both degenerated into chaos and political disorder and now both represent differential failures.

The Republic of the Sudan was the country into which many

of us were born, lived in, got education in its schools up to its finest university of Khartoum, graduated and worked in its bureaucracy, and finally participated in the process of its dismemberment. I had just published my memoirs – up from the village: an autobiography. The Sudan was both the subject and object of some of the stories I had to tell of its multiple sociocultural formations, sensibilities, and idiosyncrasies, which made up most of the narrative. This story about the Sudan and its partition generates nostalgic feelings. The partition did not trigger positive qualitative changes in the two parts to justify the partition; instead, the two parts degenerated into the worst conditions their respective leaders wouldn't have anticipated. I believe, the young man, Lado said nothing but the truth of the Sudan. What he said was a pointer to the need to reconsider some of the ideas and emotions that informed our thoughts as we struggled for secession. Evanescently and metaphorically speaking, the situation in the two Sudans echoes succinctly Mohammed Wardi's lyrics, *"alone, I did it unto myself."* The truth is that the cause of partition of the Sudan did not come *sui moto*; it was a result of myopia and/or perhaps cynical ethnocentrism of those who rose to the pinnacle of Sudanese state power particularly after the experience of the Juba conference 1947.

There were many sides to the Juba conference. First, it was an admission on the part of British colonial administration that their Southern Sudan policy had failed and untenable in face of the post WWII realities. These realities rendered untenable the colonial setup, and for that matter the Anglo-Egyptian Condominium of the Sudan catching the British administration unprepared. The British Colonial administration had not fully separated the southern provinces from the rest of the Sudan. The original idea was to annex southern Sudan politically and economically to the British East Africa. This did not happen, but the British colonial authorities failed to create the conditions for the southern provinces to stand alone independently or to be united at par with northern Sudan. The surging Egyptian nationalism forced the British to quickly reconsider its position in the Sudan, abandoned southern Sudan and opted to pursue its economic and political interests in Egypt and the Arab Middle East.

The Juba conference, on the other hand, could have been an opportunity to build genuine Sudan's unity. Both the British colonial administration and particularly the northern nationalist leaders failed to envision the importance of, or to seize on this opportunity, to build southern Sudanese confidence in the new project of its unity with northern Sudan. Most of the southern delegates were in one way or the other officials of the colonial government; and although they purported to represent the interests of the people of southern Sudan nevertheless most of them were concern about their social and economic status vis a vis their northern counterparts in terms of equalization of their salaries and other perks.

The British colonial authorities turned the Juba conference into a process of disentangling itself from the failed policy of the southern provinces and by first letting loose its grip on southern provinces the British wanted to placate the Egyptian government to its interest in the Suez Canal Company. And secondly, by reunite the two parts of the Sudan rendered asunder by the Closed Districts Ordinance, the British administration endeared itself to the emerging Sudanese nationalist movement opposed to unity with Egypt. The Southern Sudan secessionist movement has its roots therefore in the greed or rather the cynical ethnocentrism of the northern political elite. They were impatient and inherited the colonial state without genuine involvement of the southerners but instead used the state to oppress them. Between the Juba conference 1947 and the formation of the first national government in 1954, the northern nationalist leaders had enough time to win over the southerners and build confidence, trust and fraternal relations that could have prevented the disruption that occurred in August 1955.

2. Historical Roots of Political Failures in the Sudan

The history of modern Sudan begins with its occupation and becoming part of the Ottoman empire in the early nineteenth century at the height of European colonial expansion and primitive accumulation of capital. The Sudanese state therefore was founded on colonial occupation characterized by extraction, plunder, and pillage of human and natural resources of the Sudan, and confirms that exploitation, brutality of slavery, and deep unequal power relations marked the early days of the Sudan. The Ottoman state in the Sudan was an oppressive and a cruel context that denied black people their humanity.

The memories of *Turkiya* (1824-1885) and later *Mahdiya*

(1885-1898) spur among southern Sudanese of yester years anger and negative sentiments of the Arabized northern Sudanese, who made up most of the *Turkiya's* foot soldiers and middlemen in the slave trade business that witnessed the shipping away as slaves of tens of thousands of black Sudanese. This knowledge of Arabized Nubians' role in slavery and slave trade informed southern Sudanese political thought and hence their struggle to separate and become independent of the rest of the Sudan. The defeat of the *Turkiya* in a revolution that united the Sudanese people, and the rise of *Mahdiya* were momentous respite. However, although the revolution echoed peoples' fervent desire for freedom, justice, and fraternity, nevertheless, the process to achieve that desire was also pregnant with contradictions that would sooner than later shatter the unity that was achieved in the heat of the struggle against the common enemy. Differentiating or categorizing people based on race, ethnicity, faith, or skin complexion weakened the Mahdist revolution through divisions and internecine fighting. It permitted the continuation of the process that singled out for slavery the people of black complexion. This justified holding of slaves and continued slave raids into southern Sudan, Nuba Mountains and southern Blue Nile long after the demise of Turkiya. The corrupt, brutal, and oppressive regime of Abdullahi Al-Taisha generated the social and political sensibilities that weakened and fragmented the Mahdist revolutionary zeal, and eventually led to the defeat of *Mahdiya* and the reconquest of the Sudan.

In a way, the oppressive context reproduced itself as soon as its creator vanished, but the successor regime generated identical contradictions that also led to its demise. The Mahdist state inherited the Turkiya's instruments of power with all its contradictions that fitted it against the riverine Arabised Sudanese who were the initiators of the revolution. It failed or rather refused to construct a political system commensurate with the aspiration of *all* the Sudanese people in their different sociocultural formations. The old relations based on slavery, plunder, exploitation, and brutality could not obtain under changed conditions of freedom from the *Turkiya*. This would explain how and why the Chollo Kingdom (Fashoda province) broke loose of the Mahdist state and regained the independence and freedom it had enjoyed long before the Turko-Egyptian incursion into the Sudan. It will be recalled that Rath Kur Nyidhok was the Chollo sovereign when he signed the Fashoda Pact with the French military officer Jean-Baptiste Marchand in March 1898, six months before the battle of Kerrari in September which led to the defeat of the Mahdist state and the reconquest of the Sudan by joint Anglo-Egyptian expedition force. Stories of the Chollo war against the Mahdists remain vivid in the Chollo oral history preserved in songs and lyrics.

The reconquest of the Sudan leading to the establishment of the Anglo-Egyptian Sudan was by no means smooth except among the riverine Arabized Nubians who had previously rebelled against Khalifa Abdullahi's brutal rule and facilitated Kitchner's southward movement towards contact with the Mahdists in the battle of Kerrari. In the southern provinces pacification raged brutally and severely where the people offered resistance.

The rebellion or rather the insurrection that rocked parts of the southern provinces against colonial administration in Lou (Guek Ngundeng), in Aliab (Kon Abar), and in Aweil (Ariathdit) were manifestations of people's desire for freedom and justice. However, lack of unity and solidarity, as each ethnic group battled it out separately against colonial occupation for own existential survival was the determinant factor in their mutual defeat and subjugation. The enemy finished defeating each resistance one after the other, which could have been different had they joined up. Thus, the Anglo-Egyptian Condominium consolidated and entrenched its grip on the Sudanese people through trickery and deceit, winning over some communities while at the same time alienating others who refused to voluntarily submit.

3. The Condominium, the Nationalist Movement, and Independence

In northern Sudan, the British colonial administration desperate for allies rehabilitated Abdel Rahaman Al-Mahdi then settled in the White Nile area. The Mahdi followers, the Ansar, were encouraged to migrate to the White Nile as agricultural workers for the rehabilitated Abdelrahman. On the other hand, the Egyptians supported Ali Al-Mirghani and his followers, the Khatimiya sect in norther and eastern Sudan. It wasn't difficult to see reason for the two condominium powers supporting the two-family dynasties was in their colonial interest to contain, control, and direct the religious conservation in northern Sudan that triggered the revolution that led to the demise of the Turkiya.

It was therefore desirable that those sectarian groups were in support of its colonial objectives. Thus, Ansar and Khatimiya sects emerged as strong pro-colonial forces rooted respectively in the western Sudan (Dar Fur and Kordofan) and northern and eastern Sudan. And although they were both in the service of colonial interests nevertheless, they had bitter competition over leadership of the nationalist movement and later the control of the Sudanese state.

The colonial policy of 'divide to conquer' and/or rule, found expression in the dichotomous policy designs, which the colonial administration instituted to consolidate its grip on the Sudan. The first policy ran along the Ansar – Khatimiya religious sectarian fault line, which kept the two forces in opposition to each other corresponding to the divide within the condominium camp between Britain and Egypt over the future of the Sudan. It will be recalled that by the time of the reconquest, Egypt was under British occupation since 1882. One of the objectives of the Sudan expedition was to return the Sudan to the Egyptian crown. For this objective Egypt footed the bill for the expedition. Of course, Britain dishonoured that article which became the source of political friction between the colonial powers throughout the condominium era. This would explain their support for the respective religious sects. The Ansar sect was primarily pro-British, while the Khatimiya was pro-Egypt. The political parties that emerged from these religious sects namely the Umma and the Ashigga (Brothers) Party followed their sectarian patrons.

The second dichotomous policy process was along the northern

- southern Sudan socio-historical and geographical fault lines. This later evolved into the Closed District Ordinance (CDO) and formed the foundation of the problem of the southern provinces. Thus, the Sudanese society was polarized representing a contradiction inherent in the condominium between the British colonial interest and the Egyptian nationalist interest. The result of this wrangling within the Condominium was that the Egyptians supported the socio-political forces struggling for Sudan's independence and unity with Egypt. The struggle between the British colonial interests and the Egyptian national interests triggered the White Flag revolution 1924 led by Sudanese officer in the Egyptian Army. Opinion differed among southern Sudanese as to whether Ali Abdel Latif[1] and Abdel Fadhil Al Maz were genuinely Sudanese revolutionaries or were infiltrated by the Egyptian Military Intelligence to precipitate a crisis serving Egyptian political interest in the colonial regime. The backlash of this uprising was swift and immediate. By enacting the CDO, which completely sealed off, insulated, and isolated the non-Muslim, non-Arab southern provinces, Nuba Mountains, and southern Blue Nile from the rest of the Sudan and civilized outside world, the British colonial administration blocked the penetration of Arabized Muslim socio-political forces and modern ideas into these regions. Advertently or not, the CDO laid the foundations for uneven socioeconomic, cultural, and political development of the different regions of the Sudan and immediately enforced the policy of divide to rule. Little did the riverine Arabized Nubians envision that those measures, which colonialism instituted, also doubled up as foundations for future instability and eventual state failure in the Sudan.

The proximity of Northern Sudan to Egypt and civilized outside world advantaged the northern riverine areas of the Sudan; many benefited from Egyptian educational facilities up to the university level and therefore led to increased social and political awareness of northern Sudanese unlike southern Sudan where the colonial authorities relegated education and school system to the Christian missionaries whose main goal was religious proselytization. The quality of education these missionary schools provided was substandard and inferior meant to inculcate obedience to colonial authority. It was an education that promoted learning to memorize but not to trigger critical thinking and confident personality in the recipients. This would explain how social awareness and political consciousness in southern Sudan lagged that of the northern Sudan. Indeed, Sudanese nationalism and movement for independence took roots first in northern Sudan much earlier than in southern Sudan. That by 1947 southern Sudanese leaders still wanted the Southern provinces to remain under British colonial regime until they reached a certain level of parity with northern Sudan, could only indicate the level of understanding of colonialism among the southern Sudan leaders. It suggested that in nearly four decades of occupation colonialism did nothing in terms of social, economic and cultural development in southern Sudan, and indeed wouldn't have done anything in the interest of the people because its purposes were extraction and plunder of natural resources. It must be added that the people of southern Sudan apart from their resistance to colonial rule, did not have resources ready for colonial exploitation and this explains why unlike in Kenya or Zimbabwe or South Africa European colonialism transformed into settler occupation.

The interaction of the Sudanese people in their variegated sociocultural value systems with colonialism, both during the Turkiya and under the Anglo-Egyptian Condominium was differently defiant across the board. Many northern Sudanese intellectuals tend to ignore, indeed downplay, the role of southern Sudanese in the anti-colonial resistance and in the nationalist movement for independence. This was partly due ethnocentric prejudices and bias but most importantly their information accrued from the colonial records of military campaigns of pacification. Instead of unifying these racial and ethnic idiosyncrasies alienated and widened the gap and suspicion between southerners and northerners.

By the time of Sudan's independence, the forces of national democratic revolution were still feeble and therefore it was a free ride for the theocratic family dynasties and their liberal-conservative political outfits to determine the destiny of the country. Thus, the debate within the nationalist movement was either unity with Egypt pursued by the Ashigga Party or total independence pursued by the Umma Party. The notion of unity with Egypt under the guise of unity of the Nile basin precipitated a split with the Ashigga Party into the People's Democratic Party (PDP) which favour unity with Egypt and the National Unionist Party

(NUP) which favoured independence under the slogan "Sudan for the Sudanese". Under its leader Sayed Ismail Al-Azhari, the NUP won most seats in the Legislative Assembly and thereafter formed the first nationalist government in 1954.

The post-colonial state in the Sudan was not a Sudanese state founded on the sociocultural peculiarities of the Sudanese people. The state in every aspect was a relic of colonialism no wonder that serious social and political contradictions punctuated the transition to independence and therefore distorted its outcome. Although most of the Sudanese were Muslims particularly in northern Sudan, most of the Sudanese were non-Arab and therefore defining Sudanese identity on only two parameters of Arab and Islam was a contradiction that would inevitably explode sooner than later. The southern provinces, and the people in Bahr el Ghazal, Equatoria and Upper Nile provinces had not fully integrated into the mainstream Sudanese national personality. Therefore, the period prior to formal independence required politics based on correct understanding and knowledge of the socioeconomic and political engineering processes in state formation and nation building, to build trust and confidence between the different social and political formations in the country. This was where myopia and chauvinism of the Arab dominated northern political elite triumphed over rationality and Sudanese patriotism.

Political dispensation in post-colonial sub-Sahara Africa based on former metropolitan values was what most post-colonial states in Africa adopted on independence. The salient truth of this ideological-cultural implantation was that none of these states succeeded to construct authentic national sovereignty that represented the indigenous people and their institutions. The wholesale transplantation of liberal multipartyism onto a socio-culturally backward and economically underdeveloped society as the Sudan was later the cause of its perpetual political instability and civil wars. The Sudanese state embroiled in a contradiction between preponderant traditional theocratic family dynastic, feudal setup and a small burgeoning petty bourgeois representing the modern sector was bound to suffer political trauma. The post-colonial state was at sociocultural variance with the Sudanese indigenous value systems. This bags the conclusion that the failure of the post-colonial state essentially reflected the failure of the political elite at independence to construct a socio-political system commensurate with the social, economic, political, and cultural reality of the Sudan. In this case, the republic of South Sudan amplified everything that was the failure in the Sudan. This requires a digression.

The social and political processes leading to state formation in South Sudan to a large extent resembled the socio-political waves of decolonization and independence from European colonialism that swept through the breadth and width of Africa in the fifties and sixties of the last century. These processes were almost in phenomenal similarity to each other except in the case of Anglo-Egyptian Sudan. Here, the nationalist leaders exploited the differing positions and colonial interests of the condominium powers. Helped by the revolutionary government that usurped power in Egypt, the northern Sudanese political parties in a conference in Cairo reached an agreement that recognized Sudan's right to self-determination. This Cairo agreement in February 1953, excluded the southern Sudan opinion. But it enabled the Sudanese Parliament, with the participation of Southern Sudanese members, on 19th December 1955 to declare Sudan independence. The Prime Minister then only requested the Governor General to leave the Sudan with his troops on 31st December 1955.

The fatal mistake the northern Sudan nationalist leaders committed was to exclude the southern Sudanese political opinion in the Cairo Agreement. This signified deliberate political exclusion of Southern Sudan pushed by racist considerations even after the southerners had accepted in the Juba conference in 1947 that Sudan would become independent as one and united country. The politics of the nationalist movement at independence was predominantly right-wing conservative and liberal in which the northern political elite belaboured a falsehood of decolonization of the Sudan by assimilation of the non-Arab people thus tying the Sudan to the Arab Middle East rather than the rest of sub-Sahara Africa. In fact, this policy viewed the Sudanese nationality only as a transition to full integration into Arab and Muslim nationhood for the non-Arab (Dar Fur, Funj, and Beja) as well as non-Muslim (southern Sudanese and Nuba) peoples of the Sudan. This policy underpinned the politics of political exclusion, social discrimination, and economic marginalization, which rejected southern Sudanese as equal stakeholders in the Sudan until they Arabized and became Muslims.

The 19th of December 1955 indeed represented the height of the Sudanese nationalism. However, the southern Sudanese political leaders and others enlightened southern Sudanese in the know of the history of the relations between the two parts of the country, the declaration of Sudan's independence was received half-heartedly, with apprehension and lack of trust of their northern compatriots. This was because on 1st January 1956, the people in the three southern provinces of the Sudan, especially in Equatoria, were still reeling and tottering in the political and military fallouts of the events in Torit on 18th of August 1955 and the campaign of vengeance conducted by the northern army of occupation. Thus, for many southern Sudanese people, Sudanese nationalism did not mean much as they saw themselves as aliens to the Sudan. Their trust and belief in unity of the Sudan began to ebb with the events that followed the mutiny of the Equatoria Corps and the surge of the secessionist tendency. This explains how the elements of Torit mutiny remained active in Equatoria province until 1960, when Abboud's policies of Arabicisation and Islamization[2] forced students and others to swell the ranks of Anya-nya insurgency to begin operating in Bahr el Ghazal and Upper Nile provinces.

It goes without saying that the agitation for special status in the Sudan by southern Sudanese especially after the Juba conference in 1947 rooted in the condescending attitude of the Arabized northern Sudanese generally towards the African people in the Sudan. It always took a visionary and wise leadership to avert national catastrophe. No matter how simple and poor a people may appear to be[3], prompting their insulation and isolation from the rest of the country, a point in time would come for them to sophisticate, become articulate and force through their demand for freedom, justice, and fraternity. The Arab dominated northern Sudanese political leadership in the nationalist movement for independence of the Sudan overlooked and ignored the southern Sudanese, the Nuba and the Funj at the peril of dismemberment of the Sudan. Ismael Al-Azhari described the mutiny in Torit as a storm in a teacup suggesting that Torit was far away and it would remain isolated, notwithstanding that it took a short time to spread throughout the three southern provinces.

The independence of South Sudan on 9th July 2011, while war still rages in Southern Kordofan, Blue Nile and Dar Fur point to the notion of never to ignore a people inspired by ideals of freedom and justice. Ignoring people's demands could be the beginning a serious political failure. The failure starts with self-deception, myopia, vain ethnocentrism, and politics of lying, innuendo, empty promises, and dishonoured agreements. The country and its people hurt profoundly because bad politics invariably lead to desperation and frustration. The Shilluk word for politics is *'awenaweno'* which in English translates into 'moving in a circle' suggesting an unending cycle of untruths, deceit, lies, empty promises, and agreements dishonoured. In fact, political deceit, lies, and broken promises characterized the political wheeling and dealing in the Sudan since independence in 1956, and all led to political and state failure. The outstanding signatures of this failure was the wars that led to the partition, and the on-going wars in Dar Fur, Nuba Mountains, Blue Nile, which might lead to further partitioning. This particularly true when politics and economics are organized in such a manner that serves the interests of the minority instead of the vast majority who are left to languish in poverty, ignorance and destitution.

By 1956, the republic of the Sudan did have a bright future better than Malaysia or Singapore at least from economic point of view. It, unfortunately, didn't have a Mahathir or a Le Quan Yu. Sudan had Ismail Al-Azhari as the prime minister and theocratic-based political elite at the helm of state power. This would explain how both Malaysia and Singapore, whose GDP combined was then less than that of Sudan in 1956 evolved into some of the most powerful economies and democratic systems in the world, while the Sudan retarded and began to demonstrate negative social and economic indices.

The Republic of the Sudan was a very large country; two million square kilometres in area and endowed with huge natural resource potential in terms of arable land, a coastline on the Red Sea that runs into hundreds of kilometres; suggesting it could have been also a maritime power. It had sufficient rainfall to support rain-fed agriculture; the White Nile, Blue Nile with their tributaries and other rivers provided huge potential to mechanized irrigated agriculture. It had huge potential in forests, grassland, swamps, livestock, fisheries, wildlife, minerals, hydrocarbons, water, wind and solar energy, potential for tourism and above all a small population. Sudan could have become one of the promising post-colonial states in African; it had highly educated civil service. Unfortunately, it did not have genuinely patriotic and visionary leadership as in Malaysia and/or Singapore. It had a political elite whose pride in the Sudan centred in glorifying an illusion that became its unmaking; the illusion (mirage) of Arab nationalism whose ideological roots did not sink deeply in the country but also exacerbated the internal contradictions that pushed the southern Sudanese to the opposite extreme.

The partition of the Sudan into the Sudan and South Sudan came after two violent and devastating civil wars. The relics and ramifications of those wars are still visible; the two states are reeling in perpetual painful straits, and agony generated by the process partition. The racially polluted and toxic politics that eventually led to partition is rooted in the nationalist movement foe independence in the fifties of the last century. A similar parallel was again created in the war of national liberation, which ended not only in partition of the Sudan instead of democratic transformation of the Sudanese polity but also in civil war in the republic of South Sudan.

It must be admitted that the Arab-dominated northern political elite initiated the north-south dichotomization and must take the blame for the state failure. Their attitude and behaviour towards southern Sudan and its people constituted the foundation of southern Sudanese secessionist movement. It would be like blaming the victim by placing the responsibility for the mutiny of the Equatoria Corps of the Sudan Defence Force (SDF) in Torit on 18th August 1955 on the shoulders of the southern Sudanese politicians. What officially became known as the 'southern disturbances', resulted from the political failure of the nationalist government to address the concerns of the people of southern Sudan.

The relics of the Closed District Ordinance were still visible in the social, economic, and political makeup of the Sudanese state. The main concerns of the enlightened chiefs at the Juba conference were socioeconomic and political development of the southern provinces to a point they would be at par with the northern Sudan. The attempts to substitute with northerners the burgeoning southern working class in the Nzara agro-industrial complex and other forestry schemes generated the bitterness and anger against the northern Sudan that spread throughout southern Sudan in the wake of the mutiny in Torit. The republic of the Sudan became independent on the heels of a civil war in its three southern provinces. The manner Azhari and the northern administrators handled this war, and its aftermath would indeed determine the future of the Sudan and its viability as a state.

The Requiem for the Sudan (Millard Burr, 1995) was written a bit too prematurely; the disaster on the Nile had not then reached the point where it required divine intervention. The period after the signing of the comprehensive peace agreement (CPA) and the independence of South Sudan would have been the appropriate time to write the requiem, which, however, would have been for both the Sudan and South Sudan as the two are about to die. The Sudan could have been saved from the partition ordeal. However, the social and political forces whether from the north or south that could have redeemed it unfortunately remain submerged in the idiotic and cynical ethnocentrism. That was why the separatists in both southern and northern Sudan carried the day on the 9th of January 2011. I am convinced that the people of Southern Sudan, particularly the progressives among them, were pushed to the extremes to support the secession of southern Sudan by the attitude of the Islamist and their rejection of social and cultural diversity of the Sudan.

The elections for the Constituent Assembly 1957, produced an Umma Party majority and Abdalla Bey Khalil became the prime minister replacing Ismail Al-Azhari. Southerners formed the Liberal Party to champion the cause of federation. The Constitutional and Legislative Committee of the Constituent Assembly rejected the southern demand for federation on the grounds that 'federation was given full consideration and was found to be unworkable' (sic). The promise that 'federation would be given full consideration' was the bait on which southerners voted for independence on 19th December 1955. They have been given a blank cheque by their northern compatriots and were agitating for political vengeance. This rendered unstable the government of prime minister Abdalla Khalil such that on the eve of a vote of no confidence on his government Khalil handed power to the military.

Gen. Ibrahim Abboud assumed power on 17th November 1958 and installed a military dictatorship to implement the policy of Islamization and Arabization of the southern provinces of the Sudan pushed by the Arab dominated northern political elite. This military coup not only proscribed all political parties in the country thereby closing all avenues for political dialogue and building consensus on the fundamental issues of the Sudanese state, it also heightened and escalated the war against the Anyanya insurgency. The policy of Islamization initially represented by the change of weekly holiday from Sunday to Friday immediately triggered strike - the Sunday Strike in April 1960, and closure of all schools in the southern provinces of Bahr el Ghazal, Equatoria and Upper Nile. This was the second most important episode that raised social awareness and political consciousness in southern Sudan after the mutiny in Torit in August 1955. As a result, the ranks and file of the insurgency swelled with educated recruits from the two secondary schools of Rumbek and Juba Commercial as well as the grown-ups from the intermediate schools.

The resistance of the Sudanese people in northern and southern parts of the country took two different modalities. In the southern provinces, where social awareness and apparent lack of political culture or organization and action consequent to socioeconomic underdevelopment and cultural backwardness, the resistance to the military regime was armed and violent. There was little for the ordinary person to learn from political violence, for it was destruction of life and property. It wasn't a mass movement to destroy the military dictatorship, but an armed movement to separate the two parts of the country.

In northern Sudan, where urbanization and civility had taken roots for a longer period, the resistance to military dictatorship took the form of political protests, processions, strikes, and demonstrations and civil disobedience. The resultant mass movement among the workers, farmers, students, and ordinary citizens eventually morphed into a popular uprising to overthrow the military regime in October 1964. The difference between the two modalities lies in the fact the October popular uprising became a weapon and a tool in the hands of the masses; they replicated the experience in the overthrow of the May regime in 1985 and again in the ongoing revolution that overthrew the thirty years rule of the Islamic fundamentalists. In the southern Sudan where, political violence was the only tool of resistance the Anya-nya2 emerged in 1976 consequent to the contradictions triggered by the May regime in violation of the Addis Ababa Agreement and the SPLM/A in 1983 when the debate within the Southern Regional political elite shifted to re-division of the Southern Region instead of social and economic development of the Region.

In his book, 'The Paradoxes of two Sudans' (2015) Mansour Khalid put it succinctly that the political attitude and behaviour of this Arab dominated northern political elite left no option for the southern Sudanese except to vote for secession[4]. One such paradox speaks to Field Marshall Gaafar Mohammed Numeiri, the first northern Sudanese to courageously make peace with the southern rebels - the Southern Sudan Liberation Movement (SSLM), to end the war that had raged since August 1955 predating the independence of the Sudan. The eleven years interlude (1972-1983) was the only time southern Sudanese have ever had and enjoyed peace. However, it was the same peace makers (Numeiri and Lagu) for different motives and volition who abrogated the Addis Ababa Agreement, dismantled the Southern Region, and returned the country to war in 1983. It is paradoxical and indeed unbelievable that Gen. Joseph Lagu out of anger and bitterness against his own brothers in the Southern Region could join Gaafar Mohammed Numeiri in the destruction of something he spent many years to achieve while fighting the bush war. The abrogation of Addis Ababa Agreement and the dismantle of Southern Region are covered in chapter two.

The other paradox relates to the situation in South Sudan after its independence in 2011. Barely three years into its independence a civil war broke out and meted severe destruction and loss of life. At the time of writing, more than half a million lives have been lost because of war and other natural calamities. There are about one million South Sudanese living as refugees in the Sudan. Many have returned to the same squalid conditions of internally displaced people camps that sprouted around Khartoum, Kosti, and other towns in the north during the war of national liberation. This time they are refugees running away from the country for which they had struggled and sacrificed. The greatest paradox is that the same leaders who led the war of national liberation have turned against each other fighting themselves in a senseless war to create the condition for failure. The refugees in the Sudan are in addition to the tens of thousands in the UNMISS protection of civilian sites in Juba, Bentiu, Bor and Malakal, and those three million refugees in Ethiopia, Kenya, Uganda, DR Congo, Central African Republic, and in the Arab Republic of Egypt. Considering the sacrifices the people made during the twenty-one years war of national liberation, this terrible humanitarian disaster shouldn't have obtained in South Sudan; It appeared the SPLM/A political and military elite were made of the same material and treated the people as arrogantly as the northern Sudanese political elite. They were interested in power and accumulation of wealth, which they stacked outside the country particularly in Uganda, Kenya, Sudan, and Ethiopia in form of real estate instead of investing it in the country to grow the economy.

The northern political elite share the responsibility between them for the failure of the Sudanese state (Khalid: 1990). This prognosis remains to a large extent accurate. Those at the pinnacle of state political power carry the biggest responsibility than those at the bottom. But why are the southern politicians who also reached the top excluded from this prognosis? They also share in this responsibility on account of their participation no matter the minor role they played in the processes of social and political engineering of the Sudanese state. But the attitude that southerners are outsiders to the concept of Sudanese citizenship because of being non-Muslims and non-Arab accounts for ignoring their responsibility. Thus, the southern leaders and operatives of the May regime (sadnat Mayo) people like Abel Alier, Gen. Joseph Lago, Eng. James Joseph Tambura, Dr. Lawrence Wol Wol, Daniel Koat Matthews and many other southern leaders were not arrested or detained like their northern colleagues when the regime came trembling down on 6th April 1985. They were considered in the same way society treated children and women.

The preponderant role of the political elite in the state machinery notwithstanding some aspects of this failure must have emanated from the primordial and conservative nature of the society in most of the Sudan. This primordial nature of society constitutes a retardation force that prevents forwards movement generated by the socioeconomic forces triggered by interaction with modernity. Thus, the transition from primaeval society to modernity is exceptionally taking a very long time. The capitalist mode and relations of production had not completely penetrated the country and society in form of large scale commercial agricultural farming and manufacturing or animal husbandry. Thus, while the state in the centre is modern in its political and bureaucratic aspects nevertheless the dominant society lives and resonates with tradition and religious conservatism and pretends to participate in the state's socioeconomic and political processes.

The state as a colonial construct in the Sudan did not emerge from natural evolution and development of Sudanese society at least from the Marxist point of view. The socio-political forces that emerged at the helm in the Sudan represented both the traditional conservative religious society and modern democratic political ideas. Thus, every time since independence until 1969 leftist putsch, the theocratic family dynasties preponderated, subordinated, and dominated the social and political engineering process of the Sudanese state. The struggle for dominance between these forces triggered the intrusion of the military into politics. In the first instance, the government of the Umma Party under prime minister Abdalla Bey Khalil, fearing a vote of no confidence in the Parliament handed over the power to Gen. Ibrahim Abboud. Incidentally, it was under the military dictatorship that progressive socio-political forces in form of workers trade union movement, farmers unions, student movement representing the interests of the Sudanese masses started to multiply and assert themselves in a struggle that eventually led to the overthrow of the military dictatorship in a popular uprising in October 1964.

The greatest paradox in the Sudan, as Hassan Turabi would articulate it in one of his public addresses, was that the masses of the Sudanese people rise to bring down military dictatorships while the political elite's failure to manage democracy trigger military coups. This couldn't have been more correct. Military coups in the Sudan, as we shall note in the following pages, resulted from the failure of the political elite to honestly adhere to the rules of the political pluralism. It is not permissible to play by totalitarian dictator rule in a multi-party democratic dispensation. The post October 1964 transitional government conducted elections and handed power to an elected Umma-NUP coalition. In a political conspiracy hatched by the Muslim Brotherhood to exclude the political left in the engineering processes towards a permanent constitution, the Parliament voted to outlaw the Communist Party of the Sudan (CPS) and to unseat its eight members. The Umma-NUP coalition government even refused to implement the Supreme Court's ruling against the parliamentary vote. This was tantamount to inviting the political left to utilize other undemocratic methods to reach the pinnacle of the state power. liberal multiparty democracy is not compatible with political repression or exclusion.

The missteps of the Parliament and the Umma-NUP coalition government radically changed the trajectory of Sudan's political history. The left organized to infiltrate the military institution and in a matter of three years pulled a leftist coup in May 1969.

The incursion of the army into politics indeed marked the failure of liberal democracy, and the Sudan was never the same again since 1969. The leftist's regime, notwithstanding the brief period it existed (1969-1971), wrought profound changes in the Sudan. The 9th June Declaration recognizing the historical sociocultural differences of the people of southern provinces of the Sudan changed the perception of the problem of Southern Sudan. It was a right step in the direction to consolidate the countries national unity. The contradictions within the left-wing and among the revolutionary forces aborted the Sudanese revolution and prevented its logical conclusion. Marx said, history occurs first as a tragedy and then as a farce. This has bearings to the repeat of the 1969 leftist revolution in 2019 popular uprising to overthrow the NIF regime that had governed the country since 1989. The notion of the Supreme Council of the State as an institution in the Constitution Document the Forces of Freedom and Change (FFC) and the Military Council signed is the elephant in the room; it emanated from that vicious cycle of thinking since 1964 that keeps the Sudan in perpetual transition.

It has been always mentioned that southern Sudan rebelled in protest to Sudanization of the colonial posts in the bureaucracy or in the distribution of power in the Sudanese state. The issue of power relations between the parts of the nascent national state is just a tip of the iceberg. The southern Sudan political class was more concerned with the future of southern Sudan in a country now defined as an Arab country. The demand for federation, which was a scale down from secession and independence was to protect the southern Sudanese identity. This could only be ensured in a strong representation in the then formed nationalist government. The Prime Minister, Ismail Al-Azhari played the politics of 'divide to conquer' with the southern politicians playing one against the other in order to buy time. This game strayed into the hands of the colonial administrators who for their own selfish interests wanted the southern provinces separated from the rest of the Sudan. It was in this environment of uncertainty and confusion among the southern political leaders that the Equatoria Corps of the Sudan Defence Force mutinied in Torit on 18th August 1955. These politicians were already divided in the different northern political establishment to which they paid their allegiance due to economic factors.

Joseph U Garang (1961) discussed this phenomenon and the confusion Azhari cultivated among the southern politicians and succinctly proved their lack of correct understanding of the social and political forces at work. I would add that as members of the Umma Party or the National Unionist Party these southern politicians wouldn't have expressed or articulated the southern view point on the political situation than in the country. The Southern political leaders were still political toddlers in the then emerging nationalist political market place. However, this changed completely with the formation of the Liberal Party to context the 1957 parliamentary elections as the authentic representative of the people of southern Sudan. Their steadfastness and solidarity was a factor in Abdalla Bey Khalil's decision to surrender power to the military on 17th November 1958.

Gen. Ibrahim Abboud intervened to the implement the policy of Islamization and Arabisation as a means to accelerate the quick assimilation of the non-Muslims and non-Arab population of the Sudan into the Arab-Islam nationhood. It would have been difficult, if not impossible, to implement under a multi-party liberal democratic dispensation based on the Westminster model. That was why Abboud's first decree as Chairman of the Military Council was to ban the political parties and all political activities in the country. The military regime and its policies produced completely negative results in the southern provinces, which then was since 1955 still under the state emergency; insurrection was active mostly in Equatoria. The anger against the change of weekly holiday from Sunday to Friday and the threat of Islamization pushed many southerners into the insurrection: political leaders, career soldiers, students, and government officials besides the initially force of officers and soldiers of the Equatoria Corps. Political prosecution forced the members of the Liberal Party into exile to establish the Sudan African Closed Districts National Union (SACDNU) ostensibly to include the Nuba and the Funj and to continue the struggle; it later changed to Sudan African National Union (SANU). The Anya-nya started to improve its military organization and was fighting a sustained guerrilla warfare against the Sudanese army.

These political developments war in the south impacted negatively on the economy in the country and generated social and political unrests in the cities and town where anti-military rule were strongest. These social and political unrest built up into a strong resistance to the military dictatorship under the leadership of the workers trade unions led by the Sudan Railways Trade Union in Atbara, Khartoum, Kosti, El Obeid and Port Sudan, and the student movement led by the Khartoum University Student Union (KUSU). The resistance in northern Sudan took the form of political strikes, street demonstrations and processions which culminated in the political strike and civil disobedience which eventually led to the overthrow of Abboud's regime in October 1964.

The October popular uprising failed to escalate into a social revolution; the revolutionary social forces led by the communists were still weak and this gave political sway to the same right-wing political forces that surrendered the power to Abboud to take over the rein of power. The transitional government wrecked by ideological contradictions had only to programmes to implement: Convene the Round Table Conference on the problem of Southern Provinces, and prepare the country for the parliamentary elections. This was indeed to create the same political conditions that precipitated the military incursion into politics in 1958.

4. The Leftist Military Putsch, the Abortion of National Democratic Revolution and a Respite for Southern Sudan

Prime Minister of the transitional government, Sirr Al-Khatim Al-Khalifa's push the peace in southern provinces through the round table conference ended in disarray; the northern political elite particularly the right-wing liberal/conservative parties of the Umma, NUP and the Islamic Chartered Front wanted a military solution to the insurrection in the southern provinces. Hence, the Umma - DUP coalition government of Prime Minister Mohammed Ahmed Mahgoub produced by the partial elections 1965, proved ruthless in the prosecution of the war against the Anya-nya. The year 1965 was the worst year ever witnessed by the people of southern Sudan. The Sudanese army, angered by the increased casualties its sustained from the rebel ambushes and attack turned their guns on innocent civilians. In July 1965, Wau witnessed the massacre of seventy-six government officials and other civilians celebrating in a marriage party. In Juba the army went on rampage shooting and killing in the suburbs in which more than two-thousand people were killed. The army razed down nearly every village they found on the roadside or riverside throughout southern Sudan. On July 30th the Sudanese army massacred one hundred and twenty-six male inhabitants of Watajwok village not far from Malakal. It was a war of extermination and pillage.

While the war raged in the southern provinces, party politics surged in Khartoum and the debate in the Constituent Assembly was on the promulgation of the Islamic Constitution, and the contradiction apparently was between the Ansar and the Khatimiya religious sects over who of the contending Al-Hadi Al-Mahdi or Usman Al-Mirghani would be elected the Imam of the Islamic Republic of the Sudan. The Communist Party of the Sudan, now outlawed, and the entire left-wing revolutionary forces were belabouring in the political cold. Mohammed Ahmed Mahgoub refused to implement the court order against the unconstitutionality of the parliamentary procedures that outlawed the CPA. This was the greatest failure of liberal democracy in the Sudan. It reflected the pressure placed on the Umma – NUP coalition by the theocratic family dynasties of the Ansar and Khatimiya using the emerging Muslim Brotherhood to champion first an anti-communist campaign and the promulgation of the Islamic Constitution. Islamic dogmatism and the use of political violence was an explosive admixture that prompted ideological infiltration into the military institution and its involvement in state politics.

The parliamentary elections 1968 were intended to weed off the progressive social and democratic political forces in preparation for the promulgation of the Islamic Constitution. The Imam of the Ansar, Sayyed Al-Hadi Abdelrahaman Al-Mahdi was tipped for election the Imam of the Sudan and against this background the Umma Party conservative stalwarts hatched a conspiracy to rig off Sadiq Al-Sadeeq Abdelrahaman Al-Mahdi from the leadership of the Umma Party leaving the ground for his uncle Al-Hadi Abdelrahaman. It was against this background that Al-Sadiq and Dr. Abdalla Al-Turabi were both trounced in the constituencies and Sayyed William Deng Nhial was assassinated in Rumbek.

There was urgent need to pre-empt the promulgation of the Islamic Constitution; the Constituent Assembly was on the verge of enacting the constitutional bill when on 25th May 1969, the political left pulled a military coup under the rubrics of the Free Officers Organization in the Sudan Armed forces. The May revolution, as it was christened, irreversibly and qualitatively transformed the politics of the Sudan. While this qualitative change would for sixteen years (1969-1985) suppress the right-wing multiparty liberal democracy, it enabled the crystallization and differentiation of the political left into its ideological cocoons, which generated serious contradictions within and between these leftist groups, consequent to external political and ideological interferences in the Sudanese revolution.

The first victim of these contradiction was the Communist Party of the Sudan. Although the CPS did not recognize the army as means to social and political change in the Sudan, nevertheless, it enlisted its support of the May revolution on condition that it maintained its independent existence as part of the national democratic revolutionary force in the Sudan. This precipitated a split in the party (March 1970) between those who wanted the party dissolved into this amorphous thing called the May Revolution and its political outfit, the Sudan Socialist Union (SSU), and those who desired independent existence of the party. The upshot of this division was the July 19th, 1971, corrective action that removed Numeiri and the Nasserites from the centre of power on the one hand and the counter coups that returned them to power on July 22nd completely turned the tables against the Sudanese revolution. The split in the CPS exposed the dominance of the elements that climbed its ranks from purely intellectual and knowledge of theory and therefore brought into the party petty bourgeois adventurism and hunting for quick fixes. Numeiri's eventual execution of Abdel Khaliq Mahgoub, the Party's General-Secretary, Al-Shafie Ahmed Al-Shiekh, vice president of the Federation International Labour Union and Joseph Ukel Garang, was the heavy price the Communist Party of the Sudan had to pay for flirting with the military.

The summary execution of its leadership was the darkest day of the Communist Party of the Sudan and indeed retarded the progress of the Sudanese revolution many years backwards. Sudan has been gearing towards the launch of the national democratic revolution and the construction of a national democratic development state in the Sudan. The CPS methodology was that of working-class and grass roots struggle to disseminate social awareness and political consciousness among the masses. The experiment with the Free Officers Movement in the Sudanese military, a relic of colonial military occupation of the Sudan, was a precipitous truncation of that methodology that also rejected armed struggle as a way to social change. It leaves many questions of how the Sudanese revolution would spread the length and breadth of the Sudan without variation in the methodology given the uneven socioeconomic development in the different parts of the Sudan. Did humanity have to follow the experience of the Soviet revolution to effect social revolution to the exclusion of other experiences like the Chinese, the Cuban and the Vietnamese? These and many questions arise because different nations of necessity must chart their own revolutionary trajectory. This reality forces me to quote below what Fidel Castro said of Marxism:

> *In the complexity of the present-day world, where circumstances are so diverse and countries are in such different situations and at such varying levels of material, cultural and technological development, it is impossible to hope to conceive of Marxism as a kind of a church, some kind of religious doctrine with its Rome, its pope and its ecumenical council. Marxism is a revolutionary and dialectical doctrine; not a religious one. To endeavour to contain Marxism in some species of catechism is anti-Marxist. The diversity of situations must inevitably lead to an infinity of interpretations. Those who give correct interpretation and apply them logically will triumph. Those who are wrong or who do not follow the logic of revolutionary thinking will fail; they will be overturned and supplanted, for Marxism is not a private property inscribed in a land register. It is a doctrine of revolutionaries written by one revolutionary and developed by other revolutionaries for revolutionaries (Granma, English weekly edition, 12 March 1987).*

It would, therefore, mean that a country as socially and culturally diverse as the Sudan, in the absence of a national centre representing this diversity, it might as well mean that the people in different regions would take different routes and methodologies to social change. This was the case of people of southern Sudan where capitalist penetration and exploitation had not taken toots as in the Gezira.

This dramatic turn of events in Khartoum in July 1971, brought in its wing dramatic political changes in the southern provinces of the Sudan, where the civil war then raged with intensity necessitating nothing but political compromise to end it. The events of 22nd July that brought Numeiri back to power in Khartoum wouldn't have occurred without the connivance of imperialist forces. The forcing down in Tripoli of the British Airways plane carrying the leaders of the Sudanese revolution from London to Khartoum was part of the conspiracy that lobbed Numeiri into the imperialist camp. Internally in the Sudan, Numeiri had lost both the political right and left; his political isolation therefore pushed him into an alliance with imperialism. After losing both the political right (Umma, DUP and Muslim Brothers) as well as the political left (CPS), Numeiri had only the southern rebels to turn to make peace with the assistance of imperialist agents in the region. The peace talks with the southern rebels, the Southern Sudan Liberation Movement (SSLM) were held in Addis Ababa, Ethiopia, under the auspices of Emperor Haile Selassie and the World Council of Churches and an agreement was reached on 3rd March 1972 (Malual, 2022:249).

The Addis Ababa Agreement between the SSU and SSLM created a peace spell in the Sudan. However, like anything done in bad faith or undertaken to cover a temporal political isolation, the Addis Ababa Agreement was not intended to last for posterity; both Gen. Lagu and Field Marshall Numeiri could have otherwise tried their best to preserve the agreement. Acting in accordance with political dictates of the moment, Numeiri responded to abrogate the agreement, dismantled the Southern Region, and returned the country to war. But the war itself caused Numeiri's downfall in a popular uprising against the regime in March-April 1985, in a replica of Gen Abboud's fall in 1964.

accelerated by war in southern Sudan proved that war couldn't resolved the fundamental contradictions underpinning the conflict in Southern Sudan. It also proves that liberal democratic party politics cannot resolve those fundamental contradictions. The multiparty democratic election 1986 produced the same situation as 1957 and 1965 in which the same Umma-DUP coalition government usher into power, while the war raged in southern Sudan. Sadiq Al-Mahdi handed power of the elected government to his brother-in-law, Dr. Hassan Abdalla Al-Turabi, the leader of the National Islamic Front on 30th June 1989 in the same fashion and under the same political circumstances of power transfer Abdall Bey Khalil handed over power to Gen. Ibrahim Abboud on 17th November 1958.

5. The NIF takes power, prosecutes a jihad and negotiates the CPA with the SPLM/A

The dominant right-wing Sudanese political elite never learned from the fact that short transitional period after the demise of a military dictatorship or a totalitarian regime is never enough for conduct of free and fair democratic elections. This was precisely because they were not the drivers of the popular uprisings. Whether in October 1964 or in April 1985, the workers trade unions, professional associations, students' movement and other civil society groups were like women and youths were the main driving forces behind the popular uprisings. The political parties only waited to usurp and exercise state power. In this respect driven by their ambition to lead, the right-wing political forces wouldn't waste time but instead hurried to the polls knowing well that ideologically and politically they controlled the ignorant and illiterate masses.

The multiparty elections conducted just a year after the demise of the May regime brought Al-Sadiq Al-Sadeeq Abdel Rahaman Al-Mahdi as prime minister at the head of the Umma-DUP coalition, but also placated the smaller political parties from the southern Sudan, which would hardly survive economically in Khartoum without being in government. The National Islamic Front, which had already burnt its fingers alongside the May regime, still had a strong power base; its forces had not been totally disrupted or scattered and moreover it was not possible to prevent its participation in a liberal democratic dispensation. Thus, except for the defeat of its leader Dr. Hassan Abdalla Al-Turabi, the NIF won a sizeable number of seats in the Parliament to constitute a nagging opposition to the coalition. Coupled with Sadiq's obfuscation and lack of clear agenda for peace in the country, the NIF dominated the war agenda in the government paralysing Sadiq Al-Mahdi and preventing him to take decisive action on peace until they overthrew him in a coups in June 1989.

The Umma-DUP government was a very unstable coalition particularly after the meeting that took place between Dr. John Garang the SPLM/A leader and the DUP leader Ahmed Osman Al-Mirghani in Addis Ababa. This meeting and the proposed constitutional conference was the straw that broke the Umma-DUP coalition government pushing Sadiq Al-Mahdi into an alliance with the NIF without realising that its leaders were scheming for power preying on the weak performance of the Sudan Armed Forces in the war against the SPLA in southern Sudan. This was the greatest political blunder Sadiq Al-Mahdi committed and exposed his ideological and political bankruptcy. The Umma Party- NIF coalition was very unstable and attempts to save it through repeated cabinet shuffle and reshuffle gave no respite. It played out in many political episodes which included the Army memorandum, which bordered on a political ultimatum. It was a risk driven by intense demoralization of the army suffering defeats that garrisons deserted or withdrew into neighbouring foreign land. This precipitated another Sadiq's shift to the Umma-DUP coalition, which never helped the deteriorating political situation. This pathetic situation of the Sudanese army in the war zone[5] emboldened the National Islamic Front (NIF) to pull a putschist coup to overthrow the democratically elected government. The NIF coup was the price Sadiq Al-Mahdi had to pay for procrastination and obfuscation on the peace agenda.

Once at the helm, the NIF immediately escalated and transformed the civil war in southern Sudan, Nuba Mountains and southern Blue Nile into a religious war – *Jihad*. It conscripted all able-bodied Sudanese including women, school children and elderly into the war and transformed its character. The NIF intended to defeat the SPLM/A on all fronts. By amassing *jihadists*, it hoped to defeat the SPLA militarily on the battlefield. On the political front, the NIF indeed did instigate splits and divisions within its ranks of the SPLM/A[6], and diplomatically by isolating it from its main benefactors in Ethiopia and in the Horn of Africa. In it war against the SPLA, the NIF hoped to defeat the Derg, which it considered the main SPLA benefactor in Ethiopia. In this scheme it supported the Eritrean People's Liberation Front and the Tigray People's Liberation Front on the assumption that the defeat of Mengistu would eventually result in the defeat of the SPLM/A. Although not exactly as the NIF had hopes, Mengistu fled Ethiopia in May 1991 and his regime collapsed, and the SPLM/A was forced to withdraw back into the Sudan. However, after sixteen years, the *Jihad* flopped and the NIF had to negotiate peace with the SPLM.

The comprehensive peace agreement (CPA) signed on 9th January 2005 in Nairobi, Kenya by the NCP/Government of Sudan and the SPLM/A in front of international and regional mediators and observers ended the war in Southern Sudan,

Southern Kordofan/Nuba Mountains and Southern Blue Nile but not the war in Eastern Sudan or in Dar Fur. The agreement, therefore, was not comprehensive; the National Democratic Alliance, of which the SPLM/A was a part *vide* its New Sudan Brigade (NSB) based in Eastern Sudan, had to sign the Cairo Agreement a version of the CPA to allow the component parties of the NDA participate in the government of national unity (GONU). The Eastern Sudan Liberation Front (ESLF) had also to sign the Asmara agreement with the NCP to enable the ESLF participate in the GONU. The NCP played games with the NDA, ESLF and even the Abuja Agreement it signed with the Sudan Liberation Movement (Mini Arkoi Menawi) proved to be a bluff.

Initially, the NCP believed it could hoodwink the SPLM/A in the northern political elite's traditional game of "too many agreements dishonoured" it played with the southern Sudanese. The signing of the Security Arrangements during the interim period confirmed the separate existence of the SPLA, and made it impossible for the NCP to renege on implementing the CPA without the risk of returning the country to war. Things even became more complicated for the NCP when the Bush Administration sent Gen. Collin Powel to witness the CPA signing ceremony on 9th January 2005 and with a commitment to oversee the implementation process. The CPA ceased to be NCP face and time saving instruments as Numeiri and the May regime used the Addis Ababa Agreement. The NCP grudgingly had to implement its provisions albeit selectively and unsteadily, refusing to implement the Abyei protocol as well as the Popular Consultation for the Nuba mountains/Southern Kordofan and Southern Blue Nile. It's obvious for the NCP these protocols were not meant for implementation. In hindsight, they were to save Garang's face in front of his SPLM/A colleagues from those areas. The NCP acceptance of self-determination for Southern Sudan was a foregone conclusion they wouldn't allow Abyei, Nuba and Funj to go with it. The present stand offs over the three areas proves this notion.

6. Garang's tragic demise and Salva Kiir's leadership of the SPLM

July 9, 2005 was a momentous day. It was the day when all and sunder believed everything would proceed as planned; the SPLM Chairman and Commander-in-Chief of the SPLA, Dr. John Garang de Mabior took the constitutional oath of office as first vice president of the republic of the Sudan and president of the Government of Southern Sudan. A few hours earlier he had landed in Khartoum to a thunderous welcome by the Sudanese people. Sudan was not going to be the same again as the black Sudanese people saw in Garang their power and humanity; no one would exclude, discriminate, or marginalize them again. Dr. Garang set to work filling his docket in the republican palace as groups upon groups of visitors, some Sudanese African for the first time ever to see the republican palace grounds, came daily to punctuate his official duties with cultural shows of allegiance.

However, the devil was there to terminate the celebrations.

Twenty-one days into the office, Dr. John Garang de Mabior was killed in a tragic helicopter crash on 30th July 2005. His tragic death at the commencement of the CPA implementation deprived the SPLM and the Sudanese people of the adroit strategist and diplomat that was John Garang. The SPLM went into an interlude of confusion and loss of direction occasioned by its lack of functional institutions and instruments of public authority. The SPLM power rather than being an institution was personified in the leader that in the absence of John Garang, SPLM was bound to face multiple problems. The SPLM first-row leaders was not a united mass. It also comprised some radicals who out of their own volition evolved into power centres around the new leader, President Salva Kiir Mayardit. As a result, multiple power centres in the SPLM party, and in the government of Southern Sudan (GOSS) built around Salva Kiir Mayardit's leadership, sometimes preventing him to assert his powers as the ultimate authority in both institutions. More often than not, Kiir was forced to rescind his orders, directives, and even presidential decrees at the behest of some powerful power centres. President Kiir, coming from military intelligence background, had all the intelligence reports, some of which he gathered through private and personal channels, nevertheless, he never used that to take decisive actions. In many instances, he would only lay serious emphasis on the trivial matters, and at the same trivialize serious matters. President Salva Kiir was not a decision maker and many instances throughout his rule, serious matters of national interest nurd on and took their own course. This style of leadership had tremendous bearing on the working relations in the government of national unity both in Juba and in Khartoum. The SPLM and the NCP were partners in the CPA implementation, and its success imperatively required that the two partners read from the same political text.

However, there were times that the SPLM behaved as if it were an opposition party to the government in which it enjoyed 28% power at the national and 70% at the level of government of southern Sudan. Dr. Garang would have emphasized SPLM political interest more than the NCP to build predictable relations of trust and confidence to ensure that the NCP subscribed to and did its bit of the agreement. The SPLM didn't need to build side shows with the northern political parties in competition with the NCP for the simple reason that any backstabbing of the NCP could easily jeopardize its relationship with the NCP and impair the implementation of the CPA. Disagreement between the NCP and the SPLM would be good music for the Umma Party and the NUP, whose interest in the CPA was nothing but its failure.

The political blunder Salva Kiir committed was to invite Sadiq el Mahdi (Umma), Hassan Abdalla Al-Turabi (Popular Congress Party), Mohammed Ibrahim Nuqud (Communist Party of the Sudan) to a meeting in Juba. Whatever agreement the three signed behind the back of NCP was something that sent jitters to the NCP spine as an act of bad faith on the part of the SPLM smacking of back-stabbing and was completely uncalled for. The Umma, DUP, CPS except the PCP had the separate Cairo Agreement supplement to the CPA, which enabled their participation in the Government of National Unity (GONU) throughout northern Sudan. The three parties were scheming for weak points or loopholes in the SPLM - NCP relations which they could exploit to their advantage.

Another example of SPLM bad politics that bordered on political *naiveite* occurred during the midterms presidential and general elections. It demonstrated SPLM's lack of clear understanding of its strategic political interests in the Sudanese national political dynamics. It portrayed the SPLM as a big windbag steered by the political whims of some of its influential politicians. It was paradoxical that President Salva Kiir and the whole party went along with this influential group, which not necessarily was the right course of action. The midterm elections came at a time of high emotional tension in the NCP. Its leader, President Omer Al-Bashir was under indictment by International Criminal Court (ICC) for war crimes and crimes against humanity in Dar Fur. The NCP leaders were extremely nervous; they did not countenance anything internally within the country like Omer Al-Bashir failing to win the presidency, or anything that could lead to the collapse of the regime and would do anything to prevent it.

The SPLM's fielding of Yasir Sayed Arman against President Omer Hassan Ahmed Al-Bashir for the presidency of the Sudan in the midterm's election 2010 was something that worked against political decency to say the least. Nowhere in the world would someone other than the party's ultimate leader contest for the presidency of the country unless the incumbent was retiring from politics. That the SPLM nominated Yassir, and not Salva Kiir, to contest against Omer Al-Bashir was something of a conspiratorial nature reflected the internal contradictions within the SPLM. That Chairman Salva Kiir went along with this stratagem speaks volumes of the SPLM internal configuration and dynamics to be discussed in chapter three. It must be viewed as the external manifestation of the SPLM internal power wrangles and intrigues.

It demonstrated two important things. First, it exposed the Salva Kiir as only a southern Sudanese leader with no or little concerns for the rest of the Sudan. Allowing his subordinate to contest for the presidency meant that Salva Kiir had made up his mind for Southern Sudan and was interested only in the conduct of the referendum on self-determination staking his political future on the independence of South Sudan. It also demonstrated that Kiir considered or treated Yassir as a northern Sudanese not a member of the SPLM with political bearings for southern Sudan. In this respect, first vice president Salva Kiir Mayardit forgot that there was a direct link between Al-Bashir's return as president of the republic in the midterm's elections and the conduct of the referendum on self-determination. The legislation that was to trigger the referendum process required the cooperation of Al-Bashir and the NCP to enable the passing of the legislation to trigger the promulgation of the Southern Sudan Referendum Bill. This was a process that required intense diplomacy and political scheming between the two parties. Thus, if somebody other than Al-Bashir returned as the president, the likelihood of NCP refusing to cooperate with the SPLM on the legislation to trigger the referendum process was granted. The timeline for midterms elections had been overshot by more than a year. The SPLM needed, therefore, to manoeuvre carefully to secure NCP cooperation and political commitment to have the Southern Sudan Referendum Bill promulgated before President Al Bashir prorogued the National Legislature.

Secondly, it also demonstrated that Salva Kiir did not care about the political future of the SPLM northern sector. The conduct of the referendum and independence of South Sudan would not necessarily spell the death of the SPLM in the Sudan, now dubbed SPLM/A-North. President Salva Kiir was politically and morally obliged to diligently work to ensure the political existence of the SPLM Northern Sector past the secession of South Sudan. In its political adventurism, the SPLM leadership missed an opportunity to strike a deal with the NCP leadership that could strengthen and consolidate the SPLM in the Sudan after the secession of South Sudan.

Out of political expediency, not principle, the SPLM should have supported the NCP against the ICC to demonstrate its commitment to the Sudanese national security interests. At such a critical time, the SPLM should have played its politics well even though it had the back of powerful states like the USA, UK, Norway, and the European Union. I could vouch, the SPLM bargain for not fielding a candidate against President Al-Bashir would have paid back handsomely. For instance, first vice president Salva Kiir could have requested President Al-Bashir to leave the SPLM to contest the state governors of Khartoum, Blue Nile and Southern Kordofan in return for supporting the NCP against ICC and for not fielding a presidential candidate; this couldn't have been an impossible demand for the NCP to agree to. President Al-Bashir could have obliged for two if not the three states. The SPLM - North had to pay for this ambivalence and the reckless political behaviour and lack of strategic political calculation. When it became clear that South Sudan was seceding, the NCP attacked the SPLM-North and waged war in Blue Nile and Southern Kordofan before the two states could conduct the exercise of popular consultation.

7. The One-Country-Two-Systems Provision of the CPA

The idea of one-country-two systems during the six-years interim period was the cornerstone of the CPA. This was a unique political system in the Sudan, which was a radical departure from the Addis Ababa Agreement 1972 and the Southern Region it established. Although it was designed specifically to give the unity of the Sudan a chance, the manner in which it was or not implemented worked against the unity. The fact that the CPA provided Southern Sudan with a constitution and a separate army, it was a foregone conclusion that Southern Sudan was a state in waiting. This was the reality the mediators and the international community had belaboured to bring the principal negotiators Dr. John Garang and Ustaz Ali Osman Mohammed Tah to directly thrash out those details in trust and confidence. Thus, in the context of the then existing NCP totalitarianism, 'one-country-two-systems' really meant the NCP's regime would retain its legitimacy even against the CPA provision of democratic transformation of the Sudanese polity; the NCP remained intact save its 1994 constitution, suggesting that the CPA gave it a lease of life to the chagrin of the progressive and democratic Sudanese political forces. Moreover, the CPA caught the SPLM before it has evolved a functional political system. In fact, in the early stages of the war Garang favourite innuendos of Numeiri's regime was that it was a one-man-no-system-rule' but the SPLM would be worse off than a replica of May regime. It was indeed a one-man show of military, political and diplomatic gymnastics during the twenty-one years of war of national liberation. By March 2005, Garang then started the process of training SPLM/A leaders and cadres. He sent all the SPLM/A second-, and third-row leaders and cadres for training in South Africa. It was an admission that twenty-one years were spent only on military functions neglecting the development of other domains of national liberation.

For all practical purposes, 'one-country-two-system' was more rhetorical than literal. The republic of the Sudan was constitutionally still one country. There was only one system - the Ingaz system, and the SPLM conformed to that political system in everything except only in banking, which was a window in the Islamic banking system. Like the Ingaz that established the National Congress Party, the SPLM/A transformed itself into a political party, the SPLM and the SPLA adopted the conventional military ranking system, and its adopted wholesale the NCP's national security and intelligence organization to continue the brutal and heartless treatment of the political detractors in Southern Sudan. The 'one-country-two-systems' was therefore to prepare the Sudan for partition. Thus, on 9th July 2011, the 'one-country-two-systems' imperceptibly transformed into 'two-countries-one-system'.

The two countries emerged from a failed post-war political system and couldn't have been anything but two failed states. This phenomenon exactly replicates the SPLM/A metaphor. After the end of war, it was imperative that the SPLM and the SPLA separated into their respective professional domains. As I have described in my previous publications, the SPLM/SPLA evolved as Siamese twins conjoined in the head that a surgical operation to separate them into their respective professional domains would result in their mutual death. Indeed, they both belatedly died[7] in 2016. The SPLA was changed to South Sudan People's Defence Force (SSPDF) and the SPLM because a caricature of itself after the infiltration into its leadership by former members of the NCP and other Southern Sudan political parties. The manner the SPLM and SPLA died consequent to their separation into their professional spheres illustrates the case of Sudan's partition. To a careful observer, it did not take long after the partition before the Sudan (successor state) and South Sudan (seceding state) showed signs of political death immediately after the secession and independence of South Sudan.

This was to confirm that northern and southern Sudan were really one country except that the Arab dominated northern political elite desired the kind of relations with southern Sudan as that between the horse and its rider. The two parts could have existed as one country had the transitional constitution 1956 provide for freedom (liberty), justice (equality) and fraternity (solidarity) upon which to construct Sudan's unity in diversity. The Arab dominated northern political elite's definition of Sudan as Arab and Muslim warranting forceful assimilation of the non-Arab and non-Muslim was recipe for conflict and secessionism. This was the parallel the JCE acting on logics of demographic preponderance of the Dinka wanted to draw in South Sudan. The notion of ethnic or racial/religious hegemony and/or domination is something that cannot take roots in the twenty-first century in which people have become socially aware and politically conscious.

The freedom of choice exercised by the people of Southern Sudan during the referendum on self-determination shattered the myth of 'national unity' and its chorus of 'no south without north, or no north without south' sung by both sides in vain political shows since 1956. The meaning of the chorus would have been realizable had there been an organic cord binding the two parts of the country. Since that cord did not exist the two countries should coexist and develop separately into vibrant economies; it only required that each state constructed the correct mix of democratic politics and a development state to address the fundamental problems of poverty, ignorance, cultural backwardness, and superstition. This was what eluded the Sudanese political elite.

The SPLM metaphor above only tries to prove one salient fact; absence of patriotic and nationalistic leadership, the two parts of the Sudan were held together by a weak sublime inorganic cord whose ends were tied by deceit, lies, untruths, and empty promises. The overwhelming (98.3%) vote for secession casted by the people of southern Sudan leading to the death of the Sudan proved the vacuity of one-country-two-system that purported to give unity of the Sudan a chance.

On signing the CPA on 9th January 2005, the NCP and the SPLM promised the Sudanese people that in implementing the peace agreement and its six protocols they would give the unity of the Sudan a chance. It is difficult to tell whether the promise to give unity a chance would have come to fruition hadn't Dr. John Garang perished in that tragic helicopter crash. However, the writings were already on the wall indicating that both the SPLM leadership and the extreme faction of the NCP started to prepare for dismemberment of the Sudan as soon as they read the protocol that provided for the exercise of self-determination.

In a speech in Rumbek on 16th May 2005 to mark the 22nd anniversary of the battle of Bor it was apparent that Dr. Garang had absolved himself and the SPLM/A of whatever would happen if the people of southern Sudan voted the wrong way. He abandoned his usual diplomacy and spoke out clearly for everyone to hear. *"If unity is not made attractive, why would any southerner vote himself or herself into second-class citizenship? If Sudan does not sufficiently and fundamentally change, why should anybody vote to become a servant instead of being a master in his/her own independent house?"* This echoed the general mood among southern Sudanese, particularly those who remained under the oppressive regime in the southern garrison towns or those who in search of security migrated to northern Sudan and were living under squalid conditions in the internally displaced people's camps.

Notwithstanding Dr. Garang's statement, the extreme faction of the NCP started to make 'unity of the Sudan' unattractive to southern Sudanese. This trend fronted by the *Intibaha* Newspaper had daily editorial tirades authored by Mustafa campaigning against the SPLM and NCP unionists. It was not SPLM leadership's obligation though to preach the unity option nevertheless it had the duty and political obligation to build and strengthen the SPLM-North as an important step to ensure future peaceful relations between the two countries. That must have been the idea behind the concept of 'one-country-two-system' during the six-year interim period Dr. Garang and Ustaz Ali Osman Mohammed Tah negotiated as a confidence boosting measure. It was commendable that the NCP leadership kept its side of the deal and allowed the Southern Sudan referendum to happen. The NCP demonstrated responsible politics by recognizing that their survival also depended on implementing the CPA, particularly, those provisions that related directly to Southern Sudan. However, it refused to implement the three areas protocols; this would be the price the SPLM leadership paid for absence of clear and strategic thinking and planning and a visionless leadership.

On 9th July 2011, the people of South Sudan celebrated their freedom and sovereignty. After fifty-five years of shared sovereignty and nearly two centuries of common history, the republic of the Sudan partitioned into two separate entities. President Omer el Bashir was one of the hundreds of worlds dignitaries who graced the independence celebrations at Dr. Garang Memorial Grounds in Juba, and the Republic of the Sudan was the first country to grant diplomatic recognition to the nascent Republic of South Sudan - a gesture of civility and political maturity though. As Mohammed Ibrahim Nuqud had predicted that the one-country-two-systems would become two-countries-one-system, and it came to be. The prediction stemmed from the manner the SPLM conducted its politics without clear direction and strategic benchmarks and implementing NCP policies even in areas that contradicted its stance as a national liberation movement.

8. The Border War over Heglig (Pan-Thao)

The independence of South Sudan spurred completely different relations between the two parts of what was one state for nearly two-hundred years. The two states had to evolve new relations under the international law as equal members of the United Nations. The hate-love relations that underpinned the NCP-SPLM transactions became inter-state diplomatic etiquette to be handled with utmost precautions. The partition of the Sudan came before the NCP and the SPLM had cleared all the post-referendum issues, which were being handled under the auspices of the African Union High Level Implementation Panel led by President Thabo Mbeki. These issues could have been resolved amicably hadn't there been serious internal SPLM contradictions. It is worth mentioning that independence of South Sudan rekindled the internal power struggle that fitted President Salva Kiir Mayardit against his vice president Dr. Riek

Machar Teny-Dhurgon and the SPLM Secretary-General Pagan Amum Okiech. It was an old grudge linked to the structural weakness of the SPLM misconstrued as personal between the leaders[8]. One of the post-referendum issues which remained unresolved with the Sudan was most importantly the question of borders. The borders issue was on Pan Thao[9] (Heglig) and of course the oil reserves therein, which was wrongly awarded to the Sudan in the case of Abyei at the Court of Permanent Arbitration in The Hague 2009. As I said, hadn't it not been linked to the SPLM internal political dynamics, Pan Thao (Heglig) wouldn't have caused war between South Sudan and the Sudan.

Barely seven-months into this partition of the |Sudan, South Sudan and the Sudan were involved in a border war. It's unbelievable, indeed flabbergasting, that 'two-countries-one-political-system' went to war, as there was nothing so impelling as to push Salva Kiir and Omer Al-Bashir into war. True to its war time militarist subculture; whereby only one man made and executed such difficult decisions the decision to go to war in other countries / states would have required a parliamentary vote. President Salva Kiir only called an emergency sitting of the Transitional National Legislative Assembly (TNLA) just to inform its members and the nation that, 'it was at war with the Sudan', and that 'our gallant SPLA forces are advancing'(sic). No questions or comments were allowed in the midst of deafening martial music played by the SPLA Band.

The parameters of this war have not been fully disclosed, explained, or justified up to the moment of writing. They remained classified and perhaps may not see the light. The explosion could have possibly been relics of bad often tremulous relations that existed during the interim period between some SPLM and NCP leaders but that wouldn't prevent senior members of the SPLM having knowledge of it. I was a member of the SPLM and a cabinet minister for Higher Education, Science and Technology, but I can swear that like many of my cabinet colleagues I only learnt of the conflict between the two countries over Heglig (Pan Thou) and the oil fields, its escalation and eruption into violence in the president Kiir's speech addressing the TNLA to which we were hastily summoned. It was embarrassing to inquire or fish for information as to how passions could have flared up so quickly as to lead to war. Worst, it wasn't a precipitous situation to warrant keeping cabinet members ignorant of such a political development as war between two neighbouring countries. Could it have been that the unionist in the NCP had taken over the power and desired to reverse South Sudan's independence while it was still weak and wobbling? We would ask ourselves. But slowly, the parameters of the war and the quick decision to war started to appear on the screen. The war was linked to South Sudan's internal political dynamics surrounding the squabbles within the SPLM for leadership. This will be discussed at length and more succinctly in the next chapters, suffice only to say that on South Sudan side, the war was a disaster. First, the Government of South Sudan prosecuted the border war without clear political strategy; it was a war for its sake. The SPLA was poorly prepared to fight an inter-state war in terms of armament, training, and morale. Thus, instead of consolidating their initial gains due to the element of surprise on the enemy, the SPLA soldiers went on looting spree and withdrew to bring back the loots leaving the Sudan to reorganize its forces, counterattack and to recapture the area as well as to win the diplomatic battles that ensued.

The border conflagration was quickly quenched, and the two sides resumed the negotiations of the post-referendum, then post-independence, issues under the auspices of African Union Commission. These talks had stalled immediately after announcement of the referendum results in January 2011 and did not resume until after the border war. On 8th of September 2012, the two sides agreed on the question of debts, assets, compensation for Sudan's loss of oil revenue, oil transmission fees, recognition of the common borders including 'mile fourteen' in Aweil area. The SPLM Secretary-General, Pagan Amum led the government delegation. It is not clear if the delegation had been fully authorized as to what points it could freely agree on the issues. This was because back in Juba the agreement was not well received. Many SPLM leaders were bitter that the Sudan government got the best deals out of the negotiations.

A characteristic feature of the SPLM/A wheeling and dealing was that what passed as policies or strategies were not discussed in formal party meetings, and its delegations rarely relied on expertise or researched position documents. During the war, it has always been 'trial and error'. Sometimes assignments were handed out only to tease out faults, and to charge with neglect the person assigned. Having gotten a bloody nose again in the negotiation with the Sudan, Pagan Amum not only got the blame for losing out to Khartoum but there also were malicious insinuations that he had been bribed to prove why he gave in to Sudan's demands. The complaints against the agreement were not placed before the delegation in a formal meeting to analyse and evaluate the mission but expressed only in whispers and gossips. Unsurprisingly, the gossips quickly translated and escalated into political tension between President Salva Kiir and Pagan Amum in the same manner the tension with Dr. Riek Machar evolved following the failure to win the Abyei case in the Court of Permanent Arbitration.

Thereafter the relationship between South Sudan and the Sudan considerably normalized. As neighbours, South Sudan and Sudan would remain for a considerable time span entangled in social, economic, political, security, and diplomatic relations that I prefer to categorize as socio-political silhouettes because they defied rational analysis and synthesis of relations that normally would evolve between two neighbouring states with history of conflict and wars. These relations did not spring from genuine conventional inter-state diplomatic etiquette but from idiosyncrasies or unconventional attitudes and behaviours by individuals to consolidate their hold on power and authority in the respective states. At this juncture another digression is required to dissect some glitches and political hiccoughs that may have marred the SPLM – NCP relations during the interim period and in the CPA implementation. What transpired in southern Sudan from the beginning of CPA implementation in 2005 to date could be categorized as post-Garang continuation of the ideological shift from revolution to liberal/conservative/traditional rural mentality and sensibilities. This may require further explanation elsewhere in the book. However, in connection with South Sudan – Sudan's socio-political silhouettes, it is imperative to clearly understand the phenomenon that brought and catapulted Mr. Tut Gatluak Manime to the citadel of the SPLM power to the extent that his disposition virtually as the second man is the republic still poses not only an existential threat to political viability of the SPLM but also to the Republic of South Sudan itself. President Kiir's acceptance, accommodation, and elevation to the position of presidential advisor for security affairs of Mr. Tut Gatluak Minami is a matter of great concern. Tut Gatluak, functionally illiterate but knowledgeable in security and intelligence domain, was President Al-Bashir house boy who grew up during the war to become an important coordinator of the Nuer militias of Gen. Poalino Matip Nhial under the aegis of national security and intelligence chief Gen. Salah Abdalla Gosh. The rule that if one fames in being *used*, then it won't be difficult to find a *user*. After the independence of South Sudan and aware of Riek Machar power ambitions, President Salva Kiir asked President Bashir to release to him Tut Gatluak; this request was willingly accepted, and Tut came to Juba in March 2013 at the head of many of his Bul Nuer[10] warlords whom he had sponsored against the SPLA.

It wasn't feasible for the NCP to destroy the SPLM/SPLA during the war or in the course of CPA implementation even if it desired so. There were several political odds against the NCP and its regime; Sudan was considered and categorized a pariah state, whose destruction many forces in the region and far afield desired that any attempt to cold feet the CPA implementation could cost the NCP its power. Moreover, the NCP leaders were aware of the power struggle within the SPLM and that the temporary unity Southern Sudanese made around the leadership of Salva Kiir on account of self-determination and the Southern Sudan Referendum would not last for a long time after independence celebration. The SPLM leadership during the interim period provided virtually no social service or economic development for the people of Southern Sudan. Despite its several provocations and backstabbing, the NCP procrastinated on any action against the SPLM waiting perhaps for a later time when the two parties had nothing to bind them. Secondly, to destroy the SPLM, the NCP must first exaggerate the personal or ethnic contradictions in the SPLM leadership such that they become irreconcilable. As the adage goes, no matter how poorly defended, a castle falls only from the inside through the treacherous activities of those close to power. The highly personalized political contradictions in the SPLM leadership rendered it vulnerable to NCP machinations trying to endear itself and some of its leaders to President Salva Kiir Mayardit at the expense of the radical SPLM leaders who have been rocking the SPLM-NCP boat since 2005.

The manner, therefore, Tut Gatluak popped up in the SPLM hierarchy is suspicious and cannot be explained only in terms of the SPLM internal contradiction that fitted Salva Kiir against Riek Machar, Pagan Amum or Rebecca Nyandeng and others.

There must be something poignant linked to wider NCP strategy on South Sudan. The NCP leadership saw Salva Kiir as a leader whose political sophistication did not extend beyond South Sudan, and therefore was amendable to their policies of pretentious good neighbourliness between South Sudan and the Sudan. The NCP would also respond positively to Kiir's personal desires and ambitions to remain as the president of South Sudan and to come to his aide against his colleagues. It was clear from the beginning that the NCP leadership disdained the presence of certain SPLM leaders whom they identified as radicals or extremists and therefore undesirable in the new political environment of inter-state diplomacy; the NCP leaders feared these radicals were likely to rock the political boat and prevent the NCP and its leaders from realizing their political and economic objectives in South Sudan. It wasn't coincidental that these were the SPLM leaders President Salva Kiir himself resented and wanted removed from the SPLM leadership hierarchy. It appeared that both Salva Kiir and the President Al-Bashir were agreed to isolate, neutralize and elbow out of SPLM leadership these leaders, identified as Garang's boys, on account of being a threat to NCP and Sudan's interests in South Sudan. Salva Kiir turned out to be a shrewd former Sudanese military intelligence officer.

Internally, the SPLM/A hitherto during the war had been built up into what looked like a nest of vipers characterized by mutual intrigues, gossips, backbiting, falsehood, doubletalk, vanity, character assassination, etc, in their individual and collective relationships. In this configuration, trust or confidence between the leaders was in extreme deficit; and any action by one leader was viewed suspiciously to the extent that sometimes the SPLM/A might be seen sabotaging itself. Kiir's restoration of the SPLM Leadership Council in contravention to Garang's attempts to restructure the SPLM/SPLA was only tactical to win over those affected by Garang's orders and to deploy them against the Garang's orphans. Kiir knew there was no common ground between those SPLM leaders; each leader aspired to climb to the top through intrigues and shenanigans, and therefore Kiir spent much of the time warding off these intrigues. In fact, in the immediate post-Garang period it was impossible for the SPLM leadership to have a common national agenda. As a result, ethnic and regional lobbies sprouted and occupied the political space left vacant in the SPLM by the lack of political and organizational unity. Salva Kiir enclosed himself with Bahr el Ghazal elders[11] (mostly Dinka) to help him navigate the stormy sea of the immediate post-independence period; Salva Kiir's acceptance of Tut Gatluak was a case of turning an unfavourable situation into its opposite to ensure political survival.

By 2013, when Tut Gatluak arrived from Khartoum, Riek Machar had expressed his interest in the leadership of the SPLM and of the country. This did not amuse President Salva Kiir at all. Tut Gatluak hails from Bul Nuer, the largest section of western Nuer, with historical feuds with Dok section from which Riek Machar hails. Tut Gatluak controlled huge Bul Nuer militia and Kiir wanted to neutralize or win over to prevent them from attacking to devastate Warrap in case a conflict erupted within the SPLM between Salva Kiir and Riek Machar, which was then in an advance stage of preparation[12]. Managing the nascent state only on intelligence gathering to know only what political detractors did or planned to do while refusing to take decisive political actions on the issues of social and economic development was President Salva Kiir's strategy for governing South Sudan. It helped him to just sit at the helm and leave the country to dither or teeter without direction.

Kiir's style of leadership that overemphasized intelligence gathering was akin to the NCP's national security system from which Tut Gatluak had won a sabbatical leave. It suited and it enhanced his ability to wield enormous power through boot licking and flattery of the president of South Sudan. Moreover, Tut Gatluak had access to enormous amount of money. In the same manner Tut served President Omer Al-Bahir, he served Salva Kiir running Kiir's numerous errands in Sudan and Arab Middle East and this obedience endeared him to Salva Kiir. Tut undertook these errands as the presidential advisor on security affairs while clearly the political environment in South Sudan was visibly deteriorating, insecurity was heightening, and many parts of South Sudan were becoming ungovernable. Many people began to suspect that Tut's services to Salva Kiir were not in the best interest of the people of South Sudan. It was good he protected the people of Warrap state from his Bul Nuer marauders; many innocent people, women, children, and the elderly could have unnecessarily perished. However, Tut's service to Warrap did not prevent war raging in other parts of South Sudan especially in Upper Nile and

Malakal where tens of thousands of innocent people perished in the attack on the town, its suburbs and other parts of the Chollo Kingdom carried out successively by the Lou Nuer and eastern Jikany white armies in February and April 2014. In fact, the Nuer white armies' attack on Malakal was completely uncalled for save as a provocation to draw the Chollo into the civil war, which then fitted the Dinka against the Nuer. It advertently produced the opposite reaction that pushed Agwalek to the side of, and to rescue, the government. It worth mentioning that Agwalek formed as an insurgency to contest the issue of Chollo land in the wake of President Kiir's decision in April 2009 to establish 'Pigi' County in the territory of Panyikango County in the Chollo Kingdom. It must be said that many Chollo intellectuals, who wanted the land issue resolved politically, did not support the call to war in the Kingdom. This was out of the consideration that the people of Southern Sudan were preparing to vote in the referendum and war in the Kingdom would only serve NCP's objectives to destroy the Southern Referendum.

9. The Civil War - A Litmus Test of South Sudan – Sudan Relations

The republic of the Sudan remains the only country in the Horn of Africa that could play duplicitous political-diplomatic relations with the warring South Sudan leaders. This occurred twice and the two countries apparently moved close to than farther from each other in a manner equivalent to a developing weather pattern whereby a low pressure (high temperature) zone juxtaposed to a high pressure (cold temperature) zone leading to precipitation in the low pressure zone. At the height of the fighting in Jonglei in January 2014 that involved contingents of Ugandan People's Defence Force and Air Force against Riek Machar forces and Lou Nuer white army, the government of Sudan promptly airdropped military supplies to Riek Machar in Gadeang. Apart from muted public protestation from his operatives against the airdrop, President Kiir remained silent; more than anybody else, he was aware of the ramifications. However, this did not prevent both Sudan and Uganda sitting on the IGAD ministerial committee that was called to resolve the conflict in South Sudan immediately after the IGAD Heads of State and Government summit in Nairobi on 27th December 2013.

The second time President Omer Al-Bashir eschewed all diplomatic etiquette in pursuit of his objective was in August 2016 when on humanitarian grounds he airlifted Riek Machar from the UN Camp in the Congo and flew him to Khartoum. By playing the humanitarian card to rescue Riek Machar President Al-Bashir in Sudanese mannerism placed himself strategically in a position to woo President Salva Kiir away from the grip of President Yoweri Museveni. However, there must be something more to both Al-Bashir and Museveni agreeing to co-chair the IGAD High Level Revitalization Forum to resuscitate the agreement on the resolution of the conflict in South Sudan. There was the oil money in South Sudan and this came into play vigorously during the IGAD HLRF talks in Addis Ababa and Khartoum. As mentioned elsewhere, the political developments in Ethiopia forced the Sudan and Uganda to work together to push the South Sudanese protagonists achieve the revitalized agreement on the resolution of the conflict in South Sudan (R-ARCSS) in September 2018.

The R-ARCSS strengthened Al-Bashir hold on Salva Kiir through Tut Gatluak, whom Kiir had appointed, without consultation with the other parties to the agreement, chairman of the Pre-Transitional Period Preparatory Committee (PTC) to expedite the implementation of the pre-transitional processes of the R-ARCSS. Tut Gatluak went back to his old job of servicing political patronage and turned the PTC into SPLM home of intrigues and plots to scuttle, bribe, split, neutralize, and prevent political synergy between the SPLM/A (IO), South Sudan Opposition Alliance (SSOA) and the Other Political Parties (OPP) in their power tussle with the incumbent TGONU. He spent the millions of US dollars and billions of SSP earmarked for the implementation of the pre-transitional processes like the cantonment, training and feeding of the armed groups, paying off opposition leaders to support SPLM scheme to undermine and elbow certain leaders out of competition for the fifth vice president. Tut's office became an alternative ministry of finance, and many politicians, legislators, army and police generals and even ordinary South Sudanese would be seen queuing to meet Tut Gatluak to get something out of the cake.

In his position as presidential advisor of security affairs resonating or rather conflating with his role in the NCP, Tut Gatluak lubricated and smoothen the relation with the NCP leaders then holding the R-ARCSS dossier in Khartoum, and consequently became the direct link and conduit of unofficial relations between Al-Bashir and Salva Kiir. In this capacity, Tut Gatluak also served as a shock absorber to shield President Salva Kiir from political shock waves generated by the opposition leaders frustrated with the slow pace of R-ARCSS implementation. In this way, Tut Gatluak fulfilled Kiir's desire to frustrate and indefinitely postpone the implementation of pre-transitional processes, making him extremely powerful wielding enormous power that in practical terms became the effective number two man if not the one effectively governing the Republic of South Sudan.

President Salva Kiir was not interested in full implementation of the R-ARCSS in the same way he did not want, or complicated the implementation of ARCISS by introducing a legislation, EO 36/2015 dividing South Sudan into twenty-eights states against ARCISS' ten states. The reason for this obfuscation was simple; President Salva Kiir refused the implementation of the agreement because he believed it would disturb the balance of forces that left him in full control of the country. In his simplistic but complicated stance, speaking Arabic like a toddler Mr. Tut Gatluak charmed the foreign diplomats into not asking directed and critical questions and at the same time absorbed or deflected any political shock waves arising from Kiir's apparent reluctance to implement the peace agreement. In addition to anaesthetising the opposition political leaders already in Juba Mr. Tut Gatluak instigated and paid huge sums of money to Nuer SPLM/A (IO) politicians and military generals to defect to the

SPLM, desert or rebel against the leadership of Riek Machar. This included the bogus peace agreement between the SPLM (IG) and the SPLM/A (IO) Kit-Gwang group comprising Gen. Simon Gatwech SPLM/A (IO) Chief of Staff, and Gen. Johnson Thubo (Olony) representing Agwalek forces. The idea was to continuously procrastinate on R-ARCSS implementation; buy enough time to scuttle the opposition and prevent any coordination between their leaders and make it impossible for them individually or collectively to reach President Salva Kiir to engage in political consultation. The non-implementation of some of the critical provisions of R-ARCSS has caused general anxiety especially that the timeclock was then ticking towards the expiry of the transitional period pinned to 23rd February 2023.

In essence, President Omer Al-Bashir and President Yoweri Museveni took over the IGAD mediation not in the spirit to bring peace to South Sudan. It was in the context of their respective national security and economic interests in the conflict in South Sudan, and to bury the hatchet that existed between them since 1990[13]. To gain a foothold with President Salva Kiir in view of the difficult relations created by his decision to rescue Riek Machar, President Bashir had to initiate a reproachment with President Museveni. This reproachment must have been in respect of the Ugandan rebel Joseph Kony, in the same manner Bashir in 1994 at the behest of the American administration requested the Taliban to accept and accommodate Osama bin Ladin's and his men relocated to Afghanistan. In this context, it is possible that Al-Bashir could have quietly handed over Joseph

Kony to President Museveni and the rest would be history[14]. This contributed to easing the tension between the two leaders enabling Museveni to travel to Khartoum.

10. Al-Bashir Removed from Power, but his Regime Survives
On October 30, 2018, President Salva Kiir celebrated the R-ARCSS in a colourful occasion attended by the regional leaders, among them presidents Al-Bashir and Museveni, the champions of R-ARCSS. Since then, an interesting chemistry evolved between South Sudan and Sudan making the two an interesting binary joined together by what could be categorized as subterranean and deep passions by the leaders who have decided to stay on in power even though the country decayed and rotted. The IGAD region is highly volatile with several intra-state conflicts, characterized by competing security concerns that more often override regional economic cooperation. This political development, the South Sudan-Sudan-Uganda triangular relationship, wouldn't have evolved had it not been for the separate but related two political developments with regional ramifications affecting Ethiopia and the Sudan.

The first was the sudden implosion of a precipitous political crisis within the Ethiopian ruling party, which led to the resignation of its Prime Minister, Haile Mariam Desalegn and the appointment of Dr. Abiya Ahmed as the New Prime Minister. This political development shifted to Khartoum the IGAD's HLRF and ushered the Sudan and Uganda into chairing the High-Level Revitalization Forum, and the mediation talks between the government of South Sudan, and the South Sudan political and armed opposition. Both Sudan and Uganda apart from their mutual diplomatic and political contradictions, have respective national security and economic interests in South Sudan conflict. Al-Bashir became the acting IGAD chair, and the Sudan foreign minister, Dirdiery Mohammed, became assistant to the IGAD's Chief Envoy on South Sudan, Dr. Ismail Wais.

The second political development coming on the heels of the dramatic events in Ethiopia was the eruption of the mass movement in the Sudan, which eventually led to the overthrow of President Omer Hassan Ahmed Al-Bashir and his government in April 2019. For many Sudanese including some members of the Islamic movement would admit that President Omer Hassan Al-Bashir has overstayed in power and the regime had outlived its original purpose becoming a tool for the parasitic capitalist class in the political, bureaucratic, military establishment and business cartels. The opposition to Al-Bashir and the regime has been simmering for a long time since the Arab spring. It sparked protests and street demonstrations in 2013 but was brutally crushed by the regime's national security apparatus. The mass movement in the streets came against a backdrop of strong internal opposition within the NCP albeit surrounding Al-Bashir's longevity in power. Towards the end of 2018 the opposition to the regime energized, and mass mobilized to mark the 63rd anniversary of 19th of December, the day the Sudanese parliament voted for independence in 1955. The popular uprising to overthrow the regime evolved parallelly with a conspiracy within the national security and army top brass to remove Al-Bashir all in collaboration with the foreign militia force[15] (Rapid Support Forces) commanded by Mohammed Hamdan Daglo (Hemiti). However, the street protests and demonstrations moved faster that the coup plot and immediately led to the occupation of the square outside the Sudan Armed Forces GH/Qs in Khartoum, leading to further energization bringing more protesters and demonstrators from Atbara, Medani, Kassala, Port Sudan and El-Obeid. This huge mass movement inducted onto the political stage the 'Forces of Freedom and Change' (FFC) - a coalition of trade unions, leftists' groups, social movements, professional associations, women, and youth groups, at the head of the revolutionary *intifada* to eventually overthrow the totalitarian dictatorial system. The regime's nuts and bolts started to loosen and on 11th of April the army top brass, in what appeared like a coup to subvert the popular uprising, announced the fall of President Omer Al-Bashir. And indeed, it was the regime's own internal change; Gen. Awad Ibn Nahof, chief of Military Intelligence, who announced the fall of Al-Bashir was quickly changed, and Gen. Abdel Fatah Al-Burhan came on the top as the Chairman of the Military Council.

Struggling to maintain the *status quo* while Al-Bashir had been removed, the national security, the military intelligence and their foreign handlers devised a plan to abort the revolution, prevent its radicalization, and then exploit the breather to thwart African Union's freeze of Sudan's membership. It was in this context that the Forces of Freedom and Change committed the blunder of negotiating with the Military Council, which then had no legal existence. That situation reminisces April 6th, 1985, when Gen. Swar al Dahab announced the downfall of Gaafar Numeiri; it was in fact Ingaz regime minus Al-Bashir.

The constitutional document, which the FFC signed with the Military Council inadvertently legitimized the Military Council and gave its members constitutional powers and international recognition on account of sovereignty they did not deserve. It made Gen. Abdel Fatah Al-Burhan and Mohammed Hamdan Daglo respective chair and deputy chair of the Supreme Council of the State. The fact that Gen. Abdel Fatah el Burhan in quick succession replaced Gen. Awad Ibn Nahof at the head of the military establishment meant that the old regime was still in a state of disorientation and therefore the FFC could have continued with the occupation of the square in front of the army GH/Qs, and on the streets until the regime had fully given up power as happened in October 1964.

The presence of Gen. Al-Burhan at the chair of the Supreme Council of the State suggested the continuity of the old regime in a different format, and this played out exactly as expected when it came to handing over the chair and deputy chair of the Supreme Council of the State to the civilian faction; not only was Gen. Abdel Fatah Al-Burhan and the military establishment reluctant to step down but also pulled a military-civilian coup and arrested the prime minister, Abdalla Hamdok and some members of the FFC. This created another dynamic exposing the opportunistic nature of the so-called revolutionary forces of Malik Agar, Mini Arkoi Menawi and Gibril Khalil and their immediate alliance with Al-Burhan – Daglo axis and the traditional tribal leaders to elbow out and isolate the Forces of Freedom and Change.

The political development in Khartoum did not quite affect the relations with Juba regarding Khartoum's role in the (R-ARCSS). Gen Abdel Fatah el Burhan and his deputy Mohammed Hamdan el Daglo continued to relate to the Government of the Republic of South Sudan much in the same manner as Omer Al-Bashir did. Indeed, in every aspect it was Bashir's regime without Bashir thanks to the presence of the presidential advisor on security affairs. Mr. Tut Gatluak's role was to facilitate all wheeling and dealing with Khartoum generals in respect of their ploy to negotiate a peace agreement with the Sudanese rebels, while Khartoum generals managed the IGAD dossier on South Sudan This was a political game the two regimes played to buy time to lengthen their stay in power needs contextualization.

Playing the role of chief mediator on South Sudan to expedite the R-ARCSS, Gen. Al-Burhan had Dr. Riek Machar and other opposition leaders in Khartoum. However, aware that the Government of South Sudan had relations with the Sudanese rebels or at least South Sudan was a sanctuary for many of these rebels, Gen. Al-Burhan wanted to exploit the opportunity provided by his role as R-ARCSS's chief mediator to outwit the FFC and to short-change its leadership and the prime minister, Dr. Hamdok. The Sudanese military establishment requested President Salva Kiir to mediate between the government of the Republic of the Sudan and the different Sudanese rebel groups. President Kiir obliged with perhaps an added interest. Mr. Tut

Gatluak, now promoted to a Lieutenant General in the South Sudan People's Defence Force (SSPDF), became the Chief Envoy on the Sudan assisted by Dr. Dhieu Mathok Wol. Incidentally Dr. Wol and Gen. Tut Gatluak were NCP activists during the war and President Kiir's choice was not accidental. Appointing former NCP members in the guise of SPLM representing the government of South Sudan to mediate between Al-Burhan and SPLM-North and other opposition couldn't have been anything but an insult hurled at the former colleagues in the national liberation movement. Al-Burhan preferred to deal with the splinter groups than the mainstream groups and this raised suspicion regarding the military establishment's commitment to peace. These splinter groups comprised breakaway faction of the SPLM/A North (Malik Agar Eire), the Justice and Equality Movement (Dr. Gibril Ibrahim), the faction of Sudan Liberation Movement (Mini Arkoi Menawi) and a host of many other smaller breakaway factions. It was in this context that the leaders of the SPLM/A-North (Abdel Aziz Adam el Hilu) and the Sudan Liberation Movement (Abdel Wahid Mohammed) refused to deal with either Gen. Abdel Fatah el Burhan or his deputy Gen. Mohammed Hamdan Daglo[16] preferring to have serious conversation with Prime Minister Hamdok on the assumption that he represented the masses of the Sudanese people.

The political systems in the two neighbouring countries have come to mirror image each other in face of acute political and economic crisis afflicting them. In this configuration, the two regimes believed they are assisting each other in shoring up each other's internal troubles; Gen. Al Burhan or Gen. Daglo undertook the mediation between Salva Kiir and his political detractors in South Sudan while Salva Kiir conducted mediation between Al-Burhan or Al-Daglo and the Sudan's political and armed opposition including the SPLM/A-North. Apparently, the governments of both South Sudan and the Sudan present a picture of two individuals struggling to assist each other in a treacherously duplicitous political environment which they are conscious would yield them the very opposite of what they desired to achieve. Both were not interested in resolving the fundamental contradictions underpinning the conflict in the two countries; but they want to use the peace processes to maintain themselves in power. In trying to help the other, they both are likely to slip away and fall.

Let's be honest; President Salva Kiir will not countenance a situation in South Sudan, which would temper with the current balance of forces to upset his personal power and his control of the country's financial and economic resources. He is aware of the acute social and economic crisis and the dire humanitarian disaster generated by his policies. Nevertheless, he soldiers on believing that he would weather all obstacles on his way. In the same vein, Gen. Abdel Fatah Al-Burhan, and Gen. Daglo, representing the old regime have stuck their legs in the mud refusing to leave the seat of power lest they found themselves in the International Criminal Court in The Hague. The two regimes speak publicly of implementing peace agreement but in reality, they are creating conditions for their continued stay in power.

Both Salva Kiir and Abdel Fatah Al-Burhan know that implementing the R-ARCSS and the Juba agreement in letter and spirit would lead to their political demise. Like the IGAD HLRF, the Juba conference brought together different social and political groups in the Sudan. The Juba talks and agreement were modelled on the IGAD HLRF centred on power-sharing. Thus, as in the R-ARCSS, this power-sharing formula permitted every Tom and Jerry purporting to represent sections of Sudanese society got included and this complicated the implementation process to the advantage of the Military Council. The Khartoum Junta and their foreign backers, replicating the scenario between the SPLM or ITGONU and the opposition (SPLM/A (IO), SSOA and others, did not have enough positions in government to satisfy all the parties that popped up except at the expense of the FFC. The Juba Agreement 2020, and the inclusion of the so-called the Revolutionary Forces, in the Sudan Transitional Government sealed the strength of the military junta and their hold on power. They now worked together to divide and elbowed the FFC out of the transitional government, resignation of Prime Minister Abdalla Hamdok, counted as an agent of the western powers, and therefore unwanted by both the military elements of the old regime and some members of the FFC.

The Burhan - Daglo coup temporarily stalled the forward march of the Sudanese revolution and prevented it to achieve its immediate short-term political objectives. However, this created and lobbed the Sudan into a situation of perpetual turmoil. The military elements of the old regime in collaboration with the so-called revolutionary forces, the traditional and tribal administration froze the process of transferring power to the civilian fraction of the transitional government on the ground that it would only hand over power to the elected representatives of the people. But at the same time the military council has erected obstacles to prevent the civilian government to construct democratic institutions and instruments that could prepare the ground for the conduct of elections to bring the people representatives. The FFC was left with no option save to continue with the street demonstrations until Al-Burhan and the military establishment relinquished power to the masses.

Parallel to the contradiction that fits the military establishment against the FFC, and the masses of the Sudanese people there exists a bitter but muted power struggle between Gen. Abdel Fatah Al-Burhan representing the NCP military security establishment and Gen. Mohammed Hamdan Daglo representing the Rapid Deployment Force (RDF), which runs along the deep historical fissures between the *'garaba'* (western Sudanese) and *'awalad el bahr'* (riverine Arabized Nubians). The refusal of Al-Burhan and the Sudan Armed Forces to have the RDF integrated on account that most of its officers and men are foreign mercenaries (hailing from Chad, Mali, Niger, Mauritania, and South Sudan). It is a contradiction that is likely to trigger a blood bath in Khartoum as it completely disorients the Sudanese people.

In South Sudan, the political situation to some extent resembles that in the Sudan in terms of its political uncertainty generated by Salva Kiir's refusal to implement the critical provisions of R-ARCSS that should lead the country to democratic elections and power transfer to an elected government. However, the situation is more complicated. On the one side, unlike in the Sudan where there exist historical references like multi-party democratic dispensation, Supreme Council of the State, and independent Judiciary, etc., there is no such reference points in South Sudan. Moreover, there is no vibrant civil society, and the dominant political force, the SPLM, has no democratic political culture that could trigger internal struggle for change. Furthermore, president Salva Kiir is not keen on leaving power; he is aware of consequences of being out of power. Thus, the talk about elections may amount to idle talk because the condition for conducting fair, free and credible elections does not, and will not, exist in South Sudan for the next fifty years.

The absence of democratic political culture in the SPLM, which by virtue of is liberation legacy, makes it the largest and popular political party renders dim the future of positive change in South Sudan. This explains why the SPLM leaders readily went to war than dialogue to reach consensus on issues of contention. It's the ignorance of social norms and political principles combined with ethnocentrism and stubbornness that characterize social and political engineering in South Sudan. Ethnocentrism and surge of ethnic nationalism encouraged patronage, and jettisoned politics based on democratic political principles. This pushed to the fore front and leadership of state executive, legislative and bureaucratic institutions individuals with little or no concern for the state and its institutions. They have turned the state and its institutions into tools for personal aggrandisement, and South Sudan does not function in the same way the neighbouring countries do government business. As the R-ARCSS implementation time clock ticks and South Sudan tethered with uncertainty towards the expiry of the transitional period, a breather came from the presidency[17] on 24th August 2022 in form of a two-year extension of the transitional period. It was a two-years extension to give the R-TGONU another lease of life. The parties had spent four years without implementing the peace agreement; will two years extension be sufficient for processes they failed to implement in four years? Definitely, no. In fact, Dr. Riek Machar and his SPLM/A (IO), the leaders in SSOA and OPP have rendered themselves toothless and therefore have thrown in the tool. Their individual and collective interests have become identical to those of the leaders in the ITGONU and therefore are not interested in change.

There is something poignant to the growing insecurity in the country that is pushing the civilians in towns and particularly the UNMISS POCs. The exponential explosion of the population of Juba, which has outgrown its size due to influx of people mostly from Bor Jonglei and Warrap in Bahr el Ghazal correspond to the growing insecurity therein. The same is occurring in the Chollo Kingdom triggered by the marauding Nuer white army from Jonglei and Unity States. The Chollo civil population in Fashoda and Manyo Counties has been disrupted, massacred or displaced from their villages and the survivors are in Kodok, Melut or Renk.

The SSPDF or the UNMISS forces in Malakal, Wau and Kodok failed to protect the people and President Kiir's response was to airlift to Juba the Shilluk King, His Majesty Rath Kwongo Dak Padiet. This development is a pointer to the reality that the leaders in the R-TGONU have agreed amongst themselves to continue to extend the transitional period *ad infinitum* to forestall any opportunity for holding free, fair and credible elections because they are aware that the people will never again trust them or elect them back to office. There is no ideological difference between Salva Kiir and Riek Machar nor between the two of them and the leaders in the SSOA and the OPP. Moreover, there is no visible alternative political force that could force a change. Therefore, President Salva Kiir, his first deputy president Riek Machar and the other deputy presidents now organized in the presidency could extend their life at will.

11. How and Why the Sudanese States Failed

Any human civilization in a process of decline, disappears forever. It is impossible to resurrect or resuscitate and revive like a drawn person. The state and the modern state in particular is the highest form of human civilization. It is nothing but vanity that the Sudanese people, particularly the Nilotics, pride themselves in the past and place premium on those glories and contributions to human civilisation. It is vanity because it translated to relaxing the present endeavours to achieve and build more better and superlative state, Instead, unlike other nations, we are witnessing destruction of lives in the form of state failure, occurring under their watch. The Sudanese people generally are a very proud and stubborn people. This stubbornness attributes to their rural background, where life is a perpetual individual or collective struggle to survive against the adverse forces of nature. In this environment, one may always be called upon to prove one's humanity sacrificing for the community and take pride in it. In the same vein they could split hairs over the obvious simply because concession to the other would suggest weakness. This attitude of not conceding to others, rightly or wrongly pushes communities to separate and *en masse* move farther away than to cohabit the same territory.[18] In worst case scenarios, violent conflicts consume communities in mutual acts of destruction even to extinction. It would require serious sociological investigation to get to the root of this phenomenon and its incursion into the Sudan's body politics as drivers of state political failures.

Karl Marx was right; human history is a forward procession that does not repeat itself. When leaders spend their time and nation's resources on futilities of past glories instead of heeding the demands of the time they live in, they will never recover the opportunities they lost in building their countries. The Sudanese government spent most of the post-independence period politicking about Arab nationhood, Islam and the Palestinian problem and paid little attention to the issues of social and economic development of the Sudan. In the course of time, Singapore, and Malaysia, both former British colonies but poorer than Sudan when they became independent, had dominant Muslim populations and meagre natural resource base, bypassed the Sudan in socioeconomic development. In the 1970s, the Sudan had a work force of engineers, skilled labour, and administrators it couldn't make use of because there was no national plan. This work force went and built the Arab Emirates into the paradise it is today. Dr. Hassan Abdalla Al-Turabi wrote the secular constitution for United Arab Emirates and an Islamic constitution for the Sudan. It is not easy to pin to any single cause of the Sudanese state failure, which eventually occasioned its partition and the independence of South Sudan. It must have been a combination of factors some of which were discussed above.

I would say that poverty, ignorance, and stupidity constituted the amalgam that underpins state failure. Myopia and cynical ethnocentrism of the political class are products of ignorance and poverty in society, which submerge consciousness preventing a correct understanding of socioeconomic and political process in state formation and nation building. The ethnic, religious, cultural diversity of the Sudan naturally rejected their categorization of the Sudan as an Arab and Muslim; it was bound to explode, and the wars erupted at its weakness point, in South Sudan, as a testimony to this phenomenon.

The transition from sociocultural configurations (tribes) to and the emergence of the Sudanese nation state did not happen through a slow process of integration whereby the Sudanese nation would have been a product. Thus, ethnicity survives and worse caught up by democratisation in its primaeval form because assimilation through the agency of the state could not be sustained; it triggered insurgencies. In this connection, ethnic rivalry whether in the Sudan or South Sudan remains a strong and disruptive force. It underpins the political standoffs both in the Sudan and South Sudan between competing ethnic-based political – military forces. In the Sudan, the standoff between Daglo (garaba) and Al-Burhan (awalad el Neel), created a situation that blocked the Forces of Freedom and Change (FFC); ethnicization and regionalization of the politics of change created divisions that scattered the forces and aborted the revolution. The power struggle between Salva Kiir (Dinka) and Riek Machar (Nuer) that has polarized the South Sudanese people that prevented the emergence of a critical mass to transform the situation. As soon as South Sudan became independent in 2011, the SPLM, which led the war of national liberated ceased to be a uniting political ideology. This is partly because it existed as a falsehood in the memory of the people; only the SPLA existed in the reality but as soon as the war ended, the new reality was a political and ideological void called the SPLM. It's worth repeating that the SPLM/A was more of a power project rather than a project in the Sudanese revolution. The successor to Dr. John Garang could only promote it in the same manner through totalitarian autocracy otherwise it wouldn't have survived this long. Unfortunately, Salva Kiir initially was not the benevolent dictator he should have been to promote the construction of public goods. He instead turned the nascent state into a project of political and economic empowerment of the Dinka people to endear himself to the Jieng Council of Elders (JCE) that emerged in the context of political patronage and neo-patrimonialism.

The Dinka, as a sociocultural formation, do not have history of centralized power or state for that matter. Thus, arose the contradiction between the nascent state as a national and impersonal institution owned by the nationalities that inhabit South Sudan and the Dinka concept of state power as a personified than institutionalized tool of this empowerment. This contradiction played out as the civil war that erupted in December 2013. The failure of state in South Sudan therefore emanated from the failure of the SPLM political military elite to live up to the ideals of national liberation. They delegitimised and disempowered themselves as revolutionary section of the South Sudanese society by promoting the incursion of ethnic nationalism (community) into the social, economic, and political engineering processes of South Sudan. Comrade Salva Kiir has turned from a leader of the revolution to an ethnic Dinka chauvinist who believed that only the Dinka fought and died in the war of national liberation.

This is false; under the leadership of Dr. John Garang in 1984/5 Salva Kiir commanded two SPLA battalions, Tiger and Timsah, made up entirely of ethnic Nuer combatants. He derived his code name 'Tiger' from the battalion he commanded and has now turned it into presidential guards. It's this chauvinism and ethnic bigotry that pushed the policy of Warrap Dinka hegemony and domination of the state political, economic, and bureaucratic institutions. It wouldn't have mattered if the persons appointed had the knowledge and were qualified for their position, but they unfortunately were appointed to learn on the job; and the result was catastrophic. Ignorance, inefficiency, lack of patriotism and national dignity are at root of failure of state. It's catastrophic when political and bureaucratic failures run side by side and enforce each other. Corruption has become the norm, not the exception, in most government institutions; the individuals at the centre of many of these cases are presidential appointees answerable only to the President Salva Kiir, who was constantly in loop with these corrupt cartels in their pillage of South Sudan.

12. The Exact Meaning of Two Failed States - Concluding the Discourse

If this chapter were to be the court of public opinion, it might be prudent to solemnly ask; how did the Sudanese state fail, and why South Sudan failed to be a state? The Sudanese state was a colonial construct, that brought together variegated sociocultural formations to serve economic interests. This colonial was erected on wrong foundations suggesting that as a state Sudan was pregnant with contradictions from the word go. This triggered a revolution, the *Mahdiya*, but its political objectives fell short of the aspirations of the Sudanese people, and as a result, the Mahdiya as a sociopolitical system also generated internal contradictions that eventually led to its defeat. The British change of policy 1946 and the convening the Juba Conference 1947 could be counted first the steps towards the construction of the Sudan as an entity. In the Juba Conference, whether conscious of the implications, the so-called southern representatives acquiesced to the dictates of the Administrative Secretary and endorse the concept of Sudan emerging as a united country.

The failure to a build a united nationalist movement after the Juba conference is a responsibility that falls squarely on the northern political elite. Then, Southern Sudan was represented by people whose knowledge and political sophistication did not extend beyond their villages and therefore need visionary leadership among the northerners to carry with them their compatriots from southern Sudan. The deliberate decision to exclude the southern political leaders from the Cairo meeting in 1952 was unfortunate particularly that the northern leaders negotiated the right of self-determination. Southern Sudan was already an integral part of the Sudan and therefore the decision was in bad faith. It paid back later when the SPLM raise the issue of self-determination for the simple reason that southern Sudan was not part of the Cairo Agreement. It was a missed opportunity.

Sudan was such a large country, one million square kilometres in area, a multiplicity of race, language, religious faith, and cultures spread in different geographic and climatic zones. The rhetoric that 'no federation for one country' was ill-conceived to defeat the southern demand for federal system of government at a time federalism was already a working political system in many countries including the highly centralized post-colonial states in Nigeria and India. This was another missed opportunity smacking of cynical ethnocentrism sheathed in political trickery. The Round Table Conference on the problem of southern Sudan was another opportunity but was bound to flop because the democratic political forces in the country were still weak and fragile; the political left is the only social force in the Sudan with genuine desire for its unity. The putsch, which the political left hatched in 1969 could have been an opportunity to resolve the fundamental problems of poverty, ignorance, and cultural backwardness that underly the contradictions afflicting the Sudanese people. It only proved that fundamental change can only come from the people at a certain level of social awareness and political consciousness. The forces of national democratic revolution must grow within the society, mature and then sprout to the political stage by themselves not through a military coup de tat.

All these facts constitute the reasons how the Sudanese state failed as soon as it became independent in 1956. The nature of the Sudanese society prevented the progressive social and democratic political forces under the leadership of the working class to emerge and sprout onto the political stage to lead the struggle for social change. It was a failure that came in successive bounds of pro-imperialist dictatorial regimes preceded by theocratic family based dynastic civilian regimes. The failure of the Sudanese state therefore was the failure to trigger the national democratic revolution as opposed to the neo-colonialism the political elite chose on independence as the path to social, economic and political development of the Sudan. This failure ended in the partition and independence of South Sudan. The construction of the national democratic developmental state in the Sudan would have prevented South Sudan breaking away, or the current racial situation in Dar Fur escalating into genocidal war.

The failure of the revolution in northern Sudan shifted the revolutionary struggle to southern Sudan in the form of revolutionary armed struggle, and a war of national liberation to destroy what SPLM/A leadership dubbed as the 'Old Sudan' and to construct in its place a 'New Sudan' based on freedom (liberty), justice (equality and equity) and fraternity (solidarity). It was a paradigm shift that captured the imagination of African peoples in southern, central and western parts of the Sudan. It was also a radical shift in the political thinking of southern Sudanese intellectuals and political elite who hitherto concerned themselves only with issues of southern Sudan. However, the social and ideological base of the SPLM/A leadership (petty bourgeoisie) was not as radical as the Marxist ideas they championed; nor were they party of the political struggle against the May regime. Without the situation then in Ethiopia and the intense ideological and superpower rivalry in the Horn of Africa, the SPLM/A wouldn't have emerged as a force it became militarily and politically.

The military struggle in southern Sudan, Nuba Mountains and southern Blue Nile remained separate and parallel to the political struggle against the May and the NIF regimes in the cities, towns and villages in northern Sudan. Thus, after twenty-one years, the war stagnated and indeed ended in a political compromise at the expense of the Nuba, Funj and the Ngok Dinka of Abyei; because was the political compromise was to enable southern Sudanese to become independent but to democratically transform the Sudanese polity. The revolution flopped and failed to achieve its political objective. It not only betrayed and left in limbo the people who hooked their hopes on the 'New Sudan' project but also created a bitter dichotomy between the southerners and their compatriots the Nuba and the Funj most of who died fighting in southern Sudan.

Many factors contributed to this failure; however, the most important was reality that the SPLM/A leaders were at odds with the revolutionary message of socialism they proclaimed. This has always been the nature of the petty bourgeoisie; vacillating between the masses and the big capital they are likely to betray the masses and abort the realization of the ultimate goal of the struggle. South Sudan could have evolved into a modern state as a result of revolutionary management of the war of national liberation. It still has the opportunity but only consequent to the emergence of a critical mass that would trigger the launch of the national democratic revolution and the construction of a national revolutionary democratic development state. Only a national democratic developmental state could save South Sudan from repeating or going through the agony the republic and people of the Sudan went through.

ENDNOTES

1. Sudanese writers on both sides of ideological divide make claim of his southern Sudanese origin to support Sudan's unity and reject the tendency to separateness and secession among southern Sudanese. In fact, children for former slaves recruited into the Egyptian Army, indoctrinated with Islamic virtues and Egyptian nationalism did not see themselves as Sudanese or Southern Sudanese for that matter.

2. In 1960, Gen. Ibrahim Abboud in executing the policy of Islamization and Arabicisation of southern Sudanese, ordered the change of weekly holiday from Sunday to Friday. This provoked student strikes throughout southern Sudan leading to closure of schools, raising people's awareness and mobilisation to resist the policy. Many government officials deserted their jobs and joined the students to form Anya-nya units

3. The colonial Closed District ordinance to isolate and insulate the southern Sudanese, the Nuba and the Funj.

4. The people of southern Sudan to rid themselves of the third-class status imposed on them by the policies and power politics of the Arab dominated northern political elite, many other factors contributed to the dismemberment of the Sudan.

5. Brigadier Omer Hassan Ahmed Al-Bashir was commander of Mayom garrison and had first hand knowledge of the situation of the army. He left Mayom precisely to listen to the NIF leadership as how to change the government and transform the situation.

6. The Nasir Declaration on 28th August 1991 overthrow Dr. John Garang de Mabior from the leadership and the split within the SPLM/A must be viewed as part of the political efforts of the NIF to defeat the SPLM/A.

7. In the same manner the SPLM/A evolved like Siamese twins cojoined in the head (person of Dr. Garang who was chairman and commander-in-chief respectively). The truth was that SPLM, and SPLA did not exist separately Garang was chairman of SPLM central committee that did not exist and commander

in chief of the SPLA that had a chief of general staff that also did not exist. Both the SPLM and SPLA were not each other's organ, meaning that the SPLA was not the military wing of the SPLM nor was the SPLM the political wing of the SPLA, yet the two were taken as one.

8. This was the problem for which Chairman Salva Kiir convened the SPLM 2nd National Convention in 2007 to dismiss from the SPLM leadership both Riek Machar and Pagan Amum. The SPLM 2nd National Convention failed to dismiss the two, but Salva Kiir had not given up on the issue.

9. The GOSS delegation to Court of Permanent Arbitration (CPA) in Dan Haag headed by Dr. Riek Machar did not study the ABC report; they would have found out that Pan Thao (Heglig) was wrongly added to Abyei area. Once CPA made its ruling delineating Pan Thao from Abyei, the Sudan government immediately claimed Pan Thao, and this caused tension between the two countries.

10. These included Gen. Matthew Pul-Jiang, Gen. Bapiny Monytuil,

11. The Bahr el Ghazal Elders was an extension of the group that supported Cdr. Salva Kiir Mayardit during the Yei crisis 2004. The groups agitated against the policy of deploying Bahr el Ghazal youths (Dinka) in the war in Equatoria while the Murahalieen (Rezeighat and Messeriya) devastated northern Bahr el Ghazal. Now that Salva Kiir was the president of the Government of Southern Sudan, they did not power to cross the Nile to the east – euphemism for Bor.

12. When in the closing session of the SPLM National Liberation Council meeting on 15th December 2013 Salva Kiir said that "1991 will never be repeated", he meant that the Nuers will never devastate Warrap in the manner they devastated Kongor and Bor following the Nasir Declaration. He had marshalled enough forces in form of Bul Nuer to prevent it.

13. Sudan trained and armed anti-Museveni rebels of the Lord Resistance Army (Joseph Kony) and West Nile Front (Juma Oris) while Uganda gave free passage to the SPLA. However, Sudan's support to the Uganda rebels was in the context of its fundamentalist ideology to spread Islam by force of arms.

14. Joseph Kony and his rebel Lord's Resistance Army (LRA) was Al-Bashir proxy against the SPLA in Eastern Equatoria, but the situation changed after the defeat of Khartoum's offensive on the Juba-Nimule corridor. It was not clear if Kony was airlifted to Khartoum after 2005. In 2006, Uganda deployed its forces in Western Equatoria on pretext of tracking Kony leading to the formation of Arrow Boys to protect the civil population from atrocities the UPDF committed.

15. Made up of elements from Chad, Mali and Nigers the force served as Saudi Arabian mercenary force in Yemen but Al-Bashir used them against the Sudan Liberation Movement in Dar Fur but when it became an international scandal brought Daglo to Khartoum.

16. This was on account that Gen. Abdel Fatah el Burhan and Mohammed Daglo were involved in war crimes and crimes against humanity in Dar Fur. Omer el Bashir sent Daglo and

his Rapid Deployment Forces to the Nuba Mountains in 2014, where Cdr. Abdel Aziz Adam el Hilu badly defeated him

17. The presidency: that is president Salva Kiir, his first vice president Riek Machar, vice president James Wani Igga, vice president Taban Deng Gai, vice president Hussien Abdel Bagi Akol and vice President Rebecca Nyandeng de Mabior, don't represent all the parties to R-ARCSS; NDM made a statement against the extension and so did Troika refuse to attend the signing ceremony suggesting Kiir's political manoeuvre was in bad faith.

18. The Luo people of Sudan: [Luo (Bahr el Ghazal), Shatt, Bwor, Chollo, Anywaa, Pari, Acholi] meet their distant cousins in Uganda [Acholi, Ethur, Jo-Naam, Alur, Jo-Podholla], DR Congo [Alur], Kenya {Luo} and Tanzania {Luo} and try to trace their commonality,

CHAPTER TWO

THE SOUTHERN REGION [1972-1983]
SOUTHERN SUNDANESE' FIRST EVER
EXPERIENCE WITH POWER

1. Background Synopsis

On the 9th of June 1969, and for the first time in Sudan's independence history, a northern Sudanese leader, Colonel Gaafar Mohammed Numeiri, admitted publicly the sociocultural disparity between the peoples of the three southern provinces and the rest of the Sudanese in other parts of the country. In fact, this was an enunciation of a position put to the Round Table Conference in 1965 by the Communist Party of the Sudan[1]. The new revolutionary government used it to placate the southern Sudanese and to win their political support for the May revolution.

In essence this disparity was socially and politically engineered initially in the context of colonial policy which insulated and isolated the people of southern Sudan, the Nuba Mountains and southern Blue Nile from the rest of the country and the civilized world. The Arab dominated northern political elite later found convenient to continue enforcing this policy after independence in the context of political exclusion of southerners in the process of governing the country. These disparities obtained and were perpetuated as part of the policy of decolonization by forceful assimilation into Islam and Arab culture of southern Sudanese and other non-Muslim and non-Arab communities in the Sudan. In fact, on independence in 1956, the official policy defined Sudan as Arab and Muslim, suggesting that Sudanese citizenship for the non-Arab and non-Muslim Sudanese was only a transition into full integration into Islam and Arab nationhood. It was because of this disparity and the sad historical relation between the people of southern Sudan and the dominant forces in northern Sudan that on independence southerners envisaged a Sudan governed on federalism. Had, the northern nationalist leaders been sensitive to southern opinion, the Sudan could have evolved without the difficulties it went through that eventually led to its dismemberment.

Everything in nature has a flipside and out of bad things emerge good ones. Had the Equatoria Corps of the Sudan Defence Force (SDF) not mutinied on 18th of August 1955, Azhari would have transferred them to the northern Sudan and the so-called problem of southern Sudan could have died before anybody beside the wrangling southern politicians knew it. Had the theocratic traditional parties, the Umma, the NUP and the Muslim Brotherhood not conspired in 1965 to outlaw the

Communist Party of the Sudan and unseated its eight members in the Constituent Assembly the political left would not have conspired to pull the May 1969 military coup that overthrew the democratically elected Umma-DUP coalition government.

The June 9th Declaration came at the height of right-wing insurrection in the southern provinces. I call it deliberately right-wing; the political culture in southern Sudan, if it ever existed, was apolitical, right-wing liberalism or traditional conservatism conditioned by church teaching, and therefore most of the leaders that emerged at that material time could accordingly be categorized as right wing. The wave of left-wing politicism which sprouted in southern Sudan with the advent of Egyptian and hence Sudanese working-class trade union movement receded in the wake of the disturbances in 1955[2]. Only a few southern Sudanese intellectuals could be counted as left-wing or communists. Therefore, the revolutionary government needed to exert more efforts to sway the already suspicious anti-communist audience in southern Sudan as also in northern Sudan.

The alliance of political left-wing forces that on 25th May 1969 catapulted Colonel Gaafar Mahommed Numeiri to the citadel of power did not hold on for long. The ideological differences within the alliance were stronger than the revolutionary message they carried or rather the socioeconomic and political transformation of the Sudan each group in the alliance desired. In another context, perhaps the correct understanding of desired revolutionary change in the Sudan ran against the socioeconomic and political interests of some groups within the alliance. The dominant among them were the Arab Baathist, Arab Socialist, the Nasserites suggesting that they were inspired by foreign, not Sudanese, images and idiosyncrasies. These ideological contradictions played out in changes that elbowed the communists out of the revolutionary council and the suppression of its political activities throughout the country. These repressive measures included censorship of the Sudan Youth Union (SYU) and the Sudanese Women Union (SWU), which operated separately and independent of the Communist Party of the Sudan being themselves mass based organizations. The Communist Party of the Sudan had insisted on maintaining independent existence within the leftist alliance and this couldn't only unnerve the Pan-Arab groups but also triggered ideological split within the CPS in 1990[3]. The reasons for expulsion and censorship of the CPS had nothing to do with the Sudanese revolution but with political currents in the Middle East. The dominance of Pan-Arab ideology, which in general was anti-communists and anti-internationalism led to repress the communists in the Arab countries like Iraq, Syria, Egypt, and Libya. The invisible hands of the Egyptian, Libyan regimes and the British MI6 could be counted behind the counterrevolutionary coup of 21st July 1971.

However, unlike the CPS, which has large mass support behind it, the Baathist and the Nasserites didn't have a real mass following in the Sudan. This placed Numeiri in an awkward dilemma. The break with communists meant that Numeiri or the May regime forfeited its mass support base among the modern forces in the centre (Khartoum-Medani-Atbara area). The sectarian theocratic dynasties with their political establishments controlled the regions: the Ansar sect (Umma Party) controlled western Sudan, while the Khatimiya (DUP) controlled the eastern and northern Sudan and were collectively also at war with the May regime[4]. Numeiri could only count on the southern provinces for support and therefore had to enter negotiations with the Anya-nya and the Southern Sudan Liberation Movement (SSLM) under the leadership of Gen. Joseph Lagu. The negotiations between the delegation of the Sudan government led by Abel Alier Kuai and the delegation of the SSLM led by Ezbon Mundiri were sponsored by the World Council of Churches under the auspices of Emperor Haile Selassie, in Addis Ababa Ethiopia.

2. The May Regime - SSLM Peace Talks and the Addis Ababa Agreement

There is always a reason behind anything. The ideological struggle within the left-wing alliance and within the CPS triggered the movement to correct the path of the revolution leading to the military action on 19th July by the revolutionary faction of the Free Officers Organization. As if the situation in the Sudan was a grave danger, imperialism immediately marshalled forces to nip it in the bud, As mentioned above, 22nd July downing of the British Airways plane carrying the revolutionary leaders Col. Babiker Nur and Major Farouk Hamdalla was a well-coordinated crime. It was this counterrevolutionary coup and the encouragement of imperialism that pushed Numeiri in negotiation with the SSLM to end the war. It was no wonder these peace talks involved the

World Council of Churches and Emperor Haile Selassie who at that time was US main pillar in the Horn of Africa.

It is not the intention of this chapter to analyse the talks and the agreement, suffice to mention that the SSLM delegation demanded separation and independence of Southern Sudan, which its delegation led by Aggrey Jaden tabled in the Round Table Conference in 1965 in Khartoum. This demand was in any case a non-starter. Secession of southern Sudan couldn't be negotiated on the table; it could only be achieved by force of arms. The Sudan government delegation already had the 9thJune Declaration as the regime solution to the problem of southern Sudan. The talks dragged on for sometimes because the SSLM delegation wouldn't easily accept the regional autonomy presented by the government delegation, which returned to Khartoum to mobilise the southern public opinion to put enormous pressure on the SSLM to accept any agreement. It was rather absurd that southerners in the country were asked to put pressure on SSLM for something of which they never had a glimpse of, or whose parameters were not immediately available publicly. Moreover, what power did non-members had on a political military organization as the SSLM. In desperation, southerners were made to believe that local autonomy was a kind of federation, and this was accepted. While the progressive southerners rejected this explanation, it was good music to many people with low political consciousness. All in all, with the pressure from the western countries, the SSLM and the government of Sudan reached an agreement and on 3rd March 1972 both Gaafar Numeiri and

Joseph Lagu signed the Addis Ababa Agreement (AAA). This immediately ended the insurrection that had lasted seventeen years.

3. The Establishment of the Southern Region.

The Addis Ababa Agreement provided self-rule for the three southern provinces of the Sudan namely Bahr el Ghazal, Equatoria and Upper Nile then collectively and officially known as the Southern Region (SR). The Southern Region had a regional government comprising the High Executive Council (HEC) made up of a president and eleven regional ministers, and an elected People's Regional Assembly (PRA). The Sudan was under a one-party totalitarian rule, which proscribed any political activity except under the auspices of the Sudan Socialist Union (SSU). Although the agreement did not provide, the members of the SSLM automatically became members of the Sudan Socialist Union (SSU), the ruling party in the Sudan, to enable them to participate in the political process in the country. As for the Anya-nya, the agreement provided for absorption of six thousand Anya-nya officers and men into the Sudan Armed Forces, then known as People's Armed Forces. The Addis Ababa Agreement also provided for a transitional period of eighteen months after which the government would conduct the elections of the PRA, which in turn would elect the President of the HEC. The concept of regional self-rule or local autonomy was an ideological platform of the political left, and its essence could only be better understood and internalized by progressives and revolutionary democrats. By

1972, the vibrant democratic movement that sprouted onto the political stage in the southern provinces during the initial days of the May revolution had imperceptibly melted away.

The prosecutions, imprisonments and political harassment that occurred following the counterrevolutionary coup of 22nd July 1971 by the police and the regime's national security organization pushed many into hiding or abandoned political activism altogether. However, as was first introduced, local autonomy was predicated on existence of a strong democratic movement in southern Sudan. In the absence of the democratic revolutionary forces, the liberal and conservative right-wing politicians, formerly members of SANU and Southern Front now congregated in the SSU, tasked themselves with the implementation of the agreement on regional self-rule. Instead of the rebel leader, Gen. Joseph Lagu, Gaafar Numeiri appointed Abel Alier, who led the government delegation to the Addis Ababa negotiations, as the interim president of the Southern Region.

Many people in southern Sudan then hardly accepted Numeiri's wisdom of appointing Abel Alier instead of Gen. Joseph Lagu to head the interim government. It was indeed a confirmation that war leaders can hardly be peace builders. Those versed and skilled in destructive enterprises like war are hardly appropriate in constructive endeavours of peace and nation building. This was the wisdom that eluded Omer al Bashir and Dr. John Garang after they signed the CPA in 2005; the same people who planned and prosecuted or commanded the war were the same people who were appointed to build peace. In the same vein those who negotiated the peace agreement were the same people who sat down to implement it. This may explain why Sudan has never been peaceful. The leaders administered the peace agreement with the war mentality. In certain instances, they revised the agreement to suit their new thinking. The war in Dar Fur did not end despite the Dar Fur Peace Agreement in Abuja, Nigeria. The NCP waged war on the SPLM-North in Blue Nile and Southern Kordofan immediately it became obvious that South Sudan was seceding from the rest of the country. Numeiri in this respect was an angel at least from the perspective of principle.

The Interim High Executive Council and Abel Alier's presidency

The implementation of the Addis Ababa Agreement started immediately after its ratification thanks to the efficient Sudanese bureaucracy; it was then still accountable and transparent. The period that immediately followed the Addis Ababa Agreement was not without social and political glitches. Indeed, sometimes for a people who have been at war for a long time, they find it difficult to manage peace times either because of ignorance or existence of war inertia reflected in suspicion and lack of trust. Many of the political glitches resulted from ignorance, lack of experience in government and bureaucratic procedures. As was the case then, many southerners would be in possession of adequate technical and professional knowledge but would be denied administrative or bureaucratic positions. As a result many of them lacked those skills and experiences. This was deliberate policy to prevent southerners acquire administrative skills, and therefore would always remain junior to a northern Sudanese colleague. Thus, they found difficulties managing the implementation of agreement especially those processes that required impartiality, neutrality and holistic consideration.

First, the process of selection, absorption, and integration of the Anya-nya forces into the People's Armed Forces (PAF) and other organized forces of police, prisons, wildlife, and fire brigade was expected to be smooth and straight forward. On the contrary, the exercise was so opaque and flawed that ethnic exclusion, discrimination, corruption, nepotism and favouritism in evaluation of individuals accompanied the process throughout the southern provinces resulting in mutinies and assassinations of leading officers[5].

Secondly, the process of repatriation, relief, rehabilitation, and resettlement of the refugees from Ethiopia, Uganda, and Congo witnessed widespread corruption and misappropriation of relief materials and funds at the level of policy and bureaucratic implementation of the projects.

Thirdly, the process of secondment recruitment of civil servants preceded perfectly well although there were few incidences of corruption and favouritism. Whatever the social and political glitches that faced it, the interim HEC ignored or overlooked them and settled down to its business of self-government. The Southern Region recruited and built its bureaucracy from the experienced and competent Sudan Civil Service. Except for a few glitches the formation of the regional public service was successfully built on the slogan "Public Service Without Fear or Favour".

In fact, the southern provinces of the Sudan for the first time since 1955 became generally peaceful. Many southern Sudanese, particularly those born during the war, believed this new situation was a form of independence. The regional self-rule was celebrated, and Gaafar Mohammed Numeiri accepted as the only trustworthy northern Sudanese leader. Some southerners made it so personal that those individuals who opposed Numeiri and the May regime on account of ideological difference were vilified and ostracised. What many people in the southern provinces didn't objectively view, or in fact, brushed aside as undesirable truth, was the reality that the Southern Region was not a personal gift of Numeiri to the people of southern provinces. It was something they had won through struggle in which many lives were lost since the mutiny in Torit on 18th August 1955. They also did not seriously accept that Southern Region was part and parcel of the Sudan; that it was subject to the same laws governing other parts of the country. Little did they realize that sooner than later the negative realities of the May regime, which many southerners wanted to ignore or fudge, would dawn on the Southern Region in the form of Numeiri's direct and uncalled for interference in its political and democratic processes.

The founding of the Southern Region coincided with the general economic crisis in the world triggered by the sharp rise of oil prices following the Yam Kapur war in 1973. Sudan had just succumbed to the dictates of the Bretton Woods Institutions - the World Bank (WB) and the International Monetary Fund (IMF). The IMF imposed the structural adjustment programmes

(SAPs) on the Sudan and no sooner did it trigger a general decline in the value of the Sudanese currency against the US dollar, and low income from the Sudanese exports. This was reflected in government's inability to provide social services or economic development. The Southern Region was the weakest link in the system. Its huge natural resources potential notwithstanding, it depended absolutely on the central government and therefore started to show the negative indices of the economic crisis earlier than any other part of the Sudan. The HEC received only chapters one and two of its annual budget, which indeed were salaries and services, known as aid-grant, from the central government. There were hardly any funds for chapter three – development. Because of the SAPs, the HEC could not provide the social services in education and health. Most of the boarding intermediate and primary schools in the Southern Region transformed to day schools, the regional government or area council employees seldom got their salaries on time. There were times when they would spend months without salaries adding to the crisis of lack of essential commodities and growing corruption in government.

The politics in Juba revolved around allegiance to the May regime and President Numeiri. With the slogan of 'national unity', the regional ministry of information and culture assisted by the national security organs of the state hypnotized and submerged people's consciousness to prevent a correct perception and understanding of the relation between the regime's economic policies and the declining quality of life in the region.

The difficulties were blamed on the people surrounding Numeiri without thinking back how a good leader could surround himself with bad people. At times, they would put the blame for all the failures in the system on the person of the president of HEC. Abel Alier, a prudent lawyer politician, weighed issues, whatsoever, against the objective reality and what feasibly could be undertaken at the least possible inconvenience to the president of the republic. A colleague and friend, Benjamin Warille, once told me Abel Alier was visibly angry when he read in the Nile Mirror an article Warille had authored on the oil discovery in western Upper Nile. Abel Alier inquired if Warille had a combat ready contingent of army to defend what he wrote. In his administration of the Southern Region, Abel Alier seldom interfered with nor intervened to correct some of bad decision made by his ministers or his chief of police, Gen. Ruben Mach, despite the thunderous complaints against him from the people. The interim period of the Addis Ababa Agreement ended without many problems for Abel's presidency. Eighteen months was short a time that the political direction was still not clear to many people. Khartoum still controlled the Southern Regional chapter of the Sudan Socialist Union.

The regional self-rule started to show discrepancies as real power remained in the centre in Khartoum while the semblance of authority in Juba was a kind of devolution of powers rather than genuine regional self-rule. There were southern leaders; people like Joseph Oduho, Luigi Adwok, Hilary Paul Logali, and others in the Political Bureau or in the Central Committee of the SSU, but as Joseph Oduho confided to me in Debri Ziet, they nevertheless did not exercise that political authority. The president of HEC, Abel Aliet, sent Oduho, a member of SSU Political Bureau, at the head of delegation from Juba to Belgrade, Yugoslavia, to negotiate a US$ 5million contract for building government residences, offices, and the parliament in Juba. On reaching Khartoum, the delegation was shuffled and a junior member of SSU Central Committee was made to head the delegation. The Yugoslavs party leaders were amazed how a senior member of the party, Joseph Oduho, could be led and directed by his subordinate in the ruling party, Salihieen. These northern Sudanese attitudes towards their compatriots from the Southern Region invariably fuelled the secessionist tendencies. Joseph Oduho related this while we were already in the SPLM/A suggesting that his decision to join the armed struggle resulted from such slighting treatment.

The elections for the People's Regional Assembly (PRA) scheduled at the end of the eighteen-months interim period were to be conducted either in late 1973 or early 1974, when the climate in the whole southern Sudan would be dry. The PRA elections were going to be the political litmus paper that would gauge the political thinking in the Southern Region. Many of the former rebels were already disillusioned with Abel's interim administration; and indeed, problems that normally would crop up because of weak institutions had started to surface in different parts of the region warranting security considerations. There was no visible power struggle against Abel Alier and the elections were conducted peacefully. The issue of Abel Alier continuing as president of the HEC was not on the elections campaign agenda to warrant highhandedness on the part of Numeiri. Many people in the Southern Region disdained, if not resented, Numeiri emissary, Abulgasim Mohammed Ibrahim's braggadocio and naked show of unmitigated state power when he come to Juba to impose Abel Alier's candidature on the PRA for the president of the HEC.

It demonstrated that after all the Southern Region was a subset of the May totalitarian dictatorship, and therefore, regardless of the provisions of Addis Ababa Agreement for a democratic process in the Southern Region, Numeiri nevertheless could impose on Southern Region the leader he believed was loyal to him and the unity of the country. This was an uncalled-for direct interference in the democratic determination of Southern Region's leadership suggesting Numeiri wouldn't countenance any other leader than Abel Alier. For many politicians and political activists, the imposition of Abel Alier in 1974 was a precursor of what to expect if southerners desired another independent minded leader. This development echoed old relations of suspicion and lack of trust northern political establishment had in their southern compatriots based on the falsehood that southerners would secede from the Sudan if they were left alone.

The opposition to the May regime intensified throughout the country including two aborted military coups in Chaban 1974 and 1975. In the Southern Region strong voices against the digging of Jonglei canal emerged to jam the corridors of power in Juba. Many people have not forgotten the high-handedness with which the HEC suppressed the Jonglei canal protests and street demonstrations that resulted in the death of a student shot by the police, and the arrest, and detention of several members of the PRA. Many people in the Southern Region perceived Abel Alier as a weak leader who would not confront the northern political establishment in many of the issues that sprang up negatively against the Southern Region. These included the refusal of Gaafar Numeiri to implement the Abyei referendum and the plebiscite in Kurmuk and Guma Guffa areas, which Gen. Ibrahim Abboud had annexed to Blue Nile province in 1960. The agitation against Abel Alier, and the efforts to vote him out of the presidency of the HEC started to simmer in Juba especially among the youths and students. Many southerners began to feel the political hiccoughs and started to realise that self-rule did not give them the independence (freedom) they desired. It confirmed that the north would always continue to interfere and to impose weak leaders on the Southern Region. Clandestine political activities to oust Abel Alier from the presidency of HEC started in earnest.

By 1978, many southern intellectuals were already fed up with Abel's soft politics of appeasing the leadership in Khartoum. It is worth mentioning that six years of experience with the Southern Region has raised their awareness. They had totally woken up and ready for change. However, as usual, the people create conditions for change, but the leaders would let them down. After all, one party politics is about loyalty and political renting; there was nothing as struggling for people's rights to social and economic development. The SSU was an employer and every Tom and

Jerry wanted to try their luck in the political game set to be in the elections of the people regional assembly (PRA). These were SSU elections meaning that anybody desiring to contest these elections must be a loyal member of the SSU; gone were the days when independent candidature was constitutionally permitted. The PRA elections would therefore be a contest between the SSU conformists (Abel loyalists) and reformists (rebels). It would also be a test of political and organizational sophistication of the reformists if they would challenge the establishment. The lack of political space in the prevailing conditions represented by strict security surveillance to curb dissidence was indeed a risk for any kind of anti-establishment campaign in the PRA elections. This campaign had to be undertaken pretentiously as loyalists as possible across the board in the territorial, workers, and intellectuals' electoral constituencies and therefore required organizational sophistication to avoid confrontation with the establishment's security agents.

5. The Wind of Change and Election of Gen. Joseph Lagu
The elections of the People's Regional Assembly were indeed a political melee between the pro-Abel and the anti-Abel groups in the SSU regional secretariat. It couldn't have been a context in the same party had the reformist behaved as if they were an opposition. In the end, the results were dramatic ever to be expected in a one-party totalitarian regime buttressed by a huge national security apparatus. This reformist group christened 'the wind of change' identified itself as anti-Abel group long after the

declaration of the results and the struggle had then shifted to the precincts of the People's Regional Assembly where the election of the president of HEC would take place. Most pro-Abel Alier politicians had been trounced; an indication that Abel Alier had no chance of winning the contest for president of the Southern Region. In a single vote, Gen. Joseph Lagu was elected president of HEC. The people of the Southern Region told Numeiri and the political establishment in northern Sudan in no uncertain terms that they were free to elect the leaders they wanted.

Gen. Joseph Lagu was the choice of an amorphous political group that comprised former elements of the SSLM/Anya-nya, SANU and the Southern Progressives, who were not pleased with Abel Alier's six years performance as president of the HEC. Gen. Lagu was not the group's leader; in fact, the group had no clear and defined leadership hierarchy. Gen. Joseph Lagu was put forward to challenge Abel Alier only on account of his proximity to the centre of power in Khartoum and that proved to be the group's biggest weakness. The problem with such an alliance was the lack of a common and uniting political ideology. Being against an individual in the system does not whatsoever translate into true commitment to political change nor did removing Abel Alier from presidency of HEC mean that the wind of change group would escalate the struggle or transform itself into an opposition to the regime. Indeed, the wind of change group was not ideologically or politically united and didn't possess a post-elections political programme. The lack of organization and hence leadership proved a fatal mistake for the group and for the people of Southern Region who voted them into power. Although this tactic shielded them from the national security apparatus nevertheless it exposed them as an *ad hoc* body instituted for the purpose of removing Abel Alier from the presidency of HEC. Removing an individual like Abel Alier and not working to change the bad system was an exercise in futility. It's true many politicians in the region perceived Abel Alier a weak leader; he would not stand up to the northern political establishment when it came to issues southerners considered red lines, but would sooner than later come to discover that Gen. Joseph Lagu was even weaker. The political incompetence and inexperience of the wind of change group showed up in the government that Gen. Joseph Lagu pieced together immediately after his election as president of HEC. It exposed the incoherence and lack of unity within the 'wind of change' group. As it became apparent, individual members pursued personal power agenda prompting Gen. Lagu to precipitously shuffle his government removing his supporters to incorporate some elements of Abel Alier's group[6] which poised a spirited opposition to Lagu's leadership. Abel's groups in the PRA, comprised multi-party democracy era Southern Front and SANU politicians who were versed and skilled in political brinkmanship, had burrowed into and widened the gap within the 'wind of change' group leading to its disintegration. Gen. Joseph Lagu eventually paid back dearly when the elements of Abel's groups incorporated into his government moved a motion in the PRA to impeach him on flimsy and unproven charges of corruption.

The pro-establishment group meticulously worked to remove Gen. Joseph Lagu and to bring back Abel Alier as president of HEC for the second time without having to conduct fresh elections. The members of the 'wind of change' group were left licking the political wounds they inflicted on themselves. The return of Abel Alier as the president of HEC immediately on the heels of Gen. Joseph Lagu was a bad omen for many people in the Southern Region, especially when he brought back into the government some resented politicians and civil servants. It also generated ill-feelings and bitterness among many Equatorian politicians and ordinary people; they read sinister motives into the impeachment and unseating of Gen. Joseph Lagu as something against the people of Equatoria. Thus, began in earnest the provincialization and ethnicization of Southern Region's politics.

The struggle and scrambles for power in a socially and politically backward environment like Southern Region was bound to throw up raw emotions and sentiments that run along provincial and/or ethnic lines. The Southern Region and its power politics was unique in that although a part of the totalitarian regime nevertheless the politicians here played liberal democratic politics and could impeach its president even on flimsy and phony charges. It solicited envy from certain quarters with the political establishment, including Numeiri himself, to disrupt and disband whenever and wherever possible. Both Abel Alier and Gen. Joseph Lagu should have been mindful of this reality to avoid being exploited by enemies of southern Sudan.[7] The politicians in Juba were not sensitive to the implications of ethnic and provincial discords generated by their bad politics.

The regional government, whether under the presidency of Abel Alier or Gen. Joseph Lagu, did not provide the anticipated social and economic development in the Southern Region. The greater part of its budget was spent in and around Juba, the seat of the regional government where a consumption driven economy emerged. This was to the complete neglect of other provinces and created an influx into the capital and its environs of people and livestock especially from Terikeka and Bor triggering conflicts with the local Bari community. The power politics among the politicians and intellectuals permeated into and affected local community relations in and around the capital Juba. In fact, large cattle camps belonging to some government officials sprang around Juba attracting migration of Dinka Bor pastoralist, who overzealously change the Bari names of places generating another layer communal conflict. I will discuss this problem in details in the context of the re-division politics.

6. The Oil Discovery and the Unmaking of the Southern Region

When in 1979, the Chevron Oil company of California struck oil deposits in western Upper Nile little did its management know that they had detonated a land mine. A land mine remains for a long time in the earth if no one touches it. Oil in any part of the Sudan would have been a blessing than a curse if nothing so spiteful or of a spectre had not been attached to this innocent scientific discovery. The discovery of oil, and in southern Sudan immediately re-enforced the traditional suspicion between southern and northern political elite to the extent that those with power of decision making lost rational thinking and responded to prejudices. In July 1980[8], on the side-lines of the 3rd International Geological Congress in Paris, the minister of petroleum of the Sudan, Dr. Sharief el Tuhami, in a briefing, informed the Sudanese participants of the congress about the oil discovery somewhere five hundred kilometres south of Khartoum, and the government's decision to refine the oil in Kosti. Innocently, I inquired whether it would not have been economically feasible to refine oil in Bentiu than Kosti, and the Minister exploded prompting the ambassador to stop the briefing and to dismiss us. Later, a friend warned me that the National Security organization may have taken note of my question. Little did I know that this was already a political problem in the Southern Region. I was a post-graduate student in Budapest, Hungary and had travelled from there to attend the congress.

The unfortunate thing about Southern Sudanese politicians and intellectuals in general was their capacity to fragment themselves in pursuit of short-term personal rather long-term common interests. During these fracases they quickly got distracted and abandoned an earlier adopted common political position. This played out in the politics of re-division of the Southern Region, when quickly they forgot the seventeen-year war they had fought together. The discovery of oil in Bentiu and the decision by authorities in Khartoum, of course dictated by Chevron Oil

Company's economic considerations, to refine the product in Kosti stirred and united the southern politicians in or out of the regional government against the northern political establishment. The members of the PRA stood solidly in block behind the HEC in opposition to northern Sudanese attempts to deprive the people of southern Sudan of the economic benefits of the oil finding; the public in the Southern Region was also behind their government. In view of this strong opposition, Numeiri came in with a trick to scuttle and destroy that unity. Nevertheless, the politicians couldn't see the plot as soon as they could identify their personal interest behind the plot. Numeiri's ploy was to exploit the weaknesses inherent in the sociocultural diversity of the people of southern Sudan, which deflect their anger to themselves instead of the common enemy.

It will be recalled that in his appointment as interim president of the HEC, Gaafar Numeiri did not have any inkling about Abel Alier's Dinka Bor ethnic background. This consideration must have been a late discovery when ethnic differences became a factor in Southern Regional power politics. But Maulana Abel Alier was not somebody who could be described as a tribalist although many people, even those who knew him in legal defence of southerners across the board, would look suspiciously at some of his tribal appointments. However, unlike Gaafar Numeiri, Abel Alier should have been more sensitive to factor into his policies the ethnic diversity of southern Sudan and to save himself from such accusations. The presence in Juba of Abel Alier as president of HEC and his appointment as police chief in Juba of

Ruben Mach, a fellow Dinka Bor, must have been an important factor that attracted and triggered of migration of Bor Dinka with their animals to Juba and its environs. They established cattle camps and giving Dinka names to replace Bari names of those localities; some of these names are still in use now although the Bari had decided to assert their sovereignty 'Thong-Piny' is now Juba na Bari.

The Bor Dinka grazed their herds and sometimes carelessly permitted them into the Bari gardens to eat or destroy crops. The Bari whose crops have been eaten or destroyed by Bor Dinka cattle would go to report the matter to the police station in Juba only to find a Bor Dinka policeman, who locked up the Bari in the police cell instead of the cattle herder. These incidences repeated over a period marred social and communal relations and eventually built up into political crisis. By late 1980s, the relations between the Bor Dinka cattle herders and the Bari sedentary agriculturalists reached crisis point. This crisis correlated with the trouncing of a veteran Bari politician, Hilary Paul Logali, in the election of the people's regional assembly in 1978 on account of being too close to Abel Alier, who as president of HEC was reluctant to act against his Dinka Bor cattle herders who were committing profound damages on the Bari villages in the environ of Juba.

The ploy of dismantling the Southern Region, dressed up as decentralization and bringing the services nearer the people, found fertile ground in the already bad ethnic or community relations in the Southern Region. The points that would tear apart or unite the people of southern Sudan all was now in Abel's group. It was obvious, Numeiri had lost confidence in Abel Alier, and had appointed Gen. Joseph Lagu second vice president of the republic. Abel's group needed to put up a candidate to replace Abel Alier whose position as president of HEC was the bone of contention. Instead of proposing a compromise candidate, Abel Alier went for Bona Malual, a fellow Dinka, to secede him against the opinion of many members of the people's regional assembly from Equatoria and Upper Nille. This widened the divisions and made it impossible to strike a compromise. Gaafar Numeiri only needed to tighten the nuts and bolts on the regional government to achieve his goals. He dissolved the PRA, dismissed the HEC, and appointed a military caretaker, Gen. Gismalla Rasas to be in charge and to conduct the elections for the people's regional assembly. In Khartoum, Numeiri started to intimidate the southern politicians known to be vocal against the redivision of the Southern Region[9].

7. Divisions Within the Southern Sudan Political Elite: The Debate on the 'Unity' or 'Re-Division of the Southern Region'.

There was no provision in the Addis Ababa Agreement on how long the Southern Region would have lasted in that constitutional and legal status. It was also not clear if it were a permanent status, and what would happen, as it occurred in 1985, that the May regime was overthrown? With the benefit of the hindsight, the Southern Region would not have lasted beyond 1983 without something spectacular happening. Gaafar Numeiri was at the head of a social-political force that no longer existed at the top. The political power in the SSU had shifted to the Muslim Brotherhood and was clear the promulgation of Islamic constitution frozen by the May coup 1969 was back on the table spearheaded by none other than Numeiri himself at the behest of Hassan Abdalla Al-Turabi. In this context, the Addis Ababa Agreement had lost its political clout; it had served its purpose to end the war and rein peace in the southern provinces. However, the constitutional arrangement it provided, which had ensnared many people in southern Sudan to wholeheartedly support Numeiri at the beginning were considered usual Sudanese political wheeling and dealing that play out in empty promises or agreements dishonoured.

In the course of six to seven years in the life of the Southern Region, vested political interests emerged and their wings ushered political divisions which played out as power struggle between these different groups. In the absence of clear ideological differences, the struggle for power usually plays out along ethnic and/or regional/provincial contour lines. The debate that engaged the southern Sudanese politicians, intellectuals, and ordinary people in early eighties about 'unity' or 're-division of Southern Region' was not in any way linked to the question whether or not Addis Ababa Agreement had resolved the problem of southern Sudan. The debate, which was evaded deliberately, should have raised the failure of the southern Sudanese political elite to build a state, and to unite their people around that state in a period of ten years they implemented the Addis Ababa Agreement. Short of answering that question would only suggest that the Addis Ababa Agreement, which the leaders of SSLM signed with Numeiri was merely an instrument to end the war. This would explain why the debate was on something completely irrelevant triggered by raw emotions and sensibilities.

Whether or not, the SSLM leaders were aware the Addis Ababa Agreement did not address the fundamental contradictions that underpinned the civil war. The socioeconomic and cultural development of southern Sudan to address the centuries old conditions of poverty, ignorance and superstition was not in the political lexicon of the SSLM leaders. The power struggle, that tore themselves apart in sterile debate in response to Numeiri's dictates, was not for transforming the lives of the people. The Juba political elite and others who participated in the debate should have reflected deeply in the common interest of the people of southern Sudan. They would have recognized Gaafar Mohammed Numeiri signatures in the region's lack of socioeconomic development and its political trepidation.

However, in this debate about unity or re-division of Southern Region, two prominent groups emerged. The Equatoria Central Committee (ECC) and the Council for Unity of Southern Sudan (CUSS) and perhaps there was a third smaller one, which supported neither of the groups but didn't feature much in the headlines. The ECC comprised predominantly of leaders from Equatoria, and this configuration generally echoed the Equatorians' complaints of Dinka domination of political life in the Southern Region with the corresponding marginalization of Equatorians in the bureaucracy. It included some prominent leaders from Upper Nile and Jonglei. The CUSS composed of people across the board in the Southern Region including Equatorians. The two groups theoretically aligned to Gen. Joseph Lagu and Abel Alier respectively although later when the debate heated up the groups shuffled and reshuffled in response to the emerging political alliances.

To the ordinary southern Sudanese, it appeared as if Abel Alier stood for the *status quo*, suggesting that the Southern Region be maintained to preserve the Addis Ababa Agreement. On the other hand, Gen. Joseph Lagu appeared to stand for dismantling the Southern Region while also preserving the Addis Ababa Agreement. Gen. Joseph Lagu in his arguments believed re-division was enriching the Addis Ababa Agreement by generating three subregions instead of one region. This was not straight forward as it appeared. A critical analysis demonstrated that the two positions were deceptive and untenable. The target was the Addis Ababa Agreement as an instrument with regional and international legitimacy giving the people of southern Sudan self-rule. Its abrogation was the condition upon which the National Front would join the May regime as per Port Sudan Agreement 1977. Lagu's argument was therefore misleading because once he accepted the Southern Region to be tempered with it was the end of Addis Ababa Agreement. One could read into dismissal of Abel Alier and appointment of General Lagu as second vice president as a signal that he (Abel Alier) was in the know about Numeiri's intention to dismantle the Southern Region but must have given an opposite opinion to his followers. Being a very decent man Abel Alier would not discuss publicly an opinion the matter he must have failed to reach a consensus with his boss. However, it was a question of destiny of a people; he was morally bound to tell his supporters the truth that Numeiri had changed his mind and wanted to dismantle the Southern Region. The arguments put forward by the Solidarity Committee of the people's National Assembly smacks of lack of in-depth knowledge of what was on in the presidency confirming what I mentioned above that Abel Alier did not keep his supporters abreast with the political developments in the Palace.

The political undercurrents in the campaign for 1982 elections of the people's regional assembly elections resembled the 1978 political fault lines, which catapulted Gen. Lagu to the citadel of High Executive Council. However, the campaigns had a streak of party politics never played before in the Southern Region. SANU came out a better political player than Southern Front. It outsmarted the Southern Front employing the Dinka Unity card to rally and to unite all the Dinka members of PRA behind it in an alliance with the ECC, and 'wind of change' from Upper Nile and Eastern Equatoria around the candidature of Eng. James Joseph Tambura to the president of HEC. This strategy won the day, with Dhol Acuil Aleu as deputy president of HEC, and Matthew Obur Ayang as the Speaker of the PRA. However, this proved to be an unprincipled political alliance driven only by short-term personal ambition for power rather that higher long-term national interests. It did not take long before political fissures surfaced in the alliance triggered by lack of a common agreement on re-division of the Southern Region.

By the time Numeiri appointed Gen. Rasas the caretaker president of HEC, it was clear that he was intend on dismantling the Southern Region. The politicians who opposed the re-division of the region had time to build a strong alliance to defeat and thwart Numeiri's stratagem. But as it appeared ethnic consideration and power ambition blocked rational and strategic thinking. Nothing could have pushed SANU into alliance with the re-division camp if it were not power consideration and their resentment of the Southern Front. The Southern Front politicians on the other hand insisted on presenting Abel Alier as candidate for the president of HEC against clear signs that neither he nor his preferred candidate, Bona Malual Madut[10], wouldn't win the contest. This led to the formation of an unprincipled alliance that brought Eng. James Joseph Tambura as president of HEC, Matthew Obur Ayang the Speaker of the PRA and Dhol Acuil Aleu, the vice president of HEC, Mr. Charles Koat Chatim the minister of regional administration, police and prisons, HRH Prince Othwonh Dak Padiet the minister of finance and economic planning, Mr. Philip Obang Ojway as minister of education. It turned out in this alliance that there was double-talking and short-changing; those who assumed they were in the centre found themselves elbowed out to the periphery and ostracised.

Politics in a totalitarian political environment can be pregnant with surprises, shocks, double talks, and short-changing.

The government [Legislature and Executive] of Eng. James Joseph Tambura came out of the PRA all wearing signature palm leaves hats and brandishing thump salute having won the context against the Southern Front. The legislature and executive comprised powerful politicians from Upper Nile and Jonglei provinces whose social base were visibly anti-re-division of the Southern Region. This perhaps was part of the surprises of politics in a totalitarian environment. Eng. Daniel Koat Matthews campaigned and was elected on his own slogan of 'Upper Nile without Bor'. The people of Nasir who elected him didn't concern themselves much about his problems with Abel; they elected his person, and so was it with Prince Othwonh Dak Padiet and Philip Obang Ojway, who visibly were for the re-division of the Southern Region but not their social bases.

The detestable thing about the scramble for power in a politically backward environment was that it generated animosities and personal hatred which permeated and trickled down to the communities in form of explosive ethnic or communal conflicts. This occurred particularly in Juba and its environs fitting the Bari and Mundari youths against the Bor Dinka counterparts with loss of life and destruction of property, while their leaders and elites were wined and dined together in Juba pubs and bars. The Mundari people had to pay back in form of murders, rape of women and girls, looting of cattle and devastation of their area when an SPLA contingent comprising mainly Bor Dinka invade the Mundari territory in 1984/85 ostensibly in vengeance for their role in Juba skirmishes accompanying the re-division debates.

With the announcement of the election results and the formation of the government, the rowdy and hair-splitting debates on re-division, which usually culminated in stone-throwing and running battles in the streets had ceased and everything went quiet in Juba and in the provinces. It deceptively appeared as if President Numeiri had shelved his re-division project now that the Southern Region had a president different from Abel Alier or Joseph Lagu. This quiet was deceptive for nobody spoke anymore about the redivision. The regional government settled down to its business. However, it was clear Numeiri and his strategists had gone to develop other plans required for dismantling the Southern Region. The first noticeable action was disruption of air, river, and road travels and communication inside and outside the Southern Region. The Sudan Airways flights that connected Malakal to Juba and Wau had ceased. To travel from Juba to either Wau or Malakal by Sudan Airways one had to fly to Khartoum and that meant waiting for some days for the appropriate connections. Then, the Sudan Airways flights became non-existent; people travelling from Juba to Khartoum occasionally flew on Sudan Air Force Hercules planes, which were also inaccessible even for constitutional office holders; the National Security organ had to issue permits to allow travelling. The situation was becoming unpredictable.

Then suddenly, in March 1983 the vice president of HEC, Dhol Acuil Aleu, the Rt.Hon. Speaker of PRA, Hon. Matthew Obur Ayang and some other politicians were summoned to Khartoum, arrested, and detained. The national security heightened surveillance on persons suspected of opposition to the re-division. In this drive, they arrested and detained students, workers, and government officials. Surprisingly, the actions of the regime's security apparatus did not provoke mass reaction or protests. What puzzled many observers was how Eng. James Joseph Tambura an avowed re-divisionist managed to ensnare such staunch southern unionists like Matthew Obur Ayang and others into an alliance that principally aimed at dismantling the Southern Region. It was mind boggling how these unionists allowed themselves to be co-opted into the re-divisionist camp.

It was easy to explain this political behaviour in terms of lack of principle. The politics in Southern Region or politics generally in southern Sudan, was about positions in government than about political principles, or political programmes. This stems from the general sociocultural underdevelopment hence no political tradition and culture underpinned by principles of integrity, selflessness, sacrifice, and solidarity. As a result, those who called themselves politicians did not think or act on clear political principles as they struggle for political rent (office). The unionist camps comprising most members of the PRA from Bahr el Ghazal and Upper Nile and East bank Equatoria were in the majority and could have defeated the re-divisionist camp. Unfortunately, the factor of Bona Malual, a Dinka from Bahr el Ghazal and truly Abel Alier's protégé derailed the negotiations and out of expediency pushed many unionists to the Tambura camp.

That the regime's security agents targeted Dhol Acuil, Matthew Obur and others from Bahr el Ghazal and Upper Nile spoke to the split in the alliance. It was clear that SANU and other Southern nationalists, who were ensnared into alliance with the re-division camp must have decided to oppose the policies put forward by president of HEC, Eng. James Joseph Tambura. Numeiri did not want a repeat of Lagu's impeachment in the People's Regional Assembly and to pre-empt any PRA action against James Tambura, Numeiri had to summon to Khartoum and arrest both Dhol Acuil and Matthew Obur. The situation then in Juba would be described as confused. The government alliance had been thrown into confusion and dysfunctionality set in immediately. The blame game started in earnest, and this generated bitterness within the unionist camp. Moreover, the President of HEC, Eng. James Joseph Tambura and many of his ministers shifted to Khartoum their operations leaving the people in Juba to circulation of unfounded rumours and outright disinformation exacerbated by the complete isolation of Juba due to lack of regular transport and communication between it and Khartoum. I would say that the period between March and May 1983was the most difficult time in the Southern Region. The Southern Region entered a situation of motionless calm or quiet that usually characterizes the moments before a huge storm. Many of the Southern Region's politicians relocated to Khartoum in anticipation of Numeiri's decision whichever way it came.

8. The Mutiny in Bor, Southern Region Dismantled and Addis Ababa Agreement Abrogated

The deceptive calm mentioned above was not to last for long. On the 16th of May 1983 Bor town was woken to the rattle of machine gun fire. A contingent of Sudan armed forces sent from Juba attacked the rebellious soldiers of Battalion 105 in Bor town. The news of the fighting in Bor reached Juba but people shared it in small confidential circles and in whispers. At the University of Juba staff club, where members of the academic staff liberally discussed political issues related to the government, this time round nobody dared speak publicly about what transpired in Bor. However, those in the know of these events concluded that the attack on Bor marked the death of the Southern Region.

The attack on elements of the SAF battalion 105 was of course a matter of momentous political significance that would change for good the situation in the Sudan. The action was efficacious. No sooner was the country pounded with Republican Decree No. 1 dissolving the Southern Region and breaking it up into the three component subregions of Bahr el Ghazal, Equatoria and Upper Nile. The false calm that had submerged the region was broken creating a fundamentally new situation. If anybody had doubted Numeiri's intentions, it was now clear he was on a journey of no return and had no reasons to placate anyone either nationally or regionally; the man he would have been careful not to infuriate, Emperor Haile Selassie, was long dead having been overthrown by his own army. Field Marshall Gaafar Numeiri had taken stock of the southern politicians and had broken their resistance in one republican decree. Instead of protesting they congratulated him for his decision. If the southerners foolishly believed the Southern Region was a personal gift from Gaafar Mohammed Numeiri to the people of Southern Sudan, he had then withdrawn at will. How could a political victory won after relentless struggle paying heavy price in terms of human life and missed opportunities for socioeconomic and cultural development be a personal gift?

The popular narrative was to plant the blame on Gen. Joseph Lagu for championing the re-division of the Southern Region while promoting Numeiri's policy of administrative decentralization. This would be the falsification of history; besides Gen. Lagu there was also Abel Alier and his Southern Front brigade as well as the SANU and the Dinka unity group. All played the game which dismantled the Southern Region. In fact, Gen. Lagu could only be blamed for nurturing a political force he later couldn't control or arrest to prevent the destruction of the Addis Ababa Agreement, which in his words 'had brightened my image before the people of southern Sudan' and the African region. Numeiri acted out of political expedience; he entered into agreement with the SSLM to break out of the political isolation in the country. After defeating the Ansar in 1970 and split with the communists in 1971, he was in complete isolation from both the right and left of the Sudanese political spectrum. His newfound confidence and security to audaciously say that "Addis Ababa Agreement was neither the Bible or the Quran" then came from the Islamic Chartered Front, whose political agenda was the Islamic state in the Sudan.

THE PROBLEMS OF SOUTH SUDAN

When on 1st June 1983, Numeiri dismantled the Southern Region and abrogated the Addis Ababa Agreement he couldn't have done so without the cooperation and collaboration of the political leadership of the Southern Region. This leadership had, since the establishment of the Southern Region, hypnotized themselves and with them the people of southern Sudan, singing the slogan of 'national unity'. This 'national unity' song loudly ignored the socioeconomic development of the people Southern Region, the only most important factor that could have effectively contributed to the national unity of the Sudan. The northern political establishment welcomed this chorus without the slightest feeling for reciprocity. National unity of the Sudan is a shared responsibility in the form of fair and equal provision of social and economic development to all parts of the country. National unity couldn't be achieved in the context of economic marginalization, political exclusion and discrimination of southerners and their forceful removal from the capital in the resented *kasha*. Some southern leaders, people like Gordon Mortat Mayen and others who on principle refused to accept the Addis Ababa Agreement remained as refugees outside the Sudan. They had difficulty trusting the northern political elite particularly in their military uniforms. The leaders who came home with the agreement like Aggrey Jaden, Ezbon Mundiri, George Otor Akumbek Kwanai, and many others, were elbowed out of the SSLM hierarchy, marginalized and left to waste away until they died out of deep frustration and despair. Their sin was taking a rather negative attitude towards the agreement and the relations it established with the northern political establishment especially Numeiri's appointment of Abel Alier to lead the interim government of the Southern Region in 1972, hardened their attitude believing that leadership of Southern Sudan had passed into the hands of political rent-seekers and won't be long before they betrayed the people.

Ten years down the line of the totalitarian dictatorship system wasn't short a time for weak- kneed, unprincipled, and spineless leaders to shift position. The presidential decree No. 1 of 1st June 1983 dismantling the Southern Region and abrogating the Addis Ababa Agreement found many of the southern regional leaders queuing to meet Numeiri in the Republican Palace in Khartoum. They were there not to protest his dismantling of the Southern Region or the abrogation of the Addis Ababa Agreement; those leaders including those who had vigorously opposed Numeiri's project for re-division of the Southern Region, were there to congratulate Numeiri for betraying the people of southern Sudan. They were there to dispose themselves for political rent to run the government of the new weak subregions of Bahr el Ghazal, Equatoria and Upper Nile; a political attitude and behaviour that wasn't surprising at all; particularly for many of those politicians who were inside the country at the time Lagu and Numeiri signed the peace agreement. They were prone to changing sides to keep themselves relevant. It was those same spineless politicians who in early 1972 mounted enormous pressure on the SSLM delegation in Addis Ababa sending them telegrams after telegrams urging them to sign the agreement whatever its content entailed as if they were saying 'it is enough brothers, we are tied of the war'. That they went back to congregate on the corridors of power in Khartoum after the abrogation of that agreement and eruption of war in the Southern Region was something to be expected of them. They had been desensitized and become impervious to political humiliation including the abuse of their people.

The attitude and behaviour of Gen. Joseph Lagu was rather difficult to comprehend. It would be simplistic to explain it only in terms of having been re-instated into his position in the Sudanese Armed Forces or having married a northern Sudanese Muslim while retaining his Christian persuasion. The explanation must lie somewhere but I'll come back to it. The attitude of the politicians who went to Khartoum for political rents contrasted with position of principle, honour and integrity taken by the likes of Joseph Oduho, Akuot Atem, Lual Ding Wol, Martin Majier Gai, Malath Joseph, Benjamin Bol Akok, Samuel Gai Tut, William Abdalla Chuol, and many other politicians and political activists, intellectuals, students, workers and peasants who decided to follow the survivors of the Bor battle into the bushes of southern Sudan to continue the armed struggle. By 1983 when war erupted in southern Sudan the May regime was moribund. The regime's relations with the Bretton Woods Institutions, the World Bank and the IMF, and its acceptance of the structural adjustment programs (SAPs) had triggered acute social, economic, and political crisis in the Sudan, which eventually led to its overthrow.

The political opposition to Numeiri's regime had existed since its usurpation of power in a military coup on 25th May 1969.

The regime first alienated the political right namely the Umma - DUP coalition government, and no sooner did it antagonize the political left. After a ten-years honeymoon with the southern political elites, the regime braved a split on ground that the alliance with the Islamists would buy it more time. By June 1983, when Numeiri abrogated the Addis Ababa Agreement, political opposition to the regime had heightened throughout the cities of northern Sudan namely Atbara, El Obeid, Medani, Port Sudan, Kassala and Khartoum. This was the political reality Gen. Joseph Lagu, Abel Alier and their supporters failed to grasp and make use of to thwart Numeiri's machinations in the Southern Region. It was sad that the political elite in the Southern Region including the two political leaders Abel Alier and Gen. Joseph Lagu couldn't recognize Numeiri's fingers in every crisis that afflicted the country including the Southern Region and instead turned it into a power struggle among themselves. Instead of tearing down themselves and dividing the people of southern Sudan, especially after their 1980 confrontation over the oil refinery, they could have joined up with the rest of Sudanese people to rid the country of the totalitarian regime. As soon as Numeiri decreed the dismantle of the Southern Region, the opposition to the regime immediately took onto a revolutionary armed struggle spearheaded by the SPLM/A. Thus, with the armed struggle in the south and popular uprising in the cities and towns in northern Sudan, the May regime was moribund and came crumbling down on the 6th April 1985 barely two years into the death of the Southern Region

9. A Critique of 'Unity' and 'Re-Division' of the Southern Region (1981/83)

Tribalism in general or Dinka dominance in southern Sudan couldn't have been the reason to destroy the Southern Region and abrogate the Addis Ababa Agreement. The reason must be sought somewhere. This is because tribalism was and remains a post-colonial African phenomenon. It took roots and flourished in the context of neo-colonial path to socioeconomic development the African nationalist leaders adopted for their peoples (Prah, 1987). This phenomenon expressed in the form of nepotism, favouritism, and ethnic discrimination in access to resources and employment opportunities in situations like in the then Southern Region or currently in the republic of South Sudan where the government is the main important employer, could easily generate sentimentality and feelings that could be politicized to trigger discord and conflict. The mutiny in the Equatoria Corps of the Sudan Defence Force in Torit August 1955, which heralded the first civil war was triggered in part by political exclusion and social discrimination of southern Sudanese by their northern compatriots.

The dominant class in control of political and economic power in the Southern Region was part and parcel of the petty bourgeoisie class controlling the centre except that their rural background rendered them a subclass due to their attachment to their respective ethnicities. The power they wielded was not by virtue of ownership and control of the means of production, but because of education, knowledge, and control of the state bureaucratic machinery as ministers, legislators, judges, senior bureaucrats, army and police commanders. They were in perpetual competition for political dominance along ethnic and provincial lines and in this they adopted transclass ideological solidarities to strengthen their individual or collective interests in the guise of what they falsely portray as ethnic interests. During this political wheeling and dealing, the political elite inadvertently thwart the evolution of class consciousness among the deprived peasants and urban lumpen classes made up of all these ethnicities.

South Sudan is inhabited by more than seventy ethnic communities, in fact, nationalities or national groups of differential demographic weights and at different levels of socioeconomic and cultural development. These differences, social or cultural, do not constitute enough grounds for conflict among these people. In their villages and even in residential suburbs in the cities and town, these people coexisted without any problems until the question of opportunities or representation came up. The people began to differentiate, categorize themselves and discover that these differences in certain instances ran parallel to policy practices of uneven distribution of opportunities; these innocent differences become explosive and triggered conflict and ethnic animosities. The May regime was not an ideal situation to construct national unity based on freedom, justice, fraternity, and prosperity for all. The issue at hand in this discourse therefore is whether 'tribalism' in general or 'Dinka dominance' for that matter in the context of May's totalitarian dictatorship then, provided enough grounds for a section of Southern Regional elite to dismantle the Southern Region.

Social discrimination or favouritism in the distribution of opportunities obtained in the Southern Region precisely because the political system was unjust and oppressive. To address the issue, therefore, was not to perpetuate the system by distributing it to other areas as it occurred subdividing the already bad system in Juba into the three subregions. It was the same politicians that destroyed the Southern Region who then took over the rein of power in the subregions created from the Southern Region. Therefore, re-division should have instead been a process to completely transform the Southern Region to create a just political system that would not permit favouritism of any sort. In my opinion, ethnic dominance in the context of a bad political system in the Southern Region was not enough ground for destroying the Southern Region. It should have been instead to destroy that political system and to maintain the unity of the people of Southern Sudan.

The debate on re-division lasted nearly two years. During this period, newspaper publications and documentary pamphlets were freely and widely circulated ostensibly for democratic discussions in support or against Gen. Lagu's Numeiri sponsored proposal. Nonetheless, one would say that the national security apparatus stifled or indeed muted the debate to keep it within manageable parameters. Thus, the debate was not undertaken formally at the lower organs and grassroots levels of the Sudan Socialist Union, the ruling party. It was only briefly introduced in the SSU Central Committee in Khartoum and was immediately suspended to prevent passions running high or to prevent it throw out among the people raw feelings and sentiments. The debate would have exposed all those policies and the general political malaise afflicting the Southern Region, which provoked Gen. Lagu into demanding re-division of the Southern Region. The debate would have exposed the weaknesses in the implementation of the Addis Ababa Agreement, which Abel Alier's administration fudged to maintain peace and stability. Peace and stability could not be maintained at the expense of Southern Region forfeiting its share of socioeconomic development. Many central government projects in the Southern Region had either stalled for lack of funding or Melut and Mangalla Sugar cane Projects had been relocated to West Sennar or Assalaya. Numeiri's national security agents stifled the debate on account of security threats it could have stirred up[11]. The issues of 're-division' or 'unity' of the Southern Region were such important and sensitive matter that required sober and sombre reflections by all sections of the people of Southern Sudan. Whether or not the Southern Region remained one region or divided into subregions was a national issue which superseded provincial, ethnic, or personal interest or ambition for power. It should have been debated with the highest sense of responsibility and the national interests of the Southern Sudanese in mind and at heart.

In view of the above exposition it is imperative to make a review of the southern political forces that inadvertently contributed to the demise, in the guise of strengthening, South Sudan anits people. I do this with the benefit of hindsight as well as the knowledge of the current context of the republic of South

Sudan, which invokes the sentiments that the republic is a farcical replica of the Southern Region forty years ago. A critique of the democratic and political processes in the Southern Region within the 1980-1983 period reveals that politics then was not about ideas, principles, or political programmes for social and economic development of the region to address the objective reality of socioeconomic underdevelopment and cultural backwardness of the region and its people. The politics of that period were only about power and position one would occupy in government. The SSLM and the Anya-nya arrived Juba at the behest of a peace agreement, whose parameters were determined by the government delegation and the international community. The ease with which the agreement was reached in terms of its time span meant that both the SSLM and the SSU wanted a quick fix to save their faces. The relations that evolved between the subset (Southern Region priding itself for liberal parliamentary democracy) and the centre (Numeiri's totalitarian dictatorship) were incongruent and were bound to disrupt at any time. The politicians in the Southern Region did not construct a safety net to protect the region against political manipulations from the centre. It's clear from the beginning that Abel Alier's leadership of the Sudan government delegation spurred suspicion among southerners of northern Sudanese commitment to ending the war in southern Sudan, and where there is suspicion thing seldom work well. Therefore, the safety net could have been the unity of the people across ethnic and provincial lines constructed through policy that engendered freedom and justice (equality) rather than absolutely loyalty to Numeiri and the northern political establishment. This loyalty to Numeiri, for those who passionately engaged in social and political engineering of the regional politics, was only to ensure perpetual survival in power.

In this context regional politics and power engineering required no principles or personal integrity but absolute loyalty to with the president of the republic or president of the HEC whether that was Abel Alier or Joseph Lagu. It's in this context of loyalty that those who refused to tow this line of spinelessness like Aggrey Jaden, Ezbon Mundiri and others were elbowed out of the hierarchy and thrust into the dustbin.

In the beginning, two forces drove the opposition to Abel Alier in his interim HEC presidency (1972-1973) and elected HEC presidency (1974-78). The members of the SSLM and some senior Anya-nya officers opposed Numeiri's appointment of Abel Alier instead of their leader, Gen. Joseph Lagu as the president of interim High Executive Council. This opposition was, as people would say, like 'spearing the shadow rather than the elephant'. The opposition was wrongly directed at Abel Alier when it instead should have been directed at Gaafar Mohammed Numeiri, the president of the republic. In his memoirs Gen. Lagu indeed honestly alluded to his feeling that "I was not happy with Numeiri's decision to appoint Abel Alier instead of me (Lagu)[12] to lead the interim administration of the Southern Region". This would suggest that Gen. Joseph Lagu considered himself the architect of Addis Ababa and therefore should have been the one to nurse and protect it. Of course, he back down to play another important role of disciplining his officers and soldiers. The peace agreement caught the Anya-nya combatant half-way between still being civilian and a guerrilla army. The Anya-nya was not a combatant prepared unified army. Rolf Steiner[13] described them as tribal army ready to fight themselves than the common enemy. Under the guise of rejecting transfer to northern Sudan, the Anya-nya contingents mutinied in succession of each other starting with Mbili near Wau (1976), Juba (1974), and Akobo (1975) but except for Akobo were contained and ringleaders punished.

The opposition to Abel Alier in his first elected presidency of HEC and which later evolved into the 'wind of change' stemmed from his leadership style which many southern Sudanese viewed as too much compromise with the Northern political establishment at the expense of southern regional interests particularly in the domains of social and economic development. In contrast, the leadership of Gen. Lagu in the HEC did not last long. His precipitous fall from power attributed to political inexperience; Lagu was more of a soldier who was not accustomed to political sophistication of the SANU inside and Southern Front politicians of the multiparty democracy era. However, the politics of opposition to Abel Alier's leniency, and Gen. Joseph Lagu ascendancy to and subsequent fall from the presidency of the High Executive Council opening the way for Abel Alier second elected presidency including the Peter Gatkuoth Gual's and Gen. Gismalla Rasas stints as caretakers, in all their totality, constituted the drivers of ten-years social and political engineering of the Southern Region.

Abel Alier and Gen. Joseph Lagu stood out as the principal leaders upon which the future of Southern Region and the destiny of the people rested and depended. The manner the two leaders conducted themselves and managed their relationship was an important factor in the crash that occurred notwithstanding the role of Numeiri in the crash.

The Southern Region and the fate of the people of southern Sudan ranked higher in significance and protection than the two leaders. That they in different ways let the crash to happen would be unforgiveable commission. It demonstrated that personal agenda and ambition was more powerful that the concern for the country. The absence of a national (southern Sudan) agenda to trump ethnic egoism and greed, and the corresponding agility of the northern Sudanese political establishment worked to destroy the Southern Region and to trigger a war. This war was a blessing in disguise; it rescued the unity of the people of South Sudan to continue the struggle for their independence and sovereignty.

Ideologically speaking, the southern political elite were essentially liberals and the conservatives-traditionalist whose understanding and knowledge of socioeconomic and political engineering processes of the state were still condition by their respective rural backgrounds. The re-division debate therefore was within the liberal-conservatives-traditionalist camp, made up of individuals whose interests centred on positions in the government either executive, legislative or senior bureaucrats. Many of them were individuals who couldn't survive outside the state institutions; they would fight back in many ways including selling own principles. Without intellectual or other skills for business, many southern Sudanese politician remain stuck to the Sudanese state for employment and sustenance, and that was their greatest weakness. However, there were professionals who indeed survived outside political rents. These included Maulana Abel Alier, a lawyer profession, who demonstrated integrity and principle resigning from Judiciary to attend the Round Table conference on the problem of southern Sudan in 1965. Abel Alier became an advocate in the service of many people and that was honourable.

Having rightly or wrongly been kicked out of the presidency of the High Executive Council, Gen. Joseph Lagu could have returned home to farm at least to preserve the honour have having led the SSLM and brought peace to the people of southern Sudan. It was the weakness of remaining attached to the state that he proposed the re-division of Southern Region. And he did it in a manner than resembled the action of Biblical Samson, "on me and my enemies". Gen. Lagu made his proposal believing passionately that administrative decentralization, which then was being implemented in the rest of the Sudan, was the right way for Southern Region to traverse. The administration decentralization in northern provinces compensated Numeiri's abolition of the native administration in 1970, and as a means of modernizing tribal administration in northern Sudan. Administrative Decentralization was not the regionalization that divided northern Sudan into six regions, which many southern intellectuals grudged on account that it put the Southern Region at *par* with those regions in northern Sudan. In that context Gen. Lagu's arguments, as presented in his booklet, were deceptive and misleading. It particularly affected and influenced people with little understanding of political matters.

The proposal kicked off a bitter debate in the Southern Region, and because they could not assail Numeiri or the Khartoum establishment, "the southern politicians took upon themselves tearing every bid of confidence and brotherhood but left it to Numeiri to decree the division of the Southern Region into three subregions of Bahr el Ghazal, Equatoria and Upper Nile"[14]. The later generations of south Sudanese and students of history would not understand how leaders who have struggled and achieved a victory could out of personal consideration just throw away that victory. It is reminiscent of the pact the Nubians made with the Muslims to give away their victory after six hundred years of war of resistance, which they actually won. In this connection the re-division of the Southern Region was not just a betrayal of the sacrifice made by the tens of thousands of southern Sudanese who paid the ultimate price in the seventeen years struggle war; it was also a surrender to Numeiri. Dividing Southern Sudanese along their ethnic and provincial lines was also a complete retreat from a highest social and political unity the people of southern provinces have achieved in their struggle against northern domination. The southern regional political elite beat a retreat from position of honour and integrity in face of Numeiri's manipulations for easy solutions to very complex problem of nation building.

Viewing the merits and demerits of the debate and the heat it generated among southerners in Juba, Khartoum and other towns and cities, it is not difficult to demonstrate the huge personal ego that was the emotive force and the personal bitterness driving the proposal to re-divide the Southern Region as well as the unveiled ambitions for power demonstrated by the supporters of the proposal, whether they hailed from Equatoria, Bahr el Ghazal or Upper Nile. It is not difficult to see Gen. Lagu's personal anger, bitterness, and a sense of betrayal for being kicked out of presidency of High Executive Council and how that pushed him to the extreme. Anger and bitterness pushed Gen. Lagu to the point that he could not imagine that 're-division of Southern Region' was good music to the northern political establishment. In fact, to the autocrat Numeiri, who has not only lost support of the Sudanese people but also the moral compass, Gen. Lagu's proposal read 'dismantle the Southern Region'. And this resonated with the primary political objective of his agreement with the National Front in Port Sudan. This was where Gen. Lagu erred in the highest national interest of the people of South Sudan. By his own actions, he 'dimmed what had brightened his image before the world' and the people of Southern provinces (my addition). In his memoirs, Gen. Lagu brags that "the people saw me, not Abel Alier, as the guardian of the peace accord in the South, and I used that phrase when I wanted to slight Abel Alier and his ministers".[15] If the people saw him as the guardian of the peace, how could Gen. Joseph Lagu again turn round to become the spoiler of the peace agreement? And again, Lagu says, "it was clear that he (Numeiri) deliberately intended to abrogate the peace accord and that Abel Alier with his thirst for power was an accomplice, and I thought to myself "let it go, I shall fight the fools someday, one at a time separately". [16] It's clear from Lagu's own words it was not Abel Alier's thirst for power but Lagu's bitterness and vengeance that deliberately helped abrogate the peace accord. This was the bitterness that fuelled Gen. Lagu's vengeance against those who conspired against him when in 1979, he naively accepted to shuffle his government throwing out some of his trusted and staunchest supporters in the 'wind of change'. Gen. Lagu's behaviour therefore in the re-division proposal finds explanation not in his personality; in terms of cross religious marriage or being reinstate alongside his colleagues in the Sudan Armed Forces but in his quick and hot temperament, which don't augur well for a leader of his calibre. A decision of such momentous proportions as the destiny of a people couldn't be undertaken under duress, personal anger and bitterness but under solemn conditions of mind and body. The debate about unity or re-division of the Southern Region was not an academic exercise *per se* whereby there would be counts of 'valid' and 'invalid' points at the end of the exercise. It was a political discourse whose parameter were the very high stakes the people of southern Sudan attached to the final decision. And indeed, the question of validity or invalidity of arguments would be irrelevant as raw emotions drove the debate. Looking back at this episode, especially now that South Sudan is an independent country, and yet ethnicity and ethnic politics, which destroyed the Southern Sudanese first experiment with power, still reared their ugly head renders its absolutely necessary and imperative to problematize ethnic politics to gain a proper understanding and scientific knowledge about how to transform the lethargy of ethnic primordialism in which the Southern Sudanese intellectuals and their political elite are still submerged.

It is the material of politics, notably liberal democratic system, that politicians employ all kinds of tactics to acquire or retain power. Gen. Lagu trained a soldier but went to the bush before he could acquire political skills particularly that of Sudan's body politics or in clandestine movements as in the progressive and free officers' organization in the Sudan Armed Forces. His politics were traditionalist/liberal in every aspect, which defined the north-south dichotomy in terms of black and white deliberately excluding the other hues. The May regime particularly after July 1971 had established a totalitarian dictatorship, and many Sudanese people opposed the regime. In fact, it is safe to say that some important and influential individuals in the regime opposed some of its policies including the establishment of the Southern Region. It would be illogical, if not self-deceptive, to hope that a dictatorship like the May regime led by pan-Arabists would speak truth to the unity, and unity in diversity of the Sudanese people, and that it could generate policies to the best interest of all the people of the Sudan including the southern Region. It would also be illogical to hope that the bad policies and failures of Abel Alier or Joseph Lagu's respective administrations in the Southern Region were not part and parcel of the May regime failures. This is where the supporters of Gen. Lagu's proposal, many who had just returned to the country from refuge in Uganda, had gone wrong; they did not understand the political dynamics generated by Gen. Lagu's proposal regarding the north-south relationships. They thought it was straight forward issue of political and bureaucratic space. The struggle in the Sudan was more about identity in the context of pervasive Arab domination and policy of decolonisation through social and cultural assimilation of the non-Arab and non-Muslim in the Sudan. When those ignorant new arrivals jumped into the foray of re-division politics in support of Gen. Lagu proposal this created a false picture, which completely misled Gen. Lagu. The fulcrum of Gen. Joseph Lagu's case for the re-division of the Southern Region was 'tribalism' in general and in particular Dinka domination of politics and the bureaucracy in the Southern Region. This was good propaganda material for those who needed political and bureaucratic rents. They picked up bombastic arguments and spirited debate without knowing that in relations with Arab north there were always sensitive areas southerners wouldn't dare tread. Any flicker of disunity in southern ranks fed into northern political establishment's scheme for defeating the southerners and was therefore avoided.

On the other hand, the unionist presented weak counter arguments with their strongest point being their unwavering trust and support of what they called the 'revolution' centred in the president of the republic. If, as we have tried to analyse above, that was the nature of tribalism practiced in the Southern Region, then whatever arguments the unionists and re-divisionists advanced for and against the re-division of the Southern Region by their unscientific nature were faulty in the context of totalitarian dictatorship obtaining in the Sudan and the undemocratic political system in the Southern Region. Both the re-divisionists and the unionists did not address the underlying fundamental root cause, which in essence was the May regime itself. In this respect, the struggle to rid the Southern Region of tribalism and Dinka dominance should have been directed against the totalitarian regime. Tribalism was a direct product of the undemocratic political system in the Southern Region. Both the unionists and the re-divisionists cognized the dangers, which the northern political establishment posed to the Addis Ababa Agreement, which Gen. Joseph Lagu correctly said the North wanted to abrogate, while the unionists still had trust, confidence and supported what they called the 'May Revolution' in the person of Gaafar Mohammed Numeiri. The revolution that catapulted Numeiri and his colleagues in the Free Officers Organization to the helm of power in the Sudan for all practical purposes had died on 22nd July 1971 in a counterrevolutionary coup that brought Numeiri back to power.

While both the re-divisionists and unionists agreed on the importance of maintaining the Addis Ababa Agreement nevertheless, even with their sophistry in sterile debates, they did absolutely nothing to preserve it in face of Numeiri's determination to abrogate it. The unionists by praising Numeiri and the May revolution thought they would influence him to disappoint the re-divisionist driven by tribal and provincial sensibilities. On the other hand, the re-divisionists employed false arguments of tribalism and Dinka domination either deliberately or out of ignorance to pull people along into believing that Numeiri would still maintain the Addis Ababa Agreement after destroying the foundation that was the Southern Region upon which it rested. It was obvious to all and sunder that after ten years the quasi-liberal democratic experience of the Southern Region ran counter to Numeiri's personal rule, which directly felt and started to generate opposition, in northern Sudan. The regionalization of the north and the policy of administrative decentralization did not change the character of totalitarianism and Numeiri's personal dictatorship. These were diversionary stratagems to enable him to buy more time in power.

What both the re-divisionists and the unionist did not know was that the Addis Ababa Agreement had no provisions within it for resolving political disputes or different interpretations arising from its implementation either within the Southern Region or between the Southern Region and the central government in Khartoum. Thus, after all the self-shredding, which suggested that the southern politicians lacked civility, or red lines in form a common national interest, which they wouldn't cross whatsoever in pursuit of power, personal or ethnic, these politicians left the final word to Numeiri to conclude the bitter debate and to pronounce his verdict. And the verdict wouldn't have been different from Numeiri's strategic political objective for which he triggered the debate – dismantle the Southern Region and abrogate of the Addis Ababa Agreement. The peace agreement was neither the Quran nor the Bible. Caught unawares, the southerners, both the politicians and the ordinary folks, were thrown into serious confusion and disorientation. Those who trusted Numeiri would not dim something that brightened his image before the world and the people of the Sudan were shocked but were in no position to do anything; only those who were earlier assured of position in the new setup celebrated. One would have expected that the Dinka [accused of dominating the politics and bureaucracy in the region] and the non-Dinka politicians [who opposed the re-division of the Southern Region] to join efforts in opposition to the Republican Decree No.1 of 1st June 1983. It was very embarrassing seeing the two groups of southern politicians justling to secure seats on the same plane to fly them to Khartoum.

The questions that inevitably imposed themselves then, and now, was Dinka domination of politics in the regional government grounds enough to justify the dismantling of the Southern Region, and 'let go' what the people of southern Sudan had won after seventeen years of relentless struggle? Did the re-division of the Southern Region resolve the issue of tribalism in the subregions, which were created by the re-division of Southern Region, or did the re-division bring the desired socioeconomic development, which the re-divisionist purported in their sophisticated argumentations? In one such public debates the author witnessed in Juba, as if to suggest that the problem in the Southern Region attributed to the May regime, a unionist politician said, "if you realize that your house is infested by beg-bugs, the solution would be to take everything out and spray the house with a detergent to kill the bed bugs." In response, one of the re-divisionists replied, "No, you don't do that, you just set the whole house on fire". This response spoke exactly to what Gen. Joseph Lagu, in his anger and bitterness against Abel Alier, Bona Malual, Clement Mboro, etc., did to redeem his dented image and deflated ego by destroying the very thing that had brightened his image as a leader who brought peace to southern Sudan.

The re-division of the Southern Region into three subregions did not resolve the question of tribalism neither in the politics nor in the bureaucracy. The power elites then dispersed to their respective subregions continued to turn the masses of the people into mere pawns in the game of power politics whose rules were circumscribed by personal or ethnic rivalries rather than by ideas, principles, or political programmes. The formation of subregions profoundly exacerbated tribalism everywhere in southern Sudan; the 'big tribe' arose in all the subregions on account of numerical superiority to control power and wealth.

In Equatoria, the fulcrum of re-division politics, the Azande people and western Equatoria in general emerged as the main beneficiaries of this power re-alignment. Eng. James Joseph Tambura continued as the Governor of Equatoria, and Hon. Francis Wajo, hailing from Moro nationality, as his deputy Governor. It did not take long before strong voices were raised against the domineering stance of western Equatoria over Eastern Equatoria. The agitation, sooner than later, shifted to slogans of the Azande having become the 'new Dinka' of Equatoria; and this lasted until the fall of the May regime. Nevertheless, the politics of division continued to stalk Equatoria right into the Ingaz system when Central Equatoria was curbed out of Eastern Equatoria eventually to save the Bari speakers [Bari, Kakwa, Pojulu, Nyangwara and Mundari] from the Azande - Moro 'domination' in the west, or from the Otuho - Toposa speakers in the East Bank Equatoria.

In Bahr el Ghazal, the Dinka maintained its dominance over the other small nationalities being the largest nationality spread over the whole of Bahr el Ghazal including parts of western Bahr el Ghazal. But the Dinka are not a monolithic nationality with a centralised leadership and authority respected by its constituent sections and subsections. The appointment of Dr. Lawrence Wol Wol, a Rek Dinka from Gogrial exposed the structural weakness underlying kinship and the process of segmentation which characterized the Dinka and Nuer nationalities. Rek Dinka [Tonj, Gogrial and parts of Aweil] dominated the subregion's government to the chagrin of the other Dinka sections in Lake province [Agar, Ciec and Atwot].

In Upper Nile, where the three nationalities Nuer, Shilluk and Dinka were approximately of the same sociocultural configuration and therefore created a kind of desired political stability in the subregion to the effect that no complaints as those witnessed in Equatoria and Bahr el Ghazal came from the smaller groups in the subregion [Murle, Anywaa, Maaban and Koma]. This stability in the subregion forced Governor DK Matthews, a Nuer from Jikany, to swallow his word; he had campaigned in the 1982 election on re-division platform and on the slogan of "Upper

Nile without Bor." Bor was part of Upper Nile region and for that one of the most educated parts of the subregion. The notion of Upper Nile without Bor could have just been cheer nonsense to underline that Abel Alier hailed from Bor. It wouldn't become part of Bahr el Ghazal or Equatoria.

Experience in the subregions and even now in the republic of South Sudan has sufficiently proved it that re-division or federating a highly centralized post-colonial state does not resolve 'tribalism' or ethnic dominance in politics and the bureaucracy. Ethnicity or ethnic autochthony reflect the primaeval stage the people are still living in the twenty-first century. It is a social, political and an economic problem requiring a political programme to address in terms of development of the productive forces and transforming the way the people produced and reproduced their wealth. Those who argued that re-division would resolve the issue of tribalism and Dinka domination would be surprised that instead of erasing tribalism re-division triggered another level of consciousness and social awareness that brought into play the 'big-tribe' syndrome in the subregions. In this respect demographic preponderance popped up to exacerbate the practice of ethnic preference and neglect of others; the Dinka by their cheer demographic weight in an undemocratic political system as that which obtained in the Southern Region would without doubt dominate the politics and bureaucracy. However, as mentioned above re-division heightened the 'big tribe syndrome and in that respect, it was not only the Dinka but also the Azande and the Nuer as power wielder in Equatoria and Upper Nile respectively.

Once he had dismantled the Southern Region and the southern politicians have flocked *en masse* to Khartoum, Numeiri then showed his real motives. He decreed the imposition of the Islamic sharia laws or September laws as they were popularly known. The southern politicians and the people of southern Sudan found themselves in a situation they could not change, and they did have constitutional tools to fight back against the instantaneous justice and the application of the *huddud* which discriminated against the Christians and the non-Muslims. The social, economic, and political crises of the May regime multiplied, heightened and in under two years from the dismantle of the Southern Region, it came crushing down under the political pressure of the mass movement and the popular uprising it ignited. In fact, popular uprising became the tested weapon the Sudanese people employed against autocracy and totalitarianism. Unlike the armed struggle, it had the added advantage of political enlightenment and raising social awareness and political consciousness and could be replicated.

In hindsight, the southern politicians could have initiated the fall of Numeiri and his regime in the lost opportunities over the oil refinery and the Jonglei canal project. Unfortunately, the two leaders Abel Alier, Gen. Joseph Lagu, and their supporters unknowingly had rendered themselves pawns in Numeiri's chess game to install himself the Imama of the Sudan. Had they been a little bit suspicious, they would have discovered the weakness of Numeiri in 1976 and could have charted a way for South Sudan. They missed the opportunity provided by the standoff over the oil refinery crisis Numeiri himself triggered in 1980. The people of the Southern Region, frustrated by lack of social and economic development and incensed by the policy of *kasha* or forceful removal of the African people from the national capital, Khartoum, to their rural homes of origin, were ready for a confrontation with the regime but the politicians backed down. A regime that has forfeited the trust and confidence of the people could only be fought not by dividing but uniting the people and galvanizing them into a force for social and political change. An oppressive dictatorship could not be transformed by raising issues of tribalism and ethnic domination which in themselves are products of the system, but by creating and raising social awareness and political consciousness of the people and organizing them into a force capable to transforming that oppressive reality. Tribalism in southern Sudan society in general or Dinka dominance of politics couldn't have been the reasons to destroy the regional self-rule and the constitutional arrangement between the southern provinces and the rest of the country. The reasons must be sought in the nature of the southern politician himself, and how he or she interacted with the principles of freedom (independent thinking and action), justice (equality), and fraternity (solidarity) when dealing with the masses. These principles underly the foundation of a modern state. The leaders of the Southern Region (1970 – 1985) may be categorized as comprising the second-generation southern politicians. Many of them were university graduates who had understanding and knowledge of social, economic, and political engineering of state.

But there were some of the 'old schools' whose perception of these processes were still blurred by their traditional concepts and beliefs. This would explain how a Southern Region's minister could choose from a list of potential appointees to local government administration only people whose names were socially or culturally familiar to him; or in another situation when the Southern Region Police Commissioner chose police cadets only individuals from his home turf. In other incidences of lapse in security resulting in destruction of property, the police officers involved incarcerated the victim of aggression or whose property was destroyed by livestock instead of the aggressors who happened to be his relative or hailed from the same ethnicity. These were few examples to illustrate how tribalism operated in higher and lower echelon of power in the Southern Region. Some were ignored or neglected but other issues were blown out of proportion and built into political cases that ended in the destruction of the Southern Region.

What was viewed as weakness in Abel Alier 's administration of the Southern Region stemmed from his inability or refusal to discipline the notorious and recalcitrant ministers or his closed confidantes who in government committed all kinds of mischief and behaved as if they were above the laws of the country. This neglect of real issues built up into a political case that led to rebellion against his presidency of the HEC in 1978. Gen. Lagu populism lasted barely two years, as somebody said, 'Lagu was too intelligent to be advised'. That's perhaps how he lost the support of people like Aggrey Jaden, Ezbon Mundiri, Clement Mboro and his close friends Matthew Obur, Benjamin Bol Akok, and others in the 'wind of change'. No matter how difficult the political differences were, as leaders of the people Abel Alier and Joseph Lagu should have left some leeway for compromise and consensus building. The idea of heightening the debate to the extreme, as if it were a limit situation, or a competition for basic survival as to draw out the basest of instincts in vindictive outpourings that destroyed the common good smacked of reality that southern politicians invariably didn't have anything in common, which they would treat as sacrament or a red line not to be crossed no mater. In this connection, the politicians would ignore the most strategic to push for very trivial personal affairs.

This attitude of projecting trivial over the strategic national issues endeared southern politicians to the northern political establishment. The *Jinubieen* always concerned themselves with southern Sudan issues while they distanced themselves for wider Sudanese national issues. Engaging in national issues did not preclude the peculiar issues of southern Sudan but the problem with Southerners was that they don't educate themselves about the national issues including the history of Southern Sudan. Many southern politicians enrolled in the Sudan Socialist Union not because the SSU was ideologically socialist but because it was the ruling party in the Sudan and a place for political rent. The SSU indeed was a political marketplace in which loyalty to the power wielders in the centre was the commodity the regional elites and tribal barons paid in exchange for political rent. It was more conspicuous in the case of Abel Alier and Gen. Joseph Lagu alternating as second vice president of the republic between 1981 and 1985, and in the unfortunate scenario created by Samuel Aru Bol in 1985[17]

The eruption of war in 1983 was a blessing in disguise not that it erased the issue of tribalism, but that the new situation pushed tribalism to a higher level of awareness where it became repugnant even to the perpetuators of ethnic politics. Tribalism was problematic in the Southern Region. It was also problematic during the war of national liberation but in a context linked to the leaders' cult of personality, which in itself was antithetical to liberation. It became a national issue after independence in the context of state power and resources pushing the formation of the Jieng Council of Elders (JCE) as the principal agency of ethnic nationalism. Having raised tribalism to the level of national state politics, bureaucracy, and/or business, the JCE provided ethnicity with tools and the capacity to degenerate to the lower levels of society in form of sectional, sub-sectional, clan and even sub-clan conflicts. The JCE made up of self-promoted volunteer politicians and bureaucrats encouraged and promoted the idea of ministers, legislators, and senior bureaucrats becoming community leaders ostensibly to build community and state into one entity. The idea was to organize state politics based on and to ensure community participation in the guise that it brought the government closed to the people. This generated steep competition and triggered more community conflicts in Rumbek, Tonj, Gogrial, Bor and Ruweng; the competition for appointment at the national level started at lower level where politics were based more on personality than ideas or political programme and this usually ended up in violence.

As an illustration of this phenomenon the conflict between the Apuk and Aguok in Gogrial has its roots in the two communities' leaders replacing one another in succession in the same constitutional post[18]. The danger with politics based on community or ethnicity lies the position in government whether executive, legislative, bureaucratic or administrative was interpreted as belonging to that community and people would come from that community to protest removal of their person or demand a replacement with someone from the community. This resulted in certain smaller communities being totally marginalized and invisible in the state system.

Power struggle, ethnic rivalry and unprincipled alliance between the politicians leading to the dismantle of the Southern Region in 1983 did not disappear with the independence and birth of the Republic of South Sudan. The issue of Dinka dominance in politics and bureaucracy in the Southern Region that used to be applied blanketly without objectivity was not the case then as it is no longer the case now. Although, the majority are Dinka by ethnicity nevertheless this privileged class that has crystallized out from the political and military components of the national liberation movement and remnants of the NCP is made up of all the different ethnicities in the republic of South Sudan. It would be completely inappropriate to categorize them as Dinka or as persons hailing from Warrap and Aweil in Bahr el Ghazal at the helm of the political and economic power of South Sudan.

The social origin of the political elite in the Southern Region was rooted in education and bureaucracy as means of social mobility. In the republic of South Sudan, this elite has risen to the helm because of the vantage point they occupied in the liberation movement. By its nature, it is parasitic by virtue of its relation to the state. In this respect, this class does not include all Rek Dinka from which President Salva Kiir and the barons who surround him hail. It is therefore important to put things in their correct perspective lest we mis the point. The context of the Southern Region before and now in the republic of South Sudan the correct analysis of the political situation must be expressed in class terms rather than ethnicity. There has never been a government in the Southern Region or in the republic of South Sudan made up only of the Dinka to warrant the slur of hegemony and domination. Because of the primitive nature of the dominant parasitic class, it has evolved into patrimonialism to entrench political patronage whereby social, economic and political interests of communities are realized through the agencies of community lobby group, ethnic councils of elders, and business cartels in the market; they have colluded to capture the state and turned into a political vehicle of this parasitic capitalist class[19].

The parasitic capitalist class that has emerged at the helm of the state in South Sudan is backward, unproductive, and therefore moribund due to two important factors. Its money comes from the extraction and plunder of non-renewable oil deposits but instead of pumping this money into local economy through investment in productive enterprises and services it is helping in capital flight from South Sudan into economies in East Africa and far afield to import articles and commodities, which could have been produced in South Sudan. It means that sooner than later the drying up of oil wells will spell the death of this class. The other factor is that the parasitic capitalist class minds about and has placed its political survival above the state's viability or people's welfare. It continuously generates insecurity that pushed most of the peasant population into the cities where they can't engage in food production but depend on social safety networks. This overtime would lead to alienization and therefore emergence of a revolutionary lumpen proletariat class to overthrow the political set up. In comparison, the Southern Region's political class was more advanced in their political thinking than the parasitic capitalist class that emerged from the war of national liberation. The administration of Abel Alier had at least plan for exploiting the natural resource potentials of Southern Sudan in form of feasibility studies of the hydroelectric power plant in the Fulla Rapids in Nimule, Limestone - Cement factory in Kapoeta, Agro-industrial complex in Nzara, and many other projects; they only did not have the necessary funds to implement these projects.

10. The New Call for Federation was Essentially the Resurrection of the Re-Division Politics

The Southern Regional government undertook feasibility studies of some important natural resources in Southern Sudan. The importance of that exercise lies in that the execution of those projects could have triggered social and economic development in the Southern Region. This in turn could have led to raised social awareness and political consciousness of the people to stimulate changes in attitudes, behaviours and perception of reality. In a nutshell, this process of social and economic development could have transformed the means of social production and introduced new and different but higher relations of social production. Of course, the regional government did not have the financial and economic means to execute those projects and they remained changed to date. However, it is not difficult to imagine or envisage that the process could put have the people of southern Sudan at a higher level of understanding of themselves as citizens of the same country. The lack of social and economic development of the region resulting in diminished resource base of its government falsely triggered the debate of re-division of the Southern Region as a way out. This energy, instead should have turned against the regime.

It's the same falsehood and lack of correct understanding of politics and its dynamics that poignant to what was discussed above as re-division of Southern Region to address tribalism and tribal dominance, some politicians out of political expediency and opportunism have raised the slogan of 'federalism' or federal system of governance for South Sudan. The 'federation' slogan appeared in the same manner the southern political leaders raised it to their northern counterparts on the eve of Sudan's independence in December 1955 and driven by almost the same sentiments only that this time it was intended to address the failed transition from war to peace experience during the interim period (2005-2011); to address the contradictions generated by the SPLM-led government of the Republic of South Sudan reflected in corruption, political exclusion, discrimination, and selective economic empowerment of individuals from particular regions, etc., reflecting political failures of the SPLM.

'Federalism' was raised by a senior member, in fact the second in the SPLM hierarchy. This was immediately following the announcement of the referendum results in favour of secession. The Southern Sudan Legislative Assembly was debating the draft constitutional text for independent republic of South Sudan. Like the 're-division' of the Southern Region debate, 'federalism' was bound to trigger serious deceptive arguments and raw emotions. It quickly revealed that it was only a power bait; as soon as the principal proponent was promised the second position in the independence government, he immediately dropped his case, ordered his followers in the SSLA to vote for decentralized system of government leaving their colleagues feeling angry and betrayed. It is high stakes material, which the political elite interested only in power and not socioeconomic development of society would split hairs debating it.

This section is not about discussing federalism as a governance system worldwide. The idea of raising was only to question the logic, drivers, and feasibility of federalism in the Republic of South Sudan in the context of totalitarianism the SPLM constructed since 2005. It goes without saying that federalism as a governance system has successfully served many countries in the world but was also employed to suppress people in some countries. It was once a demand of the first-generation southern political leaders to federate the Sudan on account of the sociocultural differences between the people of southern provinces and the rest of the Sudanese people in the north, east, west, and central Sudan. The debate in the SSLA about federalism was not placed in its correct context that South Sudan was part of a highly centralized colonial state and the process of federating a highly centralized state is not the reverse process of is formation. The twenty-six federal states into which the NCP curved the Sudan was nothing more than centralization of power and resource in Khartoum, while the states and the people had the illusion of power and resources.

A correct analysis and scientific understanding of the socio-economic and political engineering processes of the Sudanese state could prove that the arguments employed by the southern politicians were not grounded in correct assessment of the situation in the Sudan. The Sudan is African and as the name suggests, the majority are black Africa. Those Sudanese who claimed Arab ancestry make up 31% of the population (Population Census 1955). There were no discernible distinctive differential features between the peoples in southern provinces and their compatriots in Blue Nile, Nuba Mountains, Dar Fur, and parts of Eastern Sudan. Ancient history of the Sudan would tell that those who claim Arab ancestry came into Sudan from west Africa where they had acquired African features on their way to the Sudan. Therefore, the claim of sociocultural differences as basis for federation of the Sudan was fallacious.

Deeply uneven power relations differentiated southerners from the northern Sudanese who by virtue of proximity to Egypt and modern civilisation enabled them to acquire modern knowledge and skills in state and economic management and put them at an advantageous position that became the basis of Southern Sudanese inferiority and fear of domination by the northern Sudan. The inferiority of Southern Sudanese in face of their northern Sudanese compatriots prompted their political demand for federation glossed in sociocultural arguments and prevented solidarity with other Africans in northern Sudan, which could have offset the dominance of the Arabized Sudanese. The struggle for freedom, justice (equality and equity) and fraternity in a highly centralized post-colonial multinational and multicultural state like the Sudan required social awareness, political consciousness, and unity of purpose on the part of those who felt disadvantaged by the system. This would enable them to struggle for and easily win their rights had they put their acts together. In the Sudan the, had the southern politicians, who were aware, vocal and better organized, united ranks with the Nuba, Funj, Fur, Zaghawa, Masalit, Danagalla, Halfawiyieen on the basis of pan African virtues and ideals, they could have won. It did not require separateness and lone struggle for the same political objectives. It became clear later when southerners, Nuba and Funj joined together in a common struggle in the SPLM/A on the concept and vision of the New Sudan, they were able to achieve political recognition. The protocols on self-determination and Popular Consultation were victories for the Nuba and Funj people and this attributed to unity of purpose.

South Sudan emerged from a long war of national liberation prosecuted outside its political and ideological contents. This generated contradictions and falsehood of which the failure to transition from war to peace and development has left South Sudan at the lower rungs of social and economic development. Nearly most, if not all, socioeconomic and cultural indices are in the negative notwithstanding the enormous natural resource potentials the country is endowed. The failure to provide social services and economic development generated political contradictions and a power struggle that triggered a civil war. It was in this context that many perceived these social, economic and political contradictions as Dinka ethnic nationalism and the ideology of hegemony and domination fitting the Dinka against other ethnic groups in the independent South Sudan and therefore required federation to address them. The demand for federalism therefore emerged in this context to resolve the contradictions generated by the bad political system in which other ethnicities participated.

The totalitarian dictatorship the SPLM erected in South Sudan is an oppressive, exclusive, discriminative. It's a system based on extraction and plunder of natural resources in collaboration with regional and international comprador capitalism, and has completely run down the country economically. The demand to federating South Sudan based on this system would be like reproducing the system in every part of South Sudan with the objective of complete and total destruction. Those we called for federation, just like those who called for the re-division of the Southern Region, are driven by concern for power but not by genuine concern to bring social and economic development to the people. What followed Kiir's Executive Order 36/2015 establishing twenty-eight and then thirty-two states in the republic of South Sudan proved that the political elite's desired power for its sake and for their own economic empowerment. In Melut, Renk and Akoka counties, the elite used the oil revenue to purchase real estates in Nairobi, Kenya and Kampala Uganda instead of addressing the environmental pollution in the oil field that caused many infantile deaths in the area.

The people of South Sudan have struggled together for more than two hundred years; first against the Turko-Egyptian state, then against the Anglo-Egyptian Condominium and against the Arab dominated northern Sudan in two wars; the Anya-nya war for secession and the SPLM/A led war for self-determination. The people won their independence in 2011 through the exercise of the right to self-determination in a secessionist vote in the referendum. The task before every South Sudanese patriot is the important task of building the country; its economy, triggering the exploitation and development the enormous natural resource potential the country is endowed. Building the infrastructure: roads, power transmission lines, power generating plants, building schools, hospitals, affordable decent housing, building the productive forces of the country, etc.

In fact, South Sudan does not need a large government. If there was a way of reducing the ten states to three provinces that was the southern provinces until 1976 would be appropriate. Only the political elite benefits from bloat government at the national, state and local level because they transform the financial resources into salaries, their services and other perks living the people with no social services for education, health, veterinary and agricultural extension services. It's the same elite who raise the issues of tribalism and ethnic domination when they find themselves knocked out of political competition, which in essence obtain due to lack of democratic principles in the conduct of this competition. And all this obtains due to bad government. In any way, they should not be used to destroy the country as was done to the Southern Region. Instead, people should struggle to transform the bad situation.

The Southern Region was South Sudanese first experience with government. It was in some aspects a success story, but its failure occurred partly because it was part of a bad political system in the Sudan. The May regime was a totalitarian dictatorship; it was oppressive and discriminated the citizens on the basis of religion and language and therefore only benefited a small section of the Sudanese society. It fomented crisis and triggered conflicts and therefore the Southern Region was bound to suffer negatively from these crises. Its failure was also partly because the Southern Region's political elite were duplicitously vacillating politically between national unity with the north and secession of Southern Sudan.

Now, in complete control of their state, the republic of South Sudan, the political elite demonstrate the same attitudes that led to the failure of the Southern Region. These play out in form of vacillation between constructing an authentic national state involving all the people on the one hand and recoiling to ethnic nationalism, promotion of ethnic fiefdoms that are exclusive, violent, and oppressive. This configuration of South Sudan provides opportunity for change, for more concrete revolutionary and democratic programmes for social transformation. This bad situation, in the words of Regis Debray, matters little that the aura of invincibility is obscured so long as the conditions for winning the real victories can be seen. It would be a healthy thing for a myth to crumble; and being brought back to reality is a good starting point for people who want to change that reality; it gets rid not only of false friends but also of a considerable number of false ideas.

The opportunity for South Sudan to survive all these contradictions has been provided by the experience with the Southern Region (197-1983). It therefore requires learning and drawing lessons from the experience and chart new ways of moving forwards. It also requires learning from the experiences of other peoples in the world. On our part we will require elf-sacrifice, commitment to the people's cause; political enlightenment to raise consciousness to enable a critical mass capable of organized action to sprout on the political stage to capture the initiative from the lethargic petit bourgeoisie.

ENDNOTES

1. The Communist Party of the Sudan was the only political party in the Sudan that had a scientific understanding of the problem and had developed a document, indeed a programme towards resolving the problem not only in southern provinces but in the whole country.

2. The first action of the nationalist government in 1954 was to replace the southern workers in Nzara industrial complex with northern workers. This was out of fear that these workers and could be a problem to the oppressive northern administration since they had acquired working-class consciousness.

3. The split within the Communist Party of the Sudan mirrored the ideological split between those who wanted to build authentic revolutionary working-class culture through ideological struggle and the opportunities who wanted power and therefore were ready to jump onto any political bandwagons.

4. The Umma Party attacked the regime first in Wad Nubawi Omdurman on 29February 1970 and this spread to the White Nile and culminated in the battle of Gezira Abba leading to the murder of Imam A;-Hadi Abdelrahaman Al-Mahdi.

5. The assassination of Major Matthew Pagan Nyilek in Gambella and the assassination of Emmanuel Abur around Aweil. In fact, William Nyuon Bany was absorbed captain instead of his mutinous commander whom he tracked down and killed.

6. There was no opposition sensu strictu in the PRA, but the members were branded according to the leader they followed. This was Abel's group made up of staunch supporters of the

Southern Front, while Lagu's groups comprised members of SANU and former SSLM.

7. No wonder that Numeiri exploited the Abel – Lagu political schism to styme and dismantle the Southern Region. And this took several calculated steps coinciding with his ambition to become the Imam of the faithful.

8. I was then a PhD student in Budapest Hungary and had travelled to Paris to attend the congress as part of the studies. Note that minister spoke of a place south of Khartoum. It was official policy not to mention southern Sudan as that could arose feelings in Southern Region.

9. Numeiri summoned to his office the member of People's National Assembly Aldo Ajou Deng, showed a case dossier and said would send it to the Attorney Chambers if Aldo did not immediately go to the radio to rebut that he was against re-division of the Southern Region.

10. Abel Alier's nomination of Bona Malual instead of Peter Gatkuoth, in a Dinka Unity meeting infuriated many Southern Front members of the Nuer nationality who felt let down by the attitude that only a Dinka would replace Abel Alier as the candidate for president of HEC led a walk-out resulting in the election of Eng. James Joseph Tambura.

11. The intervention of one member, Dro. Justin Yac Arop, in the PRA debate that "if the Arabs had ruled the Sudan for fifty years, the Dinka would rule Equatoria for a hundred years", was insensitive enough to provoke a flare up the passions and raw feelings that the debate had to stop.

12. Major-General Joseph Lagu (2010) "Sudan - Odyssey through a state: from Ruin to Hope", MOB

13. The German mercenary abducted by Sudanese agents in Kampala in 1971 with the assistance of Uganda intelligence service.

14. The Solidarity Committee in the People's National Assembly in Gen. Lagu. Ibid p.545.

15. Lagu, ibid, p. 317

16. Lagu, ibid, p.379

17. While the younger generation politicians of the Sudan African Congress demanded the position of Prime Minister to balance the position of President occupied by a northern Sudanese, Gen. Swar el Dahab, Mr. Samuel Arol Bol demanding the creation of the position of deputy prime minister for himself in order to circumvent another southern Sudanese becoming the Prime Minister of the transitional government.

18. The change of the post of Chief Justice from Ambrose Riiny Thiik (Apuk) to Chan Reech Madut (Aguok) was misinterpreted and quickly translated into communal conflict in which hundreds of people perished.

19. The parasitic capitalist class that has emerged at the helm of the political and economic power in South Sudan is dominated by the Aweil/Warrap cartels, but it also includes cartels and businesses from other regions and nationalities. The attempt to divide this class along ethnic lines would only represent ignorance or tactic support for the political establishment, which seems to promote it as a means of dividing the people and engaging them in futilities.

CHAPTER THREE

THE SUDAN PEOPLE'S LIBERATION MOVEMENT/ARMY: THE REVOLUTION THAT INSPIRED FEAR AND DESPAIR

1. Preliminary Remarks

The sudden and lightening appearance of the Sudan People's Liberation Movement/Sudan People's Liberation Army (SPLM/A) on the Sudanese political theatre was kind of an enigma to say the least. The acute social, economic, and political crisis afflicting the country only peaked in the Southern Region - the weakest link in the system, but was not to the point that it threatened the political viability of the regime. The May regime still held the political initiative and complete control of the country. However, the SPLM/A appeared at a time the people of southern Sudan yearned really for a spectacular episode to punctuate the drudgery of a tasteless debate triggered by politics of re-division of the Southern Region.

The SPLM/A was not Sudanese; it was southern Sudanese in everything from its genesis, leadership, its hidden political objective, and to the theatre of its war. It wasn't a Sudanese national movement. The naming, as it played out, was to fool Derg's legs into believing that, unlike the Anya-nya2, the SPLM/A was genuinely a Sudanese movement. This explosion, which occurred in Bor did not resonate with the peculiar social and political crisis around the redivision or unity of the Southern Region. If anything the timing of Bor incident has much to be said about it either as an opportunistic, conspiratorial or adventurism but nothing near to it being a revolutionary insurgency. Therefore, the misnomer did not alter its southern Sudanese character even after the arrival into it of the Nuba, the Funj and other Sudanese nationals. The use of 'Sudan' rather than 'Southern Sudan' was efficaciously to generate obfuscation in the country about its strategic political objectives, but also to create opportunity for solidarity, political and military support in the region and internationally[1].

This obfuscation was necessary and indeed imperative in case northern Sudanese for seldom did southern Sudanese politicians engage wholeheartedly in Sudan's body politics of power and control of the Sudanese state. Not that these politics were too complicated for the southern Sudan politicians, but essentially most of the time southerners considered themselves outsiders to the Arab dominated Sudanese state or consider themselves third-class citizen, whose concerns didn't extend beyond their locality or their day-to-day sustenance. As a result, southern political parties namely the Liberal Party and the Southern Front, had always worked on issues that concerned the southern provinces of the Sudan. The closest they came to projecting a national solution was in the presentation of 'federation' to resolve the multiple sociocultural differentials that existed between the peoples of northern and southern Sudan. The projection of the SPLM/A as a Sudanese and not a southern Sudan movement was intended to scare away the secessionist, who indeed didn't have any reason for fighting and losing life for the country that was already united. But in this context, it was more about power and leadership of the movement than about secession because as Garang put it, the secessionist could fight up to the border of what they categorised as southern Sudan and from there, he together with the unionist would continue the war until the total liberation of the country. It was a clever articulation to convince any doubting Thomases in northern Sudan.

In the second republic following the October popular uprising, Sayed William Deng Nhial, and his party SANU, played genuine southern Sudanese unionist who broke social and cultural barriers to construct an alliance with northern Sudanese forces. His political venture, like those of southern Sudan communists was a sharp departure from south Sudanese inward-looking attitude and political subculture of feeling inferior as not to engage in national political market place. William Deng had broken ranks with SANU main body in exile and returned to establish SANU inside the country to engage in national politics on equal terms with northern Sudanese politicians. In 1967/68, with

Sadiq el Mahdi (a breakaway faction of the Umma Party) and Dr. Hassan Abdalla el Turabi (Islamic Charter Front), Sayyed William Deng Nhial (SANU) formed the Congress of New Forces (CNF) to challenge the traditional theocratic dynasties of the Ansar (Umma) and Khatimiya (DUP). Being a modern and a progressive compared to feudal based theocratic family dynasties, the CNF threatened to overthrow the established order that kept the Umma Party and DUP in control of the state as coalition partners. This would explain the frantic efforts that triggered the conspiracy during the 1968 parliamentary elections to have Sadiq Al-Mhadi and Hassan Al-Turabi trounced in their respective constituencies and Sayed William Deng Nhial assassinated on the way between Rumbek and Tonj. This was the last time in the Sudanese political theatre that a South Sudanese politician attempted to play fair and equal national politics.

The appearance, therefore, of an armed movement in Southern Sudan calling for revolutionary transformation of the Sudanese polity leading to the creation of a New Sudan based on freedom, justice and fraternity was something completely new in the Sudanese political lexicon. A revolutionary leadership emerging out of a socioeconomically underdeveloped and politically backward southern provinces of the Sudan was indeed something that raised eyebrows in many circles in northern Sudan. In some parts of southern Sudan and among the right-wing politicians in Khartoum the attitude was that of apathetic disbelief. Submerged in their deep slumber many people concluded it was not feasible for a south Sudanese to liberate the whole country, if anything, the SPLM/A should have restricted itself to southern Sudan.

In Equatoria, particularly in Juba, the mood was not only anti-SPLM/A but also anti-Dinka or those tall black people from Bahr el Ghazal and Upper Nile; the SPLM/A conflated with the Dinka in the minds of many Equatorian intellectuals. Of course, Juba was the epicentre of the re-division and anti-Dinka politics. The re-division chorus was still at high pitch that many people in the subregion believed the Dinka formed the SPLM/A to counter the then independent Equatoria Region. It was so unfortunate that they couldn't even think beyond the regime's propaganda that overthrow of the totalitarian regime was equivalent to destruction of Equatoria Region whose stature they elevated falsely to the equivalence of an independent state. In northern Sudan, many educated and enlightened northern Sudanese including the communists also questioned the concept and vision of the New Sudan out of general mutual suspicion, but they also believed the concept and vision of the 'New Sudan' was not genuine; that it could have just been a façade raised by the SPLM/A leadership to camouflage its secessionist objective. Indeed, many northern intellectuals never trusted any call for unity of the Sudan coming from Southern Sudan.

This chapter should be the beginning of the discourse on the SPLM/A. Some of us, intellectuals, and politicians, who joined the ranks of the liberation movement as combatants are well placed to engage in this discourse. This discourse would unlock and unpackage many uncertainties the leaders, cadres and combatants glossed over in the hope that they would disappear of themselves when left unspoken of. Nothing more could have forced such a discourse than the present context the people of South Sudan find themselves after winning independence in 2011. The English saying that all is well that ends well is pertinent and the flipside is all was not well that ended badly suggesting that anything not organized and operating outside natural laws would end successfully. The current context of South Sudan points to some disconnect within the liberation movement that must have occurred up the line to the SPLM/A formation in 1983.

The debate revolves around whether truly the SPLM/A was a national liberation movement driven by revolutionary ideology and ethos, or a southern Sudanese secessionist movement just like the Anya-nya and the Southern Sudan Liberation Movement (SSLM), which spearheaded the first civil war (1955-1972). As Regis Debray would say, everything that makes a revolutionary organization a living thing: flesh, nerves, muscles, blood, etc., depends not on what you call it, but on its relationship with the people. It depends on its origin, on whether it has come into being artificially or naturally; whether its leadership was formed in a laboratory test tube on in the warmth of life and society; that's from the reality of grassroots mass movement. The discourse is to investigate, analyse, and assess the emergence of the SPLM/A against the parameters that characterised the national liberation movements in the Horn of Africa and other parts of the world.

The assumption is that the SPLM/A was essentially a southern Sudanese liberation movement and therefore no confusion should be entertained in respect of its leadership's real intentions; the falsehood could have been tactics adopted to achieve that intention. By virtue of its social composition and its leadership, the SPLM/A was a section of the national democratic revolutionary forces in the Sudan and in the Horn and Africa. Sudan as well as most of the countries in the Horn are still in the early stages of the national democratic revolution. Thus, the SPLM/A like the Eritrean People's Liberation Front (EPLF, the Tigray People's Liberation Front (TPLF) and the Ethiopian People's Revolutionary Democratic Movement (EPRDM) were all elements of the national democratic revolution, not elements of socialist revolution. It was too premature for the SPLM/A to have raised the socialist slogan. It was in this respect, and in line with Debray's statement above, which pushes the conclusion that the SPLM/A projected the cloak of 'socialism' and 'united secular socialist Sudan' slogans only as a strategy to lure into the war the Nuba, the Funj and Dar Furi, and other Sudanese who racially identified with the people of southern Sudan. In the final days of the May regime, the Africans in the Sudan identified, mobilized, and organized in the Sudan Rural Solidarity (SRS) immediately in the aftermath of May regime's overthrow in 1985. But more importantly, the notion of socialist Sudan was as well a strategy to solicit Ethiopia's political and military support.

The hypothesis that the SPLM/A was a southern Sudanese secessionist movement stemmed from several factors linked to its social configuration, its leadership and relationships, and its power politics since inception in 1983. In the second edition of 'the politics of liberation in South Sudan: an insider's view', in 2000, a question posed itself about the SPLM; about what it was and where it was. The question hasn't to this moment been answered beyond a generalised but direct accusation labelled against the author that he had exposed the movement's secrets. In his book, "Dr. John Garang de Mabior – the Man to Know", Edward Lino Abyei (2017) painted a rosy picture of what followed the mutiny and attack on SAF Battalion 105 in Bor. The diplomatic contacts and connections that were undertaken in Khartoum following the incident of Bor prompted the Ethiopia regime to immediately recognize and provide logistical support to the nascent SPLM/A. This immediate action contrasted with the treatment Ethiopian authorities meted out to Anya-nya2 which had been operating in western Ethiopia since 1978. The Anya-nya2 did not even receive Ethiopian regime's recognition let alone giving support even on a *tit* for *tat* basis against the Sudan's support for the Eritrean and Tigrayan insurgencies. It was only by projecting Sudan's unity and a socialist ideology was the SPLM/A able to receive Derg's military support. This support was first to fight the Anya-nya2 and to chase them back to the Sudan, and then to prosecute the war against the Sudan government.

In view of the above, and to understand the social and political triggers and drivers of the SPLM/A, we must raise the questions whether the SPLM/A formation was in anyway linked to the toxic political discourse in the country that eventually prompted Numeiri's precipitous action to dismantle of the Southern Region. Was there any linkage between the re-division politics and the formation of the SPLM/A? If that could be established then it would be possible to conclude that the formation of the SPLM/A was triggered by Southern Region's politics and in this respect, the discourse should look for verifiable evidence, pointers or indicators connecting the SPLM/A leader, Dr. John Garang de Mabior to either the re-divisionist or unionist in the political debate that spanned two years. Edward Lino's book is not explicit about it although it alludes to meetings conducted with certain leaders of clandestine National Action Movement, some of who became victims of the SPLM/A.

The SPLM Manifesto (1983:18), published postdatedly, was another source of information; however, it is difficult to prove the validity that former Anya-nya officers in the Sudan Armed Forces had organized into a clandestine cell that planned the insurrection in Bor with the intention to capture Juba. It difficult to make sense of the significance of capturing Juba in a political military situation controlled from Khartoum otherwise it was an attempt to falsify history.

The formation of the SPLM/A was rooted in the Sudanese political context, which generated the social, economic, and political crisis that afflicted the country. However, at that material time the social, economic, and political forces of building socialism didn't yet exist in the Sudan leave alone southern Sudan. The SPLM Manifesto, published months after the events in Bor, Pibor and Ayod, is infested with efforts to falsify history, and therefore renders doubtful its authenticity. It was therefore necessary and imperative to delve deeper into a different narrative about the SPLM/A because of what has been related verbally or in print were from people with tinted credibility. The scholars and students of history will continue to investigate and find out the truths. Forty years since the SPLM/A formation nothing should remain classified or hidden from public knowledge. This discourse therefore is an attempt to shed light on every fact, idea, truths, untruths, rumours, and gossips linked to the SPLM/A in its formative and other stages in the conduct of the war of national liberation. The analysis of these facts would inform the reasons why the SPLM/A like the other revolutionary forces in the Horn of Africa and great lakes Region namely the RPLF, TPLF, EPRDF, NRM, RPF failed to shoot itself into power in Juba or Khartoum but had to compromise with the enemy to end the war thus eschewing its vision, and the political objective of New Sudan.

The battle of Bor on 16th May 1983 and the formation later in July of the SPLM/A bring us to the gist of this discourse. As alluded to above the appearance of the SPLM/A onto the political stage in the Sudan was an enigma. It was like something parachuted from somewhere in a manner suggesting that the cause had to catch up with its effects. The people of southern Sudan had to find reasons (cause) for the war (effects) thrust upon them. The synthesis would indicate that the SPLM/A was not the trigger[2]; it was only an effect. This was because nothing was heard of it before until the SPLA first lightening military operations that closed down the Chevron oil exploration in western Upper Nile and the operations of the International Construction Company (CCI) digging the Jonglei canal in February 1984. Unlike the

Anya-nya battles, these victories quickly caught the imagination of many young people many of whom were shipped down from Khartoum in the wake of Numeiri's kasha policy and those who had been preparing to resolve their local conflicts. It is not an exaggeration to say that many of the peasants and cattle herders who joined the SPLM/A did so from a different perspective than the liberation. It is worth mentioning that in its dying days, the May regime had generated contradictions some of which reflected as conflicts among communities. The SPLM/A, as an insurrection, therefore provided opportunity for acquisition of firearms. Thus, many of the youths joined the SPLA only to acquire firearms to go back home to resolve those local conflicts. This could be garnered from the *morale* songs these peasants turned SPLM/A recruits and combatants sang in their induction into the SPLA and during their training. That the recruits into a national liberation movement spoke to the problems with their neighbours demonstrated that no political work had been undertaken in preparation for the SPLM/A formation and proves that the SPLM/A leadership has no links to the re-division politics that turned the Southern Region upside down during the 1980/82 period. It was only the lumpens that constituted the enlightened core that engaged in running battles of the re-division politics, embittered by the manner they were chased out of Juba like foreigners who were true recruits to the notion of liberation. Moreover, the SPLM/A leadership comprised former military officers of the Sudan Armed Forces with no or little connection with civilian politics.

The republic of South Sudan had just celebrated the thirty-ninth anniversary of the battle of Bor on 16th May 2022 and writing a chapter devoted solely to the SPLM/A was significantly imperative; it was the dominant player in the emergence of South Sudan as an independent country. A few South Sudanese authors published first-hand accounts of the SPLM/A and the war of national liberation it spearheaded. It was permissible in the past that some facts and truths were then deliberately hidden from the public knowledge to protect the image and integrity of the movement and its leaders. While the war raged, it was necessary to shield the movement and its leaders lest such negative information benefited the enemy. The war ended in 2005, it is not permissible to still protect those leaders in view of the distortions and diversion from the vision that occurred in the course of war of national liberation and immediately following the death of Dr. John Garang.

The people of South Sudan still reel from impacts of bad policy engineered during and after the war of national liberation. It is imperative to unpack that baggage to conduct an audit and a correct evaluation of the roles and responsibilities as basis for genuine and objective evaluation of the SPLM/A and its performance in the war of national liberation. This would also prove it or not as an element of the national democratic revolution in the Sudan and in the Horn of Africa. It would also be imperative to locate the distortion and diversion that ended in the war in the Nuba Mountains and Blue Nile as well as the civil war in South Sudan.

The SPLM/A had the support of the entire people in the peripheral Sudan, who joined its ranks and file in their tens of thousands, a typical case of mass response to the call of the leaders. However, unlike the other democratic revolutionary forces in the Horn of Africa, the SPLM/A did not organize and conduct it as a war of national liberation combining into one and the same thing - the social, economic, political, military, and cultural functions of liberation. That its leadership did not organize and conduct the war in this manner is an important pointer to whether the hyped concept and vision of the New Sudan stemmed from genuine revolutionary conviction to transform the Sudanese polity, or a concept driven by opportunism and adventurism. We will come back to it but now let us begin with the emergence of the SPLM/A.

2. The Narrative of the SPLM/A Formative Stage was Falsification of History

The SPLM/A sprouted on to the political stage at a time of social, economic, and political crisis in the Southern Region nevertheless it was not linked to this crisis except by a thin chord that betrayed some of its leaders as adventurers and opportunists. The political volcanic cauldron, that metaphorically was the Southern Region, has been smouldering and bubbling emitting pneumatic shock waves since some Anya-nya officers refused and rebelled against absorption into the Sudan Armed Forces, as provided by the Addis Ababa Agreement. There were several acts of indiscipline among the absorbed Anya-nya officers and soldiers throughout the interim as well as after the election of the PRA and Abel Alier's elected presidency of HEC in 1974. These acts of indiscipline among the absorbed Anya-nya officers and soldiers at times put the Southern Region[3] on high security level. They had no clear linkage to the political struggle occurring then among the different political forces in the Southern Region. Indeed as Gen. Joseph Lagu would say, most of them were administrative in nature and resulted from ignorance and lack of professional military experience.

The picture painted by the SPLM Manifesto, however, would appear as if somebody was there working hard to discredit the Addia Ababa peace agreement because it did not represent pan-African idiosyncrasies, and that the Addis Ababa Agreement placed the southern Sudanese permanently under Arab tutelage. These acts of indiscipline among the Anya-nya were spatially, temporally, and even politically isolated that rational analysis or synthesis wouldn't yield a coherent political picture of the forces behind them. By their nature, these acts of indiscipline wouldn't have raised the political temperature in the region to trigger much wider political action for change. The Anya-nya was a military not a political organization and it didn't evolve like other national liberation movements in Africa, Asia or Latin America. As it transpired later, most of the ex-Anya-nya who joined the ranks of the SPLM/A were those caught up by the war in southern Sudan and had been therefore forced to join because the alternative would be to move to northern Sudan. The political work undertaken by the clandestine cell bore no marks that could be attached to the mutiny in Battalion 105 in Bor.

THE PROBLEMS OF SOUTH SUDAN

In 1980, President Numeiri decided to locate the oil refinery in Kosti rather than Bentiu where the American Chevron Oil Company had discovered it. This decision triggered a political standoff with Southern Region's political elite; the discovery of oil was the only hope for socioeconomic development of the region. However, the political standoff added another level of distrust between southerners and the political establishment in Khartoum. Before this political crisis could completely sublime, another social and political crisis erupted in connection with *kasha*, a racist policy deliberately promulgated and executed in Khartoum province, the capital of the Sudan. The policy forcefully returned to their place of origin all the black Sudanese people from the south, west and central Sudan. The *kasha*, and later the application of the *Islamic huddud* through prompt justice pushed to the precipice the racial relations in the Sudan. In fact, many non-Arab Muslims in northern Sudan found themselves lumped together with their southern Sudanese compatriots.

The administrative decentralization policy that provided for the creation of Area Councils was a policy instrument to change or redraw district boundaries. This rocked the region to its core as it efficaciously conflicted and divided communities. The policy was to prevent the unity of the people in face of Numeiri's continued political schemes to the regional self-rule. The administrative decentralization created new area councils or changed the old provincial boundaries and generated frictions and conflicts between communities in certain areas. Instead of directing their frustration towards the government, the communal leaders conflicted amongst themselves and started gun running to arm their communities in anticipation of war to settle those local disputes generated by Numeri's administrative decentralization policy. On the heels of the administrative decentralization policy, and as if to accelerate its implementation in the Southern Region, the political establishment dropped another bombshell in the form of re-division of the Southern Region. However, this time the bombshell came through the agency of southern Sudanese politicians mainly from Equatoria and Upper Nile disgruntled with Abel's presidency of the Southern Region. The re-division debate coming up against the backdrop of what crystallised out as power struggle between Abel Alier and Gen. Joseph Lagu. This power struggle, playing out as conflict between the Dinka and Equatorian, worked up raw emotions and sentiments that prevented rational thinking and behaviour among the politicians and the ordinary people.

The mutiny was, therefore, triggered by administrative not political matters, and attempts to politicize or to link it to the political crisis triggered by the proposal to re-divide the Southern Region would be falsification of SPLM/A history. The attention this mutiny received at the levels of Juba and Khartoum speaks to a different hypothesis. In view of the general political situation in the country and Numeiri sudden shift to fundamentalist Islam, the mutiny in Battalion 105 was part of a strategy to accelerate the political process of abrogate the Addis Ababa Agreement and to dismantle the Southern Region. As part of this political engineering process, the security and political situation in the Southern Region quickly spiralled out of context of what apparently was becoming deceptively a peaceful environment. There were unusual movements of troops in and around Juba, with more troops flown in from Khartoum and other parts of northern Sudan.

On the 16th of May 1983, the army H/Qs in Juba ordered the attack on the mutinous soldiers in Bor. No one in the southern region political leadership, including the wrangling politicians in the regional government envisaged that the political situation could develop fast that quickly[4]. Two weeks after the attack on Bor, the President of the Republic Gaafar Mohammed Numeri issued a republican decree comprising three parts: one to abrogate the Addis Ababa Agreement, another one to dismantle the Southern Region and a further one to establish the subregions of Bahr el Ghazal, Equatoria and Upper Nile. The popular stories told about the sudden emergence of the SPLM/A including those documented in the SPLM Manifesto tended to exaggerate the political and organizational stages of its formation and therefore have been discounted [Nyaba, 1997:29]. When the founding of a movement, that claims a national character as the SPLM/A, is wobbly and people made to accept it through falsehood and innuendos, there would be a lot to be wary about. There could never be reasons whatsoever for revolutionaries committed to social and political change to lie to prove what they have or have not done. This assertion stems from incongruences and discrepancies ubiquitous in the narrative of SPLM/A formation intended to insult people's intelligence.

First, the mutinous environment in Battalion 105 in Bor and Pibor was clearly a lapse in security and military order generated by indiscipline, corruption, and embezzlement of soldiers' salaries. The embezzlement of soldiers' salary couldn't have been political action of revolutionaries desiring change of the situation. This must be the work of criminals; for embezzlement of soldiers' salaries is essentially criminal. If the soldiers had knowledge of this crime, they would instead mutiny against it. Therefore, the attempt to explain the events in Bor and Pibor as revolutionary, particularly with the rejoinder that it was planned to capture Juba, and work of the clandestine cell of the former Anya-nya officers, was to protect the criminal nature of the action major Kerubino Kuanyin and his colleagues undertook. Anybody conversant with clandestine political activities would know that it's always guided by strict discipline and ideological commitment to the cause. If there really was clandestine cell of the former Anya-nya officers planning to launch a movement for social and political change in the Sudan it wouldn't have been in isolation of other revolutionary forces in the Sudan and more closely the Free Officers Movement in the Sudan Armed Forces. The re-joinder in the SPLM Manifesto in connection with the capture of Juba was superfluous and shameful; it could only demonstrate that the Manifesto was written with a deceptive mind not known of revolutionaries. This narrative therefore speaks to an obvious falsehood from the following perspectives.

In confidence, one would insist that the attack on mutinous soldiers in Bor on May 16th, 1983, came within the regime's strategy from the time of Numeiri's break with the regional political elite in the wake of oil discovery in western Upper Nile to create political conditions in southern provinces that would eventually lead to the abrogation of the Addis Ababa Agreement and to the dismantle the Southern Region. The dismantle of the Southern Region was bound to generate serious repercussions in the country at a time the Umma-NDP faction of the National Front had kind of withdrawn from the Port Sudan Agreement, that was why Numeiri took the circumlocutious route engaging the southern political elite in re-division politics. The mutiny in Bor including the presence of Dr. John Garang and Abel Alier then on private vocation therein were final jigsaws in the puzzle.

It was open secret in Juba then that major Kerubino Kuanyin Bol was an important pawn in the execution of the strategy. Major Kerubino and major William were at the time notoriously prosecuting the war against the Anya-nya2 in eastern Upper Nile. It was also common knowledge that major Kerubino was Gen. Sadeq Al-Bana's confidante; he used to illegally hunt, kill, and regularly bring Sadeq Al Bana wildlife trophies in contravention of the laws prohibiting trafficking in wildlife trophies. In return Gen. Sadeq ignored major Kerubino's reckless behaviour and indiscipline. It is worth mentioning that Gen. Sadeq Al-Banna was Numeri brothers-in-law and therefore was posted in Juba as his confidante on account of share interest.

Secondly, if a clandestine cell or organization of former Anya-nya officers existed, it was natural that the cell leadership automatically would constitute the leadership of the nascent organization the cell had established – that is the SPLM/A. This was the practice worldwide that leadership of the party constituted its government except in rare situations. Unfortunately, this was not the case in the SPLM/SPLA leadership. It is true there were glitches during the formation of the SPLM/A and the emergence of the politico-military high command (PMHC) was not a straightforward development. The leadership line up after the ostracization of the politicians eventually was as follows: Colonel Dr. John Garang de Mabior (chairman and c-in-c), major Kerubino Kuanyin Bol (deputy chairman and deputy c-in-c) major William Nyuon Bany (chief of staff), captain Salva Kiir Mayardit (deputy chief of staff for operation) and major Arok Thon Arok (deputy chief of staff for administration). This line up was anomalous; first it excluded Lt. Col Francis Ngor, who could have been Garang's deputy by virtue of his seniority. Secondly, that captain Salva Kiir appeared in the hierarchy senior to major Arok Thon Arok. Whatever the explanation advanced, that Salva Kiir arrived at the SPLM/A H/QS first before Arok Thon didn't add up, was terribly unconvincing and should not have been advanced in the first place. This is because Francis Ngor arrived at the same time as Salva Kiir. It added to the suspicious death of Lt. Col. Francis Ngor. For such a high-profile military officer to die in a battle against the hands of armed Gaajak civilian smack of a conspiracy to resolve the leadership tussle. The only acceptable explanation could be that Lt. Col Francis Ngor was not a member of the clandestine cell, if it ever existed, otherwise he should have been second to none but Col John Garang in the SPLM/A hierarchy.

Thirdly, colonel Dr. John Garang de Mabior was the most senior officer in Bor during the attack by the forces from Juba, yet he did not take over the command of the fighting. It couldn't have been by mere chance that Colonel John Garang was in Bor. The brewing mutiny already known as engineered from Juba and Khartoum wouldn't have permitted the presence of a senior military officer of the ranks of a colonel unless on a sanctioned operational assignment. This anomaly spurs a different and a suspicious understanding of the situation. Col. John Garang did not partake in the battle; he instead climbed a vehicle with his family and headed to the Ethiopian borders. This behaviour defies all logics; that the clandestine cell in a situation of war and yet its ultimate leader abdicates the command responsibility. The absence of satisfactorily convincing explanation that neatly knits together the various parts of this narrative invokes doubts and different interpretations.

Many people now believe the SPLM/A was the cerebral gymnastics of one man, Col. Dr. John Garang de Mabior. What Edward Lino revealed in his book could have been official SPLM/A version and must interpreted differently in order to arrive at the truth. In the practice of Sudanese army, the movement of a senior officer of the rank of Lt. Col. even on a private mission is controlled to the extent that he could not be permitted to travel to a garrison town where the officer in command was suspected of mutiny. That the army top brass in Khartoum and Juba allowed Col. John Garang to spend leave at a time they were preparing to launch an attack on the mutinous unit in Bor is something to be seen in the context of a conspiracy theory surrounding Numeri's strategy on the Southern Region. There are two possible scenarios. The first could have been that Numeiri must have from a military point of view discussed with Col. Dr. John Garang the possibility of crushing the mutiny in Bor, Garang's home area. In this respect Col. John Garang himself could have been object of this conspiracy by way of exploiting his (Garang) and Abel Alier's presence in Bor for Numeiri to generate an alibi for his decision to dismantle the Southern Region. The alibi in this respect would be the mutiny of Battalion 105. In this case, therefore, Col. John Garang was on a mission either to quell the rebellion or face a military court martial for having failed to do so. He, however, changed his mind and instead decided to lead these troops into the bush. Instead of executing the orders of the military top brass, Col. Garang decided to join the rebellion but for tactical reasons chose not to take over the command – the troops didn't know him. The story of clandestine cell of the former Anya-nya officers was therefore concocted to whitewash the mission for which he was in Bor whose objectives were at cross purpose with his power ambition. It was a means of creating a grandiose self-profile, a way of falsifying history to place oneself on top of events. Falsification or exaggeration of role and responsibilities once one was outside government's precincts became a common phenomenon in the SPLM/A. This deliberately encouraged others to generate false grandiose self-profiles of themselves[5] including the fugitives of the Sudanese justice system whom the SPLM/A leadership received with open arms as revolutionaries as soon as they were outside the precincts of the Sudanese government.

3. Col. Dr. John Garang de Mabior Assumes the SPLM/A Leadership

Bitter and violent struggle for leadership marked the formation of the nascent SPLM/A between the former military officers of the Sudanese army and the veteran politicians some of who had already made alliance with the Anya-nya. It must be admitted that Colonel Dr. John Garang de Mabior was known only to a small coterie of acquaintances, relatives, and friends back in the Sudan and his bit for leadership would become a contentious issue. That Garang was known to a few people wasn't a discovery, but the nature of his job as a military officer would of course not permit mixing with politicians and other ordinary citizens. In this respect, politically, Garang interacted with only few trusted persons, and this was the source of confusion about his political life. It was after the formation of the SPLM/A that many people including the author got to know and intimate with Dr. John Garang. There was no one among those who interacted with Garang including my two political friends and colleagues George Maker Benjamin and Edward Lino Abyei would divulge a credible picture of Dr. Garang in terms of his political philosophy save that he was a revolutionary, whatever that meant. When I had an opportunity in the SPLM/A to discuss anything outside military orders and commands, Dr. John Garang did not strike me as somebody well-grounded in the Sudanese revolutionary politics.

It is impossible to start a revolutionary war of national liberation in the Sudan without knowledge and correct understanding of the Sudanese politics; having been in any of its political outfits. It would be clever guess work or one would be relying on trial and error in the prosecution of such grandiose project as war of national liberation.

No doubt, Garang was an astute, avidly articulate, and an intelligent politician with the capacity to turn white into red and vice versa. This was clear from his initial political writings. Just arriving back from his university studies in the United States of America to join the Anya-nya in 1971, his letter to his commander in chief, Gen. Joseph Lagu speaks volume of the pan-Africanist perspective and dreams among the Africans in America not on the continent. He had not yet been baptized with fire though, so to speak, when Garang started a diatribe against the SSLM negotiating with the Numeiri's regime. That letter as well as his other letter to Dr. Akech Mohammed [Paanluel, 2015:] were high profile political communications but became known only in 1984 after the formation of the SPLM; as the politicians and intellectuals struggled to know more about the man, they dug out his political past. For instance, they traced and attributed to captain John Garang explosions and grenade throwing in Wau cinema in 1972/3. It was only that these incidences became public knowledge much later; otherwise, it was possible to read between the lines of his letter to Gen. Lagu that captain John Garang did not want the Addis Ababa Agreement and therefore started to sabotage its implementation by creating insecurity and encouraging mutiny among the absorbed Anya-nya forces.

Dr. John Garang de Mabior was known to be a lone player in matters that would be public in nature and of necessity would involve other actors. He has been credited for writing the SPLM Manifesto depicting and encapsulating his political thinking and ideological orientation, which he acquired outside the context of the Sudanese reality. The political ideology of Pan-Africanism was something completely foreign to the Sudanese politics which was Arab and Middle Eastern oriented. Southern Sudanese for that matter never entertained pan-Africanism in the fashion displayed abroad; they were more concerned with the internal situation than across the borders or far afield.

By the time the survivors of Bor battle arrived western Ethiopia to form into a movement, there were already several rebel groups operating in the bushes of southern Sudan. Besides the Anya-nya2, which comprised groups operating against the Sudan government in Aweil, Abyei, Bentiu and Bilpam in western Ethiopia, the Southern Sudan Liberation Front (SSLF), a quasi-Marxist group was then operating a Che Guevara type guerrilla movement in Boma area of eastern Upper Nile[6]. Dr. Garang's obsession with power and leadership showed up immediately in relating the nascent SPLM/A to the Anya-nya2 and SSLF. He exploited the Ethiopian support to coerce these groups into organizational unity with the SPLM/A. However, instead of opening a constructive dialogue to forge an agreement on the political objectives, organizational structure and the leadership of the nascent movement, Dr. Garang decided to fight and defeat the Anya-nya2. The SSLF voluntarily joined the nascent SPLM/A but not without first disintegrating as a group to win over their leader Ngachigak Ngachiluk and alienating the radical Lokurnyang Lado, who was later executed in a fire-squad in the SPLA training camp in Bonga on flimsy charges. In fact, the charges for which Lokurnyang Lado was killed had not been impeachably proven; he was accused but was not presented to a court to defend himself or to render an appeal against the death sentence. Before the firing squad was ordered to shoot him and other condemned colleagues, Lokurnyang raised his 'complaint of injustice' but the commanding officer Cdr. Salva Kiir Mayardit told Lokurnyang in no uncertain terms to executive the order after which he could raise his 'complaint of injustice'. Many similar cases particularly brought by members of the high command like Kerubino or William Nyuon were foregone *fiat accompli* and the victim would have nowhere tp appeal to. In most cases the SPLA Disciplinary Laws (1984) provided for death penalty by firing squad or payment of a certain number of heads of cattle – indeed problematic for some ethnicities.

Dr. Garang viewed these rebel groups suspiciously as competitors for power rather than collaborators in the war of national liberation. The Derg had already decided to throw its moral, political, and military support behind the nascent SPLM/A under Garang's leadership; his academic and military credentials and his political ideology then being the determinant factors. Indeed, the Anya-nya2 was by no means a viable political movement. Like the former Anya-nya Land Freedom Army, it raised the slogan of separation and independence of southern Sudan without coherent political ideas. The leadership of the contingent in western Ethiopia had very weak relationship with former Anya-nya leaders like Gordon Mortat Mayen then domicile in the United Kingdom and this predominantly was because of ethnicity and ethnic considerations. It could be safely said that the Anya-nya2 did not have a political leadership. It was mere war-lordism, its leadership was made up of illiterate unprofessional war generals who lacked political and democratic organizational principles imperative for a movement struggling to construct a modern state. This configuration rendered the Anya-nya2 prone to internal power struggles and conflicts mainly along ethnic or clan lines explaining why although a formidable fighting force, the Anya-nya2 could not attract external military or political support, not even from the Derg on a tit for tat basis, against the Sudan[7].

Garang's desire to disperse the Anya-nya2 forces was accentuated by the impatience of the Ethiopian general who was sent to mediate between the two antagonistic leaders. The impatience of the general immediately precipitated a bloody clash with the Ethiopia fire power deciding the outcome. The Anya-nya2 were defeated and routed out of their camps in Itang and Bilpam forcing their withdrawal into the Sudan.

In retrospect, the clash with Anya-nya2 in Itang was strategically ill-advised and was a mistake the leadership of the nascent SPLM/A should have not committed. First, the Anya-nya2 was predominantly ethnic Nuer who bestride the border area between southern Sudan and western Ethiopia all the way from Maiwut in the north to Akobo in the south. The involvement of the Ethiopians in the skirmishes, which also involved heavily armed Nuer civilians in the nearby villages on both sides of the borders created immediate problems for the SPLM/A. The Anya-nya2 and the armed Nuer civilians effectively retarded the SPLA movement towards its military targets in the hinterland, because it had to battle its way through ambushes erected by armed civilians in Gaajak, Gaajok, and Lou resulting in enormous loss of SPLA life. The same hostility affected the recruits travelling to the SPLA camps in Bilpam and Itang.

It was only after the agreement and re-unification with Anya-nya2 in 1988 that the SPLA was able to move with freedom and security in the area, and this enabled it to capture (liberate) from the enemy the garrisons of Jekau, Nasir, Akobo, and a string of smaller garrisons in the border area. Unfortunately misadvised, the SPLA ambushed and killed Samuel Gai Tut who according to popular stories was returning to reconcile with Dr. Garang. That was the defining moment, the Anya-nya2 withdrawal into Sudan making a final decision to ally with Numeiri's regime. The decision to attack the Anya-nya2 or to disperse them did not serve the social, political and military purposes of the war of national liberation, which for its success and victory over the enemy demanded unity and strong sense of fraternity among the people of southern Sudan. This was imperative particularly that many southern Sudanese were still submerged in the bitterness, resentment, hatred and ethnic conflicts triggered by the re-division politics of the Southern Region. With the benefit of the hindsight, the attack on Anya-nya2 could have served one strategic political objective linked to Dr. Garang's power ambition. Although he wouldn't admit it under any circumstance nevertheless Dr. Garang harboured a deep-seated sense of Dinka supremacy over other nationalities in southern Sudan, which he projected under the guise of Pan-Africanism. This was a serious contradiction; a pan-Africanist turning into an ethnic chauvinist.

This ethnic chauvinistic attitude originated from William Deng Nhial, who in the sixties believed that unless a Dinka politician led SANU there was no way it could successfully end the war in the independence of Southern Sudan. This ethnic ideology encapsulating Pan-Africanism complicated, if not obfuscated, the nature of national liberation in southern Sudan inhabited by sixty-seven nationalities. Dr. Garang's underlying ambition was power to lead the war of national liberation. In order to achieve this ambition, Garang's primary concern was to raise an army in which the Dinka ethnicity numerically preponderated over and above all other nationalities as a guarantee for his leadership of the liberation movement. In this respect, Garang achieved his power and leadership ambition exploiting the fact that the Dinka is the largest ethnicity in Southern Sudan. This demographic factor had to be moulded into an ideology deep rooted in their past and could unite all across segmentation lines through language, poem and song.

The clause 23 (b) in chapter eight of the SPLM Manifesto speaks to 'early determination of correct leadership to prevent the movement being hijacked by counterrevolutionaries' (sic). The Derg had rejected as mild and not loudly revolutionary the manifesto version the veteran politicians: Joseph Oduho, Martin Majier Gai, and others, drafted and therefore Dr. Garang single-handedly authored the final version to meet the interests of the Ethiopian revolutionaries. Most of these veteran politicians were indeed right-wing liberals and conservatives and their world view circumscribed their politics. Garang's idea in rejecting the veteran politician's version of the manifesto was to exploit as a means to discredit, isolate and send these veteran politicians and their liberal ideas to oblivion. In this manner and with the assistance of Derg, Dr. Garang emerged the undisputed leader of the nascent movement.

This victory against the politicians would then set the trend to militarize the nascent movement. Having eliminated the threat of Anya-nya2 and the veteran politicians had been neutralized; they had been arrested and detained, the only power contesters remaining for Dr. John Garang to watch would be the leftist intellectuals and any other new political arrivals in the liberation movement. Therefore, nobody, particularly the political activists and former senior bureaucrats arriving to join the movement was permitted to undertake any assignment until he or she met and was interviewed by the Chairman. The reason was obvious; It was Garang's movement and must know each and every individual coming to join the liberation movement.

The idea of separating the political from the military, and to subordinate the military to the political authority, as was the practice in other liberation movements, became the breaking point between Dr. John Garang and the politicians. He would not accept any position in the nascent movement less than the supreme commander, meaning that Col. Dr. John Garang must have the political and military authority himself to avoid being subordinated to anyone. This was the exact meaning of the clause enunciated as the early determination of the leadership of the nascent SPLM/A. It was the caveat that generated frictions, suspicions, and lack of trust between the career military officers, I would say between Dr. John Garang himself, and the veteran politicians. To strengthen his position and endear himself to his military colleagues, Col. Dr. Garang incited Kerubino Kuanyin Bol and William Nyuon Bany against the politicians falsely accusing them of not respecting the two in the leadership because they were functionally illiterate. It did not take long before Joseph Oduho, Martin Majier, Malaath Joseph, Bol Ayualnhom, and others were all bundled up into the SPLA prison in Boma. The military officers arrested the political process in the liberation movement, and this was to have profound ramifications in the development of the war of national liberation.

Leadership, and visionary leadership for that matter, is crucial for the liberation movement to achieve its objectives and victory over the enemy. The problem in the SPLM/A was that leadership was already determined precluding any chance of improvement or replenishment. Not only that, but leadership was perceived in terms of one man – Dr. John Garang de Mabior, not an institution as it would be in other political movements. The personification instead of institutionalization of the SPLM/A leadership was the greatest fatality that would stalk the liberation right into the independence of South Sudan to become the unresolvable causes of the civil strife and the unending transition.

Leadership of an organization does not appear ready made from the blue skies. This was anti-dialectical; of necessity, leadership in a liberation movement emerges from and as a result of ideological struggle inside the movement. The self-serving clause in the manifesto read as 'an early determination of its leadership' inserted even after the SPLM/A had already been formed and recognized, missed a cardinal rule in party and revolutionary politics. It inadvertently denied the ideological struggle characteristic of a national liberation movements. It suggested lack of correct understanding of revolutionary politics and knowledge of the Sudanese reality, whereby people cherish freedom of thought. This clause also denied young and new blood in the movement rising to the top of the SPLM/A leadership hierarchy. In fact, many of the young SPLM/A leaders and cadres who bought and subscribed to the falsehood of 'an early determination of correct leadership' would live to discover that in politics as in nature there is no early determination of leadership. Leadership in the national liberation movement at a particular time is dictated by the objective reality and circumstances of the movement. Little did many comrades understand that the clause was a trap that allowed Dr. John Garang to monopolize power and control the movement without necessarily building a scientific understanding of the process of liberation to permit the emergence of new leaders, cadres, and progressive ideas in the context of the struggle.

At the material time the SPLM Manifesto was published, it was imperative and of paramount importance to have published the movement's political programme. The manifesto was an announcement of formation and that was all. What Col. Dr. John Garang forgot or indeed did not know was that the armed struggle was one of the many components of the liberation process. The personality of Col. Dr. John Garang and his obsession with military power hampered and forestalled the subordination of the military to the civilian and political authority in the liberation movement. A leadership of the liberation movement that combined political and military authority in one person was the creation of a one-man dictatorship. The over centralization, indeed, personification of the SPLM/A power and public authority accentuated not only the contradiction between the army and the politicians in movement but also, as we shall later see, generated contradictions within the military officer corps: between Garang and Kerubino, Arok, William Nyuon and finally Salva Kiir himself who survived them all.

The public image of the SPLM/A generated by the victories the SPLA scored against the Sudanese army inside the Sudan shielded or rather smoke screened the evolution of the SPLM/A from critical scrutiny and objective evaluation[8]. Many southern Sudanese in the country contended themselves with the picture created by SPLA propaganda beamed out of its GH/Qs that they ignored or overlooked the excesses the SPLA soldiers committed against the civil population. The death in August 1984, indeed, assassination at SPLA hands, of veteran politician, Hon. Benjamin Bol Akok, then the SPLM representative in the United Kingdom, rudely awoken everybody including those already in the movement to the risks involved in joining the movement. It shattered the faith and confidence in the SPLM/A leadership that many potential recruits cold footed. This exposed some hidden secrets that the veteran politicians who joined the ranks of the SPLM/A were either languishing in SPLA prisons or may have been executed.

Militarism in the liberation movement had profound consequences for the civilians especially the intellectuals and the politicians and political activists, and people who were only used to democratic intercourses. The notions of commands and orders were completely new. It meant that everybody arriving to join the SPLM/A to participate in the liberation was forced to undergo military training to become a soldier, and to be ranked and commissioned with the batch one trained in. It did not matter how experienced or qualified one was in other professional domains, which were also important elements of the liberation process, one was forced to become a military. The idea was for everyone to fit into the command system. It was paradoxical that medical doctors after commissioning into the SPLA ranks were forced to work under paramedics, whom the SPLA had earlier trained and had been promoted above the starting rank of a new comer; simply because they were senior in military ranks. This policy endured and became worst when the SPLM/A introduced the civil-military administrators to manage the liberated areas.

This deliberate policy to ostracise the intellectuals was to vain show to the illiterate officers and soldier that they were more important to the revolution than the university graduates.

In this way the SPLM/A couldn't harvest the knowledge and expertise of the graduates or post-graduates to promote the liberation process. Many of these intellectuals were administrators, office managers, senior clerks, and accountants who were well versed in bureaucratic functions. What they required to fit into the liberation movement was not necessarily military training such that they became combatants; no, what they needed was political education and ideological training. This training would help them to correctly perceive their objective reality, change their attitude and behaviour and transform into revolutionaries. The refusal to benefit from the knowledge and expertise would explain why the SPLM/A didn't build its own bureaucracy, which for all purposes would have been the backbone of the state the SPLM/A desired to construct in the areas that fell under its administration. This would also explain why the liberation could not implement the resolutions and recommendation of its first national convention 1994, its senior officers conference in Chukudum 1995, the National Liberation Council meeting in Kajo-Keji 1997 and Rumbek conference 2004. It was easy to call meetings for people to speak, and indeed they spoke their minds, drew resolution and recommendations and that was all, for they left the venue until the next meeting. In the absence of a bureaucracy nobody was there to implement whatever has been decided.

The first time the SPLM/A leadership woke up to the

importance of bureaucratic procedures was after the signing of the comprehensive peace agreement. In a move that was difficult to explain, Dr. Garang dispatched to the republic of South Africa SPLM/A 2nd row leaders, cadres, commanders to be trained by the ANC. As a national liberation movement that had captured power in South Africa, at that material time -2005, there was nothing the ANC could impart on the SPLM/A leaders and cadres at the end of the war of national liberation. This training in South Africa though for a short period wouldn't have been necessary; the SPLM/A by its nature was a school in which all kinds of professional disciplines could have been learnt. A liberation movement that spanned twenty-one years was a practical field class in which military knowledge conflated with knowledge of politics and government, culture, economics within the objective reality of the Southern Sudan. SPLM/A leaders didn't need to travel to South Africa; it was a waste of ANC resources.

4. Militarism was the De-Revolutionization of the Liberation Process

The social and political configuration of the Southern provinces of the Sudan especially after the Numeiri's suppression of the bourgeoning democratic movement in 1971 meant that any resistance to the regime would only be political violence. The SPLM/A had no way except as to kick off and evolve in the military tradition and environment of its Ethiopian benefactors - the Derg[9]. And the way the SPLM/A built relationship with the Derg suggested that there would have been no way the

SPLA could have evolved differently from the Ethiopian military institution in terms of training, tactics, armament, discipline, communication, and intelligence. It was not a relationship based on equivalence and parity; it was a relation of dependence and patronage. The Ethiopian military then, notwithstanding Derg's Marxist rhetoric, still exhibited streaks of feudal cultural legacies in terms of relations and treatment of recalcitrance and indiscipline. The SPLM/A in its first three years of life, therefore, was a combination of Ethiopian feudalist legacy of suspicion, servitude and instantaneous obedience and Sudanese colonial army mentality of hostility towards the civilians and penchant to treat as enemies any non-military persons. It was a mistake to model the national liberation movement on a standing army who traditions still were feudal in character. Thus, the SPLM/A slanted towards militarization and this registered in the promotion of militarism instead of revolutionary militancy among the combatants; the subversion of political enlightenmen. In practice, this militarism was preoccupation with military routine, hierarchies, and discipline in which the relations between the combatants or between them and their leaders ceased to be political but military orders/commands and instantaneous obedience..

This militarism in the SPLM/A was a deliberate strategy to hollow and render barren the national liberation movement of its revolutionary content. There was a logic to it - to create a disconnect between liberation theory and practice, and to project military action over and above political education, that is the SPLA over and above the SPLM. This was deliberately engineered to prevent radicalization of the movement by denying the link up with forces of national democratic revolution in the Sudan or across the borders in Ethiopia. This assertion requires critical examination and discussion. But let's first examine how militarization and militarism played out in the evolution of the SPLA officer and combatant, beginning from their arrival, training, and to the relationships that evolved between the leaders and the combatants or between the national liberation movement and the mases of the people.

In its development into a huge army, the SPLM/A leader, Dr. John Garang de Mabior, personally interviewed each and every recruit in the SPLA division under training in Bongo, Bilpam, Piny-Udo, Rahad, and other training centres. Apart from engraining his personality into the mind of the recruits, this interview created the myth of Dr. John Garang as infatigable, and a miracle. It was in these interviews that he identified and carefully selected cadres, mostly secondary school fallouts for special training as military intelligence (MI) officers and radio operators and signalists under the command of the SPLA deputy Chief of Staff for Operations, who himself was an intelligence officer in the Sudanese Armed Forces. This was where the logic of the disconnect between liberation theory and practice operated effectively to reverse revolutionary zeal with which the recruits came to the SPLM/A training centres. Cdr. Salva Kiir Mayardit built the MI and radio signalist corps into a formidable and feared force in the SPLA. They trained not as comrades trusting or entrusting each other but as competitors virtually suspicious and ready to betray the other. Thus, the strength of this force did not emanate from what they did as individuals or collectively against the enemy but from the network of lies, false reporting, intrigues, and character assassination of comrades. The MI personnel were feared because of the concoctions they were capable of manufacturing; they spied on every SPLA officer and soldier and therefore cultivated fear, distrust, and bad blood within the ranks. As if to underscore the falsehood that serious political struggle in Southern Sudan commenced with the formation of the SPLM/A in 1983, the SPLA (MI) started a smear campaign against the politicians and intellectuals in general, and a witch-hunt to weed off and eliminate potential rivals invariably identified through dubious intelligence reports collected unprofessionally and unethically, analysed to confirm conviction, and usually the suspects were summarily executed without opportunity for legal assistance or appeal. In many instances such executions were out of personal vendetta. The execution of Lokurnyang Lado was a case in this point. As a result, the MI created an atmosphere of apathy, indifference, selfishness, self-insurance and lack of solidarity among the combatants. Thus, instead of assisting each other, comrades betrayed or undermined each other as the competed for ascendency in the military hierarchy, which became their preoccupation.

I would add without guilt or remorse that from 1985 until the consummation of the CPA in 2005, the history of the SPLM/A became an account of Dr. John Garang's social, political, military, and diplomatic actions and engagement as he singlehanded led the national liberation movement and prosecuted the war[10]. This analysis couldn't be anything without touching on the personality and political thoughts of the man because whatever happened during the war of national liberation including the deadly excesses committed against individuals or groups of people occurred in the context of executing 'revolutionary' orders and commands that invariably 'came from above' – simply meaning coming from the chairman and commander in chief. In fact, anything entitled 'revolutionary' in the SPLM/A wasn't necessarily moral, ethical, or even revolutionary; it was only expedient, and must be obeyed as orders that came from above.

Militarism in the SPLM/A was intended to turn the SPLA officer and soldier into mere robots trained only on taking and executing orders (Nyaba, 1997:51). This robotization was to buttress Garang's cult of personality registered in the morale songs of the SPLA combatants. As recruits in the training centres, they spent hours singing songs in praise of Col Dr. John Garang instead of the revolution or the country. A robot is programmed not to think or ask questions. The SPLA robots faithfully believed whatever Dr. John Garang told them no matter how false it was. For instance, Dr. Garang once told the trainees that, "these university graduates with their degrees are useless. When we finish the war, you will be the directors and directors-general in government offices and they will be your secretaries and clerks, writing reports for you". This was to a thunderous applause of the recruits/trainees, but to the chagrin of some of us present in the parade. It's absolutely misleading the soldiers; nowhere in the world could and illiterate peasant become the director and a university graduate his or her secretary. But that passed as a falsehood to raise the morale of the soldiers. However, in another incident chairman Garang was carried away as to tell a passing out SPLA batch, "it is through the AK47 that you will get your food, your clothes, your wife and everything you will need in the field." This was disastrous and requires a little digression.

The training of SPLA combatants was in fact a continuum of brutalization and dehumanization that could easily pass for a reformatory of hard-core criminals not potential revolutionaries. The SPLA recruited instructors from the Sudanese army who, as though meting out vengeance, mercilessly brutalised and dehumanized the prospective SPLA combatants. It was only after being commissioned that one rediscovered self as a human being, and only through equalling out against the innocent peasants. In the trail of a newly graduated SPLA batch, they terrorized, brutalized, raped, murdered, and dehumanized the civil population in an effort to regain their manhood, dignity, self-respect and self-confidence they had lost to the instructors in the course of training. This was a contradiction, which apparently did not come in the realm of struggle and unity of opposites in the liberation movement. The explanation must be sought somewhere we hope to espouse in the coming lines.

Militarization, or robotization of the SPLA combatants was a process intended to forestall any steps towards institutionalization of the liberation movement. This would have automatically entailed building political and administrative institutions and instruments of public authority, creating institutions of accountable governance and building accountable relations between the people and the army. Militarism purported to consolidate personal power and to prevent power struggle or dissent in the liberation. Therefore, it was not in the best interest of the SPLM/A leadership to construct institutions and instruments of public authority; it worked against the logic of personified power. However, personification of public authority than its institutionalization, nevertheless, did not immunize the SPLM/A against internal power struggle and other contradictions, which the lack of institutions continuously generated due to other social, economic, and political factors weighing in.

As more people from different parts of the Sudan started to arrive at the SPLM/A, the movement grew considerably in size, and this required qualitative changes particularly in the domain of management. Apart from military formations of divisions, battalions, companies, platoons and squads, the SPLM/A had only the political-military high command (PMHC). This High Command did not conduct itself as the political authority of the movement. It had no constitution, rules of conduct of its business or other instruments of authority. It seldom met formally and therefore didn't have minutes of its proceedings or resolution. What were categorized as High Command meetings, were in fact radio conversations the chairman and c-in-c, Dr. John Garang conducted separately with each individual member of the five-man organ of the movement, and therefore could not be counted as High Command meetings. At no time in the life of the SPLM/A were the High Command members present in the same place at the same time. Only the chairman and c-in-c was at large but the others were deployed in different zones and could come to Bilpam or Itang only with the knowledge and permission of the commander in chief. In fact, the High Command was a hollow theatrical structure, and this configuration suited Dr. Garang in terms of power of decision and control of the liberation movement. The political system in the SPLM/A was akin to a one-man dictatorship. Its public authority was personified in its leader, Dr. John Garang de Mabior but as time passed, it became very difficult, if not impossible, to rectify this structural defect. This structural defeat became the trigger and driver of all contradictions within the PMHC, and generally in the SPLM/A. Garang's deliberate refusal to correct those structural defeats heightened the contradictions within the leadership of the movement leading eventually, albeit at different times, to the arrest and imprisonment of Cdr. Kerubino Kuanyin Bol, the deputy chairman and deputy c-in-c in June 1987, and Cdr. Arok Thon Arok in April 1988. It also triggered the Nasir Declaration and the split in the movement August 1991, the rebellion of Cdr. William Nyuon Bany in December 1992, and what was called the Yei Crisis, 2004, that fitted Dr. John Garang against his long-time loyal lieutenant and second in command Cdr. Salva Kiir Mayardit. It's the same structural defects, as we shall see in the next chapters, that was the very unmaking of the republic of South Sudan in terms of the civil war it engendered.

The initial split with Anya-nya2 was essentially on the

fundamental issues of organization and political objectives of the nascent movement. It didn't have to lead to military confrontation; the issues could have been resolved amicably through political tact and wisdom. After the failure of the Southern Regional experiment provided by the Addis Ababa Agreement, no southern Sudanese would countenance unity with the north. The valid point in Garang's projection of unity of the Sudan, if only to satisfy the Derg's national interest, was political empowerment of the African people in the Sudan. That didn't have to generate contradictions that tore apart the southern Sudanese. In this connection, Dr. Garang's dilemma was real and the decision to militarize compounded the dilemma; militarization shrank and narrowed instead of widening the political space, and thus prevented strategic manoeuvring and dialogue to build consensus. This consensus would have created enough space in the same movement for both the southern secessionists and unionists to prosecute the war as the strategic political objective. The arrest of Cdr. Kerubino exposed the lack of organic and political unity in the High Command and in the movement in general. In fact, without the intervention of Prof. Bari Wanji to convince Cdr. Kerubino to project national rather than regional (Bahr el Ghazal) agenda, which unfortunately brought Cdr. Kerubino to Addis Ababa, where he was arrested, the SPLM/A would have suffered its first split in June 1987, with the bulk of SPLA forces withdrawing *en masse* to Bahr el Ghazal.

The greatest problem in the SPLM/A was not that contradictions erupted and caused difficulties. The problem was that the leadership and the whole movement never drew useful lessons from these contradictions. The remedy to structural problems in the liberation movement couldn't have been military confrontation, but political and democratic opening of political space. Military solutions shrunk the social and political space and rendered impossible compromise or consensus building. The concern for personal power prevented the SPLM/A benefiting from its agreement with the Anya-nya2 (1988) in terms of rectifying the structural bottle neck in the SPLM/A to create political space for the Anya-nya2 political leaders. This was necessary after the episode that led to the arrest and detention of Cdr. Kerubino Kuanyin Bol and as a gesture of good will to the incoming Anya-nya2 after the bitter and violent split in 1983. The agreement to reunify with Anya-nya2 was unfortunately reduced to merely a *'return to the SPLA fold'* of Anya-nya2 officers and men, and this excluded its political leaders. Only Gordon Koang Chol was appointed alternate member of the SPLM/A High Command and Stephen Dhol promoted commander in the SPLA. The veteran politician Daniel Koat Matthews were forced to undergo military training and was commissioned a captain. The refusal to structurally transform the SPLM/A to accommodate the Anya-nya2 played out destructively in the SPLM/A split that was the Nasir Declaration 1991.

The *'return to the fold'* was Dr. Garang's a means of protecting his power and to forestall democratic changes in the movement by fudging the contradictions or to leave them unattended to. It is not possible to make the basis of a real contradiction magically disappear simply by refusing to resolve it politically and democratically because a debate evaded, indeed a contradiction stifled in the short term becomes an inevitable crisis and a possible split in the long term. Moreover, what led to the split and fighting with Anya-nya2 in terms of the political objectives and power structure in the nascent movement had not been resolved. This created conditions for Kerubino's actions. The reasons that forced the Anya-nya2 back into the *fold* of the SPLM/A weren't discussed internally within the movement to draw lessons to forestall and recurrence. These social and political contradictions remained unresolved indeed incubating to play out later more destructively as in Nasir declaration (1991), Yei (2004) and Juba (2013). It was mere luck that these developments did not shatter the SPLM/A completely but their social and political ramifications still stalk the people and the state in the republic of South Sudan in the form of personal enmity and hatred among the leaders translated into military confrontation. The eruption that led to the civil war in 2013 was not because politics have failed between Salva Kiir and Riek Machar but because the power struggle between them had become so personified that it could only be resolved by mutual exclusion.

5. Surge of Dinka Ethnic Nationalism in the Liberation Movement

National liberation is a complex process of societal transformation from colonial or its primordial stages of development. However, it occurs in leaps and bounds; no society ever evolved in one leap or bound because it involved physical, social and psychological transformation. The SPLM/A war of national liberation came at an appropriate time to transform the centuries old condition of sociocultural backwardness of the people of South Sudan. The People's Republic of China, Vietnam, and Cuba were successful example of prosecuting wars of national liberation ending in social revolutions and their industrialization.

National liberation involves combining military action with political enlightenment and ideological training to produce a completely different revolutionary individual whose personal interests are aligned and subordinated to those of the society. This obtains as a result of the ideological transformation that individual had undergone. The SPLM/A war of national liberation was completely different from the process in China, Vietnam and Cuba because the SPLM/A leadership separate the military training and action from political education and ideological training in what we mention above as a disconnect between liberation and its theory and practice. This translated into prosecuting the war of national liberation outside its political and ideological content. The SPLM/A leadership promoted militarisation and militarism in the liberation movement and inadvertently sabotaged mass awareness. This meant that the psychological make up and thinking of the lumpens, the peasants and the pastoralist that joined the liberation movement remain unchanged as they came from their homes. The perception of the SPLM/A remained the same; they joined the movement only to get fire arms to go back to resolve local contradictions. Political education and ideological training were absolutely necessary to change attitudes and behaviours and to impact on one's perception of reality and the very process of liberation they were involved in. Military training alone without political training and ideological orientation build relations based solely on military doctrine and discipline and produced militarists whose perception of liberation was just shooting at the enemy. The subversion of political education, social and political awareness during the training of the combatants engendered negative ethnicity. It is difficult to imagine that a contingent of SPLA combatants comprising the same ethnicity and have not been subjected to political education would always identify their commonality and as result behave like a herd of livestock. Humans hardly tolerate social or cultural vacuums; they would recoil immediately to their natural cultural environment.

In Bonga SPLA Training Centre, a batch of twelve to fifteen thousand SPLA trainees from all over southern Sudan even after thorough mixing would still differentiate into their ethnic cocoons. This occurred when they settled to eat their meals, converse, or socialise after drills and lessons. The absence of a common spoken language usually accentuated this segregation especially among the preponderant ethnicities like Dinka and Nuer. The Equatorians also had that tendency of cocooning themselves except that their association was always multi-ethnic; they always trying to speak the Juba Arabic, which unlike the Dinka, Nuer, Shilluk, united them as a distinct group. They developed affinity for each other based on this ethnic socialization, especially during the time they composed their morale songs. The problem with this ethnic segregation arises when one ethnic group preponderated on account of their numerical strength in the SPLA battalion or division and begin to hegemonize the other smaller ethnicities.

The Dinka is the largest single nationality in southern Sudan. Their lifestyle is communal and would therefore stand up to participate in any undertaking whether it was local or national like in the SPLM/A. The political circumstances that ushered the SPLM/A found the Dinka at the centre of the proposal to redivide the Southern Region on account of Dinka domination of the political system. Thus, the Dinka responded to the call to arms in large numbers that in every hundred SPLA soldiers about seventy-five would be Dinka from Bahr el Ghazal or Bor in Jonglei. There would have been no way of preventing this numerical domination particularly after the split with Anya-nya2 and the Nuer, the second largest single nationality reluctantly joined the SPLA. The SPLA training centres were far removed from the small ethnic communities in western Bahr el Ghazal and indeed very few of them managed to join but not necessarily trekking from their homes in western Bahr el Ghazal. The Azande and the bulk of western Equatoria including southern parts of Central Equatoria were also far removed from the SPLA training centres and therefore only few managed. The eastern Equatorian pastoralist joined in large numbers and trekked all the way to western Ethiopia; ostensibly to prop up their leader veteran politician, Joseph H. Oduho. In fact, absence of a leader to follow could have also been the factor underlying the lack of popular response to the call to arms in some areas.

The SPLA kicked off as a conventional rather than classical guerrilla army, and its combat engagements with the enemy were semi-conventional or conventional resonating with the Dinka, Nuer, Shilluk, Otuho, Pari, and Anywaa traditional warfare unlike most other nationalities in Equatoria and western Bahr el Ghazal. Thus, the Dinka found themselves deployed in nearly all the fronts making them the most common SPLA soldier or officer all over southern Sudan. This generated the false feeling, sometimes echoed by some Dinka leaders in or outside the SPLM/A, that the Dinka were the only ones who fought and died in the war of national liberation. Indeed, this attitude shored up as a negative element in the peasants and pastoralists primaeval consciousness.

In a national liberation movement whereby the leader, Dr. John Garang de Mabior, and three out of four most senior commanders hailed from the Dinka nationality was already a bad indicator not only for justice (equality) and freedom but also for whether nationalities other than the Dinka existed or participated in the SPLM/A. This was where omission or subversion of political education had precipitous consequences of envy and jealousy among those who considered themselves excluded in the power equation. The fact that appears as exclusion of other ethnicities could have been employed also to prove that the SPLM/A was not a national liberation movement. The leader of a national liberation movement encompassing over sixty nationalities should have been sensitive to ensure the visibility of other nationalities not only as foot soldiers but also in the leadership hierarchy of the movement. This would impress on him to construct democratic institutions in the movement to accommodate leaders of other nationalities. Garang's refusal to build democratic institutions in the SPLM/A inadvertently amounted to mimicking political exclusion and social discrimination the Arab dominated northern political elite practised against the southern Sudanese. This was a serious contradiction; the national liberation movement practiced the ideas it vehemently struggled against. The notion of 'let the sleeping dog lie' played out when Dr. Garang rejected the concept of the House of Nationalities as means to conserve the unity and diversity of the people of Southern Sudan. This action on the part of the leader of national liberation movement demonstrated not only negative ethnicity but also a false perception of liberation.

This was the genesis of Dinka ethnic nationalism and its ideology of hegemony and domination and/or assimilation of the smaller ethnic groups. In the SPLA training centres, the instructors the MI and the so-called political commissars saw to it that most if not all the morale songs were composed in Dinka language forcing the non-Dinka to memorize and internalize. Here, liberation lost its national and revolutionary content; it acquired a different connotation corresponding to training the rifle on the enemy but shooting the comrade. It generated a completely different perception of liberation. Thus, sometimes a SPLA commander or a senior officer who by force of his seniority would take possession of somebody's property like a watch, radio or even a cow, irrespective of whether that individual was a colleague in the movement, it was said that 'he had liberated it'.[11] This was not only a clear distortion of the meaning but indeed trivializing liberation.

The surge of ethnic nationalism signalled political failure in the national liberation movement; the failure to organize the process of national liberation based on principles of freedom. justice, and fraternity encapsulated in a programme of political enlightenment and ideological orientation of both the members of the SPLM/A and the masses of the people in a process of conscientization – perceiving reality together. The surge of ethnic nationalism was driven mainly by demographic considerations; the feeling that we are numerically dominant meant that we are powerful and have right to control power and wealth. This logic in essence drove ethnic nationalism but was a function of low level of political consciousness. The absence of political and ideological motivation in the SPLM/A was like a timebomb planted, which personal rivalry for leadership detonated as in 1983 (Itang), 1991 (Nasir), 2004 (Yei), 2013 (Juba) and in 2016 (J1).

It is no more than literal truth that whenever military training of the combatants takes priority over their political training their lives and those of the people are placed in serious danger. Thus, when in 1991 the political contradictions in the SPLM/A triggered by power struggle escalated into a split, many Nuer SPLA combatants read into it the traditional Nuer-Dinka ethnic rivalry and the split in the SPLM/A was immediately ethnicized.

The attack and devastation of Kongor and Bor by the combined Nuer SPLA forces of Riek Machar and the Anya-nya2 stationed in Dolieb Hill can only be explained in those terms. Nevertheless, it will remain a dark spot in the history of South Sudan for it smacked of vengeance for everything counted against the SPLM/A leadership read Col. Dr. John Garang who hailed from Kongor. The same but opposite process occurred in the elimination of individual Nuer and Chollo officers and men who found themselves in the dominantly Dinka SPLA contingents.

It was not the intention to single out the issue of Dinka ethnic nationalism – negative ethnicity as the only danger to state formation and nation building in South Sudan. The idea was to explain the genesis and surge of ethnic nationalism to occupy the political and ideological void created in the liberation movement by the absence of a liberation ideology and lack of political consciousness amongst the SPLA combatants. The peasants and pastoralists that comprised the SPLA were invariably conservative in their thoughts and action, and this would have required immense effort to transform them into a revolutionary force. Without that transformation it was impossible to erase the prejudices with which they left home to join the SPLA. Once deployed in areas different from their homes, they behaved and acted as if they had no cultural or moral instincts to prevent the bad and irresponsible behaviour they meted out to the civil population like raping of women and girls, forceful misappropriation of property, murder etc., which they couldn't have committed in their homes. This underlines the importance of political education as part of the military training of the combatants; it raises their mental capacity to enable a correction perception of the objective reality.

The absence of democracy and institutionalism in the national liberation movement stirs and steers its politics along personal, ethnic and/or regional lines. Those are the domains where negative ethnicity breeds, flourishes, and sprouts into action. Thus, in the absence of political awareness and ideological training in the SPLM/A, its internal social and political contradiction arose along regional, personal, ethnic or clan lines than ideological. This occurred and almost shattered the SPLM/A into regional pieces in 2000 when the personal quarrel between Dr. John Garang and Ustaz Bona Malual Madut was misconstrued as Bahr el Ghazal versus Upper Nile regions. Garang and Malual were both Twic Dinka; but Bona Malual was not a member of the SPLM/A, and there was nothing that should have involved the SPLM/A as an organization in a quarrel that was between two individuals. Bona supporters in the SPLM/A made it look like Upper Nile leadership of the movement had wronged Bona Malual and therefore read Bahr el Ghazal versus Upper Nile contradiction into the Bona Malual-John Garang personal quarrel.

It would have been easy to tackle negative ethnicity in the national liberation movement hadn't Dr. John Garang have vested interest in promoting it to ensure power and political leadership of the SPLM/A. His tragic death, just at the time he tried to rectify this structural weaknesses in the movement, put the SPLM/A and the people of southern Sudan in a state of terrible confusion and disorientation. The tragic helicopter crash took place in institutional and power vacuum in the SPLM/A. Neither the people of southern Sudan nor the SPLM/A had a *Loya Jirga*[12] to refer to in such a situation, the Shilluk would call *'wangi yomo'* - state of no authority. Salva Kiir was in a power limbo, so they would say; he was neither in the leadership of the SPLM nor in the command of the SPLA. He was only deputy president of government of Southern Sudan that even then had not been constituted. That, Dr. John Garang, the person who single-handedly had managed the movement and liberation process was just no more accentuated the confusion and disorientation in the SPLM/A. This profound disorientation was exacerbated by another development. The SPLM leadership ordered SPLM representation in constitutional positions in government (executive and legislature) at National, Southern Sudan and States levels based on community choices rather than party membership. This brought into the SPLM individuals who indeed were ideologically opposed to the SPLM. Dr. John Garang wouldn't have done it that way. After taking oath of office as first vice president of the republic and president of the government of Southern Sudan, Garang was already in a powerful position that he did not again require negative ethnicity to prop his authority. It was only during those uncertain times in the war of national liberation that Garang needed the overwhelming support of the Dinka.

The ascension to the SPLM leadership and the state power by Cdr. Salva Kiir Mayardit introduced a style of leadership that consolidated negative ethnicity in South Sudan body politics. It came through the agency of the communities then an important factor in political representation that pushed the formation of community elders' councils or community lobby groups instead of the SPLM grassroots instruments. Thus, instead of building democracy in the SPLM, the leadership of Salva Kiir built political patronage and patrimonialism. The Jieng (Dinka) Council of Elders (JCE) became prominent than other ethnicities' elders' councils on account of social and political proximity of its leaders to President Salva Kiir Mayardit. This proximity coupled with Kiir's own ethnic chauvinist attitude elevated JCE's programme of building South Sudan into state run on Dinka cultural values rather than on democracy and political principles of a modern state. Ethnic nationalism in South Sudan, and Dinka ethnic nationalism for that matter, is a post-war phenomenon linked to the failure of SPLM/A leadership to build a genuine national liberation movement.

At the end of the war, the national liberation movement emerged as an amalgam of liberal/conservative ethnocentric social force with no programme for social and economic development of the country. The political, military elites and business cartels in the war economy in the SPLA administered areas lubricated by the international humanitarian and relief assistance dovetailed with the NCP cartels and the competition for primitive accumulation of wealth started in earnest. It also translated into competition for the control of the state and its political and economic resources, generating social forces that proved to be the very unmaking of the state they won through heavy sacrifices in life and destruction of people's livelihoods. It quickly degenerated into violence and a civil war, whose parameters apparently became ethnic political and economic empowerment to occupy other non-Dinka communities' ancestral lands and habitats. Salva Kiir's decision in April 2009 to give the Shilluk lands east of the Nile to the Padang Dinka sections of Luach and Paweny (Atar County), the migration of tens of thousands of Bor Dinka with their huge herds of cattle to Madi, Acholi and Kuku lands was not in isolation. It was linked to JCE demographic policy of Dinka presence in every state in South Sudan including occupation of the border lands with neighbouring Kenya, Uganda and DR Congo never mind if that pushed the indigenous people over the borders into refuge. This couldn't be anything but twenty-first century colonialism. Dinka ethnic nationalism driven by Jieng elite has pitted the Dinka nation against nearly all other nationalities and has put South Sudan in a state of perpetual instability and conflict. The surge of Dinka ethnic nationalism came as a result of subversion of political education and ideological training in the liberation movement on the one hand, and ascension of a Dinka ethnic chauvinist to the helm of the state in South Sudan on the other hand.

6. Political Failures in the War Pushed the SPLM/A into Political Compromise with the National Congress Party

The war of national liberation started on an uncompromising high-pitched note of complete destruction and transformation of the Sudanese polity dubbed the 'Old Sudan' and the creation in its place of a 'New Sudan' based on freedom, justice, fraternity, and prosperity. The regimes that governed the Sudan since independence practiced political marginalization, economic neglect and social discrimination based on faith, race and culture. These contradictions underpinned the conflict that any revolutionary change must address them to the satisfaction of the Sudanese people in their different regions and the SPLM/A leadership was therefore on the right path.

However, given the manner the SPLM/A leadership organized the liberation movement and prosecuted the war the achievement of this political objective was bound to be a difficult, if not, impossible task. This sentiment stems from the reality that liberation, and national liberation for that matter, is a process that involves intertwining together the social, economic, political, military, and cultural functions of the struggle to create organic unity between the combatants and the masses of the people. It's this organic unity that enabled the NRM (1986) the EPLF and EPRDF (1991) to shoot themselves into power in Kampala, Asmara and Addis Ababa respectively. These liberation movements did not have to negotiate peace but the incumbent regimes imperceptibly melted away.

The SPLM/A led war of national liberation spanned twenty-one years. The was prosecuted predominantly in Southern Sudan, Nuba Mountains and Southern Blue Nile subregions with a brief extension in Eastern Sudan. In the end, the SPLM/A leadership had to negotiate and finally strike a political compromise with the National Congress Party (NCP) to stop the war and rein peace in the country. Simply stated, the SPLM/A failed to destroy the 'old Sudan' and also failed to create the 'New Sudan' in the territories that came under its control in southern Sudan, the Nuba Mountains and in Southern Blue Nile; it did not achieve its strategic political objective. Not only that but this political compromise, unlike the Obote II regime in Uganda or the Derg in Ethiopia, also left the Ingaz completely intact, entrenched and consolidated NCP's hold on the political and economic power of the Sudanese state. However, this political compromise placed the SPLM/A in complete control of Southern Sudan; this control of Southern Sudan could have been SPLM/A leadership's *raison d'être* for the insurrection. This circumlocutious route to Southern Sudan after twenty-one years of war involving war between southern Sudan unionist and secessionists reveals something suspicious and different from liberation, destruction of the 'old' Sudan and construction of the 'New' Sudan. Dr. John Garang de Mabior in 2005 struck with the NCP a political compromise for which he disparaged Gen. Joseph Lago as a jobbist when he signed the Addis Ababa Agreement in 1972.

The consummation of the political compromise was inevitable. Many factors contributed to force the political compromise; nevertheless a great majority of these factors were intrinsic to the SPLM/A and how it conducted the war of national liberation. As Chairman Mao would say, victory cannot be achieved simply by wanting it; it requires many specific conditions like adequate preparation, seizing the opportune moment, concentration of superior forces, etc. By the time the SPLM/A signed the CPA in

2005, it had built an army of more than two hundred thousand man and woman; it had liberated large swaths of territory in Upper Nile, Equatoria, Bahr el Ghazal, Nuba Mountains, and southern Blue Nile. The war reached a stalemate and the SPLA did not possess a reserve force to turn the tide against the enemy. It's leadership had to negotiate and sign the peace agreement; the SPLA couldn't anymore continue the war.

Two or three critical factors stand out to explain why the SPLM/A unlike the national democratic revolutionary forces in the Horn of Africa and the Great Lakes Region had to compromise to end the war.

6.1 Reliance on External Resources Turned the People into Spectators

The revolutionary forces in Eritrea, Tigray, and parts of Amhara regions we referred to above prosecuted the war based on the principles of a people's war. Wherever they were, whether in their villages, in enemy garrison towns or in the refugee camps across the international borders the Eritrean and Ethiopian masses were organized to participate and indeed these were people's war in objective reality. It's more than literal truth that without the Derg and Col. Mengistu at the helm of the Ethiopian political system, the SPLM/A would have not kicked off. However, incidentally, it's Mengistu and Ethiopian people's benevolence that pushed the SPLM/A to neglect the cardinal principles of self-reliance in the process of national liberation, and to conduct the war of national liberation outside the context of the laws of revolutionary people's war. That Dr. John Garang directed his forces to trek to the Ethiopian borders instead of withdrawing to the rural hinterland pointed to a misconception of the war he wanted to prosecute.

The SPLM manifesto 1983 spoke to the formation of the SPLA to conduct a protracted revolutionary war. It is important to underline 'protracted' because it is loaded with concepts that underpin a people's war of national liberation. A deeper understanding of the concept of a protracted war wouldn't have push the SPLM/A into political compromise with the Ingaz regime; it would have meant taking the national liberation process to its logical conclusion. In fact, the social and political circumstances in southern Sudan under which the war erupted meant that it would be protracted suggesting that it would have required a long time to build up a formidable force to challenge the Sudanese army. However, knowing circumstances under which the SPLM/A was formed in Itang with the assistance of the Ethiopian government, and in hindsight that the manifesto was written after SPLA's formation, the notion of a 'protracted war' was superfluous to say the least. Anybody conversant with leftist lexicon and classical guerrilla warfare would dismiss the notion of a protracted war in the SPLM Manifesto as a bluff or a joke.

Immediately after the battle against Anya-nya2, the SPLA began mobilising recruits, organizing, training and forming them into army units. The first to be formed in 1983/84 were the elements of Battalions 105 (Bor and Pibor) and 104 (Ayod), Jamus (Buffalo) Battalion, Tiger and Timsah (crocodile) Battalions. These were then followed by the training of SPLA

Divisions: first Jarad (Locust) (1985), Mour-Mour (1985), Kazuk (1986), Zal-Zal (1987), Intifada (1990). In the conventional army formation, the squad would comprise nine (9) men but because of large numbers of recruits the SPLA squad comprised seventeen (17), its platoon was made up of fifty-one (51), its company comprised two-hundred-forty-four (244), while its battalion comprised one thousand four-hundred and forty (1440) men. The SPLA battalion was equivalent to a brigade plus in the Sudanese army. This configuration was a guerrilla formation for a protracted war. The SPLA started as a conventional army without tanks, artillery, and aircraft. There wouldn't be grounds for a guerrilla or a protracted warfare whose objective would have been attrition to wear down the enemy. The SPLA attacked with a brigade sized (Battalions: 104, 105, Jamus, Tiger and Timsah) army when its launched its first attacks on the Sudanese army in Malual and other enemy's delaying elements.

The author trained in Zal-Zal (earth quake) division and so was conversant with this configuration. Zal-Zal was made up of seven battalions that added to about eleven thousand troops[13]. To source such a force; that is to provide field armaments, ammunitions, shells and explosives uniforms, food and medicine would be a logistical nightmare for a third-world government, leave alone a guerrilla army which had no economic and financial base. The funding of the SPLA over the first seven years must have been in hundreds of millions of US dollars. If Mengistu provided the funding through the efforts of the Ethiopian people, it meant that he was essentially fighting three wars: one in the southern Sudan, one in Tigray and the third one in Eritrea (northern Ethiopia).

This initial large force had serious logical implication in terms of armament, uniform, food and medical supplies for an insurgency that didn't have own stores but relied on the beneficence of Ethiopian government fighting two wars in the north of the country. Some of the initial weaponry the SPLA received came from Col. Moammar Gadhafi who supplied it on account of his fallout with Numeiri but as soon as Numeiri was overthrown in the popular uprising in April 1985, Gadhafi stopped his assistance to the SPLA. This was the time the SPLA had training and passed out the Koryom and Mour-Mour Divisions a total of about thirty thousand troops. The logical question that imposes itself would be about the logistics in all its dimensions; reliance on external resources is something that could easily sour relations between friends. We will come back after the digression.

The SPLM/A was not a guerrilla army *per see*; perhaps only in the context that it acted outside the laws of the Sudan. It prosecuted a conventional and semi-conventional warfare, which did not precede according to laid down concrete own plan. Not only that, but also the SPLA victories were invariably pyrrhic; it deployed large forces against a small enemy force, indeed acting against the strategic principle of war to destroy the enemy and preserve own forces. Thus, sending three thousand SPLA combatants in waves against an enemy company of one hundred twenty men and officers entrenched in bunkers in Jekau, a very small and limited space, was a strategic blunder. Many SPLA combatants suffered from both enemy and friendly fire in an operation that was obviously a deliberate waste of human resources. In the battles of Jekau (1985) and Malual Gahouth (1984) the casualties' ratios was three hundred or more SPLA combatants to one enemy soldier.

In the first two years of war, when Cdr. Kerubino and Cdr. William commanded the Jekau -Nasir corridor, there was unacceptable waste of human life. Kerubino and William behaved and treated the SPLA combatants like robots without humanity in them[14]. This was an attitude also driven by negligence and carelessness towards resources which one acquired without labouring for them. The war of national liberation particularly a protracted one as Garang had wanted it did not warrant such waste of human life or generating traumatic incidences which required hospitalization. The fact that the SPLA had its support bases in western Ethiopia compounded its total reliance on external resources it did not care to conserve.

The Derg really spoiled the SPLA in the same manner a child could be spoiled by kindness of its guardians. The Derg overlooked building SPLA's capabilities to fend for itself and this was detrimental to its long-term sustainability. The Eritrean People's Liberation Front (EPLF) -*shaabia*, fought their war of liberation with minimal support from the Sudan. *Shaabia* organized itself and the people of Eritrea until they became one body whether they were in the front line in Eritrea fighting or outside in the refugee camps in the Sudan or in the Diaspora working for the cause that it depended on the Eritreans than on external resources provided by its sympathizers. In all this, it was impossible to see an Eritrean fighter anywhere in the Sudan in the same fashion SPLA fighters could be spotted openly in Gambella and even in Addis Ababa crowding, boasting and brandishing their rifles as if they were part of the Ethiopian security system or as if they were in the SPLA controlled areas in Southern Sudan. Most of the SPLA combatants had never been exposed to foreign lands and different cultures and in their simplicity considered anywhere they went to as if they were in their environment and behaved exactly as they would in Southern Sudan. That's why I say the Derg, and the presence of Mengistu Haile Mariam spoiled and de-revolutionized the SPLM/A[15]. Coming from sociocultural background not shamed or embarrassed by becoming a burden of a willing benefactor, the SPLA combatants easily and inadvertently abused the Ethiopian generosity.

It goes without saying that the society in southern Sudan by its nature was still rural, socioeconomically underdeveloped, and culturally backward, which to a large extent conditioned their perception of the places other than their homes they set foot in. This required intensive does of political enlightenment and cultural orientation to transform them.

It was not only that they need enlightenment and cultural orientation but the notion of having the SPLA rear bases in western Ethiopia was completely wrong. The correct thing was for the SPLM/A leadership to transform the SPLA into a genuine people's army and to create conditions inside Southern Sudan for stable secured rear bases to support the war fronts. Had the

SPLM/A done that revolutionary task, it wouldn't have been necessary for the SPLA to have any showing in Ethiopian villages, towns and villages. Thus, the unfortunate episode was for the SPLA to train in Bonga, Piny-udo, Bilpam, Dimma and Assossa and went back into the Sudan like an army of occupation while its malingerers remained loitering in Ethiopian towns and villages.

Of course, had the SPLA prosecuted a people's war, the methodology, strategies, and tactics the SPLA employed would have been profoundly different. This in the word of General Giap, the progress, escalation and intensification of the war in Southern Sudan would have gone hand in hand with the gradual withdrawal of the training and support bases from western Ethiopia into Southern Sudan, and to construct a strong rear base and satellite bases in the regions of southern Sudan. Yambio the capital of western Equatoria state and the whole territory of western Equatoria was a classic example of capture, not liberation, from the enemy. This SPLA contingent that arrived western Equatoria was not different from the Sudan Army contingent stationed therein. However, unlike the SPLA, the national liberation army, the Sudan Army was commanded by a local Azande general Isiash Paul and had contact and communication with the people.

By 1989, the SPLA was operating in different parts of Equatoria and its daily radio broadcast, Radio SPLA was heard throughout the Sudan. It's impossible that the people of western Equatoria could have been shielded off from the SPLA or its operations in other parts of Southern Sudan. However, when the SPLA set foot in Yambio, it took both the enemy and the local Azande people by surprise, and they all ran away for their dear lives; only that the people ran in a different direction. The element of surprise was superbly adhered to but at a political disadvantage. The enemy army's commander, Gen. Isaih Paul, with his forces ran to Wau while the Azande people ran into the bushes and into Zaire and Central African Republic. The people trickled back into the town days later to find that their houses had been repossessed by SPLA officers and soldiers.

The SPLA's liberation of Yambio found Gen. Samuel Abu-John Kabashi and other Azande intellectuals in town. Like others, Abu-John had to run to Dungu in the Congo to save his life. A former general in the Anya-nya, about whom the SPLA command should have known from intelligence gathering, was definitely a potential SPLA recruit, as indeed he later became a senior member of the SPLM/A leadership. I am sure with secured communication established Abu-John could have joined ranks even with many other Azande intellectuals, soldiers, policeman, wildlife officers and civilians present in Yambio. In the way Western Equatoria was liberated without the participation of the Azande, the Mundu, Moro, and Avkaya people, which could have been in form of information sharing, providing SPLA with clothes, food, drinks, and other necessities as they advanced to contact with the enemy. The SPLA combatants came from somewhere ready-supplied and needed nothing from the people. It's this coming ready-made that disqualified the SPLA from being a people's army.

The war of national liberation is a people's war by the simple fact that they participate in its every aspect for this war combines mass social, economic, and political struggles, and the people's armed action to neutralize or defeat the enemy. In the words of Ernesto Che Guevara, any attempt to conduct a war of national liberation without the support and participation of the masses of the people is a prelude to inevitable disaster. Therefore, a war of national liberation must be prosecuted in accordance with scientific knowledge of war and processes that underpin it. In such a war, in a country as vast as southern Sudan and this vastness is expressed in terms of people's actual participation, the enemy is always in danger of losing ground if he concentrates his forces in garrison towns and villages or losing strength if he disperses them as cover every square kilometre of the country. The most important feature of a people's war relates to the organic unity between the people and the people's army that the only differences between the two in a particular location, say a village, would show theoretically and in practice in their different tools. The SPLA combatant would be carrying a rifle while the peasant or worker/artisan would be carrying a net, sickle, or hammer all to the service of the people's war.

In the first civil war (1955-72), the Anya-nya forces fought classical guerrilla warfare. This was mainly ambushes and way-laying government troops in motion. Seldom did the Anya-nya forces engage the government army in conventional battles. Their light weapons and small arms dictated the manner vide which they engaged the enemy. In fact, in most cases in Equatoria they used traditional weapons like bows and arrows, and spears. In

Upper Nile, particularly at the beginning of the war in 1962, it was possible to find that in a force of three hundred men only about ten men would be carrying mark five rifles and the rest carried spears. This meant that the Anya-nya forces operated in their immediate habitat. Through the traditional institutions of governance, chiefs, sub-chiefs, rainmakers or monyomoji leaders, the Anya-nya collected peoples' contributions to the war effort in which a household would pay in kind or in cash. This money was collected and sent to Congo, then the main source, to purchase firearms and ammunitions[16]. That was how the Anya-nya survived until the late sixties when the Arab Israeli war 1967 brought the arms windfall. But most importantly, the Anya-nya units built good relations with the civil population in the rural areas among whom they lived as well as with workers and government officials in garrison towns, who usually made monetary contributions through the networks.

The Anya-nya experience underscores the relevance and significance of self-reliance as a very important principle in any struggle political or armed insurgency. This principle encouraged and glorified self-sacrifice, volunteerism, commitment to the national cause. Many of the successful national liberation movements in Africa, Asia and Latin America cultivated and conducted their struggles with minimum support from their internationalist friends. The support to the liberation movement based on international solidarity while a necessity nevertheless is amenable to abuse or exploitation when it comes to enter-party political and diplomatic relations. Parties or liberation movement desire to develop independent positions and actions in international relations irrespective of their friendship. That is why many liberation movements prefer to rely on themselves except in cases of extreme necessity. The SPLM/A in its relation with the Ethiopian Workers' Party departed from the classical ways in which a guerrilla army emerges and develops.

This relationship located the SPLA training camps and support bases (refugee camps) located far away from northern Bahr el Ghazal, western Bahr el Ghazal and western Equatoria where from the bulk of its recruits hailed. The potential recruits spent months on the way to the training centres by the time they arrived, they were completely exhausted. It would have made a difference had the SPLA training centres been western or southern part of eastern Equatoria as they were during the Anya-nya war. There is more than words to the concept of SPLA 'rear bases' and their location inside Southern Sudan. Theoretically and even practically, SPLA support base or SPLA rear-base is very important component in the prosecution of the war of national liberation. It is impossible to envisage the SPLA operations without support bases. The social, economic, political, military and cultural functions of the support bases and their location in the process of liberation can't be overemphasized. The problem with the SPLA rear bases was their location in western Ethiopia and the fallout from that in terms of their social and economic dynamics.

We mentioned above the several divisions the SPLA training and passed out from Bonga, Bilpam, Piny-Udo and Dimma.

These were recruits that had registered with the UNHCR as refugees returning away from war in the Sudan, thanks to the Ethiopian government manipulation. As long as these recruits/refugees remained in the training camps inside Ethiopia no problem arose because their food rations taken out of the UNHCR would register as going to them. The problem arose when these recruits/refugees passed out as SPLA combatants; it required similar numbers recorded. In this the SPLA encouraged, indeed forced, mass exodus of the civil population to the refugee camps and thus made the people food coupons for the army. That the people of Southern Sudan had to migrate *en mass* to become refugees in order to sustain the SPLA war of national liberation was the beginning of dependence on external resources in the prosecution of the war of national liberation. It engendered the tendency among the SPLA combatants to look down on the people; they came ready-made with their weapons, uniforms, food, and medicine and needed nothing from the people except as porters.

This would have been different had the SPLM/A based its insurgency inside Southern Sudan. Liberation would have acquired a different connotation for the SPLA combatant and the masses of the people among whom they moved and operated because people's participation would have kicked into every liberation process. The whole of Southern Sudan would have transformed in the SPLA support base or rear base. The rear base would therefore fulfil the economic functions of food production and other necessities for the liberation army. It would fulfil the political functions of political enlightenment to raise social awareness and political consciousness of the people creating the condition for conscientious participation in the liberation. It would be in the rear base and its environ that the people and the people's army would have created a new culture commensurate with the evolving means and relation of social production. It would have been here that people created a new culture across ethnic lines in terms of language, theatre, dance, song, and poetry, entailing whole national heritage and forging national unity of the southern Sudanese people. The rear base would also have military functions of recruitment, recreation for the combatants returning from the front and treatment of the casualties. In this rear base the combatants would eschew their outlaw mentality and begin to operate like normal citizens simply because they are in control.

The SPLM/A did not perform as it should have, and this requires investigation and explanation. It is possible that the Derg, on account of huge investment it committed to the SPLM/A in form of training, armaments, and uniforms, wanted to keep a grip on its activities and development inside Ethiopia. In fact, the presence of SPLA and others counted as refugees was a source of foreign exchange to the Ethiopian economy. Most of the supplies to the refugees who numbers were controlled by the government institution rather than the UNHCR made it easy to inflate. Thus, the idea of trekking the recruits all the way to western Ethiopia was not for lack secure bases inside southern Sudan. The government of Sudan had its presence only in certain towns; while the rural areas was open to the insurgency to traverse at will.

The placement of SPLA training centres in western Ethiopia was to serve Dr. John Garang two important purposes: first, his concern for personal safety and security. Dr. Garang was very careful about his security and would not travel places until there was sufficient escort. He also liked comfort and has never moved on foot since becoming the leader in July 1983. And secondly, being inside the Ethiopian territory made it easy to meet Col. Mengistu Haile Mariam to secure him military logistics and air transport. The benevolence of the Ethiopians was the SPLM/A weakest point, and this created the undesired dependency syndrome. The presence of SPLA rear bases in western Ethiopia therefore had economic and security dimensions which could not be ignored without the risks of negative ramifications; they ran against the principles of self-reliance in national liberation though.

In the context of superpower rivalry in the Horn of Africa, I have the feeling that Ethiopia's enemies must have planted the SPLM/A to quickly deplete its meagre national resources such that Ethiopia could kneel to the insurrection in the north. The feeling stems from the hypothesis above that Mengistu could have been fighting three wars: one in Eritrea, the other in Tigray and a third one in Southern Sudan on account that the SPLA got its military logistics from Mengistu's military stores. Col. Mengistu fled Addis Ababa on 21st May 1991, and the SPLM/A withdrew into southern Sudan while its leadership relocated to Kenya. It was a case of hitting two enemies with one stone. But one was not an enemy; it was essentially being used to bring down the real ideological enemy.

Mengistu's Ethiopia did the logical thing in its relation with the SPLM/A although that action militated against the important concept of 'rear bases' in revolutionary warfare. It distorted the SPLA nature as an insurgency, and a national liberation. The Ethiopian Derg helped build the SPLA into a formidable force but made the international community to foot the bill. Between 1984 and 1990, refugee camps were established in Assossa (Blue Nile), Itang (southern Sudanese and Nuba), Piny-udo (Jonglei and Bahr el Ghazal), Dimma (Upper Nile, Bahr el Ghazal and Equatoria) and Rahad to welcome recruits and children (ages between eight and eleven years) forcefully taken away from their parents. They registered as refugees and provided for by the UNHCR, UNICEF and the Red Cross. They were not refugees in the real sense; they were in transit to the SPLA training centres.

Free external resources could be addictive particularly for people with low or no cultural inhabitation to reception of free things; they did not see anything wrong with receiving, if anything, it was perceived as a right particularly among certain communities whose traditions and cultural mores promote such practices. This perception might have formed the background for the SPLM/A leadership to accept the tripartite agreement *vide* which the United Nations Operation Lifeline Sudan (UN/OLS) coinciding with the shift of its logistical base to Lokichogio in Kenya. By 2005, there were three hundred and twenty (320) relief air strips under the aegis of the UN/OLS, a multi-billion humanitarian business managed from Nairobi Kenya. The amazing paradox of the international humanitarian intervention in southern Sudan, as we shall see in chapter four, was that it was a blanket intervention covering even areas where people could provide for themselves.

The war of national liberation was supposed to be a dual process; the process of defeating an oppressive regime militarily and transforming the people's means and relations of production leading to transformation of their lives, their attitudes and behaviours. The liberation process presumably starts with building a strong synergy between the people and the liberation army leading to emergence of a counter society in the areas under the control of the liberation army. This would be social, economic, and political system completely different from the system under the oppressive system. As Mao Zedong once said, "war and in particular war of national liberation is developmental", indeed in executing the liberation dual processes, the SPLM would not be only fighting the enemy but would also be creating conditions for the development of people's productive forces – all elements involved in the productive actives to transform their lives for the better.

The SPLM/A leadership unfortunately fell short of this cardinal principle of liberation. As a result, the people in southern Sudan, Nuba Mountains, and southern Blue Nile were forced into relief aid dependency instead of relying on their efforts. The attack on Yambio epitomises the link between militarism and reliance on external resources., it did not dawn on the SPLM/A leaders, cadres and combatants that the war of national liberation meant freeing people's intellectual and physical energies to transform the reality that surrounded them and their lives in freedom, justice and fraternity. Many combatants treated the process like rescuing people from a burning house; the people had to do nothing but just wait to be taken out of the conflagration. This attitude explained how in a stealthy manner the SPLA contingent arrived Yambio without the Azande people having knowledge of their movement or participation in their own liberation. It meant the SPLM/A did not want their participation; the Azande people had to be 'liberated'. But this is false; no one liberates another or is anybody the other's liberator. People liberate themselves or rather participate in their own liberation, and any person who says, has liberated the other is a liar or is parading his ignorance of the concept of liberation. It underscored combatants' lack of political consciousness, which pervaded their relations with the civil population wherever in the war zones they set foot. This attitude prompted the establishment of the military-civil administration in the so-called liberated areas, just in the same way the British colonial administration initially deployed military instead of civil personnel to brutally pacify the people. In the same manner the SPLA brutalized the civil population particularly if those soldiers did not hail from the area or if the people didn't put resistance to such treatments. It was a process contrary to the customary meaning of liberation as would be perceived by political scientists.

6.2. Militarism and Robotization of the SPLA Combatant

The second critical factor that inadvertently led the SPLM/A into the political compromise with the National Islamic Front government was militarism in the SPLM/A. Militarism essentially is what military action degenerates into when executed outside the context of its ideological purpose. Stated in another way, when the SPLM/A leadership evolved and promoted vertical authoritarianism in the liberation movement, and dissociated the political from the military functions, it was indeed mutilating both and with them the liberation movement.

Militarism in the SPLM/A was meant to subvert revolutionary consciousness in the combatants and also among the masses of the people with the intention to tie them down to their indigenous traditional concepts and beliefs. The dominance of traditional beliefs in movement in turn subverted and trumped the emergence of patriotic nationalism envisioned and envisaged in the concept and vision of the 'New Sudan'. It was a complete recoil to the starting point. It was rather a negative confirmation that the masses who create history will not be stirred into action, unless their hearts are stirred by some basic image or feeling rooted deeply in their past. In this respect, it was a struggle to separate from the Arab-dominated northern Sudan, for the simple reason that national liberation was contextualized only in Southern Sudan

The notion of self-determination for the people of southern Sudan, which preoccupied the SPLM/A leadership in the last three years of the war, did not come from the blue skies. It was definitely linked to the initial idea engineered to prevent from merging and dovetailing the two parallel processes in the two parts of the Sudan: SPLM/A insurrection in Southern Sudan and mass political and democratic movement in northern Sudan. The platform for common action would be political, but since the SPLM/A subverted political work among its members it meant separate and parallel development of the two processes, which instead of touching and enriching were cancelling each other. The intention therefore was to make SPLM/A the vehicle to separate and govern 'southern Sudan' from the rest of the Sudan. This idea would have landed Dr. John Garang in direct problem with Col. Mengistu Haile Mariam the SPLM/A benefactor. It was therefore necessary to conceal the secessionist content and the power project, which concerned only Southern Sudan. Hence, Dr. John Garang had to undertake ideological and political circumlocution in the form of the New Sudan and other innuendos to continue access to the Derg's logistical support.

This circumlocution included the apparent initial lukewarm concern for the proxy war the Arab Baggara *muraliheen* (Misseriya and Rezeighat) fought against the Dinka in northern Bahr el Ghazal. On this account Dr. Garang ignored the devastation caused in northern Bahr el Ghazal lest it exposed his real intentions about Southern Sudan. Dr. Garang publicly acknowledged very lately the right of the people of southern Sudan to self-determination, and only after the Derg had been defeated in Ethiopia, and the SPLM/A had long shifted its operational base to Kenyan borders. It was a convenient and his clever way to abandon the concept and vision of the 'New Sudan', which indeed was only a bait to attract into the Nuba and the Funj people; it was not the ultimate political objective. Nobody dared to question the political and ideological shifts Dr. John Garang beat and proves the efficacy of militarism or robotization of the combatants. In this respect, there is therefore a direct connection between militarization or militarism in the SPLM/A and the political compromise.

This political compromise, coming twenty-one years of war of national liberation, was not a result of SPLM/A having achieved its political objective in form of creating conditions for the transformation of the Sudanese polity to construct the New Sudan; was not also a result of military stalemate between its forces and the Islamists forces. No. it was a political compromise dictated by external and foreign interests. The political and ideological subversion in the movement and promotion of militarism rendered it possible for Dr. John Garang to change track without the risk of political opposition or rebellion. Militarism had indeed turned the SPLA combatant into a robot.

The explanation is simple. If the whole idea of SPLM/A formation was to separate southern Sudan from the rest of the country, Dr. John Garang did not have to fight to the last man. He had already made the point and could achieve the rest through political and diplomatic skills. That was how the donors pushed the idea of negotiation by principals: Dr. John Garang and Ustaz Ali Osman Mohammed Tah to take over the negotiation of the most sensitive parts of the agreement. In this respect, the connection between the political compromise and militarism in the SPLM/A kicks-in the following manner that militarism meant conducting the negotiations, like in the war, without the active participation of the masses. In twenty-one years fighting conventional and semi-conventional warfare the SPLM/A had exhausted its foreign supporters and could no longer continue with the war without further support; it had to make peace with the enemy. The SPLM/A leadership had efficaciously subverted not only the revolution but also its vision of the New Sudan leaving as orphans the Nuba and the Funj, while the Southern Sudanese knew eventually got what they wanted. The political compromise was therefore necessary to facilitate the treacherous exit from the concept and vision of 'New Sudan'.

6.3. The Evolution an Elitist Officer Class

The third critical factor in the political compromise was the emergence of an elitist group within the SPLM/A top political and military leadership. The split occasioned by the Nasir Declaration and internecine fighting that followed within the SPLA has had profound impact on the combatants and many had left for the refugee camps in Kenya and Uganda or migrated to USA, Australia and Europe. However, some remained in the internally displaced people's camps in Equatoria. The operations to liberate Central Equatoria in 1997 was undertaken with the heavy support of foreign troops and artillery fire. It was a clear indication war fatigue had set in among the SPLA officers and combatants alike, but the truth was that many senior officers had registered and established businesses in Uganda and Kenya in the name of the army and were engaged in money making. It was in this context that some senior SPLA officers deployed whether in the H/Qs or in the front lost interest and war stalled.

Militarism in the SPLM/A produced an elitist class completely isolated from, and whose social, economic, and political interests don't align with, the masses of the people; it was a class interested in primitive accumulation of wealth than taking the liberation to its logical conclusion. Thus, by 2002, the war of liberation had virtually grinded down to only isolated sparks. It was not accidental; during the dying days of the war, the SPLM/A leaders, and cadres, particularly the senior officer corps, tended to see themselves as separate and independent of the poor peasants, who made up the bulk of the SPLA and the masses in the villages and cattle camps. They stuck or rigidly dedicated themselves to militarism as the only means to protect their privileges in the movement.

This triggered the competition for wealth and its accumulation through coercion and extortion taking different forms and dimensions. The most common was herding of cattle to marry many wives. In a SPLA division for instance, the commanding officer would just apportion for himself part of the herds contributed by the community as rations for the SPLA contingent. In other instances, the SPLA officer took over the function of the traditional court president or the paramount chief to settle traditional cases and pocket the taxes and fines. In some places, the SPLA commanders erected roadblocks and extorted taxes from passing vehicles or individuals walking on foot or at the relief airstrips to collecting landing fees from the relief planes. In a more audacious way between Nimule and Aweil town there could be as much as four hundred roadblocks or checkpoints in which the truck drivers and traders had to pay lest their trucks were impounded for a very long time[17]. The paradox is that the money didn't go to government treasury.

Many of these illegal practices were known and were reported at the highest level of the SPLA GH/Qs but nothing was done to restore legality. Perhaps, those at the GH/Qs were themselves also involved in looting and therefore kept their peace by not reporting the matter. That Dr. John Garang kept those commanders posted to continue the loot wasn't surprising; it was deliberate, not only to prevent them from rebelling but to also for them to develop an appetite for wealth and in that become endeared to him. It was when the practice reached embarrassing proportions in the form of slave redemption project did Garang intervene but also inadvertently generated a contradiction that threatened a rebellion in northern Bahr el Ghazal. The impact of such practices would only be felt immediately after the end of the war in the form of resistance to reform or transformation of the SPLM/A into its different professional spheres these generals put up.

The demise of Dr. John Garang aborted the reform process he started as soon as he took oath office. Alas, the wasted time, those reforms should have started immediately in 1988 after ridding himself of both Kerubino and Arok Thon. On taking over the mantle of authority, President Salva Kiir surrounded himself with the same looters and undisciplined commanders who then continued to behave as if they were the law to themselves. They helped themselves to any public utility, occupied government departments as director, directors-general, or even under-secretaries without the necessary qualification or expertise. It was worst in the army, where commanders would refuse to pay their soldiers.

For the first time in the history of the Sudan accounting officials in government departments and in the army harboured and inserted fictious name into pay-lists with the intention to pocket their salaries. As corruption and abuse of power increased so did the public services and utilities deteriorate and indeed became dysfunctional. The former revolutionaries who at the beginning of the war executed their comrades for petty crimes now settled down to self-aggrandisement and wealth making, and forgot about the promise they had made to the people during the war. They forgot about their disabled comrades or widows and orphans of their fallen comrades as they stampeded to quench their thirst and hunger. The oil money was there to line their pockets. In a ceremony to honour the war heroes on 13th of September 2019, Cdr. Kuol Manyang Juuk, the Minister of Defence and Veteran Affairs said its succinctly.

> *[T]his ceremony to honour and decorate the war heroes and heroines should have been down earlier, and not in this manner where there is nothing to accompany the medals. Let me be honest with you, we forgot. When we arrived Juba in 2005, we were hungry and thirsty but found there was a lot of money and we sat down to*

eat and drink, and when one got satisfied, we started to throw back, even without seeing what one was throwing back to our immediate relatives. That was how we forgot. I am sorry that it happened like that."

These words, said without remorse or guilt, were not meant as an apology but only demonstrate to the audience that there was nothing they could do; the abuse of power would continue unabated. The liberation leaders' lack of care and indifference to the people was staggering.

For instance, when the war ended and the leaders of the national liberation movement set foot in Juba, Malakal and Wau, they found such public utilities like land line telephones, tap water and electricity still functional, but no sooner and with bad management these utilities deteriorated and completely failed. Juba, for instance, became a 'generators' city', may be a noise city because the electric generators produced more noise than electric power. It would be interesting to ask who imported the generators and the answer would be obvious. The water taps dried up, and in their place came the water tankers driven by Ethiopian and Eritreans but ownership belonged to the SPLA generals and others[18]. The Gem-Tel and Viva-Cell initially were GOSS investments approved by the Southern Sudan Legislative Assembly (SSLA) but nobody could speak with certainty how these investments were privatized to be owned by some SPLM politicians or to explain how they were sold to foreign investors. The truth got lost in the leaders' verbal skirmishes and personal wrestling for ownership and control leading to the cancellation of their licences.

7. Liberal Multi-Party Democracy and the Parasitic Capitalist Class at the Helm

When a social political force takes to arms to pursue revolutionary transformation of society as the SPLM/A announced in its manifesto, seldom does that force voluntarily acquiesce to demands recoil to sharing power in a liberal democratic setting. This occurs under strenuously difficult conditions as that imposed by USA on the Sandinistas in Nicaragua (Dolack, 2018). The essence of the war of national liberation in an unindustrialized poor country but potentially rich in natural resources like South Sudan is to capture power and develop these resources to transform the conditions of poverty, ignorance, and cultural backwardness of the people. The task, therefore, of any revolutionary national liberation movement is to launch the national democratic revolution to capture power and construct a national democratic developmental state; trigger the agrarian reform or revolution in agriculture, in education and the cultural revolution. The Tigray People's Liberation Front, as soon as it captured power in Addis Ababa, embarked on the construction of the national democratic developmental state in Ethiopia, freed the productive forces of the Ethiopian people and put the country on an industrialization trajectory.

Unlike the TPLF, the SPLM/A organized politics along community and ethnic lines rather than on the basis of political parties, and organized economics on the basis of liberal and free market as dictated by the Bretton Woods Institutions. The result was that South Sudan is now a liberal multiparty democracy in politics and liberal policies and free market in economics. This was a radical departure from the path of national democratic revolution and was consequent to political and ideological shifts the SPLM/A leaders beat since 1990. It disqualified he SPLM/A as a section of the nation democratic revolution in the Sudan or in the Horn of Africa.

This was not only a complete negation of the principles on which the SPLM/A leaders prosecuted the war of national liberation, but also a betrayal of the national democratic revolution of which the SPLM/A purported to be a section and, on that basis, received political, material and moral support from Ethiopia, Cuba[19], Libya, Yemen, Zimbabwe and other countries and liberation movements in the regions.

Since it's then obvious the SPLM/A was not a section of the national democratic revolutionary forces in the region, and there was no sharp ideological difference between it and the regime in the Sudan, the political and ideological shifts its leaders beat in the course of the war were necessary to prepare the ground for the SPLM/A leader to seal the political compromise with the Islamist regime in Khartoum. It was not clear how it would have played out had Dr. Garang not perished in the helicopter crash, but for Salva Kiir, at the helm of the SPLM and the government of Southern Sudan, it was predictable. He never demonstrated any socialist or revolutionary democratic credentials, if anything Salva Kiir remained a rural Dinka man with no urban sophistication, and therefore was likely to be attracted to conservative ideas on managing the state.

It is important at this point to recall the notion of robotization of the SPLM/A combatant as a prelude to render impossible any internal resistance or dissidence. It enabled the leader to make unpopular decisions without the risk of triggering internal opposition. Indeed, robotization in the SPLM/A engendered the subculture of fear, self-insurance, indifference and lack of solidarity among comrades. For instance, something outrageously wrong or bad could happen and nobody dare speak, each keeping own peace against any backlash. Thus, President Salva Kiir got free sway over every nitty-gritty of the party, government and state; the corruption and abuse of power that was practiced in the liberation movement transferred to the government and the state institutions. Moreover, the political compromise or the comprehensive peace agreement (CPA) landed both the SPLM and NCP leaders into the same boat of power-sharing. The NCP was managing its own corrupt regime and the CPA brought the political elites on the two sides one-country-two-systems regime quickly merged into one interest class. In South Sudan, the SPLM political and military elite, former NCP functionaries, business, and commercial elite now evolved into a parasitic capitalist class at the helm of South Sudan political and economic power.

The class is parasitic because it doesn't control any means of production but its elements accumulated their wealth respectively from relations to the state as ministers, legislators, justices, generals in the army, police, and national security, and senior bureaucrats in the state machinery, and business cartels in the market. They did this in collaboration with regional and international comprador capitalists in the context of extraction and plunder of South Sudan's natural resources: hydrocarbons, livestock, forestry plantations, minerals, fisheries, and wildlife. This class erected a totalitarian dictatorship buttressed by NCP styled brutal and ruthless national security services ready at hand to suppress any dissent.

The Transitional Constitution of South Sudan 2011 provides for a multi-party democratic dispensation. But in practice, Salva Kiir erected a totalitarian dictatorship and shrunk the political space considerably as it implemented the liberal and free market economy policies under the tutelage of the World Bank and the IMF. Under this liberal regime the SPLM-led government of South Sudan withdrew completely from social and economic development of South Sudan leaving it to market forces. It had the opportunity to at least utilize the oil revenue money in the construction of the Fula hydroelectric power plant whose feasibility studies was undertaken by the Southern Region's government in the seventies of the last century. The government of South Sudan was duty bound to construct roads and highways, lay railway lines, which like the hydroelectric power plant no capitalist could put money into such long-term investments in a country that is politically unstable. Investment in long term development plans that positively affect the lives of the masses could only be undertaken by the national democratic development state.

The SPLM-led government has also completely withdrawn

fron provision of social services in education, healthcare, agricultural and veterinary extension services leaving them to the market forces with profound ramifications for quality and standards particularly in the absence of government supervision and control.[20] It is so paradoxical because those in control of the market sent their children to schools in Kenya and Uganda, travel abroad for medical attention. This parasitic capitalist class has turned South Sudan into a shadow state, which according to William Reno defines as 'an informal network of domestic and international actors, any of who are not operating in their official capacity but collude to wield political, social and economic authority to their own benefits.'[21] The dubious transactions were visible more particularly in the oil industry where shiploads of crude oil officially reported missing were in fact awarded to certain individuals in the establishment. From the preceding lines it would appear that the SPLM led government had embarked on building capitalism, but it must first manufacture the local capitalists -the parasitic capitalist class.

The revolution of despair and fear, the subtitle of this chapter, might have been a little bit too harsh a description of the SPLM/A, but for those who have lived the experience, this categorization fitted perfectly during and after the war of national liberation. First, there was this scenario in which the defenders of Numeiri's oppressive regime were the first to arrive at the insurgency. It was psychologically atrophying for some political activist who have been in Numeiri jails to arrive to find that at the top of the SPLM/A hierarchy the same intelligence officers who tortured them in the Sudan. Not only did they enthusiastically carry out Numeiri's orders to suppress dissent but were also still driven by the same attitude of ethnic arrogance. Despair and fear overwhelmed many progressive intellectuals and political activists who in the Sudan had struggled against Numeiri's dictatorship and who believed joining the SPLM/A was their natural abode, but sooner than later to discover that there had not been a break in the oppressive system. The one in the bush was exactly an extension of that in the Sudan.

There was a draw back; For the revolutionary democrats in the SPLM/A it became difficult to pursue the same strategies and tactics to counter the political right and other reactionary forces through ideological struggle. It exposed them to extreme danger. Dr. John Garang, the chairman and c-in-c was not disposed to this kind of political and ideological activity. It was also possible he didn't understand the meaning of ideological struggle in the movement. He dealt with his detractors administratively rather than ideologically, which indeed ended in total inimical, if not, volatile separation. Moreover Garang, weary and apprehensive of the political right, did not want any confrontation whatsoever while they were still in numerical strength. They really posed a threat to his leadership.

In such a situation, while Mengistu still supported him, Garang could have resolved the contradiction with the political right by organization and institutionalization of the liberation movement to build structures and instruments of public authority with clearly defined democratic principles. Instead,

Garang chose to play the tactics of deceptive weakness and fear which enabled him to manoeuvre these leaders out of power. Understandably, Garang was also afraid of the political left which made him operate in a state of intense fear relying on very few trusted lieutenants. It's a question of life or death in the liberation movement; death that easily could come from comrades than from the enemy. Therefore, self-insurance to cover one's back whether in the war front or in the refugee camps became the pre-occupation of many combatants and cadres alike. This self-insurance against intrigues, lies, gossips, false framing, blocking, or double-crossing and outright elimination by colleagues did not inspire trust or confidence and prevented the evolution of solidarity and spirit of genuine comradeship. In this configuration of things, comrades subverted instead of offering supportive assistance to each other; this sometimes included sabotaging strategic and tactical operational orders relating to military action against the enemy, and which passed without investigation. This behaviour among comrades translated into cutthroat competition to win the confidence of the leader for promotion; and in this they tried to outdo each other in flattery, bootlicking, gossips, etc., as ranks, promotions, and hierarchies suddenly became a important factor in the relations.

It was not an overstatement that the SPLM/A leaders, cadres, and commanders were not very friendly with each other, and apparently this was engineered and promoted for a purpose to maintain what in classical mechanics is called 'unstable equilibrium'[22] in which sense the same relations that existed between the comrades can't be sustained once spoiled by some suspicious encounter. This served Dr John Garang well that his close lieutenants were perpetually suspicion of each other; it prevented them from colluding and conspiring to hurt him or his power. This was the kind of relation Dr. John Garang maintained in the movement with Kerubino Kuanyin, William Nyuon, and Arok Thon, until he had them arrested and detained, or as in the case of William Nyuon, provoked him into rebellion. But finally, this strategy did not even spare Cdr. Salva Kiir Mayardit. It precipitated the Yei crisis just on the eve of signing the CPA, Salva Kiir reacted violently forcing Dr. Garang to pull back.

The sudden demise of Dr. John Garang ushered into power Cdr. Salva Kiir still disoriented, angry and bitter. Garang had unceremoniously and without clear explanation removed him from the hierarchies of the two branches of the liberation movement; he had no position or office in the SPLM and was not in the command of the SPLA. Garang's order to transform and separate the national liberation movement into its professional domains on the start of GOSS had caused serious consternation in the SPLM/A ranks and heightened the level of frustration and bitterness among those officers negatively affected. It could have been worse had Garang survived the tragic helicopter crash; the writings on the walls indicated some SPLA units were ready to rebel against the transformation. This would have replicated the mutinies in the Anya-nya units following the Addis Ababa Agreement but this time it would have been the NCP leadership and SAF military intelligence driving the rebellion with the support of the Nuer tribal militia of Paulino Matip Nhial with the intention to reverse or obstruct the CPA implementation[23]. The immediate post-Garang period was the most critical time for the liberation movement, the people of Southern Sudan and Cdr. Salva Kiir's stewardship of the SPLM/A ship abandoned with neither a compass nor a political radar. The shock of loss of the leader was profound, but the SPLM internal political situation was also dangerously confused and pulled in many directions by power ambitions.

The SPLM/A had not fully absorbed and internalized the hastily prepared programme of war to peace transition; precisely because the bureaucratic instruments for implementing this programme were not there. It was also obvious that Cdr. Salva Kiir was not in the loop when the SPLM team working like a civil society organization prepared the document as if it were a military secret. This was the negativities of militarism and the refusal to institutionalize the movement playing out ruthlessly in vengeance. As it would always be in a situation of no system, the contradictions generated by this confusion were profound, most of the leaders including Salva Kiir were used to Garang working habits, whereby he undertook all the mental and intellectual work, leaving all others to perform the errand functions. This new situation demanded more intellectual gymnastics of thinking, strategizing, planning and action, which meant long hours of meetings and consultations.

If there is any one thing that would peel off 'revolutionary' cloak from the SPLM/A, it is 'corruption' in government and society that invaded the moral and ethical foundations of the SPLM. It is a truism that corruption started during the war, however, it became rampant after the CPA and the formation of GOSS in 2005 until corruption became synonymous with 'right' or 'normal'. There is no time President Salva Kiir would speak to the nation without mentioning his 'zero tolerance to corruption', nonetheless there has never been conviction of corruption cases brought up in the annual reports of the Auditor General. It was through corruption that the SPLM/A political and military elites submerged and disappeared into parasitic capitalist class at the helm of the political and economic power of South Sudan.

8. The SPLM/A was Just a 'Power' Project

The popular anecdote in the Sudan in the wake of Numeiri's ideological shift to the counterrevolution was that he indicated to the left but turn the revolution's car to the right. Many political parties and movements whether civilian or military the world over started as political left but in the course of time change their political orientation; only few parties or movements have remained consistent with their original ideological objective. The Sudan People's Liberation Movement/Army was not exception. It had been discussed since its inception and the stages it went through until the consummation of the comprehensive peace agreement. There were indeed discernible qualitative changes in the nature of the movement that would be used as a yardstick to measure its progress towards achieving its strategic political objective. Read from its manifesto, the strategic political objective of the SPLM/A was the destruction of the 'Old' Sudan and the creation of the 'New' Sudan. It would be against this objective that the SPLM/A and its leadership could be judged to have realized in its twenty-one years of war of liberation.

We have established clearly that the SPLM/A, the revolutionary armed struggle, was Garang's brainchild and has remained so after his death. Dr. John Garang generated the idea; but as an idea it could have become the collective property of the people of the Sudan and therefore would cease to belong to Garang as an individual. At the beginning, that's if the SPLM/A had started normally as insurrections started, the people would have owned and internalize the idea through a process of ingestion and political mobilization in anticipation of condition conducive for the launch of the idea, either in the form of a political party or a military insurrection. It appeared that Dr. John Garang kept the idea to himself until the political situation in the Southern Region imploded, and other political and armed movements sprouted onto the political stage.

The problem that immediately followed Dr. Garang's initial refusal to own the people his idea was that he could not accept any other person to lead or share in the leadership of the nascent movement. In retrospect, Dr. John Garang made use of his knowledge of military counterinsurgency - trigger contradictions the resolution of which would eventually leave him in the centre to control the process. Thus, the conflict with Anya-nya2 over the strategic political objective was resolved violently to his advantage by raising the socialist and unity of Sudan slogans. This victory over the Anya-any2 strengthened DR. John Garang's grip on power over the veteran politicians and successfully subordinated the SPLM/A political power to its military authority. This action was a textbook application of Mao's dictum that political power comes from the barrel of the gun; whoever commanded the army controlled the political power of the liberation movement. A question that would arise was whether it's people's or personal power; for the two power categories organized differently being at cross purposes.

The refusal to organize and build political institutions in the liberation movement reflected Garang's egocentrism and power ambition. It was a means of denying the existence of SPLM as a political entity and also a way of denying the veteran politicians' participation in the liberation process unless they enrolled as SPLA combatants and in that respect would give him opportunity to deal or interact with them vide military discipline, commands and instantaneous obedience.

Dr. John Garang did not refute my assertion that the SPLM did not exist because it would raise the obvious questions. The attitude of reducing political work in the liberation movement to the leader's public relation tool was adopted by some leaders of national liberation movements in the region particularly those who reached revolutionary standpoints and attitudes through purely intellectual ways. In their journey to revolutionary positions, they carried with them the germs of petty-bourgeoisie spirit, ethnic chauvinism, and egocentrism. The dominant logic was militarize and promote militarism to buttress the cult of personality and suppression of human sensitivity. It's in this way that the SPLM/A – the revolutionary armed struggle, morphed from a national liberation movement – Garang's brainchild, to a 'power project' for governing not the Sudan or New Sudan but Southern Sudan.

Unlike the concept and vision of the New Sudan, the SPLM/A as a power project would only be personal and short term. Therefore, the political compromise with the NCP was to buy Garang time to actuate this power project. It led to jettisoning the idea of united socialist Sudan because socialism would be at odds with his petty bourgeoisie class origin. The political compromise accelerated the recovery of his social reality. In the words of Regis Debray, the revolutionary wheel had gone full circle to its original position. The wheel had gone full circle is both literal and metaphorical and it wasn't unexpected only that the political and ideological shift left an indelible legacy. It will be such an impossible task for the people of South Sudan to extricate themselves from this legacy – the liberation falsehood, which like the scars on the face of smallpox survivor will remain to remind us of the SPLM/A war of national liberation. South Sudan is an independent country, which is the very incarnation of the Sudan from which it seceded in terms of the system of political patronage based primeval ethnic idiosyncrasies. There is a government, a corrupt brutal ethnic based government run in the sovereign name of the people of South Sudan. The head of Dr. John Garang de Mabior is on the money, the value of which is less than the paper it is printed on, it also hangs in every office in South Sudan and its embassies abroad along sides that of President Salva Kiir Mayardit. This juxtaposition doesn't in anyway indicate glorification of Dr. John Garang, but Kiir finds it impossible to undo the falsehood. The false historical narrative has ossified and calcified in the minds of the ordinary folks and like a religious belief is likely to endure into posterity.

Unlike in the early days of the national liberation movement, when the SPLA was preponderant than the SPLM, the SPLA has imperceptibly disappeared; it has transformed into the South Sudan People's Defence Force. The SPLM is nothing more than but a caricature of its war time effigy heavily infiltrated by former NCP functionaries and other political defectors, it now serves as a medium for political renting. The SPLM/A was not a national liberation movement; it was a power project. In this respect, the project died with its author. The reason is simple; Garang died before he could complete the SPLM/A transformation. This triggered serious internal political contradiction and power struggle, which two years into the independence and birth of the republic of South Sudan culminated in a civil war and an unending transition from war to peace.

9. A Requiem for the SPLM?

May 16th 2023 will mark the fortieth anniversary of the battle of Bor. This violent event heralded the formation of the SPLM/A, and the beginning of the revolutionary armed struggle. It's a day that every South Sudanese annually celebrated until the political establishment stopped celebrating the day because of regime's dissidents in the person of the Red Card Movement (RCM) and the People's Coalition for Civic Action (PCA) emerged demystify and delegitimize Kiir's regime and to expose SPLM's misrule of South Sudan. It would be ironical if the fortieth anniversary passed without the leaders' usual self-gratification and chest-thumbing about the invisible achievements in the country. However, it's not certain whether the ceremony to mark this day would be celebrations or a requiem for the soul of the liberation movement.

A requiem for the soul of SPLM would be a preferable fete. The SPLM as a political organization never existed separately from its military alloy. A requiem will finally lay to rest the two falsehoods that were the 'national liberation' and the 'liberation movement'. For sure, there was no 'national liberation' in the true meaning of the words. The SPLA, to which the 'M' was added to give semblance of political existence, fought the war. This was essentially shooting, killing enemy soldiers and capturing territories. But the SPLA didn't engage in the process that could have enabled the masses of the people to liberate and extricate themselves from poverty, ignorance, and superstition that for a long time submerged their consciousness. This would have been the function of the movement involving political education and ideological training of the combatants and the people to raise their social awareness and political consciousness to change people's attitudes and to enable a correct perception of reality.

But, the SPLM/A as we mentioned earlier didn't permit political enlightenment or organization meant that the combatants didn't transform into revolutionaries, and the war didn't become a people's war involving all sections of the peasantry in the rural areas and urban dwellers. This could be gleaned from the current context of South Sudan. It is unbelievable that after twenty-one years of common struggle the people who once considered and treated themselves as comrades in arms were now enemies fighting each other and have plunged the nascent state into political avalanche. The masses have recoiled back into their respective sociocultural configurations. At no time in contemporary history have the people of South Sudan been fragmented along ethnic, sectional or regional fault lines. It's a clear testimony to the fact that the people of South Sudan became independent and have a country but national liberation didn't place. The surge of ethnic nationalism completely uprooted the South Sudan national consciousness that the liberation rhetoric engendered during the war.

The national liberation myths might have sustained had the author lived. However, immediately after his death, Garang's enemies, mostly right-wing politicians, went on to urge and encourage President Salva Kiir Mayardit to dismantle the SPLM and to form own political outfit; that would become his legacy. They perceived the SPLM/A, and rightly so, as Dr. John Garang's edifice and that Salva Kiir should build his own edifice. This became a tricky issue for Salva Kiir. To dismantle the SPLM meant dismantling his authority and delegitimizing himself; Kiir would countenance that risk. He therefore developed cold-feet on the matter preferring the use the SPLM internal contradictions and power struggle at the top echelon to paralyze the party and retards its political and organizational development into a political party. As president of the republic and as SPLM chairman Salva Kiir operated the two authorities as if they were one and the same institution, sometimes without reference the SPLM Secretary General or the SPLM National Secretariat. The formation of the Jieng (Dinka) Council of Elders (JCE) accelerated the demystification of the liberation movement and power shifted imperceptibly from the SPLM to the JCE via the office of the President Salva Kiir Mayardit.

How was it that the notion of the SPLM sustained and people clamour to be members although it was known that it did not exist as a political entity with a constitution, regulations and a political programme. This could have been permissible before the CPA, but not after the SPLM leaders took over the reign of power in Southern Sudan; it was then difficult to access inner confidential information about the SPLM/A and its internal political configuration. People flocked into the SPLM/A after the formation of GOSS for the simple reason and explanation that many of them were political rent seekers. Some left their membership of NCP, USAP, PPP and other *tawali* parties to join the SPLM because it provided opportunity for employment, power and wealth.

It was convenient for President Salva Kiir to paralyse the political functions of the SPLM than to dismantle it as was demanded by the JCE politicians. In its twenty-one years of war, the combatants and the masses of the people have not trained to the culture of political organization and activism. The few activists in the movement and many others who enlisted after the CPA became disillusioned due to the phenomenon of ethnicity, instead of SPLM party affiliation and membership, becoming the criteria for appointment in the national, GOSS, and State constitutional positions. Some NCP activists and political operatives found themselves in senior position in the government representing the SPLM on account their ethnicity. It is worth mentioning that in some areas the people didn't care much about political or ideological issues; they therefore chose on the basis of social relations,

The notion of ethnicity or community-based representation in government instead of political affiliation or membership entrenched the creation of ethnic or community-based lobby groups, councils of elders, and student ethnic and community associations in the universities and schools leaving the SPLM as an empty façade to smokescreen these political patronage networks that sprouted around Kiir's leadership. This coincided with the complete breakdown of law and order in the regions, and the surge in ethnic nationalism creating another dimension that completely erased the social capital that united the people in the struggle for national liberation.

What appears as the death of the SPLM is the logical consequence of subversion of political and ideological preoccupation in the liberation movement. It has been hallowed of its original ideological content as a national liberation movement and ethnic nationalism invaded to occupy the resultant ideological void. This has raised the danger of ethnicities or communities breaking up into autochthonous groups. The creation of Pibor and Ruweng as independent administrative areas ostensibly to protect the Murle from Dinka Bor and Lou Nuer on the one hand and the Ruweng Dinka from western Nuer is a pointer to promotion of ethnic autochthony. It's a dangerous development given the weak nature of South Sudan state.

The falsehoods and myths of national liberation, and the SPLM itself as a vacuous political outfit attracting new members notwithstanding its lack of a political programme might endure and survive beyond its current leadership. This is because of its linkage to the South Sudan state as the main source of power and wealth. The IGAD peace making process, as we shall see in the coming chapter, forced the SPLM into a coalition with some small parties at a very high price at its expense. The survival of its leaders is now dependent continued support of these parties, and who without the SPLM could exist because they would be out of government.

The coalition comprising elements of the burgeoning parasitic capitalist class has now erected a totalitarian dictatorship buttressed by the national security apparatus. In this configuration, the government of South Sudan has ceased to be SPLM-led coalition but an amalgam of these parties united by common social, economic and political interest in the extraction and plunder of South Sudan natural resources.

In summary and conclusion of this chapter on the SPLM/A, it was fair to say it's a revolution of fear and despair. At the end of the war, only Southern Sudan political elite benefited out of the political compromise; the rest of Sudanese got a raw deal, and this explains why the war rekindled in the Nuba Mountains and Southern Blue Nile. The twenty-one years of war did little to positively transform the lives of the people in Southern Sudan. As a result, it was easy for the people to recoil back into their sociocultural formations, and the nation-building process stalled. The SPLM/A political - military elite, the elements of the NCP and other Southern Sudan political parties formed into a parasitic capitalist class at the helm of an oppressive totalitarian dictatorship. The SPLM/A was engineered away from the concept of a genuine national liberation movement precisely because it was a power-project.

ENDNOTES

1. Southern Sudanese were generally noted for their secessionist tendency. The emergence of a nationalist movement is Southern Sudan notwithstanding its pronouncements was received and accepted with a pinch of salt in the Sudan even among the progressive Sudanese.

2. In most cases the world over a party electing to rebel and take up arms as its means of struggle establishes an armed wing that prosecutes the war. The SPLM was launched after the war has already erupted in southern Sudan and would constitute an anomaly.

3. The most spectacular were the disturbances in Battalion 116 (Juba) in March 1974 whereby the soldiers and NCOs arrested

their commanding officer, Lt. Col. Peter Cirilo; the Akobo crisis 1975 in which the mutineers executed their commanding officer Col. Abel Chol, a career soldier; and the Wau crisis 1976 in which Capt. Alfred Aguet secretly vanished into the bush with his soldiers, this led to murder of brigadier Emmanuel Abur

4. It was first time experience for many in southern Sudan that a political situation deteriorated to a point of armed explosion. Many were still very young when the mutiny in Torit occurred in August 1955. The implication were too great to comprehend or contemplate.

5. It appeared many government bureaucrats who went to join the SPLM/A were interested in military ranks and commands and therefore inflated and falsified the grades and titles including unbelievable stories about their ordeal travelling to join the ranks of the nascent movement.

6. In March 1983, Southern Sudan Liberation Front fought and capture Boma and taking hostage some Christian missionaries who were proselytizing the Murle (Nyalaam) and the Suri (Kachipo) in the Boma plateau. This was before the battle of Bor.

7. The Ethiopia army was then fighting wars in the north against the Eritrean People's Liberation Front (shaabiya) and the Tigray People's Liberation Front (wayene) both separatist movements.

8. Many people in southern Sudan had in their memories of the first civil war as the Sudan Army leaving their garrisons to track the Anya-nya in the bushes. The Anya-nya were poorly armed and therefore relied on ambushes. The SPLA had modern

automatic and heavy artillery pieces that they attacked the garrisons frontally and scored victories, which were broadcast on Radio SPLA or confirmed by BBC or other broadcasting service.

9. The Derg overthrew Emperor Haile Sellasie in 1974, and the SPLM/A formed in 1983, a difference of about eight years. However, within the period, the Derg had implemented to important programme of liberation of land from the feudal lords and distributed it to the peasants; it had also implemented alphabetization whereby literacy rate reached eighty (80) percent. Nevertheless, culturally the more than two thousand years feudal heritage and legacies were still visible in the attitudes and behaviour of the Ethiopians.

10. Those assigned to diplomatic functions were mere errand of the Chairman and were not permitted to get of the text given to them.

11. Some of these incidences were crazy and unbelievable. In Itang, a certain SPLA officer conducted a marriage party in his house and invited the member of High Command who happened to be in town, who obliged but after sometimes decided to leave and no sooner did his bodyguards come back to collect the bride to the chagrin of the bridegroom and everybody in the party.

12. A traditional institution of authority in Afghanistan convened in a situation of political vacuum. It was convened immediately after the defeat of the Taliban in 2003 to authenticate and legitimate the government of Ahmed Karzai.

13. This included a battalion of minors, the Red Army, seldom deployed to the front line. This was Garang's reserve force as

their allegiance was to the commander in chief and not to the revolution.

14. A mentality derived from culture among the Dinka, Nuer and even Chollo when in childhood and adolescent life they build mud cows which they used for mock bull fights or mock marriages.

15. I worked as a field geologist in the Red Sea Hills of the Sudan and in 1975 worked in the iron exploration project in the border area with Eritrea when one day Ethiopian jet fighters almost bombed our drilling machine which appeared like rocket launcher. I can swear I never saw an Eritrean fighter in combat gears in Port Sudan, Tokar or Gaderef until I left the Red Sea Hills.

16. Through clandestine networks in Malakal, the Anyanya contingent under the command of Daniel Chwogo used to purchase Mark IV ammunition.

17. Peter Schouten, Ken Matthysen and Thomas Muller (2021) Checkpoint Economy: The political economy of checkpoints in South Sudan ten years after independence. International Peace Information Services vzw and Danish Institute for International Studies.

18. The water tankers became a lucrative business throughout South Sudan. In Juba city, a study has revealed that there were three hundred seventy water tankers owned by former SPLA commanders, legislators and senior bureaucrats, with one individual, a very senior member of the executive alone owning seventy water tankers employing his Ethiopian in-laws as the drivers.

19. The Cuban government opened a school ostensibly for SPLA martyrs' children as a sign of solidarity. Some of South Sudan's medical personnel came from that school.

20. The elements of this class resisted any regulations. In 2012, the then minister of higher education, science and technology ordered to close down some bogus universities that sprang up in the residential suburbs of Juba and offering courses to individuals, some of who had never been to school. He failed to solicit the support of the minister of justice and constitutional affairs, the minister of interior or the minister of information, who all resisted the order; they were members of boards of directors of some of those universities, which operated illegally without the approval of the higher education.

21. Quoted in Nic Cheeseman et al (2021) The Shadow State in Africa: DR Congo, Uganda, Zambia and Zimbabwe." A report

22. A body is said to be in unstable equilibrium when it does not regain its original position after experiencing an external force.

23. In a conversation of Gen. Oyay Deng Ajak, the former SPLA Chief of General Staff, in Nairobi at the beginning of 2022, Oyay said that on 30th July 2005, he was in Rumbek transporting SPLA troops to Bentiu because Paulino Matip had precipitated a political crisis with his order to his forces to prevent SPLA deployment or to raise its flag in Unity state capital, Bentiu.

CHAPTER FOUR

INTERNATIONAL HUMANITARIAN INTERVENTION IN SOUTHERN SUDAN DISTORTED THE LIBERATION PRINCIPLES OF RESILIENCE AND SELF-RELIANCE

1. Introductory remarks

The international humanitarian and relief intervention in southern Sudan under the aegis of the United Nations Operations Lifeline Sudan (UN/OLS) began six years into the war and when the SPLM/A had shifted its operations from Ethiopia to Kenya. This operation could count as one of the war's unintended negative consequences. The war of national liberation, which the SPLM/A waged was unique in every aspect, thanks to the solidary internationalism; without the Derg's prompt logistical intervention on the side of Dr. John Garang de Mabior, the SPLM/A wouldn't have survived its first six months.

In chapter three we discussed the early days of the SPLM/A

and how the Ethiopian government political and military support sustained the nascent movement. However, we continue here to discourse how the notion of dependence on the benevolence of others was a complete negation of the principles of self-reliance in the war of national liberation. It's against common sense to start a war hoping that somebody would come to your aid with arms and food for your fighters. This was exactly what the surviving mutineers of Bor did when they trekked to the Ethiopian borders. The idea was to solicit and receive political and military logistical support.

When war erupted in southern Sudan in 1983, relief and humanitarian assistance was already topical in the Horn of Africa region due to wars and accompanying environmental catastrophes in famine, draught and desertification in Ethiopia and Somalia and Dar Fur in the Sudan. These were catastrophic disasters that defied any cultural mores to resist the temptation of receiving external resources. The situation in southern Sudan was completely different from the humanitarian disasters in Somalia, Tigray, or Eritrea. The people of southern Sudan had been used to floods, famine, wars and they knew how to live with them without national or foreign intervention. They knew how to survive in the bushes or in the swamps to avoid Sudanese army raids on their villages and cattle camp. Dr. John Garang de Mabior, Kerubino Kuanyin Bol, William Nyuon Bany and Salva Kiir Mayardit, who as former Anya-nya officers, at least should have had the advantage in terms knowledge of guerrilla warfare, and therefore could have laid down the correct foundation of prosecuting the war.

The SPLM Manifesto spoke to waging a protracted war. The prosecution of a protracted was presupposed many important social, economic, political and psychological factors had been considered and necessary preparations put in place. This unfortunately turned out not to be the case, and the war of national liberation became wholesale dependence on external resources from the beginning until the end. Not only that, but it also involved mass uprooting of the people from their villages in Southern Sudan, and their exodus to refugee camps in western Ethiopia, and later to Kenya and Uganda. It's difficult to cast any doubts or apparitions on the sincerity of the Ethiopian peoples' benevolence and generosity towards southern Sudanese who were running away from prosecution in the Sudan. It was well intended. However, in the situation obtaining then in the Horn of Africa characterized by conflicts and competition for resources, the enemy of your enemy becomes a friend. The mass exodus of people to seek refugee when they could have stayed in the villages was a phenomenon whose moral weight and ethical responsibility must fall on the SPLM/A leadership than on the Derg that offered sanctuary in solidarity.

This statement above about UN/OLS being one of the unintended negative consequences of war sounds cynical, but to a large extent it reflected the true picture. Any good thing has its negative side; if the negative side of the intervention preponderated over the good things the intervention provided, the intervention itself became the unintended negative consequence of the war of national liberation. This was not because of the manner the humanitarian assistance was delivered or managed, but in that it distorted the notion and essence of the war of national liberation. Some people would dismiss the statement perhaps with the rejoinder that, "people would have died if we did not intervene." That is true though, but is equally wrong because people in Southern Sudan died despite the relief aid, and sometimes due to the relief intervention. It shouldn't be surprising to anybody that during certain times in Southern Sudan particularly in the aftermath of 1991 violent split in the liberation movement relief compounds and the presence the *kawajat* in them attracted death from the opposing splinter armed groups. On the other hand, certain aspects of western aid, humanitarian or otherwise, were problematic especially when they deployed to push or promote certain attitudinal and behavioural changes in the recipient communities. These issues deserve discussion and proper understanding.

This discourse is not intended to criticize the international humanitarian intervention during the war in southern Sudan. The humanitarian principles are above impeachability, but human beings are fallible, and the best of intentions could be abused, misused, or squandered for selfish ends. It's also not a criticism of the humanitarian and relief workers; if anything, this is a tribute to the many young foreign women and men who risked their lives in the service of the people of southern Sudan at the most critical times in their history. This discussion like others in the book was triggered and driven by the problems of South Sudan. However, we discourse it in the context of resilience and principles of self-reliance in the war of national liberation. Most of the facts are product of personal experience as a civil society activist, researcher, and situation analyst for the humanitarian agencies operating in different parts of southern Sudan, Nuba Mountains, and southern Blue Nile between 1994 and 2005.

This chapter, therefore, is a critique of the SPLM policy failures and the leaders' apparent ignorance of the principles that underpin the prosecution of the war on national liberation. One of these principles is that of self-reliance, building support bases which perform social, economic, political, cultural and military functions of liberation. The discourse challenges and exposes SPLM political inadequacies that induced relief dependence in a people who have not known relief in their lives even during natural catastrophes. It is a criticism directed at the SPLM/A leadership, that gleefully glossed over its own failures in the process of liberation.

The international humanitarian intervention in southern Sudan evolved into a multi-billion-dollar business which integrated into the economies of the Horn of Africa [Ethiopia, Kenya and Uganda] in terms of commodity supplies, air and road transport, and delivery. It also became part of the Sudan's war economy that it tended to produce conditions for its continuation instead of its exit. As a result, vested economic and political interests appeared on the theatre which incessantly pushed for perpetuation of the condition of emergency that forced the humanitarian intervention into a vicious cycle without a window for exit. In fact, relief and humanitarian assistance had not exited South

Sudan even after the end of the war in 2005. Right now as we write these lines, nearly eighty per cent of South Sudanese live on humanitarian assistance whether they are refugees in the neighbouring countries of Ethiopia, Kenya, Uganda, DR Congo, Central African Republic, Sudan, and Egypt, internally displaced persons in UN protection of civilian sites in Juba, Bor, Bentiu, Wau and Malakal or in the towns and cities receiving health and education services provided by the international and indigenous non-governmental organizations or development partners like USAID and British DfID paying teachers' salaries or incentives for girls' education. These facts reflect and confirm that external aid had not exited South Sudan since 1983 and no hope in sight for it to exit in the near or distant future, because the government of South Sudan has completely withdrawn from providing these essentials services while the political leaders engage in violent power games.

2. The Genesis of SPLA Relief or Foreign Aid Dependence

Looking back to the narrative beginning with the reception of the survivors of the battle of Bor at the border up to the confrontation between them and the Anya-nya2, to the intervention of the Ethiopian army providing support to Dr. John Garang that consolidated his power in the nascent movement it would appear as if the SPLM/A was Derg's brainchild. As discussed in chapter three, the SPLA started its war relying absolutely on Ethiopia. It began life living considerably above its means depending and on massive injection from other parties and from other countries.

It is important and imperative to underline 'living considerably above its means' because this had profound negative impact on the evolution of the SPLM/A as a national liberation movement.

The Anya-nya fought its war relying in everything on the people of Southern Sudan. In the case of the SPLM/A it was different and this impacted on the conduct of the war; on the relations that evolved within the liberation movement between the military leaders and the veteran politicians, between the leaders and the combatants, and between the SPLA combatants and the civil population wherever the SPLA set foot in Southern Sudan. It was disastrous where and when the majority of the combatants didn't hail from the place. It was invariably a catalogue of irresponsible behaviour which wouldn't be expected of a liberation army.

This was not difficult to explain. A liberation army with deep roots in the society like the Anya-nya was, would treat the civilian population and their property with due respect. The Anya-nya had administrative structures on the ground to address their social needs. The SPLA did not have these structures, and like the government army, the people would first run away until they were assured that they were safe. Late Cdr. Martin Manyiel Ayuel was a true revolutionary. He was the commander of SPLA Bee Battalion deployed in the Didinga Hills, eastern Equatoria. Most of the combatants hailed from northern Bahr el Ghazal. Away from contact with the enemy forces in Kapoeta or Torit, some of them sneaked in the villages raping women and girls, stealing animals and destroying property. After a few days, the Didinga youths brought fifty-one rifles to Cdr. Manyiel to report their death for the bad things they did in the villages. Instead of acting like an imperial army commander ordering his troop to avenge the death of their colleagues Cdr. Manyiel requested the GHQs to transfer the battalion to Bahr el Ghazal and was granted.

In 1984, two years after the eruption of war, the Southern Sudanese student and political activists and others then domicile in the United Kingdom came together to form the Sudan Relief and Rehabilitation Association (SSRA) as a vehicle to provide humanitarian assistance for the victims of war in southern Sudan. While this was a noble initiative, it appeared to haven't been coordinated with the SPLM/A leadership on the ground in terms of laws governing the organization in the UK. However, it became the relief wing of the SPLM/A to provide necessities behind the SPLA lines, but no sooner did it run into difficulties with its donors as well as with the SPLM/A general headquarters.

The difficulty with the donors revolved expectedly around observance of the principles of transparency and accountability. The SSRA did not provide transparent and accountable reports for the funds it received from their donors and this created problems that prevented further funding. The organization also had difficulty with the SPLM/A GH/Qs on the issues of ownership of the organization, its resources and the authority to dispense them. This created frictions between the SPLM/A GH/Qs and the SRRA bureaucrats in the United Kingdom. This was quickly streamlined and the SRRA shifted its operations to Nairobi Kenya. The upshot of this apparent contradiction between the

SSRA and the SPLM/A GH/Qs was an order prohibiting gainful employment of southern Sudanese, or if they were volunteers or employed with international humanitarian agencies, should be remunerated in kind rather than monetary terms. It was indeed an expression of jealousy rooted in ignorance.

Thus, for instance, the movement forced Southern Sudanese medical professional who were combatants in the SPLA to work only as a volunteer, not an employee, of the NGO operating a health care service, under a foreign paramedic (nurse) who was less qualified than him, and at the end of the month would receive bars of watching soap, kilos of sugar and salt, litres of edible oil and some used clothes as incentives. This was a deliberate policy to discourage and prevent southern Sudanese engaging in any humanitarian function otherwise remained an obedient SPLA combatant. The policy also prohibited Southern Sudanese whatsoever access to SPLM/A administered areas[1] if they were not *bona fide* SPLM/A members. However, some SPLA officers circumvented this rule to give access to their kins.

In November 1994, the UN/OLS commissioned the author to study the employment practices of the NGOs and humanitarian agencies operating in war-torn southern Sudan. The results of the study shocked many international organizations who had provided assistance in the belief that humanitarian intervention must contribute to economic recovery and growth in the war torn southern Sudan. The practice of remuneration in kind that originated from the SPLM/A was heavily criticised forcing a change of the SPLM/A policy. The renumerated employment of southern

Sudanese in different functions of the humanitarian operations was regularized in accordance with international labour laws, and was monetized across the board. There were many qualified southern Sudanese to fill the positions occupies by foreign relief workers. The SPLM/A later appreciated the report for it widened the tax base enabling the SRRA, RASS and FRRA to collect sufficient funds for their other operations. This positive opening, however, wouldn't have come about without the Nasir Declaration and the 1991 split in the liberation movement and the emergence of competing political military factions with their relief branches; the SSIM/A established the Relief Association of South Sudan (RASS) corresponding to and competing with SRRA in the SPLM/A areas, while Fashoda Relief and Rehabilitation Association (FRRA) operated in the SPLM/A-United areas in the Chollo Kingdom.

The new situation created a semblance of political liberalization and democratisation in the SPLM/A administered areas, which allowed southern Sudanese to establish indigenous NGOs (INGOs) to operate alongside the foreign NGOs and relief agencies in the delivery and distribution of humanitarian assistance in the war-torn southern Sudan. The involvement of southern Sudanese in humanitarian actions to a limited extent opened up and widened the political space allowing a semblance of free speech and organization of community-based organizations (CBOs), and civil society groups by women and youths, which impacted positively on the political environment in the SPLM/A. The practice was different in the SPLM/A-United

(Chollo Kingdom) or in the Southern Sudan Independence Movement/Army (SSIM/A) administered areas. The enduring feature of the humanitarian intervention was that it drew many combatants away from the liberation process as some of them sought resettlement in USA, Australia and other places. It was mass desertion.

The international humanitarian intervention had a positive role. Vide the Tripartite agreement the SPLM/A authorities dealt with the international humanitarian agencies in clear principles and guide lines that also helped expose and opened up the opaque political environment that existed in the SPLM/A administered areas in Southern Sudan. This was a complete departure from the practice in the refugee camps in western Ethiopia whereby the SPLM/A was part of administration of the camps. The gross human rights violations committed were completely unknown to the world outside the SPLA precincts until the split in the liberation movement became a blessing in disguise.

It was in the context of international humanitarian intervention that the New Sudan Law Society (NSLS), the precursor of the South Sudan Bar Association (SSBA). Bahr el Ghazal Youth Development Association (BYDA) and other civil society groups sprouted to push for democratic reforms in the national liberation movement and enlarging the political space to win more freedoms and human rights. The NSLS operated like an NGO in the domain of legal aid and counselling to victims of violence and human rights violations in the context of the international humanitarian law and international human rights.

BYDA organized the women and youth in Bahr el Ghazal to engage in self-employment and in such cottage activities as soap and body lotion creams production from shea (lulu) fruits. The women sold their products to the markets in southern Sudan or in Uganda and Kenya.

The proliferation of the indigenous NGOs, CBOs, Women and Youth organizations led to the evolution not only of clear policy guidelines and procedures, but also helped clarify the relations between the SPLM/A political military authorities and the civil society as a result the institutions of the Civil Administration of the New Sudan (CANS) were established in the form of regions, counties, payams and bomas. In a way, the expansion of the international humanitarian relief intervention also pushed positive changes in the areas under the administration of the SPLM/A but without much impact on the liberation movement itself, which remained militaristic and repressive particularly towards the civil population.

Of course, it must be admitted that the shifting of the SPLM/A operational base to Nairobi Kenya spurred difference in the behaviour of the SPLA compared to their attitude and behaviour when it was still in Ethiopia. The SPLM/A leadership had direct links to the government of Ethiopia and that made things very difficult for those considered dissidents or were not in line with the policy. In Kenya, the situation was quite different as it gave voice to the NGOs and civil society groups and generated negative feelings of disgust and unease in the SPLM/A leadership. This disgust with the international humanitarian agencies was expressed in the SPLM/A - Humanitarian and Relief Agencies conference entitled Humanitarian Assistance to the New Sudan - A Partnership for New Sudan, held in Chukudum in September 1995. Cdr. Salva Kiir Mayardit summarized the general frustration and anger with the international humanitarian intervention in the following words.

[Somebody] said that we should not throw out the baby with the bath water. The way things are, we are not only going to throw away the baby with the bath water, but also with the bath basin."

It was meant to register that things were not as they were when we were in Ethiopia, where the SPLM/A had everything its way. However, the threatening language, the SPLM/A was in no position to throw away the humanitarian assistance, which also fed its army; it had not trained itself and the people of southern Sudan to be self-reliant and therefore must put up with the conditionalities erected by the humanitarian agencies. The people of southern Sudan are generally proud, arrogant, and defiant – an attribute to a culture of resistance to foreign occupation and rule. However, this 'pride', 'arrogance' and 'defiance' without embarrassment or shame mingle freely with 'dependency' on foreign relief assistance.

This was a contradiction occasioned by lack of correct understanding of liberation both in theory and practice. Essentially liberation is a process of social, economic and political self-empowerment through conscientization and arriving together at the truth. It, therefore, cannot be achieved through the agency of another person or with borrowed material resources. It is false when people speak of having liberated others; each person liberate self period.

3. Misunderstanding the Essence of the People's War

Not any war is a people's war or any liberation movement genuinely a liberation movement. These have been proven by several of the anti-colonial wars in sub-Sahara Africa; they proved more oppressive and exploitative as the colonial regimes they supplanted. The quest for power and wealth pushed many political adventurers and war entrepreneurs to the crest of, and turned into a power project, the people's cause for freedom, justice and fraternity. A people's war culminates in a people's power and control of the state. This is because the the principles and methodology employed involve the people at every stage of the struggle more particularly in the unity forged in the heat of the war between the urban and rural populations. This unity is achieved through mass political mobilization and education to raise social awareness and political consciousness.

Although it had the characteristic elements of a people's war, the SPLA war of national liberation did not evolve into a people's war or a genuine national liberation war. It was essentially an elitist war notwithstanding the mass mobilization of the peasants and pastoralist in Southern Sudan and other parts of central Sudan. This mass mobilisation created conditions to make up for the inferiority in armament and sophisticated military training nevertheless it failed to create the political condition for the unity of these masses. It deliberately deprived the masses of the revolutionary ideology for that unity, and that was the source of its internal contradiction. According to Mao Zedong, fighting a people's war of national liberation without an ideology, which essentially is political, would be like wishing to go 'south by driving the chariot north' and the result would inevitably be to forfeit victory. In the same vein as Che Guevara once said, any attempt to conduct this type of war without the support, participation and organizational unity of the populace would be a prelude to an inevitable disaster. A people's war in the bushes, swamps, and villages of southern Sudan prosecuted by the peasants and pastoralists would be an equivalent of a mass political movement involving strikes, demonstrations and picketing undertaken by workers trade unions, students and political activists in the towns and cities.

The SPLM/A leadership ignored, misunderstood, or possibly did not know the exact meaning and how to organize a people's war. This is easy to explain; as soon as the leaders of the insurrection arrived the Ethiopian borders, they found readily available the political, military and economic resources they needed to start an insurrection. It was their belief that Ethiopian government on account of international solidarity would continue to provided that pushed the SPLM/A leaders into ignoring the basic principles of war of national liberation and a people's war for that matter. The result of this over-sight was that these leaders committed grave mistakes some of which could have destroyed the national liberation movement at its infancy. Dr. John Garang was absorbed into the Sudanese army having been in the Anya-nya for a few months before the consummation of the Addis Ababa peace agreement. He had not been a guerrilla fighter; coming back from studies in the United States of America in late 1971, Garang joined the Anya-nya movement when the war had virtually ended; that was the beginning of the peace talks between the SSLM and the government of the Sudan. He therefore did not experience practical fighting and therefore had no knowledge of the initial stages of guerrilla formation and development. This may explain his decision to start the war of national liberation without sufficient political preparation and organization. He and his colleagues put themselves on the war path hoping that somebody (Ethiopia) would source all the needs for the prosecution of the war. Thus, they trekked to the Ethiopian borders intending to start a people's war but counting on the solidarity of Ethiopia and the Socialist camp. This was the complete misunderstanding of the meaning of solidarity internationalism.

The Vietnamese and the Chinese communist parties provide treatise of people's war. They fought wars of national liberation in accordance with the principles and laws of war; in the words of General Giap, "if you override the laws of the objective development of things, the laws will soon override you". Dr. Garang wished to place the whole centre of gravity of the revolutionary effort on the armed struggle ignoring the establishment of social and economic infrastructure as well as political organization of the people. In doing so, Garang inadvertently transferred the centre of gravity of the armed struggle itself onto setting up of maintenance service units in the refugee camps and in friendly capitals. I underline service units in the friendly capitals made up of two radio signalists, not a political representative, who would periodically convey to their contacts checklist of required military and financial demands.

The SPLM/A set up refugee camps in western Ethiopia to receive the people rooted out of their villages to these camps (Assossa, Itang, Piny-Udo, and Dimma), which indeed became SPLA support bases in western Ethiopia.

In a people's war the rear bases are usually located in the theatre of war for they serve multiple functions in the liberation struggle. They have the economic function of production, whereby the people organize the production of food and other necessities for themselves and the people's army. The rear bases have the political function of raising social awareness and political enlightenment and organizing the masses into political units of struggle. They also have the cultural function of increasing people's appreciation of their whole popular national heritage - language, theatre, dance, and poetry to force national unity from the diverse ethnic communities that is southern Sudan. The rear bases have the military function of caring for the casualties, providing repair services for the arms and like with the Eritreans, manufacture ammunitions and bombs. That's the essence of a people's war, suggesting that a people's war in southern Sudan would have also aimed at creating a national consciousness that would trump over the parochial ethnic nationalism.

It is true the Ethiopians, the Libyan, Cubans provided the initial support; the Cuban government even opened a school for the children of the fallen heroes in the Island of Youths. This support, however, provided on the basis of solidarity would not continue indefinitely particular when it turned out that there was petty bourgeois deliberate attempt to abuse this solidarity[2]. The support was bound to stop at one point or the other. The idea of locating the SPLA training and support bases outside the country demonstrated that the SPLM/A leadership did not understand the totality of the clause in the SPLM Manifesto, the "establishment of a Sudan People's Liberation Army (SPLA) ...., to wage a protracted armed struggle".[3] Waging a protracted armed struggle implied prosecuting the war in the real meaning of classical guerrilla warfare, which necessarily wouldn't have required the SPLA to raise, train and arm all those eight to nine divisions.

The SPLA started off fighting a conventional war instead of guerrilla ambushes and waylaying the enemy. This premature conventionalization of war forced SPLA's heavy dependence on external military logistical support but also triggered massive exodus to the refugee camps in western Ethiopia as a means to procure food for this huge army. This distorted the nature of the war and compromised the SPLM/A preventing its evolution into a genuine national liberation movement. According to Mao Zedong, the "laws of war are developmental and unless one understood the actual circumstance of war, its nature, and relations to other things one will not know how to direct war or win victory". The objective laws of peoples' war are specific and define the strategies and tactics applied to war theatre and with dealing with the people. The fact the SPLM/A leadership prosecuted the war outside the context of its objective laws leading to premature conventionalization meant that it was an elitist rather than a people's war. It corresponded to Garang's personal wish for quick victory leaving the people virtually in their original social, economic underdevelopment, and cultural backwardness. Indeed, after twenty-one years of war of national liberation neither the people nor the SPLM/A leaders, cadres and combatants had undergone ideological or psychological transformation. The situation in South Sudan goes to prove that the SPLM/A was more of a power project than a project in Sudan's revolution to transform the conditions of poverty, ignorance, superstition and cultural backwardness of the people. As an elitist power project, the SPLM/A leaders didn't have to obey the natural laws of war; the prosecuted the war in the most adventurous fashion that led to unnecessary of human resources.

4. Negative Consequences of Relief and Humanitarian Intervention

The world has become a global village in the African meaning of a village, and anything occurring in one part is quickly felt or becomes known quickly in the other part. With this came the sensitivity and readiness to intervene to help in order to alleviate the suffering. Relief and humanitarian intervention therefore are part of human sensitivity. However, anything in nature, whatsoever, has two sides in dialectical balance that the good, the positive side counters the bad and the negative side in order to maintain an ecological balance. The people's war had the positive aspects of freeing the people from oppression, raise their awareness and develop fraternal relations but it also had negative sides some of which we are about to discuss.

Since there were no preparation before the eruption, the SPLM/A logics of war ran against the conventional wisdom of a people's war. The SPLA encouraged mass exodus of people from southern Sudan into the refugee camps in western Ethiopia, where the international community provided and served them free relief resources some of which was availed to the army. The negative aspects to exodus to the refugee camps in Ethiopia showed up when the SPLM/A was forced to withdrew back into Southern Sudan following the defeat of the Derg. The people the SPLM/A had forced to become refugees were equally vulnerable as the army.

Back into the areas they left, the people could not again engage in agriculture, to tilt the land they used to do before the war. Many years of dependence on international benevolence had rendered them unfit for self-reliance. This created an emergency condition for intervention; thanks, that the tripartite agreement between the United Nations Children Fund (UNICEF), the SPLM and the Government of Sudan had created the United Nations Operations Lifeline Sudan (UN/OLS), and was operational and its planes were already dropping food and other supplies wherever the refugees had return to settle or in transit to other areas. This relief intervention operated while the war raged as the Sudan Air Force planes rained bombs on the returnees constituting a perfect emergency situation and condition for continued international humanitarian intervention.

As mentioned elsewhere, humanitarian intervention or development assistance from the donor country carries in it religious and cultural values intrinsic to that society. In many instances humanitarian or development aid is employed to propagate and inculcate some of those values in the recipient community resulting in serious contradictions we categorize as negative consequences of relief and humanitarian intervention, although in essence many of them were unintended, but accrued from human agency. One of the unintended negative consequences was the prolongation, escalation, and intensification of war in southern Sudan. Although the escalation and intensification could have resulted from the in-roads the NIF regime built into the SPLM/A backyard that provoked the Nasir Declaration, the split within the SPLM/A and the resultant internecine fighting in 1991. The NIF regime found it expedient to attack the SPLA at its weakest moments as it withdrew back into the Sudan But, the Tripartite Agreement 1989 was the main cause of the prolongation of the war.

Dr. John Garang, the SPLA commander in chief, accepted the tripartite agreement to allow relief and humanitarian assistance, and announced the cease fire on May 3oth 1989 at a time the SPLA was on the verge of defeating and rooting out the Sudanese army from Southern Sudan. The SPLA had 'liberated' the stretch of territory east of the river Nile from the international borders with Kenya and Uganda in the South to the southern bank of river Sobat in the north. The SPLA offensive in Eastern, central Equatoria, and Jonglei that resulted in the capture of one garrison town after the other in a space of a few days completely demoralised the Sudanese army to the extent that they voluntarily withdrew from their defensive positions in Torit and Nimule well in advance of the arrival of the SPLA. The Sudanese army *morale* was at its lowest, while that of the SPLA was at its zenith, and was ready to continue the thrust to capture Juba and Malakal.

With the tripartite agreement, the SPLM/A leadership couldn't have more committed an error of judgement. It stopped the war when the enemy's army was already defeated and withdrawing in disarray; this error paid back negatively on the SPLM/A both militarily and politically. The then prime minister of the Sudan, Sayyed Sadiq Al-Sadeek Abdelrahman Al-Mahdi, was shrewd a politician who valued Sudan's (read Arab) national interest more than his personal power; he tricked the SPLM/A leadership through the auspices of the international community to sign a cease fire. This not only allowed the Sudanese army to regroup and re-equip itself while plotting change of government with his brother-in-law, Dr. Hassan Abdalla Al-Turabi, leader of the National Islamic Front (NIF). Indeed, the NIF pulled a military coup and turned the table on the SPLM/A leading not only to the escalation and intensification of the war but also to the split in the SPLM/A instigated by the new regime. The split in the SPLM/A enabled the Sudanese army recaptured Pochalla, Pibor,

Kapoeta and Torit and later Nasir from the SPLA then engaged in internecine fighting. The tripartite agreement was therefore a factor in the prolongation of the war.

The UN Operation Lifeline Sudan and the humanitarian intervention were an open-ended operation undertaken without a strategy for its exit contrary to known practice. No emergency should exceed a certain threshold of six months, but if it is to extend beyond that period then arrangement should be made such that the recipients could live with dignity producing for themselves. This was the policy the Ugandan government enforced from the time Southern Sudanese arrived there in the sixties, and similarly when Ugandans and Congolese were in refugees in Equatoria; they were offered land to construct their houses and to cultivate food and other cash crops enabling them to engage in economic activities. In southern Sudan, international humanitarian intervention lasted many years that it induced relief dependency in the recipient communities. Of the people forced back from western Ethiopian into southern Sudan in 1991 only very few went straight to their villages in Upper Nile and Bahr el Ghazal. The bulk rerouted themselves to refugee camps in Kenya (Kakuma) or Uganda (Kiriandongo or Rhino camp) where they could only survive on international humanitarian assistance.

Back in their villages the people had the opportunity to produce their own food, become self-sufficient and food secure, due to land fertility and availability of tools and seeds. Nevertheless, there was marked reluctance to engage in cultivation and tilting of land; they had become used to free food dispensed by the humanitarian agencies. However, there was also another factor of the armed groups, who strenuously prevented people to engage in food crops production ostensibly to keep running the wheels of international humanitarian and relief intervention. Of course, much of the food provided by the world food programme (WFP) went to feed the SPLA, SPLA-United or SSIM/A. In Leer, western Upper Nile, a Kenyan WFP worker was frogmarched, and his film destroyed for taking photo of sorghum field with prospective good harvest.

> *[Nobody] should be seen engaging in cultivation. If the UN saw people ready to work for themselves, they will stop bringing food and what will we do if the UN stops the food delivery?*[14]

This was exactly the genesis of the 'relief dependency syndrome' and its attendant psychology of 'expectation to receive' in many parts of southern Sudan. When a *kawaja* came to the village people expected to receive something. With this preponderant attitude relief ceased to be something to mitigate a temporary emergency but became a permanence in the lives of the people. It became a manmade disaster, which at another level of negativity, gradually morphed into a lucrative business for self-aggrandisement and wealth accumulation. Some rebel commanders with the connivance of some unscrupulous relief workers hoarded or diverted relief food and non-food items, which they sold for their self-fish ends. This also involved inflating to a large margin the number of the recipients in certain relief centres, and the surplus items accrued to the officers manning the centre. This robbery went on for so long that some relief workers and the area commanders became so rich from the exchange of relief resources for livestock and/or money. This was outright corruption.

5. Corruption and Evolution of Unequal Power Relations
In the southern Sudan like in many other parts of Africa, education was the only means of social mobility. Those who successfully completed the education cycle found themselves as government officials or politicians in higher social status than their kins or relatives left in the villages. In a sedentary agrarian village, the peasant had to labour hard to generate surplus agricultural produce for exchange in the market. A pastoralist like the Dinka, Nuer, Toposa or Chollo would acquire more cattle only through marriage and individuals with many marriageable relatives became rich in that manner. This situation changed drastically as a result of the raging war and the international humanitarian intervention. The free resources brought into the community created condition of unequal power relations, where what mattered was not the education or social relations but the possession of the gun. This broke all the norms and new antisocial attitudes, and behaviours submerged the traditional society.

It was necessary to discuss the abuse of power with impunity that came with war and proliferation of firearms. Corruption that now became a common feature in government and society in South Sudan has its roots in this culture of impunity that emerged in the context of reception and distribution of international humanitarian relief assistance. The impunity took the form of diversion and outright theft of these relief resources, and the culprits were never made to account or punished. In this way, the individuals corrupted and with it they corrupted the national liberation movement until corruption was not only glorified and immortalized but was also weaponized consequently leading to the evolution of an elitist class who later carried the virus of corruption into the government institutions. We have so far discussed relief in relation to the recipients or beneficiaries. If we go by the notion that there was a government in the Sudan, which had direct responsibility for its people on account of sovereignty, it then become incumbent for the government of Sudan to explain what occurred to the resources freed in its budget by the international humanitarian intervention. In fact, the government of Sudan treated as rebel anybody outside the garrison towns and automatically absolved itself of responsibility towards them. But, this government benefited from the international humanitarian intervention; it freed the internal sovereign resources at its disposal towards war efforts like purchasing weapons. With those resources, the government of Sudan energised its troops, escalated, prolonged, and prosecuted the war with vigour and determination to defeat the SPLA. Thus, in the reference we made above, Sadiq el Mahdi exploited the opportunity provided by the tripartite agreement to twist the hand of SPLA to bring a halt to its advance in the war zone. The ceasefire came because of mounting international pressure on Dr. John Garang, who was then visiting the United Kingdom and, in a BBC, interview declared the SPLA GH/Qs was with him in Bush House. With this announcement, Dr. Garang placed himself in a situation he morally couldn't dodge the mounting pressure, and had to acquiesce to cease fire even before soliciting the opinion of his field commanders.

6. Conflict of value systems in humanitarian intervention

Every human society has in-built core values vide which they live and interact. The international humanitarian system derived from and built most of its principles, guidelines, procedures, and practice on European and American cultural values rooted in individualism and liberalism. This stemmed from their dominance in the world order and the United Nations system and the rest of humanity follows this system when situations arise that prompt international intervention humanitarian. Sometimes, due to some international humanitarian principles and the manner this international humanitarian intervention is delivered, clashes with social, customary, and traditional values of the recipient communities; this usually occurred in southern Sudanese or other African countries.

The first biggest problems with the humanitarian assistance relates to its lack of democracy; the recipients or beneficiaries were never asked about the assistance they would have preferred. Instead, relief assistance was decided elsewhere and was delivered and distributed without regards to its suitability and acceptability by the recipients. It was delivered on the assumption that people were in distress and therefore would accept anything given to them. The relief agencies seldom undertook research to ascertain what the people in emergency would have preferred. Thus, for instance, the relief agencies sent food to western Equatoria and western Bahr el Ghazal, where the people were food secured but because of the raging war, there was a complete disconnect in transport and communication with the markets in Juba and Wau. Their needs, therefore, were items other than food.

In most cases, the humanitarian and relief agencies sent to the recipients communities young workers who were ignorant of the culture and traditional practicies of the people. The principle of equality or treating alike members of the recipient community irrespective of their social and biological relations whether they were men, women, and children or elderly, chiefs and notables without due consideration for social status of certain individuals in the community engendered friction tensions and sometimes conflicts. This therefore underlines the importance of local knowledge for the humanitarian agencies before embarking on their projects. A pig farming project failed and huge project funds went to waste in Yambio, western Equatoria, simply because the Catholic Relief Service (CRS) management would not take the advice that the Azande people never ate pork meat.

Sometimes, certain western humanitarian and relief agencies overzealously use the relief items to proselytise their ideals, or promote certain values they consider 'human rights', which often offended the sensibilities of the recipients leading to rejection of the commodity or conflict with the local people. The linkage of western liberal values system to western aid whether humanitarian intervention or bilateral aid in southern Sudan is the elephant in the room. It engendered difficulties some of which are under discussion. In August 1995 the Norwegian People's Aid (NPA) commissioned the author to investigate the impact of humanitarian assistance on the Agar, Ciec, Aliab and Atwot communities in Rumbek, Lakes in Bahr el Ghazal revealed. The results of the study revealed some discrepancies in, and outright contradictions that cropped up between the international humanitarian principles and practice on the one hand, and the culture value systems of the recipient communities on the other hand. That the *kawajat* (white men) came along to be part of consumption of the assistance they brought was rather flabbergasting to many people in the area. The people perceived the *kawajat* relief workers had followed the assistance they brought from Europe or America, which they shouldn't have done.

This perception stemmed from the practice among the Nilotic people (Dinka, Nuer, Chollo) in times of great stress like famine, if one donated a milking cow to a distressed family, one was not expected to follow to get some milk or butter from the same cow. Another important observation was that most traditional leaders in the area felt they were being slighted by the relief workers. Because of their status in the community, they viewed as their responsibility and function the tasks the relief workers undertook, and therefore had expected that the relief items were handed over to them to distribute. This would be in conformity with their responsibilities and authority in the community; what would be the role of the chief or the respected individual in the community if he was not seen distributing the relief items? The people would ask. It was important that they played a role in the distribution as that would endear them to their people.

The *targeting* of the vulnerable groups or individual in a recipient community was problematic in its moral and ethical dimension. Before they distributed their relief items, the humanitarian agency would go on a campaign to identify and target the vulnerable individuals in the community. This was a tricky exercise in the Dinka society that is communal or live together as clans and families who would assist each other in times of distress. Among the Agar people in Rumbek, this targeting of individuals generated tensions and friction in the community; first with the traditional leadership of the community who felt their responsibility for individual members of the community had been usurped by the humanitarian agency; secondly the rest of the community despised and scorned the targeted group, composing provocative songs that disparaged and shamed them. This precipitated violent conflict in the community and led to loss of life and destruction of property. From a moral aspect, individuals targeted and received relief items automatically absolved the traditional authority in the community of any responsibility to assist its disadvantaged members leaving them vulnerable when the humanitarian agency exited the area.

The distribution and reception of a relief items, from the perspective of the humanitarian agencies, necessitated one's presence in the compound or its neighbourhood. The people therefore form into a *queue* for easy and quick distribution of the relief items. *Queuing* was something new and most embarrassing thing to many people in southern Sudan, particularly notables detested this practice; it lowered their self-esteem and dignity in the community. The practice of queuing ran against the norms of many communities that it became the general complaint against the international humanitarian intervention. If there was anything people resented in the relief reception and distribution as this queuing to be registered, queuing to receive relief items; in which irrespective of social status in the society, age or physical strength the people were required to queue. It was humiliating and therefore resented.

7. Distinction Between People 'Inside' and 'Outside' the Compound

The defining feature of humanitarian and relief agencies' presence in different parts of southern Sudan was the 'relief compounds' they established. The compound doubled as their working and living quarters usually not far off from the 'relief airstrip' that serves the people in the area. The security architecture of the area determined the proximity of the airstrip to the compound. It was usually a security consideration in case of evacuation in times of danger. The 'emergency level' four would require immediate air evacuation back to Lokichogio in Kenya. Unfortunately, this evacuation was only for only some of the people who resided in the compound. The Southern Sudan nationals were rarely evacuated for security reasons; they were advised to mell into the community. At the end of the war there were more than three hundred relief airstrips throughout southern Sudan servicing over a hundred international and local NGOs as part of the UN/OLS consortium. The relief compound in some areas served a large population extending several tens of kilometers from the airstrip. And since there no means of transport, the people, therefore, clustered around the airstrip a distance from the 'relief compound'. This was the genesis of the visible distinction between those 'in' and those 'outside' the compound. The people 'inside' and 'outside' the compound were different and interacted differently; they were the relief 'deliverers' and 'recipients' respectively.

Among the compound residents, apart from the *kawajat* or the Kenyan and Ugandan who served as drivers, paramedics, clerks, storekeepers, or accountants, were also South Sudanese, who after 1995 started to receive monetary renumerations from the relief agencies working as cooks, watchmen, cleaners, interpreters, and others. These categories of the local community were different from the rest of the relief beneficiaries in that they had monetary remunerations and therefore had access to cash in US dollars, Kenyan or Ugandan shillings. This configuration corresponded to the emerging social stratification in the community defined by accumulation of financial and/or economic resources, and therefore were in a position to purchase items which the other couldn't afford. They, therefore, became object of envy and jealousy in the community. In certain cases we recorded disparaging poems and insulting songs composed against the South Sudanese relief workers. It created enmity between individuals and triggered violent conflict and serious divisions within the community.

These were the unintended negative consequences of international humanitarian intervention. The relief assistance linked interactions and relations contrasted with other interactions and relationship that emerged in commercial transactions between individuals in the community who worked with the *jellaba* or Greek merchants selling their wares in the community. Those who associated with the jellaba or Greek traders in their commercial businesses did not suffer the same treatment as the relief workers although in this there were aspects of exploitation and clear case of unequal power relations consequent to property ownership.

There were times in Southern Sudan when the presence of relief assistance in form of food in a particular locality became an unintended negative consequence of humanitarian intervention. This occurred in the context of the splits and splinterism in the SPLM/A that followed the Nasir Declaration in 1991. Armed groups proliferated and became a nuisance as they attacked relief centres just to deny the other faction access to relief food. Relief compounds attracted violent attacks which led to death or other fatalities to the relief workers. In April 1992, Cdr. George Athur attacked, dispersed, and killed women and children returning from Ethiopia and were camped in a place south of Ulang. His objective was to prevent relief food reaching the Nasir Faction forces in the area. Similarly, the SPLA attack on Panyagor in 1993 was to prevent the neighbouring civil population converging on the WFP compound servicing the Relief Association of South Sudan (RASS) the relief section of the SPLM/A-United.

The international humanitarian intervention in Southern Sudan during the war of national liberation saved lives, but it also generated negativities some of which have become permanent legacies now in the republic of South Sudan more specifically among the agropastoral communities. One such legacy engendered by relief dependence was that in many areas in Upper Nile and Bahr el Ghazal people have abandoned agriculture and the practice of tilling land that South Sudan has become a net importer of agricultural produce from Uganda and Kenya. This situation coinciding with the failure of the state because of civil war and widespread insecurity in the states jeopardizes South Sudan's chances for socioeconomic development.

In conclusion, the international humanitarian intervention in Southern Sudan under the auspices of the United Nations Operation Lifeline Sudan had positive as well as negative sides to it. Most of negatives linked to the absence of exit strategy; no emergency could be permanent. However, the Southern Sudan leaders had a duty to protect the people from its negative consequences.

ENDNOTES

1. The SPLA refusal of Dr. David Bassiouni but acceptance his deputy, a foreign national, was both sickening and embarrassing. David, a former minister in the High Executive Council of the Southern Region, a senior Director in UNICEF, was refused entry to Kapoeta simply because he was from Equatoria. Had

he been a Dinka he would have had no difficulty SRRA permit notwithstanding.

2. The idea of being a school for the orphans was completely abandoned and the SPLM/A leadership sent to Cuba children and relatives of senior SPLA officers thus instead of a melting pot of Southern Sudanese ethnicities it rather consolidated the ethnic identity of those children and generated contradictions.

3.Chapter Elven, section 23 (a) the SPLM Manifesto, July 1983.

4.SPLA-United commander of Western Upper Nile speaking to explain to me the reason for frogmarching David Waweru the WFP officer after photographing the sorghum field.

CHAPTER FIVE

THE REPUBLIC OF SOUTH SUDAN: A SHADOW STATE IN THE HANDS OF BUSINESS CARTELS AND COMMUNITY ELDERS

1. Why is South Sudan Only a Geographic Entity?

This is not an innocent question; it will reverberate through the minds of this and the coming generations of South Sudanese; something spectacular must occur to change the name of the country. The people of the southern provinces of the Sudan started their agitation for independent statehood as early as 1947. This was at the crest of nationalist movements for freedom and independence that swept through Africa and Asia following the second world war. Although the people's voices were then feeble and uncoordinated nevertheless their will to freedom and justice was unbendable. This was in spite of the physical and psychological forces the colonialist and nationalist leaders used to mute the voices. With the politics of exclusion, economic marginalization and social discrimination pursued by the Arab dominated northern political elite, the people grew more aware and conscious of their rights and their voices grew stronger and stronger. The southern Sudan political leaders became more articulate and with clarity presented their case in different national and international or regional fora: The Juba Conference 1947 and the Round Table Conference on the problem of the three southern provinces in Khartoum 1965, or in regional and international platforms like the IGAD, AU and the United Nations in which these leaders participated as observers. Indeed, and eventually the people of southern Sudan won their independence and are a sovereign people building the youngest state in the world.

The nascent republic of South Sudan is in political doldrums. It's transition to peace, stability, social cohesion, economic development and political stability remains challenged by its own political inadequacies. What puzzles many observers of South Sudan political theatre is the attitude and behaviour of South Sudan political leaders towards their nascent state and its people. This attitude doesn't seem to reflect the long and relentless struggle they and the people undertook to achieve the present status. It's the kind of attitude akin to a sentiment that emerges after completing an errand one was not fully convinced of the justness of its message. It may be possible that the true patriots may have died or have been elbowed out of limelight much earlier, and the self-seekers and opportunists sprouted onto the stage masquerading as the 'liberators'. They cared less about the country, its people, and even its standing in the region and in the world.

The words of the UN secretary-general, Antonio Guterres, speaking at an UN/AU meeting on South Sudan on 18th March 2018 in Addis Ababa, Ethiopia, that, "first, it is clear to me, and I am sorry to say so, but I have never seen a political elite with so little interest in the wellbeing of its people", echoes an honest opinion and reflect the reality of South Sudan political leadership in their different political groupings. The current crop of South Sudan political leadership trifurcates into three groups: The SPLM is the largest; its only credentials are having spearheaded the war of national liberation and its leaders and cadres were military with little or no political experience and organization. They are suspicious of each other and don't trust one another, but are all interested in power and wealth. The NCP, which ruled the Sudan for thirty years based on Islamic fundamentalist doctrine and principles. Its leaders and cadres are politically organised experienced and crafty having been well trained to the practice of leader worship, flattery, and bootlicking. Thus, through sweet talk they were able to capture, influence and turn President Salva Kiir against his colleagues in the SPLM. The third group comprises several small rent-seeking, briefcase political parties organized into Umbrella Parties and National Alliance Parties. Many of these southern Sudan parties were tawali parties that surrounded and buttressed the Ingaz regime core, the National Congress party, The three groups constitute South Sudan political elite - the ruling coalition defined not by individual party programme but by personal relationship each leader built with the president of the republic, comrade Salva Kiir Mayardit, chairman of the SPLM.

This relations between the different members of the coalition started to acquire a different content following the split within the SPLM in December 2013 and in the context of the IGAD peace process and the agreement on the resolution of the conflict in South Sudan (ARCISS) in 2015.

This chapter is about the republic of South Sudan, the youngest country in the world that became the 194th member of the United Nations General Assembly and the 54th member of the African Union on the political good will of the world. In writing this chapter I couldn't miss to raise the widespread but muted concern about the name of the country. At independence, the nascent state was recognized as a geographical entity as though it was an armistice[1] realty awaiting reunification at some later date with the Sudan. That Southern Sudan became independent on a name that indicates its geography without history after such a long-drawn-out struggle is not only an omission but a commission of a political blunder of historical proportion.

In discussing why, the country is recognized only as geographic name, I categorically pin this terrible omission on the SPLM/A leadership. It was one of its several political failures. But I would quickly add that although for Dr. John Garang the idea of Southern Sudan as a potential separate entity was his central thrust nevertheless, he deliberately ignored it to come out like an afterthought because he was pursuing the agenda of socialist united Sudan, and had otherwise to protect himself from being misunderstood by his main benefactor, Col. Mengistu Haile Mariam. The notion of South Sudan as a country came out forcefully much latter in the context of the right of the people of southern Sudan to self-determination, not only because the national liberation as an ideology as well as the concept and vision of the 'New Sudan' encompassing the whole Sudan had flopped, but also because Mengistu like the Soviet Union was no longer there. The independence of South Sudan presented a scenario in which the SPLM/A leadership seemed to have been frogmarched back into its natural background of Southern Sudan in what appeared like a shift from the revolution to the traditional southern Sudanese demand for self-determination.

Had the SPLM/A started and prosecuted the war as a separatist movement like the Anya-nya2 or any of the other previous southern Sudan liberation movements, perhaps it could have been an easy exercise to name the anticipated country. The Anyanya Land Freedom Army, and the different political movements and 'governments in exile' the politicians established, each had its name for southern Sudan upon liberation. Thus, there was the Azania republic, George Kwanai Akumbek[2] plagiarized from Pan African Congress of South Africa and on the assumption that the two struggle were similar. There was the Anyidi republic, the Lado republic, and the Sue River republic. Without questioning the motives behind each name, suffice to say it was in order to have a name to the country one aspired to. Indeed, naming was a statement of fact that men and women who create history are only steered into action when their hearts are stirred by some basic image or sentiments rooted deeply in their past. The names mentioned above could have echoed the home turf of the respective authors. Anyidi is a village in Bor area, but I believe only the author may divulge the significance and relevance of Anyidi republic as a name for Southern Sudan; perhaps he wanted to impose his locality on the country, the same could have been true also with Sue River republic and I believe the author must have been an Azande because there was nothing particular about Anyidi or Sue river in the history save that they are names in southern Sudan. As for Lado republic, its significance derives from the 'Lado Enclave' which until 1910 combined parts of central Equatoria and west Nile district of Uganda governed as part of the Belgian Congo. The name echoed some separatist sentiments expressed by central Equatoria intellectuals when they got frustrated with the violent and toxic ethnic politics of the Nilotics of Bahr el Ghazal and Upper Nile subregions. It was understandable that the SPLM/A leadership didn't openly entertain the notion of Southern Sudan as a potential independent and sovereign country; It had pre-occupied itself with the concept and vision of New Sudan.

The CPA provided for the people of Southern Sudan to exercise their right to self-determination and it's clear that the general opinion was for secession. Why was it that nobody among the Southern Sudanese separatists came up with a name for the country? Assuming that the SPLM members did not want to embarrass themselves calling for secession in the last moment when they championed unity for twenty-one years, why wouldn't the separatists have taken the mantle of secession including clearly naming the country that would be birth on July

9th, 2011? The six years' interim period established the subnational entity called the Government of Southern Sudan on the basis of one-country-two-systems; a political and constitutional arrangement that made Southern Sudan a state only awaiting international diplomatic recognition and the general sentiment among the leaders and people of Southern Sudan was just to wait for the conduct of the Southern Referendum on 9th January 2011. The Southern Sudan leaders including the SPLM leaders unfortunately perceived this preparation for the conduct of the referendum as an event taking place on 9th January 2011, not a long-drawn-out process that entailed construction of institutions and crafting symbols and instruments of public authority that would become operational only on 9th July 2011 as the leaders stood to raise the South Sudan colours and lowering of the Sudan's flag. There was enough time between 9th January 2005 and 9th July 2011 that whatever was necessary for the nascent republic in terms of its name, insignia, coat of arms, national anthem could have been prepared, crafted and produced well in advance of the Independence Day.

Dr. Garang was conscious of the importance of such symbolisms and that was the reason he commissioned the SPLM/A flag, copied from the Kenyan and Sudanese colours, which later was adopted as the flag of the nascent republic. Garang still wore the Sudanese Army insignia and travelled with SPLA Music Band that played Sudanese national anthem wherever he set foot in the liberated areas in Southern Sudan, The name of the anticipated republic eluded Dr. Garang perhaps deliberately not to alert the NCP of his real intentions not only because there was still an opportunity to give unity of the Sudan a chance but also did not want to embarrass himself in front of colleague from the Nuba, Funj and other African people in northern Sudan. The SPLM leaders had six years to prepare for the 9thJuly 2011, but they only began running about everything including the independence transitional constitution only after the announcement of the referendum results. They spent the entire interim period partying, dollying and aggrandising themselves. Whether it was mere negligence or brain lazy, none in the SPLM leadership initiated the question of the name of the country, not even when the SPLM and the GOSS officials discussed post-referendum issues. It is worth mentioning that a name for the three southern provinces has always been problematic as could be gleaned from the different name proposed by the Anya-nya leaders and politicians. I believe the process of naming would have been acrimonious hair-splitting exercise as ethnic bigotry stymied Southern Sudan nationalism or patriotism. I could imagine the debate about the following three proposals: Fashoda, Lado or Nile, how the Equatorians would go easily for Lado republic or Nile republic but not Fashoda; while the Dinka would only accept Nile republic if it would be translated into Kiir republic. It's sad that at the end of the struggle in which more than five million lives had been lost to war and war-related ailments and catastrophes the leaders of Southern Sudan could not give themselves time to reflect on their history and build consensus on how to precede thenceforth. Thus, the national anthem came out like a church hymn, and the national emblem had other local ingredients except the bird, fishing eagle, which doesn't domicile in Southern Sudan.

The Government of Southern Sudan (GOSS) in Juba, unlike the NCP led government of national unity (GONU) in Khartoum, had the vested interest and the financial means to grudgingly implement the CPA chapter on reconciliation and national healing. It was a chapter that was purposely inscribed verbatim in the Interim National Constitution, the Interim Constitution of Southern Sudan and in the constitutions of the states in Southern Sudan. Its significance laid in the process to translate the CPA from what it was a political compromise to peace and social harmony in and between the communities affected by the war. The war fragmented communities between the SPLM/A and the government of the Sudan and therefore needed internal reconciliation. The building of peace and stability would create an atmosphere of unity, and therefore a step in the direction of nation building in Southern Sudan, and to reverse the trend of fragmentation triggered by the politics of re-division of the Southern Region that preceded the eruption of war in 1983. It was in the interest of the SPLM more than the NCP to implement the provision on reconciliation and healing to help in state formation and nation building processes in Southern Sudan. The SPLM/A hadn't much during the war and therefore should have obliged to create conditions for unity of the people of Southern Sudan.

In the six years interim period, GOSS coffers received monthly between US$ 600 and 700 million from its share of the oil revenues. It also had the option of raising US$ 500 million in non-oil revenues. The non-oil revenues unfortunately drained into a sinkhole; certain untouchables in the government lined their pockets with the non-oil revenues - a practice that continued to date the recent establishment of the National Revenue Authority (NRA) notwithstanding. My point and emphasis were that GOSS had the financial and economic means to provide social services and initiate social and economic development projects especially those projects whose feasibility studies had been undertaken by the High Executive Council before the eruption of war. Such projects like the Fula Rapids hydroelectric power generation plant, Kapoeta limestone and cement, Tonj kenaf, Malakal paper and pulp, Yei forestry, tea and coffee and many others could have been funded to provide socioeconomic development of those areas and employment of the people especially those returning from the diaspora with skills and knowledge. With that economic prowess GOSS could have not only transformed the SPLA from a guerrilla army into a professional standing army, police force, prisons, wildlife, and civil defence forces, GOSS could have also re-established strong local government institutions in the states and counties buttressed by the traditional authorities.

The SPLM had a problem that prevented it undertaking these projects. As mentioned elsewhere, militarism in the SPLM/A ostracised innovation and generation of knowledge. This was underpinned by the marginalization of the educated and qualified cadres preventing their deployment to cerebrally challenging functions of the liberation. Only chairman Garang had the privilege to intellectual and reflective activities in the movement, all the rest were minions who performed menial and errand functions suggesting that the leader was the only thinking person. In consequence when the war ended the SPLM had leaders who could only execute not initiate orders and plans. The SPLM/A became a contradiction between the revolutionaries who desired transformation of the oppressive reality in the country and those who just wanted power and exploited the revolutionary zeal of the people. Everybody in the movement became just a tool to help achieve this political objective of the leader, who didn't desire thinkers or university graduates but only robots to implement his plans.

It is not possible to make an educated person ignorant; however, a useless piece of knowledge could consciously be unlearnt in the process of learning and unlearning. By placing an ignorant individual to boss over a learned colleague was tantamount to denying his knowledge. We saw this in the previous chapter whereby a medical professional was placed under the command of a paramedics. Marginalizing, and sometimes ostracizing, the professionals in the national liberation movement showed immediately at certain critical moments. In 1989, the SPLA captured or liberated Katire, a forestry station in eastern Equatoria, which produced timber in a swan mill driven by power from a small hydroelectric turbine placed on Kinyetti river. Instead of leaving the plant to those who were running it effectively and efficiently the SPLM/A leader put in command an SPLA officer and in two months the plant broke down never to function again. When in 2005 the SPLM/A leaders, cadres and combatants set foot in the government-controlled garrison towns of Juba, Malakal and Wau, the condition in which they found these towns was by far better than what they had in the so-called liberated towns in terms of physical infrastructure and social amenities. In Juba, the pipe water ran in the residential suburbs, powerhouse still generated and distributed electricity and the postal service and telecommunication were functional, and the telephone land lines were operational that one could call anywhere in the world at a reasonable cost. I remember receiving in Malakal an express letter coming from Holland[3]. Three months into the formation of GOSS, things started to change for the worst and suddenly everything collapsed. The water pipes dried up and Ethiopian or Eritrean driven water-tankers carrying untreated water crisscrossed the city to the residential suburbs; Juba became a noisy city as the Chinese made small power-generating machines became common sight in the city. What happened? It was possible then to conclude the SPLM-led government was being sabotaged by the NCP operatives. But the opposite was the truth; it was the SPLM that was sabotaging itself. In the SPLM/A deployment of its cades, military rank took precedence over experience and knowledge, consequently it ran down the sawmill and the small hydroelectric power plant in Katire (Torit District) and the Nzara Agro-industrial complex that was producing cloth, soap and edible oil at the time of its 'liberation' by the SPLA in 1990. The SPLM/A had in its ranks university graduates in such fields as medicine, engineering, veterinary, agriculture etc., but instead of deploying them where they could make difference, no one desired them. I recalled after the liberation of eastern part of east bank Equatoria, I sent to Chairman Garang a proposal to organize and work the alluvial gold deposits in the streams draining the Didinga hills and surrounding areas in Kapoeta district. The verbal response I got from his office manager was that "it was too theoretical", to which I asked, but what on earth does not start from theory? The office manager was trying to behave politely.

For all purposes, GOSS was run by its vice president, Dr. Riek Machar Teny-Dhurgon, a PhD holder in strategic production management and who doubled up as the minister of housing and public utilities. Riek Machar never worked before in government bureaucracy. Upon graduation in 1976, the University of Khartoum administration sent him to Bradford for post graduate studies and on completion joined the SPLM/A where he was trained, commissioned, and was given command of western Upper Nile zone, where he performed administrative functions through 'trial and error'. As vice president of GOSS and minister of housing and public utilities, Riek Machar poured billions of dollars into projects, which ten years later had not relics, or which like Juba streets and roads project[4] continue to menace vehicles and pedestrians alike. Some professionals and intellectuals in the SPLM/A succumbed to being brain lazy or 'dead woods' out of their inability to engage in cerebral functions.

2. Salva Kiir Mayardit Assumes Leadership of Southern Sudan

It doesn't matter whatsoever if ever Cdr. Salva Kiir Mayardit had harboured any ambition for leading the people of Southern Sudan in the manner Dr. John Garang, Dr. Riek Machar or Dr. Lam Akol Ajawin visibly displayed their ambitions. Until he was ushered onto the throne following the tragic death of Dr. John Garang, Salva Kiir had always displayed indifference, lack of interest in limelight and soldierly loyalty to his commander in chief except on one occasion in the meeting of the SPLM Leadership Council in 2004. When Salva Kiir in a violent mode held onto the chair saying, "I won't leave this chair", suggesting that he would rather leave the SPLM/A than allow Dr. Riek Machar to become the second person in the national liberation movement. Perhaps, testing the waters, Dr. Garang, had wanted to accommodate Dr. Riek Machar in the second position in the SPLM/A hierarchy.

Many people have power and leadership ambitions notwithstanding their ability to deliver. In political parties, particularly in parties that practice democratic centralism, individual's capability to lead is usually concealed by collective responsibility practised in the party and they rise to the apex to create serious difficulties. In autocracies, totalitarian and authoritarian parties where there is a powerful leader it won't be surprising that the second in command and other leaders would remain oblivious; their presence were scarcely felt outside the party. Salva Kiir was the nominal deputy of Dr. John Garang, and from the manner he conducted himself privately or publicly he always didn't seem to care whether or not he was the second in command. This attitude coincided with Kiir's benign character as a down to earth individual. President Salva Kiir Mayardit began his tepid leadership of South Sudan in a manner that surprised many people. His attitude and behaviour towards many people in and out of the SPLM/A echoed the bad blood that emerged between him and his predecessor on the eve of the peace agreement. The truth was that Dr. John Garang de Mabior, whom Salva Kiir Mayardit succeeded, in his leadership was like an individual re-enacting the mythical primeval scenes of power fashioned by his infantile imagination. This had little relevance to the objective reality in the liberation movement; suggesting that Garang had prepared himself for the task of leading the 'revolutionary' armed struggle and did what it took politically, militarily, and diplomatically to be at its citadel. Thus, Garang behaved as if he was implementing a pre-determined psalmody.

The succession of comrade Salva Kiir Mayardit to the leadership of South Sudan contrasted by a wide margin with Garang's leadership. He didn't provide satisfactory leadership and his lacklustre was apparent and this could have been an inherited phenomenon or could have been an attempt to conceal the intense anger and bitterness which usually accompanies a situation when one fails to undertake what he should have done. The feeling of being marginalized by Dr. John Garang, and being slighted by his subordinate colleagues in the movement bottled up anger and bitterness in Kiir. Whichever way, I believe Kiir's problem did not originate from his feeling of marginalization, which was relatively recent. It must have stemmed from his relationship with Dr. Garang as the SPLA chief intelligence officer and the avid executioner of Garang's orders. The relation with Dr. John Garang wasn't genuine collegial and comradely relationship premised on democratic political principles in the common struggle, but based on deceit, lies, trickery, and intrigues against other colleagues in the leadership. Cdr. Salva Kiir witnessed and probably was privy to the intrigues that removed from the SPLM leadership hierarchy Cdr. Kerubino Kuanyin Bol (1987), Cdr. Arok Thon Arok (1988) and Cdr. William Nyuon Bany (1992), and possibly must have felt quivers running down his spine when the same intrigues turned against him in what transpired as Yei crisis in 2004. In fact, Salva Kiir was a bitter and angry man when he took over the leadership on the SPLM, the first vice president of the republic of the Sudan, and presidency of the government of Southern Sudan. Though a lengthy digression, it is worth shedding some light on the genesis of Kiir's anger and bitterness.

Dr. Garang's refusal to organize and institutionalize the SPLM/A was linked to his political objective of personal rule. This made everybody else in the liberation movement dispensable or exchangeable but that became the source of contradictions and instability in the liberation movement, and in the nascent republic of South Sudan. The last two years to the signing of the comprehensive peace agreement (2005) were the most dramatic time in the life of the SPLM/A. In 2002, Dr. Riek Machar stormed out of the republican palace in Khartoum to re-join the SPLM/A. In a little more than a year later, Dr. Lam Akol escaping a coup in the

SPLM/A-United in the Chollo Kingdom also came and re-joined the SPLM/A. In northern Bahr el Ghazal, the slave redemption project undertaken by the Christian Solidarity International (CSI) therein was at the centre of growing dissatisfaction with Garang's leadership among Bahr el Ghazal politicians in and outside the SPLM/A. However, it was a problem exasperated by lack of democratic dialogue and political consultation otherwise it wouldn't have escalated beyond the immediate individuals concerned. In this configuration of things where leaders communicated only vide radio messages, spoilers and agents provocateurs jumped into the fray to accentuate the friction and escalate it into a political crisis. A second incident that added fuel to the growing disenchantment with Garang's leadership was Garang's dismissal of Cdr. Aleu Ayieny Aleu as director of Operation Save Innocent Lives (OSIL) a demining NGO affiliated to the SPLA through the SRRA. Cdr. Aleu had built OSIL into a successful demining business in the SPLA administered areas. Not only that but also the appointment of Jur kuch Barach, who hailed from the same home area as Dr. Garang inflamed the situation further. A third issue, which circulated as a rumour was that Dr. Garang had decided to remove Cdr. Salva Kiir Mayardit and to appoint Cdr. Nhial Deng Nhial in his place as SPLM deputy chairman. This was the time Dr. Riek Machar, and Dr. Lam Akol had re-joined the SPLM/A and the positions they would occupy in the reconstituted SPLM/A Leadership Council was stirring up rancour and resentment within the ranks of the liberation movement[5]. Riek Machar's demand to occupy the second position in the hierarchy added fuel to already tensile and inflammable political environment. It did not take long before the smouldering amalgam exploded into what became known as the Yei Crisis 2004 fitting Cdr. Salva Kiir against his commander in chief, which almost shattered the SPLM/A into pieces. The delegates to the SPLM.A senior officers' conference in Rumbek, convened specifically to resolve what appeared like an imminent confrontation between the two leaders, misdiagnosed the nature, triggers and drivers of the Yei crisis. The conference decided on reconciling the two leaders as if the problem was something personal between Salva Kiir and John Garang. What reflected as personal was indeed a deep-seated structural contradiction. In fact, the contradiction underpinned all the other contradictions in the liberation movement since 1983. It exploded several times in different forms. First, in the battle of Itang in July 1983 between the Anya-nya2 and the surviving elements of the insurrections in Bor and Ayod. Secondly, in the arrests and detention of Kerubino Kuanyin and Arok Thon. Thirdly in the Nasir Declaration 1991 leading to the split within the SPLM/A. Fourthly, in the rebellion of William Nyuon Bany in December 1992. Fifthly in the Yei crisis 2004, and finally in the 2013 implosion that triggered the civil war. These contradictions in their different manifestations were, therefore, reflection of the SPLM/A structural weaknesses. Thus, the crisis generated by these contradictions endured, escalated and reproduced themselves in different forms and intensity simply because the liberation movement did not possess the necessary democratic tools for addressing them.

In the SPLM/A, Cdr. Salva Kiir Mayardit was known for his botched military adventures in Kurmuk (1989) and Rumbek (1990), which were both disasters for the SPLA and Dr. Garang was very cautious in both cases not to rebuke or reprimand Salva Kiir but fudged the matter to keep the movement united lest it was negatively interpreted through regional lenses. On the heels of Derg's defeat in June 1991, the SPLM/A leadership ordered the evacuation of refugee camps in western Ethiopia (Assossa, Itang, Piny-Udo, and Dimma) and withdrawal of the SPLA through Pochalla back into Southern Sudan. Instead of southern bank, Cdr. Salva Kiir, who commanded the operations ordered that the entourage camped on the northern bank of Abobo river. In a stampede to avoid an advancing contingent of EPRDF forces, thousands of women, children, and SPLA soldier perished in the river.

Cdr. Salva Kiir Mayardit became the supreme commander of the SPLM/A and president of the Republic of South Sudan without any kind of achievement in the political or military domains to buttress people's trust and confidence in his leadership. It was important that the people and particularly his subordinates had trust and confidence in his leadership. It is usually a bad omen that people, especially those closed to the leader are aware of his weaknesses. It generates in him intense fear, withdrawal or recoil into the self, vindictiveness, vengeance, paranoia, and dictatorial tendency. Salva Kiir doesn't forget and his character as a quiet, soft-spoken, slow to react, and sometimes introvert has helped him to withstand those psychological irritants. The deceptive tepid commencement of his presidency find explanation not in people's knowledge of his personal weaknesses but in the political developments in the three weeks following Dr. Garang's constitutional oath-taking as first vice president of the republic of the Sudan and president of the government of Southern Sudan. Acting in his capacity as chairman and commander in chief of the SPLM/A, Dr. John Garang de Mabior instituted radical changes in the structure of the liberation movement in preparation to transform them from guerrilla to their professional domains. He dissolved the SPLM Leadership Council and appointed its members caretaker governors of the ten states in Southern Sudan; separated the SPLM into northern and southern sectors and appointed Cdr. Abdel Aziz Adam el Hilu to head the SPLM northern sector, and Cdr. Pagan Amum Okiech to head the SPLM southern sector. In the SPLA, Dr. John Garang decommissioned all the SPLA officers who were senior in rank to Gen. Oyay Deng Ajak, whom he appointed SPLA Chief of General Staff. He transferred all the decommissioned SPLA officers to the police, prisons, wildlife, and civil defence services. It caused an initial stir and consternation within the ranks of the liberation movement particularly among those who learnt of these changes. These changes, as the practice in the SPLA would indicated, must have as usual been carried in radio messages tagged 'Top Secret' to prevent their open transmission or their discussion by unauthorized individuals otherwise the decision to decommission officers who were the backbone of the movement could have triggered immediate mutinies and rebellions in the different SPLA divisions. This could have been led by none other than Salva Kiir Mayardit himself. It confirmed the rumours that it was just a matter of time and Dr. Garang would dump him. It was by malice of fate, as Machiavelli would say, it was Garang's death in a tragic helicopter crash that forestalled and saved the SPLM/A and Southern Sudan from imploding.

Cdr. Salva Kiir Mayardit became supreme leader not on account of his long history in the SPLM/A; he no longer had position neither in the SPLM nor in the SPLA. He became leader of South Sudan because was deputy president of the government of South Sudan. It was not a fresh beginning being deputy to Garang. However, it was a beginning that carried huge baggage of grievances, insubordination, and indiscipline of some of Garang's close lieutenants and relatives. Salva Kiir Mayardit took over the leadership of Southern Sudan a very bitter and angry man but never displayed combative mood; silently but quickly reversed Garang's orders to restructure both the SPLM and the SPLA, reinstated the SPLM Leadership Council and reinstated into the SPLA all the officers previously decommissioned by Dr. Garang. Kiir's action helped calm the situation and prevented the implosion. However, Kiir confirmed Gen. Oyay Deng Ajak as the SPLA Chief of General Staff. Not only did President Salva Kiir quench the flames in the SPLM/A but also in an effort to endear himself to the other sections of Southern Sudan society outside the SPLM/A, President Salva Kiir reached out also to Gen. Paulino Matip Nhial, the Nuer militia commander, appointed him deputy commander in chief, whatever it meant, and absorbed all his forces even with their inflated ranks into the SPLA. This action, good only in the context of peace making and confidence building in the war-torn country, was later to become the stumbling stone to SPLA reforms, depoliticization, de-ethnicization, and professionalization. The exponential increase of Nuer ethnicity in the SPLA became a source of great concern to the Dinka leaders mainly from Warrap. The end of war and formation of Southern Sudan as a subnational entity spurred the question of power and its distribution. In fact, some Nuer politicians used this numerical strength of the Nuer in the army to agitate for Nuer presidency of South Sudan, and it was part of this agitation that led to the December 2013 eruption of conflict.

The absence of Dr. John Garang was immediately felt in the SPLM/A and throughout Southern Sudan, and in the slow rise to prominence of his successor, Cdr. Salva Kiir Mayardit, who in the first few months demonstrated a nonthreatening posture to any group in Southern Sudan. President Salva Kiir Mayardit made himself accessible to all; the kind of attitude he always displayed even at his weakest moments. But of course, Salva Kiir was now a different person, first vice president of the republic of the Sudan and president of the government of South Sudan. It would not be long before the trappings and responsibilities of power would weigh down on him to eschew the pretence and limit his accessibility. President Salva Kiir would now, if he never thought so before, understand, and define himself *vis á vis* all others in the SPLM/A; at the same time others would then begin to treat him as the supreme leader. There was no joke. It was in this respect that the parameters of his leadership style began to crystallize and cast itself on the public screen.

Initially, like most successful dictators, President Salva Kiir surrounded himself with trusted friends and family members and worked hard to rid himself of ambitious SPLM members most of whom were Garang's trusted lieutenants. Unlike Dr. John Garang, Salva Kiir's close associates, and networks that teamed around him, the so-called Bahr el Ghazal elders, hailed from his home turf in Warrap but mostly from Gogrial and part of Aweil. Some of them doubled up as intelligence gathering networks, Salva Kiir is a practicing Catholic nevertheless he solicits the services of diviners, sorcerers, witch doctors, and medicine men/women from the different ethnic communities of South Sudan as well as far afield as Nigeria including the late Nigerian prophet, Temitope Balogun (TB) Joshua[6] to buttress his power.

Starting from a trust and confidence deficit with his colleagues in the SPLM, President Salva Kiir decided he must survive in power against all odds and machinations. He knew very well that in the twenty-one years of war, the SPLM/A had not developed further than Garang's original idea, and with his demise on 30th July 2005, the SPLM/A as an idea had also died, and nobody in the movement could challenge whatever he did. The desire and urge to survive politically at the helm, therefore, shaped Salva Kiir's key policy decisions from that time to date; he has never wavered.

President Salva Kiir amazingly proved ingenious and inventive; quickly learnt the rules of power and logics of politics to help to manipulate SPLM politics work to his advantage. The first rule of power President Salva Kiir embraced was that power is never about doing the right thing; it is always about doing what is expedient. Thus, when he surrounded himself with Bahr el Ghazal elders or when he appointed his trusted friends, relatives, and business associates to South Sudan's financial and economic power hubs obviously that ran against civil services regulations. It was not the right thing for the president to do, it was only expedient for his political survival. Since the civil war broke out in December 2013, President Salva Kiir spent government revenue on buying the loyalties of a few cronies and bribing regional and foreign dignitaries at the expense of general welfare. Thus, legislators, judges, academics, the civil servants, diplomatic missions abroad, the army, the police, and other organized forces, except the national security officers[7] would go for more than ten months without being paid their salaries not because there was no money in the coffers, it's part of dictatorial politics to make people suffer such that they don't think about the government because they are always running to make ends meet. Thus, in twelve years since independence the result stares us in the face in the form of corruption, racketeering, breakdown of social mores and morals, prostitution, drugs trafficking, organized criminal gangs, insecurity, community conflicts, land grabbing, etc.

Delay in payments of salaries and remunerations has consequences for the low income government employees. Due to delayed payment of salaries those low-income workers, soldiers, elements of the SPLA, police, prisons warders, wildlife officers, who also poached the animals they were supposed to protect , were all pushed into cutting wood and burning charcoal for the local market or export.

The reasons they gave was to make ends meet since the government was not paying them. They undertook this business with the knowledge of their seniors, whom they also had to bribe to allow them to utilise their rifles to protect themselves and their wares from other criminal roaming the forests. The question that imposed itself was to where or whom did they money go? Then, the government still had oil revenues still pouring into its coffers, yet the employees were not being paid suggesting that it was deliberate policy to enrich a few loyal cronies and pauperize the rest of the population. The problem then was that these cronies did not invest this money in the economy, they stashed it in foreign banks in the region or purchased real estates in Kampala, Nairobi, Addis Ababa or far afield as Sidney or Melbourne.

Salva Kiir's presidency of South Sudan was and remains an anti-climax of the national liberation of which he was a prominent actor. He reduced Southern Sudan to the caricature of what it was before the war broke out in 1983. The people of southern Sudan have never been so divided along ethnic and regional contour lines as today when they are independent and a sovereign people. Many people, particularly those who had experience with the SPLM/A, never imagined that the republic of South Sudan would become what it is. There were high hopes that a country better than the Sudan would emerge especially that most of its leaders had been exposed to the social, economic and cultural environment of the East African countries of Ethiopia, Kenya, Uganda and Tanzania.

President Salva Kiir struck many people as visionless, clueless, and a don't care leader who believed that his appointees to constitutional dockets should perform in their duties as expected although many of them had no prior experience with the jobs thrust at them. President Kiir relied on unofficial reports to make his decisions, and although he would have the details information about all that which unfolded in his realm whether bad or good, right or wrong, nevertheless won't make the appropriate decisions. As a result, South Sudan dithers, teeters, and cackles without his attention. Indeed, some parts of South Sudan and certain communities have never seen peace since 1955 either because of government soldiers or rebel actions. In some areas life approximates Hobbes' state of nature: being solitary, poor, nasty, brutish, and short. President Salva Kiir governs over a dysfunctional state, in which nearly all the institutions of the state have deliberately been rendered ineffectual and inefficient because of political patronage, promotion of parasitic relationship and corruption. The republic of South Sudan is in state of fractal politics – a never ending pattern of political fragmentation driven by power struggle, depicting a situation of chaos and chronic insecurity. The state legitimacy as the only possessor of the means of coercion has been sufficiently eroded; some communities are armed better that the SSPDF that other security organs wont subdue them. Paradoxically, those arms used against the army originated from army stores sold by unscrupulous officers, who although are known couldn't be apprehended because of ethnic relations and considerations.

The republic of South Sudan has deliberately been plunged into perpetual political instability. The IGAD peace agreement provided no respite; it is an unending transition renewed periodically by the government and the political and armed opposition groups at least to keep peace and order in Juba, the capital. The recent extension of the transition period suits President Kiir's objective to prolong his presidency whichever way South Sudan dithers and teeters. In fact, if there is anything President Kiir loathes it is life outside the office of the president. It conjures on him the prospect of being held to account for the failures and the crimes committed under his watch. The political patronage and intelligence gathering networks surrounding President Salva Kiir operate diligently to prevent exhausted politics reining-in because that could easily lead to disruption. It allows President Salva Kiir to keep continuously shuffling his cronies to demonstrate his keen interest in peace, placate the international community and to ensnare into the patronage system the weak knees in the opposition and hold-out groups.

The political system is overtly kleptocratic with an interesting feature of absorbing into it those who don't see any faults in the system, and at the same time prevents envisaging anything better. For some people in the so-called opposition, it is better to join because it has become a question of physical survival. Those who critically peep into it conclude that South Sudan is an example of an undying organism undergoing cellular decomposition and emitting stench which attracts regional and international vultures to scavenge, extract and plunder. The informal flight of capital from South Sudan is unbelievable and can be measured by the numbers and frequency by which these local, regional, and international vultures so-called investor arrive and leave Juba international airport.

South Sudan's plight has grown larger than President Salva Kiir Mayardit and renders it too complicated for him to handle. He closed all the political avenues in the SPLM and hence no genuine political consultation and dialogue to find a solution. This is partly because Kiir has become paranoid about his presidency making him suspicious of any initiative to assist him politically forcing him ironically to depend on individuals who are digging his political grave. In the absence of a credible alternative political force, the people of South Sudan have been plunged into an unending cycle of violence. Dr. Riek Machar, who commands the second largest grouping provides no positive remedy. He falsely believes that as first vice president he could inherit the throne; he would if only there were to be elections, but as long as R-TGONU is run on the peace agreement only James Wani who could inherited power should Salva Kiir submit to his poor health. Riek Machar has now taken to vindictive measures mobilising his Nuer followers in Fangak and Ayod including some Padang Dinka now opposed to Salva Kiir, to attack the Chollo Kingdom.

The destiny of the republic of South Sudan and the fate of its people hangs in a precarious crossroads or balance between being or not being. Each day that passes inspire no hope for change or improvement. The feeling that there is no government in South Sudan is becoming general and widespread to the extent that even senior ministers now admit that President Salva Kiir has lost it to the kleptocratic cartels some of whom are his close blood relatives.

3. Liberal and Free Market Economic System – South Sudan's Pitfall

How did South Sudan come to this pathetic situation? The answer to this question lies in the fact that it is not possible to copy-cat a political system and expect it to function efficiently or effectively. This means that any political system must have its roots in the social and economic of society and because societies and countries are at varying levels of cultural development they would respond differently to natural laws of development.

South Sudan and its people are still at the lower rungs of socioeconomic development. It emerged as a country from a brutal war of national liberation that spanned twenty-one years. Therefore, the choice of the socioeconomic and political system of South Sudan should have been dictated by the objective reality of the country, and not by the wish of a few elites at the helm of the liberation movement or the dictates of the Bretton Woods Institutions and its Multi-Donor Trust Fund established as economic advisors to GOSS immediately before independence. Socioeconomic trajectory is a political as well as an ideological decision and the choice the SPLM leaders made could not be separated from the political and ideological shifts they beat during the war. That it was wrong from the beginning would be the correct assessment of the social and political evolution of the republic of South Sudan.

It followed the development trajectory path traversed by the post-colonial African countries and that reflects in the evolution of national consciousness, social cohesions and human security in those countries. The significance of a visionary political leadership and the social, economic and political path they chose for their people couldn't be overemphasized particularly for a nascent poor country but potentially rich in natural resources like South Sudan.

The greatest mistake many nationalist African leaders committed that landed their countries in poverty and perpetual dependence on the donor countries, was their failure to link political independence of their countries to the social, economic and cultural development of their peoples. South Sudan fell into this trap from the early stages of the war of national liberation. The ideological shift from revolution to liberalism and populism registered in the offer by the SPLM/A leadership to send SPLA combatants to join the western alliance in the first Gulf war in 1990. It was a political bluff of course, but it exposed and shredded the socialism pretence of the SPLM/A leader clearly pointing to the direction the SPLM/A was treading[8].

It wouldn't have surprised anybody that the government of Southern Sudan adopted liberal multi-party democratic system and free market economy that allowed the apologists of the Bretton Wood Institutions to take over the economic planning in the nascent state. The SPLM was already in the capitalist camp by virtue of joining the western alliance. This radical shift to the right the SPLM leaders made was not only bewildering for an organization that continued to call itself a liberation movement. I would absolve President Salva Kiir of the libel of pretension; he was neither a socialist ideologue nor an economist so to say, unlike those who chanted socialism to the top of their voices and went to train in Cuba only to come back reactionary and apologists of capitalism.

During the last few years of the war of national liberation, indeed, after the liberation of the territories bordering northern DR Congo like Yei, Maridi, Yambio up to Tambura, the resulting security triggered extensive economic activities and market relations with Uganda and Kenya started to mushroom. Some SPLM/A political leaders and military commanders started to show interests in business, wealth making and accumulation. They incorporated companies and businesses in Uganda and Kenya whose ownership in the absence of transparency and accountability wavered between public (SPLM/A) and private (individuals managing those companies). The operated lucrative businesses in petroleum products, tobacco, sugar and alcohol imported duty free but smuggled back into markets in Kenya and Uganda to extract huge profits. Indeed, at the end of the war no public audit of the millions of dollars in public assets these businesses and companies transacted. It was in this context that the SPLM/A political and military commanders evolved and crystallised into an elitist class completely alienated from the masses of the people. This elitist class combined with the NCP cartels and business tycoons to form the parasitic capitalist class at the helm of South Sudan political and economic power. The class is parasitic because its elements don't own or control any means of production but accumulated its wealth from relation with state as ministers, legislators, judges, generals in the army, police, national security, prisons, wildlife and civil defence force, senior bureaucrats, business cartels, and speculators in the market.

The social, economic and political interest of this class ran counter to those of the people of South Sudan, who yearned for social services in education, health and agriculture as well as economic development and construction of physical infrastructure like roads, hydroelectric power generation and transmission, this parasitic capitalist class was only interested in extraction and plunder of South Sudan natural resources. It run down the country in the numerous financial and economic scandals like the Aweil – Mairum road (2006) that cost GOSS two hundred eighty million dollars, the 'dura' saga in which GOSS loss nearly five billion dollars although tens of thousands of people died of hunger in Warrap, Lakes and Aweil due to undelivered food contracts meant to build strategic reserves for the states. The letter of credit (LCs) saga was the blatant abuse of the international trade payment facility in which the government of South Sudan lost billions of dollars to business cartels. The Auditor-General in his report had this to say:

"Instead of giving an opportunity to the people of South Sudan to reap the benefit of the government effort in availing credit facilities (LCs) to the commercial and investment community to provide essential commodities and services to them at affordable prices, some few officials and fake 'traders' with apparently, assistance and collaboration from officials in authority turned this noble international trade payment facility to a mere mean for personal benefit that draws for them quick foreign exchange earnings at the expense of the poor South Sudanese who is languishing and crying to secure daily bread supposedly the credit facilities were intended to secure. I believe that the performance and management of the letters of credit under my current audit has caused the country huge financial losses most which ended up enriching very few individual companies and probably some individuals at the expense of the majority of the populace of the country." [9]

The auditor-general's report quoted above came at the heels of President Salva Kiir's refusal to let him audit the SSP 800 million GOSS released in March 2014 to the Crisis Management Committee (CMC), headed by Vice President James Wani Igga, formed to relieve the victims of war in Jonglei, Upper Nile, and Unity states. Instead of visiting Bor and Malakal where atrocities were reported, the members of the CMC pocketed the money and refused to visit the affected areas.

It is not just corruption *per se* but that the emerging parasitic capitalist class won't subordinate its selfishness and greed to the interest of the people of South Sudan. It can't be anything but greed and patriotism deficit that pushed them into stealing public funds. The SPLM/A revolutionaries behaved exactly like the former CPSU party apparatchiks as they transformed into the present Russian oligarchs, accumulating wealth through theft and shady deals in collaboration with regional and international cartels. They stashed this stolen wealth in foreign banks, purchasing real estate in Uganda, Kenya, Dubai, Australia and USA instead of investing in social and economic scheme that could bring development and transform the lives of the majority of people in South Sudan.

The Transitional Constitution of South Sudan (2011) provided for a multi-party democratic political system. This was when there were no political parties in the true meaning of the words. The SPLM was still somewhere halfway between a political outfit and a military organization. Its modus operandis were still commands, orders and instantaneous obedience. The only other Southern Sudan political party was the Union of Sudan African Parties, (USAP), which purported to be SPLM/A in the country although essentially it had become an Ingaz's tawali party. None of these parties or those that sprouted onto the political stage practiced democracy or operated on democratic principles. Since the SPLM had not completely demilitarized and its leaders remained military commanders, the political system in South Sudan drifted towards a totalitarian kleptocracy buttressed by a ruthless, brutal, and corrupt national security apparatus. The power struggle at the SPLM leadership considerably shrunk the political space in the party as well as in the country; President Salva Kiir Mayardit transformed into a dictator at the head of totalitarian kleptocratic dictatorship. The National Intelligence and Security Services (NISS), an Ingaz's relics of the CPA interim period, was legitimized in the republic of South Sudan in a bill imposed on and passed into law by the Transitional National Legislative Assembly (TNLA).

In order to protect itself from internal dissent and insurgencies, the regime in 2016 assented to the Pact on Security, Stability and Development for the Great Lakes Region only to isolate and declare the SPLM/A (IO) and any other political or armed opposition to the regime 'negative force' warranting intervention on the part of the Great Lakes Region countries. In the same vein, and without knowledge of international trade and its dynamics, the regime or rather the parasitic capitalist class forced the TNLA to assent the republic of South Sudan to the protocol that established East African Community (EAC).

The EAC is not a tea-party or a humanitarian relief organization dishing out goodies. It is a trading block and to join it one must have communities to trade in its markets. The bill to join the EAC was pushed down the throat of the members of TNLA by individuals who did not study it or had knowledge of international trade organizations. International trade is war, which in this connection and according to Yash Tandon, trade is war, not in the ordinary sense of the term, that is war with bombs and drones, but "trade in the capitalist-imperialist era is as lethal, and as much of a 'weapon of mass destruction', as bombs. Trade kills people: it drives people to poverty; it creates wealth at one end and poverty at another; it enriches the powerful food corporation at the cost of marginalizing poor peasants, etc.(sic)"

In debating the EAC Bill in the TNLA, the national security elements were deployed to intimidate the honourable members forcing them to pass the bill without delay. According to the Bill handlers it was the policy of the SPLM leadership (read the parasitic capitalist class) to assent to the EAC and those who either dissented or wanted the bill deferred for further study were muzzled. It was clear, the parasitic capitalist wanted to ensure the safety of their looted wealth stashed in banks in Kampala and Nairobi or the property they purchased in form of estates and palaces.

The republic of South Sudan joined the East African Community market without any commodity to sell; its oil is sold in the open market through the agencies of cartels and middlemen/women but so it would not have been available in the EAC market. South Sudan has no manufacturing enterprises, indeed, as I write these lines no product of South Sudan is worthy of accountable and transparent trading across its borders. This is not to say that South Sudan has nothing to export; there are exports from South Sudan but what happens is monkey business.

The study of charcoal production and trade referred to above revealed that hundreds of thousands of tons of charcoal imported into Saudi Arabia and Arab Gulf countries originated from South

Sudan. Although there were strict rules against random trees cutting and charcoal burning, the civil war and general breakdown in law and order has enable all those pushed out formal employment and jobs including petty traders to go into the forest and engage in charcoal burning. Much of this charcoal is smuggled to Uganda from where it is shipped overseas. The consequence of this business is extensive deforestation, ecological disaster and a general environmental degradation and a disturbed rainfall regime in central Equatoria.

In 2019, Ebony Centre for Strategic Studies commissioned a study on the risk assessment of the mining industry in South Sudan in the context of enforcing transparency and accountability. The study revealed that there is extensive artisan gold mining in Kapoeta undertaken by some senior officials in the government of South Sudan unfortunately there is no reliable information regarding gold production whether with the office of the governor, which gave artisan mining licences, or in the ministry of mining which has the constitutional mandate to oversee this business or in the ministry of commerce and trade, which authorized export. It is unofficially known that most of the traders: Chinese, Somalis and Europeans involved in the gold production in Kapoeta smuggle it to Uganda. In 2019, President Museveni commissioned a gold refining furnace in Kampala when it was globally known that Uganda does not have gold mines. One would suspect that the gold refining furnace services the gold smugglers from South Sudan but also confirms what Yash Tandon said of trade as war. In this manner unfair trade accumulates wealth in Uganda and leaves South Sudan poor, its environment polluted and degraded due to informal mining and use of toxic elements like mercury in the extraction of gold.

The ruling parasitic capitalist class has not only reduced South Sudan to a shadow state, conceptually an informal network of domestic and international looters and plunderers, but also to a dumping ground for surplus agricultural and manufactured products from East Africa and other parts of the world. This context obtained because the SPLM/A leaders abandoned the liberation and the path to the national democratic revolution confirming what Amilcar Cabral said of the petty bourgeoisie as a service class, and that for it to lead national liberation to its logical conclusion, must commit class suicide to rise in the guise of revolutionary worker and peasant. Through liberal economic and the free-market policies underwritten by the Bretton Woods Institutions, the leaders of the SPLM/A have promoted unequal distribution of power and wealth leading to stratification of South Sudanese society with serious consequences for ethnic relations and social stability in the country.

The republic of the Sudan became independent under a liberal democratic constitution and it did not take long before the political proved they were not ready for the principles than underpin the system. The political system generated contradictions that led to military intrusion into politics. The lesson from the Sudanese experience is that a political system must be homegrown or has its roots in the social, economic and cultural configuration of the people, otherwise it won't operate or function efficiently to the satisfaction of society. Liberal democracy can obtain only in a liberal society or where there is large critical mass capable to influencing policy, not in a traditional conservative society in South Sudan where the majority of the people are rural, illiterate, apolitical, and engage in subsistence production. In such a situation, it is not easy to conduct free and fairs elections to choose leaders as an exercise in democracy. In fact, for South Sudan in its current context in which political consciousness is at its web, political pluralism would be a luxury; many people are concerned with how to live. This explains the reality that President Salva Kiir has built himself in a totalitarian dictator and nobody including those in political opposition has ever raised a finger against it.

4. The Parasitic Capitalist Ruling Class and the Deteriorating Ethnic Relations in South Sudan.

Historically, in post-colonial Africa, the petty bourgeoisie comprising different sociocultural groups constituted the dominant socio-political force that led the struggle for freedom and independence, and in some countries created conditions for social and economic development and nation-building. In South Sudan, the evolution of the ruling parasitic capitalist class comprising different ethnic and linguistic groups initially appeared a progressive historical development. The assumption was that the end game of all the contradictions, it engendered as a parasitic class, would drain into a strong economic and political system that could consolidate the unity the people of South Sudan.

This was not destined to be so; unfortunately, the highly

personalised contradictions between the elements of this class triggered by power struggle and competition for primitive accumulation of wealth translated into inter-, and intra-community[10] and ethnic conflicts. The people of South Sudan have never before been so fragmented coming in response to the growing inequality between different social groups. This emanates from unfair distribution of political power, opportunities, financial and economic resources undertaken in preference to individuals and groups from particular ethnicity and region. As a result the social capital built in the course of war of national liberation has been completely shattered. Even within this parasitic capitalist class the cartels hailing from Warrap and Aweil are well sourced than others from other ethnic Dinka sections. There is a growing bitterness and hatred among the Apadang Dinka in the oil fields in Upper Nile against the Rek Dinka who have usurped senior positions in the oil sector. section,. This inequality in the distribution of power and wealth doesn't only differentiate people along ethnic lines but also along regional lines. This is the great weakness of South Sudan dominant political class; it plunged the country into a precarious situation of perpetual conflict and civil strife. The prejudices, hatred and resentment has become not only sociocultural but also personal. It is the kind of situation that became triggers and drivers of genocide in Rwanda in 1994.

The situation is further accentuated by the false affluence the elements of this elitist class display driving latest models of the most expensive cars, and staying in posh hotels. Instead of investing this stolen money into the economy to provide social services and economic development, they stash the money far away that they have become part of the capital flight from South Sudan. The deterioration in ethnic relations is a matter of deep concern. For a people just emerging from the war of national liberation ethnic fragmentation confirm what we have been saying all along that the SPLM/A prosecuted the war outside its ideological context. The primary strategic objective of liberation was the unity, and indeed organic unity of the people. But that after twenty-one years of common struggle, the SPLM/A leaders and cadres fragmented themselves and the people along ethnic and regional lines demonstrates that as combatants in the liberation movement, they had no common understanding or conviction in the message of liberation they carried. This played out in 2004 when the SPLM leader rejected of the concept of the 'House of Nationalities' (HoNs)[11] on the ground that we were trying to awaken the sleeping people (Nyaba, 2022:311).

But liberation, essentially is about waking people up and raising their awareness against submergence in ignorance, superstition, and cultural backwardness. Embedded in the HoNs was the liberation concepts of identity, humanism, respect for and acceptability of others on the basis of equality and fraternity. It is so unfortunate that the liberation movement failed to inculcate these values as vehicles for unity of the people. The war of national liberation was the opportune moments to forge the unity of the different sociocultural groups in South Sudan; once that was missed, and peace rein before a complete unity had been achieved, the social capital achieved in the course of fighting quickly eroded. This would explain why certain parts of Jonglei, Warrap, Lakes and Central Equatoria have not had peace.

The manner the heavily armed pastoralists from Jonglei defiantly and arrogantly moved with their herds into the sedentary agrarian community lands in Eastern and Central Equatoria destroying their crops was a demonstration of complete lack of human sensitivity and has contributed to deterioration of relations between the different ethnic communities in the country. It is even unacceptable when the pastoralist attack on a weaker community appears they were escaping from, or avoiding contact with another marauding pastoralist intending to grab their cattle. This situation echoing weakness of the state and its inability to provide protection and security, obtains because the dominant political elite pursues its narrow interests while neglecting the higher interests of the people of South Sudan. The parasitic capitalist class is interested only in the extraction and plunder of natural resources and not in state or nation building. It is a contradiction of historical dimension that as a modern social and political force it is unable to fulfil its mandate.

5. South Sudan's Uncertainties and Fatalities

Leaders appear and disappear; definitely Salva Kiir's era as president of South Sudan is bound to come to end someday. This would be the most precarious moment in the life of this country. With a first five president and four other vice presidents, a special presidential advisor, a president advisor for security affairs, a quiet, powerful and ambitious director-general of national security, presidential relatives respectively commander of the presidential guards the Tiger Battalion, and the chief of general staff of South Sudan People's Defence Force, it is impossible to envisage a peaceful post-Salva Kiir period in South Sudan. These are competing power centres that their unmitigated ambitions could land the country into a post-Tito situation in Yugoslavia, which eventually produced six countries instead of one.

The recent episode in Terikeka County raised the issue of President Kiir's health, and along with that also the question of succession. The republic of South Sudan is in a transition, governed by a clause in the IGAD revitalized agreement on the resolution of the conflict in South Sudan that puts the SPLM in a dominant position to decides who takes over from President Salva Kiir in case anything occurred before the elections scheduled for December 2024. There would be no problem if President were there to contest the elections; this would minimize the power scramble in the SPLM, but whether Kiir or somebody else won the contest, would definitely trigger disputes about the credibility, fairness and freedom in the election process,

The greatest danger is poised by President Salva Kiir's insistence as president of the republic notwithstanding his failing health. This obstinacy will push Kiir to extend the transitional period beyond 2025 precisely because he does not envision himself out of power. He told his colleagues in the SPLM that he would leave power in the same way Dr. John Garang did in 2005, meaning that he would die in office period. This puts the people of South Sudan in a dilemma. One horn of the dilemma is that they either must tolerate him as their president and he would continue to extend the transition to keep South Sudan in peace. He has embarked on building a presidential palace and has launched road construction projects in greater bahr el Ghazal and Greater Upper Nile to connect different parts of the country and has asked the people to keep peace. These are plan of somebody who wants to stay in power.

The other horn of dilemma is Kiir's unexpected demise due to poor health, and in the absence of clear rules and guideline for succession in the Revitalized Transitional Government of National Unity, given that the only SPLM candidate, vice president James Wani Igga is too weak to compete or is too risky for him to become the president of the republic. It is likely that James Wani could easily surrender power to the senior presidential advisor, Kuol Manyang Juuk because there would be no Equatorians to support his bid. A return of power to Bor could provoke negative reactions from the people of Aweil -Warrap from where hail the three generals in command of the forces, as well as from the Nuer ethnicity fronted for by the first vice president Dr. Riek Machar Teny-Dhurgon who could easily close ranks with vice president Taban Deng Gai. And presidential advisor for security affairs Tut Gatluak Manime. In both cases, South Sudan could be plunged into a war of all against all,

The political crisis that could plunge South Sudan into a war of all against all could be the exact interpretation of Salva Kiir's words to Pagan Amum in March 2013, that "this thing (power) you are clamouring for, I won't give it or allow any of you to have it. I will work on it until its stench becomes unbearable, then will I throw it far away such that you run after it, and whoever gets it will never benefit from it." It's a terrible attitude of jealousy, cupidity, rapacity, and possessiveness, of a person who is ready to save himself and betray the people. It is the attitude that made Salva Kiir to ignore the papal gesture of feet-kissing and refused to implement the R-ARCSS. It will be recalled that in April 2019, the Holy Father, Pope Francis invited President Salva Kiir, Dr. Riek Machar, Taban Deng Gai and Rebecca Nyandeng de Mabior to the interdenominational prayers for peace in South Sudan conducted in the Vatican, where he kissed the feet of the four leaders in the hope that they would come back and implement the peace agreement in good faith.

Back in Juba, President Salva Kiir waited until 20th February 2020 to appoint Riek Machar the first vice president and to form the revitalized transitional government of national unity. President procrastinated on the implementation of certain critical provisions of the revitalized agreement until he was forced to request a two year extension of the transitional period. Incidentally, Pope Francis is visiting South Sudan in February 2023 to impress on South Sudan leaders to mind the suffering of their people. This is the dilemma in which many people in South Sudan find themselves particularly those forced to put up with the biting economic condition in Juba and the major towns because of insecurity and ethnic conflicts in their rural homes.

It is possible to trace Kiir's apparent and perversive, bitterness to the power struggle at the top echelon of the SPLM/A, and its politicisation to become deadly ethnic conflict[12]. The refusal to implement the peace agreements for four years speaks to the reality that the political class wouldn't engage in democratic political dialogue to build consensus on important national issues including peaceful transfer of power. The recent political military situation in Upper Nile has shown that while implementing the peace agreement, the political class nevertheless engage in undermining each other It is worth discussing the contradiction that emerged between Dr. Riek Machar, the SPLM/A (IO) leader on the one side, his chief of staff, General Simon Gatwech Dual and his deputy Gen. Johnson Thubo (Olony) on the other hand, and how this contradiction morphed into a Chollo-Nuer war of wider ramifications. The idea here is to prove that the political elite still links with, and recoils to the ethnicity from which it sprouted. As a backdrop to the contradiction between him and his generals, Dr. Riek Machar always had the penchant to abandon his commanders in embarrassing situations. In 2001, he fled Khartoum without knowledge of his commanders who had to find their own ways out of Khartoum. In February 2020 in Juba, two years after signing the R-ARCSS, Dr. Riek Machar took oath of office as first vice president and got stuck in Juba leaving the president advisor on security affairs and the director-general of national security to scavenge on his commanders in Khartoum until they rebelled, delinked and split from his leadership and in what became known as SPLM/A (IO) Kit-Gwang faction.

Kiir's intention could have been to denude Riek Machar of his forces. But the manner Tut Gatluak manoeuvred the two generals in breaking away along the same lines as the Nuer militias before, it meant that the scheme served Sudan's political and economic interests in South Sudan than the survival of President Salva Kiir in power. This was because no sooner had the two generals delinked from Riek Machar did Gen. Johnson Thubo declare he had overthrown Gen. Simon Gatwech; the reason being that Gen. Gatwech did not want to travel to Juba to implement the agreement.[13] Then war erupted in Tonga, Gen. Olony's stronghold in the Chollo Kingdom. The Nuer officer among the Agwalek rebelled and attacked their Chollo colleagues. The conflict in Tonga escalated to Fangak and all SPLM/A (IO) areas in a development that quickly united Riek Machar and Simon Gatwech forces in what appeared to be Nuer unity and solidarity against the Chollo people. The first campaign against the Shilluk (not Olony) was at the behest of the commissioner of Atar country was defeated in August. The second campaign in November involving the people of Ayod and Duk county in Jonglei was still now under way and had escalated to Fashoda and Manyo counties in which three thousand was reported dead and tens of thousands displaced. These were innocent civilians. President Salva Kiir ordered the evacuation to Juba of the Chollo King, Rath Kwongo Dak Padiet, and the SSPDF to take position against the marauding Nuer white army. It has been established that this was the work of Dr. Riek Machar trying to force Salva Kiir to implement certain critical provisions of R-ARCSS.

The contradictions within the political class reflecting its failure to manage the state poses great danger for the organic unity of the people of South Sudan. It marks the inevitable collapse of the state. The indicators of state failure include the standoff in eastern Equatoria between the Dinka Bor pastoralists and the sedentary agrarian communities of Bari, Acholi, Madi and Kuku; the fighting between the Dinka and Maaban over land in the oil fields; the conflict between the Twic and Dinka Ngok of Abyei; the conflict between the different clans of the Rek Dinka in Warrap. All these security breaches might in fact echo the absence of the state and its instruments of coercion, but could have also been deliberately engineered for political survival of the political class in the fashion discussed by Chabal and Daloz (1999) or by Bayart, Ellis and Hibou (1999). The situation in South Sudan is a direct consequence of power struggle at the top of the SPLM translating into political violence at the ethnic and clan levels. The fragility of the state could eventually translate into state failure, collapse and fragmentation. The conflict in the Chollo Kingdom illustrates the role of the state in instigating disorder and breakdown of law and order to serve certain political interests. The Chollo people have not since the eighteenth century experienced such disorder and were therefore caught unprepared. Many of them are having a second thought about being part of South Sudan, and this sentiment is shared by some of the smaller ethnic communities. This could have been the factor underlying the creation of Ruweng and Pibor as independent administrative areas as a means of protecting the Dinka and Murle respectively in Unity and Jonglei states. In itself, the decision was completely wrong and could escalate the already toxic relations between the communities. What plays out as the protection of the Ruweng and the Murle is essential the failure of the state to rein in its authority.

The predicament of smaller ethnic communities in the context of the failure of South Sudan is discussed in chapter seven. It is a frightening situation that leads to insecurity and conflicts. It is also invoking the call for federal system of government by some elites hailing from medium to small ethnic communities as a means to free themselves from the hegemony and domination by the 'big tribe' in face of a weak South Sudan state. The SPLM as a liberation movement and as a ruling political party has completely failed to live to its mandate. The regime of President Salva Kiir Mayardit will not sustain for ever. The worrying post-Kiir scenario is not difficult to predict.

ENDNOTES

1. Following the World War II, Germany was partitioned between the allies into East and West Germany, which later became German Democratic Republic (DDR) and Federal Republic of Germany (FRG) but in 1990 they reunited under the name of FRG. North and South Koreas, and similarly North and South Vietnam were armistice arrangements. Vietnam reunited after the defeat of the American backed government of South Vietnam. South Sudan is not waiting to reunite with the Sudan.

2. George Otto Akumbek Kwanai "The Azania Liberation Front Manifesto 1966. Comboni A/107/2/94

3. Surprisingly, the date stamp showed that it was posted just six days before I received it. In spite of the terrible condition due to war nevertheless patriotism triumphed.

4. The road shoulders were open and shallow ditches like rural road. They were hazardous for crossing vehicles and people as they became water canals during the rainy season.

5. Both Riek Machar and Lam Akol hailed from Upper Nile subregion and their return to the leadership was construed as Upper Nile subregion increasing its portion in the Leadership Council and the Bahr el Ghazal politicians and commander in the SPLA rejected the plan.

6. This relation with TB Joshua caused embarrassment which in other countries could have caused political rancour. Joshua flew into Juba and refused to disembark unless President Salva Kiir, under flashlight of cameras, crawled into his plane. Kiir did as was told to the chagrin of many people...

7. They were the privileged of all the organized forces; modelled on the NCP national security and intelligence organization and operating exactly on the same principles, the national security service in South Sudan has grown into a huge military and economic power executing contracts for the purchase of armaments etc, and have companies in the oil fields, telecommunication and some other shady enterprises.

8.It was a contradiction that must be viewed in its ideological context. Joining the imperialist alliance against Iraq not only exposed Garang's socialist and pan-African pretence but was also intended to announce the shift away from the revolutionary camp at a time it becoming clear that the imperialist camp was winning the cold war.

9. The report of the Auditor-General, 2015

10. The community conflicts in Gogrial, Tonj and Rumbek echoed the power struggle and competition among the political and military elites therein. In Gogrial, the conflict between Aguok and Apuk attributed to former chief justice Ambrose Riiny Thiik and the current chief justice Chan Reech Madut. In Tonj, it was the struggle between Nhial Deng Nhial and Akol Koor Kuch, etc.

11. This was in New Site (Natinga), during the SPLM/A conference convened in June 2004 to thank the traditional authorities: chiefs, kings, rain makers, diviners, etc. for the support it received from the people in the years of war.

12. The Anya-nya2 – SPLA conflict (1983) became a Dinka-Nuer war in which many unsuspecting Dinka recruits into the SPLA were ambushed and murdered on the way to the SPLA camps. The split in the SPLM/A in 1991 resulted in Nuer devastation of the Dinka land in Bor. When Dr. Lam Akol differed with Dr. Riek Machar and separated in1994, about seven Shilluk soldiers in Nasir were murdered in cold blood by their Nuer colleagues. In 2013, the split in the SPLM fitting Salva Kiir against Riek Machar resulted in the massacre of twenty thousand ethnic Nuers in Juba and the eruption of the civil war.

13. Splitting the two generals from Riek Machar was more of Tut Gatluak's design linked not to political survival of President Salva Kiir but most probably to Sudan's national political and economic interests in South Sudan.

CHAPTER SIX

THE IGAD PEACE PROCESS ON SOUTH SUDAN: THE 'IMPOSED' AGREEMENT ON RESOLUTION OF THE CONFLICT IN SOUTH SUDAN (ARCISS) AND THE REVITALIZED AGREEMENT ON THE RESOLUTION OF THE CONFLICT IN SOUTH SUDAN (R-ARCSS)

1. IGAD Mediation in the Sudan: A Brief Background

The inter-Governmental Authority on Development (IGAD) started the peace mediation process between the government of Sudan and the SPLM/A in 1993. It's a complete departure from its mandate as an intergovernmental organization for drought and desertification. The powerful actors therein were Ethiopia and Eritrea, who themselves then just emerged from their wars of liberation. It was then possible to conflate the peace agenda with the drought and other humanitarian issues in the Horn of Africa. Ironically the initiative and invitation of IGAD came at the behest of the National Islamic Front (NIF) fundamentalist government that had then usurped power in a military coup the Sudan. The SPLM/A had split into two factions a year earlier and were engaged in fierce internecine fighting. The NIF government supported the Nasir faction with military logistics in an operation the NIF leaders believed would render moribund the mainstream SPLM/A under the leadership of Dr. John Garang de Mabior[1].

In hindsight, the initiative and the call for IGAD mediation in the war appeared a benign diplomatic gesture, but essentially was part of a well-choreographed strategy to completely knock out the SPLM/A mainstream by isolating it from the Horn of Africa region. On the other hand Kenya and Uganda were both in the NIF cross-hairs for propagation of Islamic fundamentalist ideology in East African[2]. The IGAD committee on the Sudan conflict comprised Ethiopia (chair) and the membership of Eritrea, Kenya, and Uganda. Except for Kenya and Uganda, Eritrea and Ethiopia had just emerged from their wars but did not go through any peace processes themselves. In fact, the two countries had intimate knowledge of the situation in the Sudan, were both weary of Sudan's quickly collapsed peace agreements. The north always did not honour their side of any agreement with the south. The Ethiopian and Eritrean foreign ministers were adamant to pin the peace negotiations to clear principles that addressed the root causes including Sudan's multiple diversities. In September 1994, the committee tabled the 'Declaration of Principles', which the government delegation disdainfully rejected as blatant interference in the affairs of a sovereign state with a rejoinder that Sudan, including the people of southern Sudan, had exercised self-determination in 1953 hence there was no need to include self-determination in the declaration of principles. The Sudan government walked out of IGAD process in search of other mediation avenues.

It was only after successive SPLA military victories leading to the liberation of most of Equatoria and Lakes province in Bahr el Ghazal that the Sudan government in 1997 returned to the IGAD negotiations process. This return underscored an important point that peace could be achieved only when there is parity in the balance of military forces between the antagonists. The IGAD process ended in the signing of the comprehensive peace agreement (CPA). The two most important of the six protocols were the exercise by the people of southern Sudan of their right to self-determination, and democratic transformation of the Sudan. Against the background of 'too many agreements dishonoured', the CPA's affirmation of the separate and independent existence of the SPLA must be counted as the real guarantee to its implementation.

This IGAD peace process on the Sudan successfully completed its task notwithstanding the political glitches in the implementation matrix erected by the National Congress Party (NCP). These included the referendum in Abyei, the exercise of popular consultation in the Nuba Mountains and in Blue Nile regions. The NCP completely rejected the concept of democratic transformation of the Sudanese polity exploiting its grip on power to subvert any moves towards democratisation. The issue of democratic transformation might have played out differently had Dr. Garang not perished in the tragic helicopter crash. However, the NCP behaviour was a registration of political bad faith. The new SPLM leadership was not keen on democratic transformation of the Sudan leave alone the issue of democratising the SPLM and transforming it from a militarist movement into a political party *sensu strictu*. Moreover, as mentioned elsewhere in the book the immediate post-Garang period, the SPLM internally was marred by confusion, power struggle and serious internal political frictions and personal vendetta.

2. The Eruption of Conflict in South Sudan (IGAD 11)

Notwithstanding the enormous political task to conduct the referendum on self-determination, the SPLM leadership and power squabbles never abated; they were too intimate and personal that in spite of such political development as the independence on 11th July 2011, or the negative event as the border war with the Sudan in March 2012, these internal contradictions never eased or ceased. When political contradictions in a political party or liberation movement take on personal rather ideological grounds, they acquire an irreconcilable dimension and become zero sum conflict – a win or lose situation. This situation does not allow for compromise or building consensus. While occupying the top leadership of the SPLM and government of South Sudan, President Salva Kiir Mayardit and his deputy Riek Machar Teny-Dhurgon tried to excluded each other in a manner few people could understand. This exclusivity exploded on 23rd July 2013, when without warning President Salva Kiir dismissed Riek Machar and the entire cabinet.

President Kiir acted on a provision derived from the SPLM constitution stealthy sneaked, without care of its negative ramifications, into the Transitional Constitution of South Sudan 2011. Riek Machar was Salva Kiir's running mate in the 2010 midterm elections and the action of President Salva Kiir to dismiss his deputy was the height of a serious political contradiction. This contradiction erupted violently on 15th December 2013in the form fierce fighting in the presidential guard unit, the Tiger Battalion apparently between ethnic Dinka and Nuer in the force. However, shooting extended into the suburbs of Juba joined by forces, which apparently were not SPLA, with orders to shoot to kill targeting only ethnic Nuer men, women, children and even the elderly. Dinka with facial marks Agar, Ngok, Luach, Nyarweng and Hol who looked like the Nuers were also targeted and killed or were humiliated to dance or sing in their language to escape death. Ethnic cleansing was the singular act of inhumanity, and the people of South Sudan sunk to the lowest point in their proud history of resistance.

Apparently, the fighting that erupted in the Tiger Battalion could have just been a trigger to detonate the volcano that had been smouldering since March 2013. The power struggle in the SPLM leadership surfaced fitting chairman Salva Kiir against Dr. Riek Machar the vice chairman, Pagan Amum, the Secretary general, and Rebecca Nyandeng de Mabior each showing interest in leadership of the SPLM and of the country. It is a constitutional right of a party member to aspire to the highest office. But, Kiir's reaction was to paralyze the functions of the SPLM, suspend the state congresses scheduled for April 2013 , which should have ended in the SPLM third National Convention in May 2013. The third National Convention was to elect the SPLM flag bearer for the presidential and general elections scheduled for April 2015. Kiir's action to freeze the political process in the SPLM was tantamount to a political coup t put an end to all democratic processes not only in the SPLM but also in the whole country. The nascent republic of South Sudan entered into an era of uncertainty. It was a great surprise to many people when Dr. Riek Machar Teny declared he was leading a rebellion a few day after the fighting in the presidential guards unit. He was joined by fellow Nuer commanders and their troops in Bentiu and Bor, this was followed by a general mobilization in Lou Nuer and eastern Jikany. The civil war erupted in Juba but had effectively started to devastate areas of Upper Nile Region [Jonglei, Unity and Upper Nile states]. However, Riek Machar directed his forces to destroy Malakal instead of Juba, to create a another level of contradiction.

The IGAD extra-ordinary summit of the Heads of State and Government over the conflict in the republic of South Sudan convened in Nairobi, Kenya on 27th December 2013, and the IGAD II process on the conflict in South Sudan began in earnest. The IGAD Committee on the South Sudan conflict comprised Ethiopia (Chair) with Ambassador Seyoum Mesfin as the IGAD Special Envoy on the conflict in South Sudan, deputized by Gen.

Lazaro Sumbeiweyo of Kenya with Uganda and Sudan as auxiliary members of the committee playing lukewarm roles in the process. Addis Ababa was then the venue to which both the Government of South Sudan and the rebellion were requested to send in delegations to start the talks on cessation of hostilities (CoHs).

Dr. Riek Machar responded positively to the invitation to send a delegation. The response was surprising; in just under two weeks earlier he had declared himself leader of a rebellion, and the rebellion had not established itself permanently on the ground. This issue nevertheless is not our concern here although we may come back to it elsewhere in the text. The problem of great concern was that IGAD search for quick fix to a problem they did not have time to study.

The Special Envoy had not established the root causes of the conflict, which indeed made it difficult to formulate a correct strategy towards resolution or to contain its outward manifestations. The war in South Sudan barely three years into its independence was a great concern to the African Union and the United Nations whose mission, the United Nations Mission in South Sudan (UNMISS) was established to help build the state in South Sudan[3]. The sudden eruption of violence eluded the Special Representative of the Secretary General although she was fully abreast with the political developments in GOSS, the SPLM, and the power struggle that ripped its top echelon. It was a conflict within the same party and between individual leaders who have been together in the struggle for nearly the age of the liberation movement. We mentioned elsewhere the attempts earlier to help save the SPLM from itself but the power struggle and the concomitant toxic relations between leaders were were powerful; indeed being a carryover from the days of the war of national liberation. That they were in armed struggle neither erased their differences nor brought unity between them; indeed, the dynamics of the armed struggle and the militarization in the SPLM/A incubated the differences of these leaders until the point of explosion.

The contradiction in the SPLM/A was essentially structural and deep-rooted dating back to the formation of the liberation movement in 1983. The militarist character of the movement did not dispose its leaders to democratic discourses. but they always preferred to deny the existence of any problems between them[4] rendering it difficult to assist them. It is always impossible to assist people who are in perpetual denial of the problems afflicting them. Both the African National Congress and the Norwegian Labour Party attempted to help the SPLM leaders resolve the power struggle. They both left in disgust.

The African National Congress leaders of South Africa were right in their assessment of the situation in South Sudan, and the personalized nature of the conflict between Salva Kiir, Riek Machar, Pagan Amum and Rebecca Nyandeng, all members of the SPLM Political Bureau. ANC's proposal was a different modality to involve only the ANC and the Ethiopian ruling coalition, EPRDF to tackle the issue with the SPLM leaders instead of the IGAD mediation. The IGAD process was already complicated by the presence of both republic of Uganda and the republic of the Sudan as mediators suggesting that the notion of too many cooks spoil the broth could easily kick-in. The two countries were deeply involved in the South Sudan conflict inadvertently on account of their respective national security, economic and political interests. The ANC proposal didn't stand or rather suffered malicious sabotage.

In such situation involving IGAD region, Ethiopia would be driven by her national security concerns, and would use IGAD instruments only as the vehicle to further than concern. In this respect, IGAD[5] mediation with Ethiopia as the Special Envoy carried the day. Indeed, for all practical purposes, IGAD served Ethiopia's national interest in the region more than peace in Sudan or Somalia. The reasons became clear later why the ANC proposal for inter-SPLM mediation and dialogue flopped. The IGAD Special Envoy was more interested in Ethiopia's national and territorial security than peace to South Sudan. He acted authoritatively to direct the mediation process while the deputy and the other envoys watched in disbelief or perhaps in tacit approval; none of them had interest in a peaceful South Sudan. It appeared the Special Envoy used the IGAD mediation to experiment a hypothesis 'how a successful state like Ethiopia could live in security with failed states like South Sudan or Somalia'. This had nothing to do with mediating peace in South Sudan but theoretically the end game of IGAD mediation in South Sudan conflict would be to create a situation that would perpetually make South Sudan a buffer zone to protect Ethiopia against

Egypt and the Sudan over the Great Ethiopian Renaissance Dam (GERD)[6].

This experiment played out in a drama, which depicted the IGAD Special Envoy as visibly favouring the government of South Sudan, when in fact he did everything to block the scientific understanding of the conflict. The insistence on 'power-sharing' and the so-called 'critical reforms' in the system was a deliberate attempt to block identify and earth out the fundamental contradiction underlying the conflict to enable the mediators and negotiators to craft a resolution. The IGAD mediation agenda of power-sharing and critical reforms was such that it had to involve all stakeholders in the country. This was erroneous and diversionary; who would take what percent of the power bogged the mediation from July 2014 to August 2015 and in the end it was an 'imposed agreement on the resolution of the conflict in South Sudan (I-ARCISS).

The negotiations over the cessation of hostilities between the Government of the Republic of South Sudan and the rebellion, which still called itself the SPLM/A didn't take much time. Riek Machar announcement that he was leading a rebellion was a bluff. The SPLA soldiers, the Lou and Jikany white armies had already melted into their homesteads with war booties from Bor, Malakal and Nasir. He had to quickly send a delegation to Addis Ababa to redeem his credibility as a rebel leader. The agreement on the cessation of hostilities (CoHs) between the SPLA (government) and SPLA (rebels) was signed to enable the talks on the substantial issues to begin. For practical purposes it was imperative to differentiate between the two delegations that claimed the same name - the SPLM/A. It was preposterous then that Riek Machar claimed the name SPLM against which he was leading a rebellion against the SPLM. It took sometimes before an agreement was reached that the government would claim SPLM/A (IG) and the rebellion called itself SPLM/A in Opposition abbreviated as SPLM/A (IO) to avoid confusion with the SPLM/A in Government.

3. Power-Sharing a *Recipe* for Perpetual Strife

The greatest mistake, indeed, the inconsistency the IGAD mediation committed was to introduce 'power-sharing' as the remedy to the unescapable power struggle that had rocked the top echelon of the SPLM since 1983. It was inescapable due its structural character, and because of that, it bound to recur almost immediately every time the SPLM/A leadership attempted to resolve its contradictions without addressing the organizational structure and institutionalization of the liberation movement. The power-sharing recipe the CPA provided for NCP and SPLM was not a panacea for resolving the power struggle in the SPLM; this was a completely different situation. However, the saying that, 'who pays the piper sets the tone', underscored what transpired in the IGAD mediation process.

The IGAD region itself is an intersection of national, regional, and foreign interests and most of the time these foreign interests preponderated over the regional and national interests due to enormous financial and economic resources they bring in to set the tone. In February 2014, a group of European NGOs and donors met in Nairobi and decided that the former SPLM political detainees hosted by the Kenyan government were a better alternative to Salva Kiir and/or Riek Machar, and therefore should be included in the negotiation process. Like the SPLM/A (IO), this group, eleven in number, renamed themselves SPLM Leaders Former Political Detainees abbreviated SPLM-Leaders (FPD) and they joined the peace talks. In the same vein, other political parties in and outside the government, the civil society organizations, the women groups, youths, faith-based group and eminent personalities were included in the negotiation roster.

Although this IGAD power-sharing formula purported to emulate the CPA power-sharing between the different political forces in the Sudan, nevertheless the CPA was negotiated by only two warring parties namely the NCP and the SPLM. The National Democratic Alliance (NDA) had to negotiate a separate agreement with NCP in Cairo; the Dar Furi movements had to negotiate a separate agreement in Abuja; the Beja negotiated the Eastern Sudan Peace Agreement in Asmara. The real power-sharing was between the NCP and the SPLM. The logic of this arrangement was that peace agreement can only be negotiated effectively by parties to the conflict. The involvement of the other groups not participating in the war like the political parties, civil society groups, women groups, which were not in government and were not with the rebels, but have vested interest in security and constitutional rule in the country would participate appropriately in the constitution making process. The SPLM Political

Leaders (FPD) who initially were part of the power struggle that triggered the war, but refused to participate in the war, the civil society, women and youth groups and the faith-based groups and the so-called eminent persons did not have to participate in the peace talks at all. The area for their effective participation would have been in the constitution making process.

However, the Special Envoy jammed the peace talks with these groups and rendered more complicated the peace process. Those talks served something else rather than bringing peace to South Sudan. It was his determination to do the negotiations his way that prompted the SPLM/A (IO) delegation to boycott the talks soliciting threats of retribution from the Special Envoy.

On another level, the IGAD mediation was bound to run into difficulties due to the participation of Sudan and Uganda; the two countries were proxy to the war. In one of the IGAD extraordinary assembly of Heads of State and Government, the Special Envoys proposed to the summit that President Salva Kiir and the chief rebel Riek Machar be barred from participation in the anticipated transitional government; and both Salva and Riek were requested to submit names of their respective nominees. President Museveni intervened to torpedo the proposal but already the rumours were in the air about the prospective candidates. The Special Envoy definitely overstepped his authority; nobody in the IGAD region, African Union or even the United Nations Security Council had the powers and authority in the international law to bar the president of a state. The Special Envoys charged with the responsibility of mediation by the same by the summit, which included Salva Kiir, had no authority to make such a proposal. This attitude of the IGAD Special Envoy and the ensuing diplomatic glitch pointed to the unstable internal political dynamics in the Ethiopian governing coalition; It did not take long before it showed up dramatically in the resignation of the Prime Minister and the change of government leadership in Ethiopia. The precipitous situation in Addis Ababa had profound impact on the quest for peace in South Sudan; coming after the collapse of the imposed ARCISS the changed situation in Ethiopia introduced new South Sudanese actors in form of South Sudan Opposition Alliance (SSOA) and new regional mediator in the person form of the Sudan's foreign minister Dirdiery.

The question of ratios in this power-sharing arithmetic generated heated debate particularly between the SPLM Leaders (FPD) and the Other Political Parties (OPP) comprising the Umbrella Group and the National Alliance. It was unthinkable that the SPLM Leaders (FPD) made up only of eleven members got more than the OPP, which comprised more than thirty registered and unregistered political parties. The government decision to prevent the delegation of the National Alliance from travelling to Addis Ababa saved the Special Envoys the embarrassment into which they had lobbed themselves because of bad arithmetic. But it demonstrated the futility of the IGAD mediating; President Salva Kiir could arrest in Juba the delegates of other political parties and neither IGAD nor the African could raise a finger in protest. Surprisingly, the sanctioned political parties still got their ministerial shares on the implementation of the imposed agreement of the resolution of the conflict in South Sudan.

4. The SPLM-Reunification Process
International and regional diplomacy could be complex because it is pushed by conflicting and competing national interests. We have above alluded to a joint attempt by ANC and EPRDF to resolve the inter-SPLM conflict. The IGAD Special Envoy torpedoed the effort in favour of IGAD mediation. However, before the IGAD mediation could run its course to a logical conclusion, the project of SPLM reunification sprang up suggesting that there were high-stakes games at play. The manner it sprang up was rather suspicious coming on the heels of the torpedoed IGAD proposed non-participation of Salva Kiir and Riek Machar in the anticipated transitional government.

The SPLM reunification project was a veiled anti-IGAD mediation, and indeed the IGAD Special Envoy, Ato Seyoum Mesfin, was deeply unhappy with the initiative. The reunification involved the three SPLM factions participating in the IGAD process namely the SPLM (IG), the SPLM/A (IO) and the SPLM Leaders (FPD), and the invitation to travel to Arusha arrived while the delegations were attending an IGAD sponsored workshop in Bahr Dar. The SPLM (IG) and the SPLM leaders (FPD) seemed aware and were in knowledge of the initiative while the SPLM/A (IO) was in complete darkness. Dr. Riek Machar accepted the invitation to attend before even subjecting the proposal to an internal study. It's apparent, some people were playing high stakes game behind the scenes but pointing to a conspiracy to isolate the IGAD Special Envoy, seen by some of those players as an arrogant autocrat.

It's obvious, the ANC had not completely abandoned the idea of SPLM reunification. It was indeed an ANC - EPRDF initiative but the IGAD Special Envoy shelved it in favour of the IGAD initiative supported by Ethiopia. It now surfaced as a project driven by Chama Cha Mapinduzi (CCM) the ruling party of the United Republic of Tanzania. The presence at the signing ceremony of the SPLM Re-Unification Agreement presided over by President Jakaya Kikwete in Arusha of the Ugandan President, Yoweri Museveni, the Kenyan President, Uhuru Kenyetta and the ANC vice president, Cyril Ramaphosa and the corresponding absence of the Ethiopian Prime Minister, Hail Mariam Desalegn spoke to the growing disenchantment between ANC and EPRDF spurred by diplomatic blunders of the IGAD Special Envoy. Behind the curtains Uganda was not pleased with the Ethiopian led mediation and President Museveni could have been in the loop either through President Salva Kiir or deputy president Cyril Ramaphosa to support the Arusha process. Occurring between states these blunders could make things not only sticky and difficult to unpack but also completely change the direction things flowed. The SPLM reunification process indeed isolated Ethiopia although she still held the IGAD dossier on South Sudan. It would later turn out that Kiir and Museveni played games to embarrass both the ANC and CCM leaderships.

These were then two parallel processes that touched each

other only through the parties at war. Instead of enriching each other through mutual understanding and co-operation the two processes tended to cancel each other rendering both of them almost sterile. The lack of co-operation between the two managers could only mean delay in expediting peace for the people of South Sudan and the reunification process would also be meaningless. This became clear after signing the reunification agreement; only two factions namely the SPLM (IG) and the SPLM Leaders (FPD) continued to pursue the process to Pretoria and Juba. The two factions found it expedient to isolate the SPLM/A (IO). In a ceremony in Juba attended by President Museveni and President Kikwete, the SPLM Secretary General Pagan Amum was re-instated into his position in the SPLM leadership. However, it did not take long for Pagan Amum to realize that the SPLM reunification was a hoax. Insecure and afraid for his life, Hon. Pagan Amum stormed out of Juba in disgust and went into exile where he now leads the Real SPLM[7]. The notion of SPLM reunification was just a charade. Chairman Salva Kiir disdained returning the SPLM to the status ante, did not want Riek Machar and Pagan Amum back in the SPLM hierarchy, but at the same time Kiir was apprehensive of the Special Envoys tactics in the negotiation process. However, President Kiir relied more on President Museveni to rescue him and this could then be gleaned from the deteriorating diplomatic relations between Kampala and Addis Ababa. Had President Kiir been honest and genuine about the SPLM reunification this would have dealt a death blow to the IGAD process. It was not permissible for President Salva Kiir to play tricks with the two processes. The obfuscation and procrastination with the SPLM reunification automatically led to the imposition of the agreement on the resolution of conflict in South Sudan (ARCISS) in August 2015. In a threatening voice 'take it' or 'leave it', the IGAD Special Envoy threw the draft ARCISS to the parties. This behaviour on the part of the Special Envoy was rather ludicrous; it gave President Salva Kiir the latitude to accept to sign or reject the agreement.

5. Peace Agreement is Only Useful When its Provisions are Implementable

On 17th of August 2015, the parties namely the SPLM/A (IO), the SPLM Leaders (FPD), the OPP, the women groups, the youths, the civil society organization, the faith-based group, and the eminent personalities signed the 'imposed' agreement on the resolution of the conflict in South Sudan (ARCISS). President Salva Kiir, who happened to be in the hall at the beginning of the signing ceremony refused to append his signature. And as he and his government delegation left the hall, this triggered hysteric wailing among the South Sudanese women; perhaps they never expected him to refuse to sign the peace agreement. In South Sudanese traditional and indigenous cultures women wailing signified the death of somebody; indeed, the peace agreement – ARCISS died at birth. In a little than two weeks later, on 26th of August, President Salva Kiir signed the agreement but with twenty-three reservations, suggesting that the agreement would not be implemented. Not only that but on 1st October he dropped a bombshell in the form of Executive Order 36/2015 dividing South Sudan into twenty-eight (28) in contravention of the ten (10) states upon which ARCISS was constructed. The issue of twenty-eight states was in reaction to Riek Machar's twenty-one states proposal he distributed even before the SPLM/A (IO) delegation had discussed and accepted. The Padang Jieng community in Upper Nile whose two districts, namely Renk and Bailiet, had been erased by Riek Machar in his proposal to the mediators, wrote a petition to President Salva Kiir, who endorsed their twenty-eight states proposal.

President Salva Kiir's reservations and his executive order creating twenty-eight, which later increased to thirty-two states completely rubbished the IGAD mediation process. It demonstrated his determination to prove that the ARCISS would not be implemented by reaching out to the Jieng Council of Elders, which was openly hostile to the notion of power-sharing; they believed power-sharing watered-down Dinka power in the republic of South Sudan. But this was also to prove that IGAD Special Envoy couldn't have it roughshod over the head of a sovereign. It also proved that the IGAD mediators did not correctly appreciate the complexity of South Sudan situation or as we have alluded elsewhere in the text the Special Envoys was experimenting with the South Sudan peace process.

Two regional forces driven by economic and security interests pull on South Sudan. The one force [Kenya and Uganda] pulls South Sudan to join the East African Community, while the other force {Ethiopia} towards the completion of GERD and isolation of Egypt. President Salva Kiir knew all this, but his concern was not about South Sudan's national interest like the other leaders; he was concerned about his personal power. In this respect, Salva Kiir had expected the region to help get rid of his detractors particularly Riek Machar and Pagan Amum. That the ANC and CCM through the SPLM reunification process returned Pagan Amum as SPLM Secretary-General, and IGAD Special Envoys through the IGAD mediation had imposed Riek Machar on him as his first vice president incensed President Salva Kiir and pushed him to a point to destroy the ARCISS as well as the SPLM reunification agreement.

The ARCISS was vulnerable from the word go. It was constructed on fallacious assumptions with little bearings on reality in South Sudan. The region (Ethiopia) falsely assumed that Riek Machar was the political military force they could rely on to achieve their interests in South Sudan. In fact, he wasn't. He could have become that force had the SPLM Leaders (FPD) joined him to form into a formidable political and military force, but the international community forced them on Uhuru Kenyetta in the vain belief that they would be the alternative force to Salva Kiir and Riek Machar. All this did not occur as planned but left President Salva Kiir to bask in the weakness of his political enemies. The region assisted Salva Kiir by appointing the former Botswana President Festus Mogae to chair the Joint Assessment and Evaluation Commission (JMEC); he could not ensure the implementation of the pre-transitional processes. President Salva Kiir quickly seized on this apparent weakness of JMEC to build in-roads into the SPLM/A (IO) to frustrate the implementation of key provisions of ARCISS in collaboration with Riek Machar's Advance Team leader, Gen. Taban Deng Gai[8].

6. The Collapse of ARCISS

In view of the preceding lines, it was inevitable that the imposed agreement on the resolution of the conflict in South Sudan would collapse anytime into its implementation. The writings were already on the wall when the parties signed the agreement on August 17th, 2015, in Addis Ababa, Ethiopia and Salva Kiir signed it with reservations on 26th August in Juba. However, ARCISS didn't collapse only because Salva Kiir desired it so, it collapsed also due to Riek Machar's lack of strategic political thinking. Salva Kiir only accentuated and exacerbated Riek Machar's weakness by hatching a conspiracy in collaboration with Riek's lieutenant, Gen. Taban Deng Gai to derail the implementation of the peace agreement.

In dealing with the peace agreement, Dr. Riek Machar thought signing the paper was enough and did not need further elaborate thinking to ensure that President Salva Kiir did his part to the implementation of the agreement. He therefore committed two grave errors of judgement in a row. The first error of judgement was against the advice of many senior people in the SPLM/A (IO) leadership meeting in Pagak. Dr. Riek Machar appointed Taban Deng Gai instead of Alfred Lado-Gore to lead the SPLM/A (IO) Advanced Team (AT) to Juba to oversee the arrangements toward ARCISS implementation. Cdr. Alfred Lado-Gore, a revolutionary of the first order did not have other interests beside the interest of the SPLM/ (IO), unlike Taban Deng, who valued the social than political relations with Riek Machar, would have loyally stuck to the terms of his assignment and would have denied Salva Kiir or his agents such games that Gen. Taban Deng did play with the SPLM/A (IO) delegation in Juba.

The Second error of judgement was to deny Taban Deng Gai the petroleum portfolio in the transitional government of national unity (TGONU). This created the condition for Kiir-Taban alliance against Riek Machar and the SPLM/A (IO). Taban Deng had scuttled the ministerial lottery to prevent the petroleum docket falling to another party, and Dr. Riek Machar should have taken bote of this fact; he instead listened to his wife, Angelina Teny to appoint Dak Doup Bichok instead of Gen. Taban Deng, and immediately hell broke loose. Gen. Taban Deng Gai and Gen. Paul Malong Awan combined efforts to chase Riek Machar and SPLM/A (IO) forces out of Juba, and usurped Riek Machar position as first vice president. The whole episode was a child game played without serious reflection or consideration for the country and the destiny of the people. Riek Machar's suffered his own folly; couldn't save himself or South Sudan.

The chair of JMEC declared the ARCISS was wounded but still alive; the IGAD under the pressure of Obama Administration recognized as *de facto* the new situation in South Sudan while Riek Machar was running for his life in the bushes of Equatoria. This situation could have been avoided had Riek Machar been strategic in his thinking and left Taban Deng to scuff whatever money he wanted from the petroleum docket. Indeed, that was the reason he scuttled and outstepped the ministerial lottery against the provisions of ARCISS implementation matrix. For the people of South Sudan ARCISS was one step forward to peace and development, its collapse was ten steps backwards to darkness and despair. It triggered an escalation of war throughout South Sudan and led to the proliferation of political and armed opposition to Salva Kiir and his regime.

With the resumption of war, the IGAD mediation reaped what it sowed. Because it rejected the discussion of the root causes in favour of power-sharing it forfeited the correct understanding of the conflict. The IGAD Special Envoys would have learnt that the conflict had structural causes and could not be resolved by sharing power. They would have discovered that the lack of democracy and functional institutions in the SPLM were the triggers as well as the drivers of the conflict, and that the responsibility laid with the SPLM leadership in the person of President Salva Kiir Mayardit, who when he came up with the twenty-three reservations against ARCISS, he wasn't joking. Kiir sincerely believed that ARCISS was imposed on him to change the precedence the SPLM/A had established during the war whereby power and public authority was personified in the leader. He stuck to this system that he could audaciously tell off his colleagues in the SPLM Political Bureau that "I will only leave power in the manner Dr. John Garang did"[9], suggesting that he would die in office to receive state funeral.

7. The National Dialogue – A Misplaced and a Wasted Opportunity

President Salva Kiir is an interesting personality when it came to political survival; come to him with a project and will immediately accept the idea only to refuse the responsibility should the idea flop or boomerang. Following the collapse of ARCISS in July 2016, one local think tank, the Sudd Institute, came up with the concept of the National Dialogue as a means of stimulating national conversation for peace. In fact, national dialogue should have begun immediately after the formation of the Government of Southern Sudan (GOSS) in the context of the CPA chapter on national reconciliation and healing. This was to transform the CPA from the political compromise it was to peace and social harmony among communities affected by the war. President Salva Kiir endorsed the idea of National Dialogue, appointed its two co-chairs, Maulana Abel Alier and Angelo Beda, both veteran politicians of the Southern Region. President Kiir launched the National Dialogue, and promised to implement its recommendations and resolutions.

As an idea, the National Dialogue was plausible, but its timing was inappropriate. The civil war still raged and indeed the scope for genuine dialogue could be limited to a few connected individuals or entities. However, its copycat nature notwithstanding[10] the National Dialogue would have been a very good idea to back up ARCISS in consolidating peace and social harmony. Unfortunately, ARCISS collapsed rendering untenable the National Dialogue. Incidentally, the form in which it was presented and executed; the national dialogue was a misnomer. Instead of sustained discussions and debate of the fundamental deep-rooted social, economic and political problems afflicting the people of South Sudan, it was reduced to facts finding in the communities. The National Dialogue Steering committee replicated the facts-finding exercise the SPLM National Secretariat conducted among its grassroots in 2012. The findings and recommendation of the SPLM National Secretariat heightened the contradictions in the SPLM leadership[11] which eventually translated into violent conflict on 15th December 2013. Democratic principles provide for sharing out responsibility although the leader would take much of the responsibility for any failure or success. The National Dialogue Secretariat conducted regional conferences, meetings of the civil society groups, business community, faith-based groups, women and youth, which discoursed the findings and recommendation of the regional conferences. Finally, the National Dialogue process was capped with the concluding National Dialogue Conference that took place in Juba Freedom Hall. This conference incidentally came after the formation of the revitalized transitional government of national unity (R-TGONU), which added another important political dimension that it served better the peace purposes and that the political class would now implement its recommendations.

An independent assessment and evaluation revealed that there was no genuine political dialogue between the different social and political groups; as a result the process failed to bring out into the open the fundamental issues underpinning the conflict.

The most interesting recommendation of the National Dialogue prevented the participation of President Salva Kiir and his first vice president Riek Machar in the election anticipated at the end of the transitional period. It was like a leaf from the IGAD mediation in 2014. And indeed, this recommendation was the straw that broke the camel back, and as was expected ended the National Dialogue.

8. The IGAD High-Level Revitalization Forum was a Missed Opportunity

The implementation of ARCISS showed negative signs from the point President Salva Kiir refused to deploy the Regional Protection Force (RPF) and prevented the SPLM/A IO) to bring into Juba not more than One thousand three hundred troops armed only with personal weapons. In his calculation, President Kiir wanted Riek Machar to come to Juba with a small force and no support weapons rendering him susceptible to capture and execution. Thus, in his procrastination and doubts in mind, President Kiir and his co-plotters failed to win the dogfight in J1 on 8th July 2016 or the attack on Riek Machar H/Qs in Jebel Kujur on July 10th. Instead, these failures created condition for the escalation of war to other hitherto peaceful areas like central and western Equatoria, and western Bahr el Ghazal.

President Salva Kiir deliberately ignited the war in these areas as part of his counterinsurgency tactics to destabilize them, disperse the civil population, and to prevent their occupation by armed opposition forces. Instead of winning over the people, he alienated them and the brutality of the government forces led to emergence and proliferation of new rebel groups. In central Equatoria, National Salvation Front (NAS) sprouted under the leadership of former SPLA deputy Chief of Staff, Gen. Thomas Cirrillo Swaka. In western Equatoria, the Azande established the Southern Sudan National Movement for Change (SSNMC) under the leadership of former elected Governor, Joseph Bakasoro. There were also remnants of Riek Machar SPLM/A (IO) forces scattered in the area when Riek Machar retreated into Congo. In north-western Upper Nile a rebel movement, National Democratic Movement (NDM) under the leadership of Dr. Lam Akol emerged in competition with the SPLM/A (IO) and its ally Agwalek over territorial rights.

A split occurred between President Salva Kiir and his SPLA Chief of General Staff, Gen. Paul Malong Awan who ruthlessly prosecuted the war against the insurgency in Upper Nile and Jonglei. This fall out between the president and his general added another layer of conflict; Gen. Paul Malong Awan established an armed group, South Sudan United Front/Army (SSUF/A). It's worth mentioning that most of the SPLA forces in and around Juba hailed from Malong's home turf and this worried President Kiir prompting increased recruitment of personnel mainly from Warrap into the National Security under the command of Gen. Akol Koor, who was Malong's nemesis. The proliferation of the political and armed opposition compounded the complexity of the political architecture in South Sudan and therefore rendered intractable the resolution.

The failure of Riek Machar to create condition for unification of the political and armed opposition, or to create conditions for an effective alliance and cooperation against the common enemy complicated the political architecture leading to further splits and splinterism. Unity of purpose would have served the opposition better but as it transpired many of these groups were political shopping bags in the IGAD power-sharing political marketplace. The peace negotiations that involved all and sunder was a bad diplomatic exercise. It encouraged the formation of briefcase liberation movements and parties. It was in this context that the IGAD mediation and the chair of JMEC came up with the idea of resuscitating the peace agreement on the resolution of the conflict in South Sudan. The High-Level Revitalization Forum was conceived along the same lines as the ARCISS modality and that would be its failure.

In August 2017, the IGAD Special Envoys conducted a preparatory workshop in Bishoftu in Ethiopia and that involved some South Sudanese intellectuals and researchers close the political establishment in Juba. As a result, the organizers could not entertain fresh or new ideas being introduced into the process. But, shortly after the process kicked off, a precipitous political crisis imploded within the Ethiopian ruling party leading to the resignation of its Prime Minister, Haile Mariam Desalegn and the appointment of Dr. Abiy Ahmed the Prime Minister forcing a change in the configuration of the IGAD mediation; Dr. Ismael Wais (Djibouti) became the Special Envoy on the conflict in South Sudan[12] deputized by the Foreign Minister of the Sudan,

Dirdiery Mohammed Ahmed. President Omer Hassan Ahmed Al-Bashir and President Yoweri Kaguta Museveni co-chaired the HLRF. The talks shifted to Khartoum. The shift of the talks to Khartoum worried many of the southern Sudanese armed and political opposition groups. They were right. They were housed in the premises of a Sudanese National Security and Intelligence Institute, and were suspicious that President Omer Al-Bashir and President Museveni were likely to buttress Kiir's position in the peace negotiations. The role of the two leaders was not about peace in South Sudan; they were driven more by their respect national interests in the South Sudan conflict. In fact, the Sudanese foreign minister, Dirdiery Mohammed Ahmed threatened to deport to Juba any group that did not tow the schedule of talks which slanted more in favour of the government of South Sudan. It was like gun-boat diplomacy; no wonder that NAS, Real SPLM, NDM PF and others, now categorized as 'hold-out' groups, refused to sign the revitalized agreement during the signing ceremony on 12th September 2018 in Addis Ababa, Ethiopia.

It would be grand folly to continuously keep applying the same formula to the same problem hoping to achieve different results. This was IGAD power-sharing formula to resolve the conflict in South Sudan notwithstanding the complexity it had grown into consequent to Kiir's power attitude that led to the escalation of war and the proliferation of the political and armed opposition was a foregone conclusion of failure. The conflict had outgrown its initial dimension as a power struggle within the SPLM/A leadership involving Salva Kiir and his deputy Riek

Machar from where it dithered into a Dinka-Nuer ethnic conflict following the massacre of ethnic Nuers in Juba in December 2013. The collapse of ARCISS in July 2016 accentuated the collapse of the SPLM reunification and rendered intractable the resolution of the political conflict within the SPLM. This created another social and political dynamic, which required a paradigm shift in the political thinking.

The IGAD high-level revitalization forum could have indeed been a missed opportunity to resolve the myriad problems that afflicted the people of South Sudan. The current problems have their roots in the history of colonialism in the Sudan and that only a solution based on correct understanding of the fundamental contradictions underpinning the conflict would have been viable and sustainable in terms of implementation. In this respect, the IGAD mediators profoundly erred by adopting the power-sharing modality hoping that the results would be different from the collapsed ARCISS. A correct prognosis of the conflict would have revealed all its dimensions: social, economic, political, and cultural, and would point to where lie the fundamental contradictions of poverty, ignorance, and cultural backwardness of the people and the means to resolved them. It would reveal that South Sudan is a poor country but potentially rich in natural resources, suggesting that the poverty and ignorance of the people stemmed from lack of development of the productive forces. And therefore the solution lies in socioeconomic development, and not in power-sharing. Solution to poverty and ignorance lies in the development of these natural resources to transform the conditions of poverty, ignorance and cultural backwardness of the people.

Simply expressed, the people are poor, ignorant, and backward because they have not developed their productive forces and as a result generated secondary contradiction, which now drive the conflicts. This means that the fundamental contradiction that underlies the conflict revolves around the issue of social and economic development of the productive forces: land, human and the enormous natural resource potentials in human resources, agriculture: livestock, crops, horticulture, forestry, fisheries, and wildlife sectors; water, aquaculture, water electric power; energy sources: hydrocarbons, solar, wind, and biogas, etc. minerals and other natural resources. The solution to this fundamental contradiction does not lie in power-sharing formula proposed by the IGAD but lies in crafting a socioeconomic developmental programme.

The crafting of this socioeconomic development programme could have therefore been the task of the IGAD High Level Revitalization Forum envisioned as a long-drawn-out conference of all the social and political forces in South Sudan assisted by professionals in the field of economics, law, and humanities to workshop these issues of social and economic development far away from power-sharing modality. The HLRF process should have not been about peace negotiation but about drawing out the programme for resolving the fundamental contradictions underpinning the conflict and building consensus around them.

9. The Revitalized Agreement on Resolution of Conflict in South Sudan (R-ARCSS)

The precipitous political situation in Ethiopia forced an unexpected change in the leadership of the IGAD HLRF making the republic of the Sudan assisted by the republic of Uganda chair and deputy of HLRF and shifted the venue of the talks to Khartoum. This was a political development that worried many opposition leaders; they were apprehensive of the attitude of President Bahir and President Museveni towards the opposition to President Salva Kiir Mayardit. It would be recalled that both Sudan and Uganda were proxy participants in the conflict in South Sudan and therefore wouldn't be difficult to perceive the role they would play in the negotiation.

The IGAD HLRF process didn't depart much from ARCISS process except for the chair and the inclusion in the process of the newly formed political and armed opposition. The opposition reported bullying, threats and intimidation of its members by the Sudan Intelligence and Security Service agents meant to give them protection. After four months of engagement, the revitalized agreement on the resolution of the conflict in South Sudan (R-ARCSS) brokered by President Omer Hassan Ahmed Al-Bashir and President Yoweri Kaguta Museveni was signed in Addis Ababa, Ethiopia on 12th September 2018. The agreement had congenital defects, which the mediators deliberately ignored. As a result, some members of SSOA refused to sign. Troika refused to sign as guarantors and Mr. Festus Mogae, the JMEC chairman declined to continue working for IGAD and opted to leave.

The only two individuals upbeat about the R-ARCSS were Dr. Riek Machar Teny-Dhurgon, the leader of the SPLM/A (IO) who had just been released from nearly two-year incarceration in South Africa, now appointed first vice president, and Mrs Rebecca Nyandeng de Mabior appointed one of the five vice presidents. The government threw a big party at Dr. Garang's Memorial Grounds in Juba to celebrate the R-ARCSS on 30th October attended by six heads of state and government. That occasion wasn't impressive as it should have; opinion was ambivalent, but it settled down to depression when Riek Machar, Lam Akol and other leaders who had come to celebrate the peace agreement flew back to Khartoum that evening with Al-Bashir. It was indeed an anti-climax of the whole peace drama.

The reasons for this sobriety were already in people's faces; the country was in acute social and economic crisis and the government in eight to ten months had not paid its employees including its diplomatic missions abroad for reasons known only to President Salva Kiir Mayardit. The government of the republic of South Sudan was not brook; the oil and non-oil revenues on which the country depended, were, under the watch of the president, lining the pockets and bank account of a few strong individuals in government. The R-ARCSS and its implementation was going to be another economic burden for the economy. It provided for a bloated government: an executive of thirty-five cabinet ministers and ten deputy ministers, a legislature of six hundred fifty members of the reconstituted Transitional National Legislative Assembly (R-TNLA), and one hundred representatives in the Council of States (CoS), ten state governments, and seventy-nine County Commissioners. It was obvious, the R-ARCSS wasn't a respite from despair and agony. The people resigned themselves to 'wait and see' if the leaders would implement this agreement.

President Salva Kiir was still adamant about working with Riek Machar in any capacity, worse as his first vice president. He had openly said it, and blamed the region for again imposing Riek Machar through the R-ARCSS. However, President Salva Kiir had some individuals in his government who had government cabinet portfolios as abodes for permanent residence. They were not *bona fide* SPLM members but in the run up to the split with the SPLM leadership in 2013, President Salva Kiir co-opted them and they became his faithful lieutenants fighting political wars on him behalf. Because these politicians wanted to maintain their positions in government, they together with the presidential advisor on security affairs made sure to render it difficult the implementation of the revitalised peace agreement, providing a breather for President Salva Kiir.

The R-ARCSS didn't have inbuilt punitive measures against reneging, obfuscation, non-implementation or procrastinating the implementation matrix. Everything in the process hinged on the good will of President Salva Kiir and his lieutenants some of whom were bent on sabotaging the implementation of the pre-interim processes. The exponentially pivotal role Mr. Tut Gatluak, the presidential advisor on security, played in sabotaging the implementation of the pre-transitional processes was remarkable that it led to six months, three months, and again another one hundred-days extension of the pre-transitional period. This repeated extension of the pre-transitional period could only point to President Salva Kiir's reluctance to assume his responsibility as the principal actor. However, finally, on 20th February 2020, he deftly summoned Riek Machar and others to take oath of office leading to the formation of the R-TGONU. The struggle then shifted to SSOA to provide the fourth vice president. Of all the SSOA leaders only Dr. Lam Akol had the credentials to occupy the vice president docket. Mr. Tut Gatluak through bribery, arms-twisting and other pressures made sure that SSOA nominated somebody politically weak and would not constitute a threat to President Salva Kiir and his government. In this manner President Kiir succeeded to scuttle the opposition and prevented their unity.

The lack of unity within SSOA or their cooperation with SPLM/A (IO) played out negatively in the implementation of the pre-transitional processes particularly in the incorporation of the R-ARCSS into the TCSS 2011 amended 2016. This task assigned to the National Constitutional Amendment Commission (NCAC) ran into difficulties over the thirty-two (32) states configuration of South Sudan, which President Kiir had decreed against the provisions of ARCSS, and the government delegation to the NCAC was under instructions never to give into the ten (10) states that existed before the civil war. President Kiir and his lieutenants deliberately procrastinated on this issue with the objective to prevent the process from triggering the constitution making and other processes that would finally drain into conduct of election to end the transition. If there is anything President Salva Kiir resented was fair and free elections, which he did not control or was not sure would win. It was cheaper for Salva Kiir to procrastinate or postpone completely the R-ARCSS implementation than to risk losing the elections, and this became tenable when Riek Machar agreed to relocate from Khartoum to Juba. The regional incarceration apparitions still hung over Riek Machar as an active blackmail bait for him to accept the R-ARCSS even in the face of procrastinations.

The formation of the RTGONU on 20th February 2020 demonstrated that President Salva Kiir had succeeded in his plan to completely scuttle the pre-transitional processes but kept in place the Pre-Transitional Preparatory Committee under the leadership of Mr. Tut Gatluak to continue singing the chorus of 'graduation of the Necessary United Forces' that had been cantoned for the last three years. While the R-ARCSS implementation matric remained stagnant and somehow frozen due to lack of political good will, nevertheless, its time clock continued to tick steadily towards the expiry of the transition slotted at 20th February 2023. The international community continued to put pressure on Salva Kiir to implement the agreement but without success. The US Government stopped funding the R-ARCSS supervision and monitoring mechanisms. Suddenly, the R-TGONGU woke up to the warnings. President Salva Kiir announced the agreement in the presidency to extend the transitional period by two years up to 20th February 2025. The preparations started in earnest for graduation of the necessary unified forces: comprising the army, police, national security, wildlife forces, prisons service and civil defence forces on the thirtieth of August 2022 in a ceremony conducted on Dr. John Garang Memorial Grounds attended by regional leaders and members of the diplomatic corps accredited in Juba[13].

This was like child game, President Salva Kiir played with his five vice presidents and the people of South Sudan. The underlying reason for Salva Kiir to sign the R-ARCSS remained the same; going along with everybody knowing that he would not implement the agreement. The two years extension is pointer that the other provisions of the R-ARCSS like the establishment of the Hybrid Court, etc., will never see the light during Kiir's presidency. With Riek Machar in Juba and his SPLM/A (IO) forces in disarray in Upper Nile, Salva Kiir continued to dodge the regional and international community to keep South Sudan in a state of permanent instability. This served President Kiir two purposes: first, prevent internal dissent against his totalitarian regime coalescing into a critical mass, and secondly continue to collect the oil and non-oil revenues to line the pockets of his political cronies and security networks to keep him in power.

President Salva Kiir cleverly exploited the IGAD mediation to prolong his stay in power. Two factors underpin this situation. The political and security architecture of the IGAD region was such that respective national security and economic concerns of the countries preponderated over the conflict they were attempting to mediate and resolve. We have already alluded to how the

IGAD Special Envoy experimented with his hypothesis that a successful state (Ethiopia) could live alongside the failed states (Somalia and South Sudan). The power-sharing formula did not address the fundamental contradictions in the South Sudan conflict but would keep South Sudan in perpetual instability because the struggle for power in South Sudan would continue *ad infinitum*, while Ethiopia through IGAD would in perpetuity continue to mediate.

The second factor was the IGAD Special Envoys and the apparent unequal power relations that emerged between them. It was clear from the beginning that Ambassador Seyoum Mesfin of Ethiopia called the shots, while Gen Lazaro Sumbeiweyo (Kenya) and Gen. Mohammed Ahmed El-Dabi (Sudan) perfunctorily followed his dictates. In fact, had the Special Envoys been patient and taken time to listen to the SPLM/A (IO) delegation the situation could have been saved from reaching where the agreement had to be imposed on the negotiators. Linked to the IGAD Special Envoys was the chairman of the Joint Monitoring and Evaluation Commission, Mr. Festus Mogae, who appeared guided by the principle of bureaucratic discipline in favour of the establishment. He lacked impartiality and therefore contributed to hardening the government positions towards the deployment of the Regional Protection Force as well as the SPLM/A(IO) forces coming to Juba with their heavy weapons alongside personal armament.

The enduring difficulty with the IGAD mediation, and the agreements it sealed, was the false premises upon which the mediation constructed the process. Power-sharing and critical reforms, whatever that meant, in a totalitarian system would never have resolved the conflict underpinned by poverty, ignorance, and cultural backwardness of the people. These three categories, underpinning the conflict, require revolutionary transformation not reforms in the system that has sustained and exasperated them since the 2005. The situation in South Sudan requires a completely different social force to drive a paradigm shift in the political thinking[14]. This failure of the parties to expedite R-ARCSS' implementation within the prescribed timeframe vindicated the need for a paradigm shift. It required the political class to first place South Sudan and the destiny of its people at the centre of their political thought otherwise as long as the leaders only think about power and their share in it would mean that South Sudan won't transition out of this vicious circle of peace and political violence.

10. What the IGAD High-Level Revitalization Forum Should Have Done

The collapse of ARCISS suggested that another agreement based on the same formula was bound to suffer the same fatality. The HLRF should have been innovative at least to encourage generation of fresh and new ideas. We had discussed above the political hurdles into which the revitalized agreement ran into leading to two years extension of the transitional period. I can vouch, even if the transition were to be extended for another ten or twenty years, the same difficulties would still obtain. The real problem centres on the leaders and personal egos rather than ideological contradictions, their existence at the helm of South Sudan state, and their inability to make personal compromises in the highest interest of the people of South Sudan. In this respect power-sharing is not appropriate a remedy where the leaders Salva Kiir and Riek Machar perceive themselves as complete opposite of the other. The two-year extension of the transitional period is testimony to the failure of the power-sharing formula and further extensions would not create any difference. It would be difficult to anticipate a change of heart and leaders' attitude towards themselves. Perhaps the papal visit and the interdenominational prayers in the second week of February might create the desired change in the South Sudan leaders.

The revitalized agreement notwithstanding, the security situation deteriorated throughout South Sudan. The issue of cantonment of forces and graduation of Necessary Unified Force engaged the R-TGONU without meaning outputs because the incumbent SPLM government wanted the international community to foot the bill and lift sanction on importation of armaments. The IGAD HLRF couldn't move any further; this pushed President Salva Kiir back into the centre to control the process.

There were many South Sudan intellectuals, political scientists and civil society groups ready to provide ideas to move the peace process steps further ahead. The IGAD HLRF and its revitalized agreement exasperated the situation further probable to the liking of President Salva Kiir; the political instability generated would help him stay in power. The idea of five vice presidents, a cabinet of thirty five ministers and ten deputy ministers, a revitalized transitional national legislative assembly of six hundred fifty members and a Council of States of one hundred representatives at the national level in addition to ten state governors, state legislative assembly and many other position was indeed a bloated government, which was not what the people of South Sudan wanted.

In fact, as soon as the government and opposition had agreed to the cessation of hostilities, the HLRF should have transformed itself into a long-drawn-out conference of the stakeholders to thrash out the fundamental problems underpinning the conflict in South Sudan. The first most important step was for the HLRF leadership to push for the deployment of the Regional Protection Force (RPF) as the only guarantee for the cease fire to hold and ensure security and observance of law and order until the graduation of the Necessary Unified Force and its deployment. That the IGAD HLRF and the IGAD mediators left the loose ends of the R-ARCSS open speak to their lack of commitment to resolve the conflict. It was already bad diplomacy bordering on lack of trust and confidence that the R-TGONU discussed and agreed on extension of the transitional period in the absence of the IGAD Special Envoy, JMEC, and the other R-ARCSS implementation mechanisms. They were only requested to endorse the extension suggesting not only their irrelevance and redundance but also that in President Salva Kiir's perception the role of IGAD in the peace process had ended. The role of the IGAD HLRF was not envisaged to terminate with the signing of the revitalized agreement on the conflict in South Sudan. Like any peace instrument its life ends with the last operations in the agreement's implementation. However, the IGAD HLRF should have been designed differently from the IGAD peace talks which produced the ARCISS. It should have been designed as a process of political consultation and democratic dialogue than peace talks in which the stakeholders were jostling for position and power ratios.

Once the parties had signed the cessation of hostilities, the HLRF leadership should have taken an innovative step to engage the parties in the substantive issues underpinning the conflict. It goes without saying that power and its sharing among the stakeholders is not the fundamental issue. The fundamental contradictions underlying the conflict in South Sudan including the ones that underpinned the war with northern Sudan was not power and whoever wielded it; it was the centuries old condition of poverty, ignorance and cultural backwardness of the people of South Sudan. The solution to these fundamental contradictions is not found power-sharing between the political elite, but the solution lies in social and economic development of the enormous natural resources South Sudan is imbued with. In this connection the IGAD HLRF should have put to task all the stakeholders and challenged each and every party to produce their respective perception as how to address the issues of socio-economic development of South Sudan. Thus, after signing the R-ARCSS on 18th September 2018, the HLRF should have transformed itself into an all-stakeholders conference to workshop the different perceptions coming from the parties. The eight months pre-transitional period could have been spent in the conference to thrash out the most difficult parts in respect to good governance, law and order, social and economic development, peace and social harmony. Once the parties have agreed and consensus built around these issues, the HLRF leadership would then codify them into a political programme to be implemented by the revitalized transitional government of national unity (R-TGONU).

With the formation of R-TGONU, the next phase in the search for permanent peace would have been a long-drawn-out political consultation and dialogue process, which the HLRF correctly categorized as the transitional period defined as the period between the formation of R-TGONU and the time just before the conduct of elections. This period could have been as short as five years or as long as ten to fifteen years, to allow the stakeholders to thoroughly thrash out all the nitty-gritty of democratic governance, social, economic, and cultural development, national cohesion and unity, repatriation and resettlement of the refugees and internally displaced people, national reconciliation and healing, etc. Thus, in discussing or debating the appropriate governance system for South Sudan; whether South Sudan would be a parliamentary democracy, a presidential system or a combination of both systems, the parties would be treated to different examples in the world to make informed choices. The choice of the political system would determine the constitutional order; it was therefore imperative that the stakeholders were guided to choose the least conflictual political system.

This *inter alia* would include depoliticization and professionalization of the army, police, national security, prisons, wildlife, and civil defence services. This process of developing the armed, security and law enforcement agencies must be accompanied by the disarmament of the civil population accompanied by deployment of effective police force and efficient local government administration to operate in cohorts with the traditional authorities. This would improve security in the villages and between the communities. In fact, without complete disarmament of the civil population particularly among the pastoralist communities it would be difficult to rein peace and bring socioeconomic development to them. The political survival of the republic of South Sudan as a viable state could only be assured if the government and society work together towards peace and stability.

The nine years spent in political lachrymose could have been avoided had the SPLM leaders opened the political space for consultation and dialogue immediately after independence; indeed, immediately after the announcement of the referendum results in January 2011. The people of South Sudan are now being treated to the processes they should have gone through during the interim period [2005 -2011] or even before that during the war of national liberation. The had time immediately after independence to build national consensus on the desired political system in order to rein-in a political dispensation built into a permanent constitution.

The internal political situation in the SPLM was not disposed to consensus building. That's usually the difficulty with populist movement sheathed in militarism and ethnic nationalism. The leader choses to stifle the debate and that's it. The resultant standoff between the leaders ultimately shrinks the political space, and raises the political temperature until its exploded or imploded. This would be the recount of the political process in South Sudan from August 2005 to December 2013. Thus, the political consultation and dialogue would in fact be rekindling the state engineering and nation building processes in South Sudan, which the civil war truncated in 2013.

The IGAD mediation in South Sudan conflict was a painful failure in terms of its perception and the neutrality of the mediators. The nature of the conflict and the character of the leaders required deeper research in order to first resolve the conflict between these leaders. It goes back to what we said earlier that hadn't South Sudan been part of a pariah state called the Sudan, the powers that be wouldn't have countenanced the exercise of self-determination. The presence of a permanent undisputed leader respected by all shades of opinion in the SPLM/A and whose suitability have been proved to everyone's satisfaction was what pushed the region and the international community to support South Sudan's cause for self-determination. It didn't, however, indicate there would equally be leaders equivalent to Dr. John Garang de Mabior. This reality of lack of equivalent leadership could have been proved if the tragic death of Garang occurred before the signing of the comprehensive peace agreement. The power-sharing formula therefore wouldn't have addressed the fundamental contradictions underpinning the conflict. The collapse of the ARCISS, and the procrastination on R-ARCSS implementation leading to a two-year extension of the transitional period are lessons IGAD mediators didn't heed; they are a pointer to the fact that the ANC-EPRDF initiative 2014 remains the best option to resolved the highly personalized contradiction between President Salva Kiir and his deputy Riek Machar Teny-Dhurgon that the power-sharing formula of the IGAD mediation.

Both President Salva Kiir and Riek Machar are the obstacles to any peace agreement on account of their obstinacy and incompatible chemistry. Kiir's attachment to power is profound and personal caring for nothing save remaining in power even if the country and its people slide into oblivion but knowing that he could do nothing positive to save it; loss of power would mean loss of personal and family security. He resents and very open that wouldn't work with Riek Machar if he could prevent that, and therefore, prompts him to trumps any solution brought by IGAD mediators. On the other hand Riek Machar failed to remove Kiir by force of arms yet he thinks he could take over power through the peace agreement and therefore accept to remain his deputy. Had Riek accepted to nominate somebody else to deputize Salva Kiir and to wait for elections, it could have been possible to know whether or not President Salva Kiir would have genuinely implemented the R-ARCSS. This puts the people of South Sudan in a catch 22 situation; President Salva Kiir remains the president and Riek Machar his deputy but South Sudan the country decomposes without dying or any attempts to change this configuration unleashes more uncertainty, while the IGAD mediators and all the implementation mechanism are there watching on haplessly. The political leaders whether in the ruling coalition[15] or in the opposition SPLM/A (IO), the SSOA and the OPP have all been absorbed into the system. Like President Salva Kiir, they have hooked their political survival on being part of this dysfunctional regime even in full knowledge that their presence does not add value to the system. Insecurity and indeed communal conflicts have increased since the formation of the R-TGONU. The desertions with the SPLM/A (IO) and ensuing communal conflicts in Upper Nile have been instigated by the government of which it is a member. It is also fighting back in Western Equatoria and instigating Chollo-Nuer war in Tonga and Panyikango suggesting that R-TGONU is fighting itself by proxy leading to total destabilization of the country.

There is no credible alternative political force to rescue and lead the people of South Sudan. The 'hold-out' groups are fragmented and struggling within themselves for power and leadership. Internally, the civil society remains weak and can't constitute the critical mass that could trigger change through mass action. The rational thing to do perhaps is for all the stakeholders to work together during the two-year extension of the transitional period on a political compromise within the R-TGONU that allows the building of institutions and instruments of accountable government to implement a social and economic development programme. The most important of which would be a professional national army, professional national and states police, prison warders, wildlife, civil defence forces and transformed civil service. I have deliberately left out the National Security; it is unconstitutional and therefore has no existence in law. This would mean that the two years' extension should not be timed on holding elections but should be extended for a longer period to enable passions to cool down, people embark on reconciliation and healing, building social and physical infrastructure and engage in social production of their livelihood.

ENDNOTES

1. It was indeed paradoxical; the NIF supported the Nasir faction calling self-determination for the people of Southern Sudan while at the same time fight the Mainstream SPLM/A which called for unity of the Sudan.

2. The National Islamic Front seized power in the Sudan to promote and support Islamic groups fighting the governments in the region. In Uganda it supported the Allied Democratic Forces and West Nile II Front, in Kenya it supported the Islamic Party of Kenya and the Islamic groups in Ethiopia and Eritrea as well as the Shabab in Somalia.

3. United Nations Security Council Resolution No.1966 of 8th July 2011

4. Both Salva Kiir and Riek Machar never accepted there was a problem between them when Cyril Ramaphosa came in November 2013 to mediate.

5. Initially it was Inter-Governmental Agency on Draught

and Desertification (IGADD) but changed in 1993 to Inter-Governmental Authority on Development (IGAD) when the IGAD Special Envoy on South Sudan, and Ethiopia's ambassador to People's Republic of China, Seyoum Mesfin, was then the Ethiopia's Foreign Minister and together with Petros Solomon, the then Eritrean Foreign Minister, were instrumental in streamlining the talks between the government of the Sudan and the Sudan People's Liberation Movement (SPLM/A)

6. Seyoum Mesfin and Abdeta Dribssa Beyene (2018) "The Practicalities of living with failed states." Daedalus Vol.147 Issue No.1, 2018 p 128-140.

7. In the contradiction that afflicted the SPLM leadership, the SPLM Leaders (FPD) believed they were closer to President Salva Kiir and decided to betray Riek Machar by refusing to join the armed rebellion although until 15th December 2013, they were politically in one camp. That they did not have the blood of the people of South Sudan because they did not join the rebellion is false; Kiir continued to shed the blood of innocent South Sudanese while he was president of the country. In fact, had they joined the rebellion the chances of changing the situation would have multiplied.

8. The proposal to bar both Salva Kiir and Riek Machar from participation in the transitional government had indeed whetted Gen. Taban Deng's appetite for power. As leader of SPLM/A (IO) advance team to Juba, he started to scheme for power. It should be known that Taban Deng was Salva Kiir's personal friend and had kept him as governor of Unity State against the wishes of its

people. His scheme involving working for the petroleum docket in the transitional government of national unity (TGONU) by plotting with the SPLM (IG) to outstep the lottery meant to choose and allocate ministerial portfolios.

9. Daniel Awet and Kuol Manyang had wanted to impress on Salva Kiir that they the former members of the SPLM Leadership Council have had their time and it was appropriate to leave the power and leadership of the country to the younger generation.

10. The NCP had conducted a similar process earlier in Khartoum but which yielded nothing in the end because the debate and recommendations pointed to the need to change the political system, and NCP wouldn't give in.

11. The report of this exercise pointed out clearly that the SPLM had deviated from the concept and vision of the New Sudan; its government had failed to deliver social services and to provided social and economic development and must therefore change that trend. Instead of accepting collective responsibility for failure some members of the leadership hung the responsibility on the Chairman Kiir and things were never the same again in the SPLM.

12. The political crisis in EPRDF leading to the precipitous resignation of Haile Mariam Desalegn and ascension of Dr. Abiye Ahmed to the throne of the Prime Minister led to the removal of Ambassador Seyoum Mesfin as the Special Envoy on South Sudan but shifted the H-LRF talks to Khartoum

13. It was another charade; it turned out that most of the forced that were graduated were just collected from the residential

suburbs of Juba. That they were not trained was clear from the display watched live on TV. Tut Gatluak and Salva Kiir managed to fool the region and the international community.

14. A shift that places the people in the centre of their political thinking. The parasitic elite occupying the citadel of South Sudan's political and economic power care only about their interests.

15. This ruling coalition established after July 2016 included the SPLM in Government, the Umbrella Group of Parties fronted for by Southern Sudan Democratic Forum (Dr. Martin Elia Lomoro), USAP, and Democratic Change Party (Onyoti Adigo Nyikwech)

CHAPTER SEVEN

LIVING AMONG THE GIANTS IN A WEAK STATE

A spectre haunts the people of South Sudan; the spectre of ethnicity is more dangerous than or even equivalent to any weapon of mass destruction. What makes ethnicity profoundly awful is that it surges in the context of hegemony and domination, which in the absence of a strong or powerful state would translate into zero sum conflicts between ethnic communities. The republic of South Sudan is the youngest state in the world nevertheless it is politically the most unstable state in the region. A civil war erupted in 2013, barely three years into its independence from the Sudan. Some of its preponderant communities have yet to accept and internalize the concept of state as a superstructure above the society, and belongs to all the people of the country. Some view the state in their traditional beliefs and practices that the state is the strongest individual in society to whom everything belongs and therefore dispenses at will. This confusion about the state and its role is further compounded by the power struggle among the political elite for the control of the state and its resources. This casts dark clouds over its destiny as a viable modern state.

Independence and with-it democracy came to South Sudan before its numerous sociocultural formations (nationalities or ethnicities) had attained a minimal level of social and economic development or have reached measure of national integration to support a modern state. Such situation generates attitudes of exclusivity and discrimination even in the management of state institutions. Thus, members of a certain ethnicity or a section thereof tend to crowd and monopolize particular departments of government to the exclusion of others. In chapter two we discussed how the political elite destroyed the Southern Region leading to another war. It really demonstrates that management of state is a serious matter and should never be left to ignorant and politically immature individuals. The republic of South Sudan is at risk of following the experience of the Southern Region because at its helm is an ignorant and politically immature leadership.

There are sixty-seven nationalities at different levels of socio-economic and cultural development and at varying demographic weights. The Dinka is the single largest nationality, while the Makaraka is the smallest nationality. Each and every group count as sovereign in their own right suggesting that the people of South Sudan in their different sociocultural and linguistic groups have equal rights irrespective of their demographic weights. By no reason could they be denied their rights as citizens of South Sudan. This is to say that what has now become a practice in which certain nationalities or sections thereof control the pillars of political and economic power of the state because of their demographic preponderance contradict the principles of justice, (equality and equity) freedom and fraternity, which underpinned the struggle for national liberation.

'Living among the giants', speaks to the reality in the past in which autochthonous large or small ethnic communities' juxtaposition themselves in the same locality and they lived peacefully because there was a powerful state. The emerging social, economic, and political realities in South Sudan rendered this situation untenable; the failure of the state may not for long sustain this autochthony and peaceful coexistence. The unfolding situation in Central Equatoria summarizes it. It might not have been obvious to the communities, but the gradual ecological imbalance driven by the long war of national liberation has its impact reflected on the post-war behaviours of communities. For the first time in the history of Southern Sudan communities witnessed conflicts over land, water, and pastures among the pastoralist and their encroachment onto the territories of the sedentary agrarian communities in search of pastures. This phenomenon is widespread in Jonglei, east bank Equatoria and in Bahr el Ghazal and echoes an emerging reality that the state has weakened

Historically, in the nineteenth and twentieth centuries, the Sudanese state grew in strength and territorial occupation at the expense of the autochthonous nationalities which succumbed to the new dispensation of law and order. The people irrespective of their ways of life, customary practices and beliefs or opinion of government acquiesced to this law and order, respected the law and security rein in the country for everybody. By the time the Sudan became independent, banditry and lawless behaviours had almost ceased except in the peripheral areas where cattle rustling, child and women abduction occurred among the pastoral communities.

1. The Predicament of the Small Tribes in South Sudan

The eruption of civil war in 1983 transformed the existing order. The war of national liberation didn't mean destruction of, but transformation of the oppressive situation, to create a new revolutionary order. In the preceding pages, we discussed the SPLM/A failure to transform itself into a national liberation movement. This meant a lot in terms of people's attitudes and behaviours and their interaction with law and order. It was clear that in some areas in South Sudan the presence of the SPLM/A retarded the people's perception of the state and its institutions. It was like two centuries backwards into the eighteenth century. In March 2009, President Kiir's made an outrageous verbal[1] decision to name 'Pigi' and relocate the Padang Dinka County of Atar in Panyikango County, and to create Akoka County in Fashoda County all in the Chollo Kingdom. The Chollo King remains flabbergasted by the decision of the President of Government of Southern Sudan to dispossess the Chollo people of their ancestral land on east bank of the river Nile. In December 2012, the police shot and killed eleven demonstrators in Wau, capital of Western Bahr el Ghazal State; they were protesting a decision cooked in Juba to relocate the Jur River County headquarters to Bagadi against the wishes of the people. There were no clear demographic pressures to warrant both decisions, however, creating more territorial space for the Dinka was the common denominator suggesting that a plan must have been drawn for demographic engineering of certain areas in anticipation of land speculation for capitalist ownership in the independent South Sudan.

Historically, humanity survived and developed at the expense of its co-species driven by the instinct to stay alive and to multiply in numbers. These instincts translated into wars of conquest to acquire resources, dominance, and control of territories, and in this process meted out insane cruelty that many nations became extinct. It might be said with confidence that the nations that exist today on this planet are survivors of horrendous crimes committed against them by foreigners who invaded their land in search of resources in a process euphemistically known as 'discovery'. The European were notorious in this enterprise; scavenging for resources was intense in the era of primitive accumulation of capital leading to enslavement of large populations particularly of the Africa people and their shipment to the Americas and the Middle East. The Arabs were the worse in that they prevented procreation among the black slaves by castrating the male slaves and turning the women into *hareem*, concubines for sexual pleasures. That the Africans have survived all these inhumanities could only prove their physical and psychological resilience more than any other race. It's only recently that Pope Francis apologized to the indigenous people of Canada and the US in the rare acceptance of these historical injustices, I hope did apologise for the white race: English, Germans, Spanish, Portuguese, and the French; but the cases of reparation and restitution remain.

In a paper read at the Sudanese Studies conference in Durham, England in June 1999, I spoke of the 'Chollo predicament', detailing prospects and the threat of physical and cultural extinction of the Chollo people in the context of the then ongoing war in the Sudan. The key word in that discourse was 'predicament' and for people who are conversant with history of slavery and slave trade, the word 'predicament' invokes deep sentiments of fear, premonitions, including memories of ethnic cleansing and genocide in the recent past during the war of national liberation or in the small state of Rwanda in 1994. The notion of the president of the republic of a multi-national, multi-cultural, and multi-lingual country, making outrageous decisions like the division of the country into thirty-two states to favour his Dinka ethnic community wherever they may be in South Sudan was not only disgraceful but also frightening. The massacre of ethnic Nuers in Juba in December 2013 at the hands of Dinka militia, *dutko beny*, amounted to genocide and ethnic cleansing of the Nuer people. This invoked the writing of this chapter as a means to raise awareness of the impending catastrophe in South Sudan occasioned by state failure, which translates into collapse of its ability to defend its weak and unarmed citizens from marauding heavily armed pastoralists or organized tribal militias. The other objective was also to problematize and find solutions to the myriad of contradictions inherent in the social and cultural multiplicities of South Sudan.

'Living among the giants', reflecting the predicament of South Sudan's smaller ethnic communities speaks to ongoing social, economic, and political crises deliberately engineered to promote Dinka ethnic hegemony and domination of the independent South Sudan. The concepts and policies that underpin the notion of Dinka hegemony and domination were put in place by the Jieng Council of Elders in the context of dividing South Sudan into thirty-two (32) states, which awarded to the Dinka nation forty-two (42) percent of South Sudan territory and made that co-habitant of all states of South Sudan. Although that policy had imploded and boomeranged nevertheless its relics still drive the current social and political crisis in the country. The recent fighting in Chollo Kingdom in Upper Nile State between the Chollo and the Nuer is a pointer to nagging truth of living among the giants. It also demonstrates how contradictions at the political level permeate down and translate into communal conflicts to resolve the struggle for power among the elites in Juba. The rare unity forged recently between the Nuer (Lou, Gawaar, Laak, and Thiang) and the Dinka (Luach, Nyarweng, Rut and Ruweng) to form a force that attacked the Chollo displaced people in Adhidhiang and which extended to Fashoda and Manyo Counties came against complex and interlocking political dynamics between the parties to the revitalized agreement to the conflict in South Sudan. The R-ARCSS and the formation of the R-TGONU forced President Salva Kiir to reverse the 32-states and returned South Sudan to 10-states. Some Padang Dinka leaders bitterly opposed this and shifted their support and allegiance to the opposition against Salva Kiir, and encouraged insecurity in Upper Nile, where most of Riek Machar forces were based.

While they implemented the R-ARCSS, Riek Machar and Salva Kiir still played political intrigues against each other. This came to the surface first in a split within the SPLM/A (IO) that witnessed Gen. Simon Gatwech, Riek's chief of Staff and his deputy Ge, Johnson Olony, breaking with their leader Dr. Riek Machar, the SPLM/A (IO) chairman and commander in chief, and forming a splinter group – SPLM/A (IO)-Kit-Gwang. No sooner did this Kit-Gwang group sign a peace agreement with the SPLM in government. This agreement has proved farcical; it was clear from the beginning that SPLM (IG) won't implement the agreement, but used the agreement to separate the two generals from Riek Machar, and to instigate split and internecine fighting among them along ethnic lines. In no time, differences popped up between Gen. Simon Gatwech and Gen, Johnson Olony leading to the fighting in Wic-Panyikango, triggered by the Nuer elements within Agwalek force but escalated into Tonga involving SPLA (IO) in Fangak and Padang Dinka militia in Atar (Pigi) County. This rare unity forged between the Dinka and Nuer against the Chollo has wider dimensions more than the notion of Kiir's side of the R-TGONU acting to exploit the contradictions within the SPLM/A (IO) of Riek Machar. This unity was at the behest of the commissioner of Atar (Pigi) Country to pointing to the growing rift within the Jieng. However, the execution was driven by three different motives.

First, as mentioned above the Padang Dinka turned against President Salva Kiir for returning South Sudan to ten instead of thirty-two states. It will be recalled that the thirty-two states configuration gave the Padang Dinka the possession of all the Chollo land on the east bank of the Nile River but alone and by themselves without the support of Kiir, read Dinka of Bahr el Ghazal, the Padang sections combined couldn't confront the Chollo and therefore had to opportunistically instigate the Nuers of Fangak to assist. The Nuers are known to fight even without a reason or political objective; their motivation in this case was resources (Chollo cattle).

Secondly, Dr. Riek Machar and Gen. Simon Gatwech each for different reasons both wanted to prevent Gen. Johnson Thubo coming to Juba to join the R-TGONU of which Riek Machar is first vice president. While Dr. Riek Machar was part of the R-TGONU, he still wanted to use the presence of both Gen. Simon Gatwech and Gen. Johnson Olony to pressure President Salva Kiir into implementing the remaining critical provisions of R-ARCSS. On his side, Gen. Simon Gatwech didn't want to relocate to Juba as provided by the agreement he signed with Gen. Tut Gatluak and Gen. Akol Koor in January 2022 without guarantees or guarantors. This created the friction between the two general and hence the fighting in Wic-Panyikango.

Thirdly, there was a growing perception among the Nuer nationality about a Nuer presidency of South Sudan after President Salva Kiir left power. This has become a driving force uniting the Nuers across political and territorial divides; surprisingly the invisible hands of the presidential advisor on security affairs appear in the form of provision of ammunitions to the Nuer forces of Simon Gatwech coming from his political networks in the republic of the Sudan.

The combined force of Padang Dinka and Nuer in Upper Nile and Jonglei could pose an existential threat to the Chollo people and their Kingdom. In fact, without the intervention of the SSPDF and its helicopter gunships, the devastation in Fashoda and Manyo would have been total. However, more importantly this illustrates the danger posed to the small tribes living with large tribes in the dysfunctional South Sudan. In fact, 'predicament' in this context is mild compared to some of the experiences these small nationalities face both physically, culturally, and politically. The predicament consequent to a dysfunctional state, deliberately engineered to allow the larger tribes predominantly the Dinka and the Nuer to hegemonize and dominate the other nationalities is a serious phenomenon in South Sudan. This raises the obvious question why has the interaction between the larger and the 'smaller tribes' become a problem now than any time before? Does the independence of South Sudan render the larger tribes uncivilized and atavistic towards their neighbouring smaller tribes?

The Dinka (Jieng or Muony-Jiang) is the largest single

nationality domicile as autochthonous sections, subsections and clans in Bahr el Ghazal (Aweil, Gogrial, Tonj, Rumbek and Yirol) and Upper Nile (Bor, Fangak, Bailiet, and Renk) subregions. The Nuer forms the second largest nationality, and like the Dinka domicile as confederation of chieng, wut and clans in Upper Nile subregion (Bentiu, Fangak, Akobo and Nasir). The Nuer are also found in western Ethiopia region of Gambella whose individuals relocate easily into the South Sudan when necessary or forced by conditions in Ethiopia. The Dinka and Nuer share a history of acephalous existence, and this is the source of social and political straits in South Sudan. The Zande, the Chollo, the Otuho, the Murle and Toposa may be counted as following in demographic strength the two largest nationalities. The rest of nationalities or ethnic communities, fifty-seven in number [table1] demographically range from a few hundreds and tens of thousands, which qualifies them as 'smaller tribes'. The problem may not exactly be the extermination and possible physical or cultural extinction of the smaller tribes. The growing inequality in the distribution of power and wealth promoted as a policy leads to marginalization even total exclusion and invisibility of some of these peoples. There is growing insensitivity and careless statements made by some leaders that "we were the ones who died in the war" and hence have automatic entitlement to power, wealth, and land. It's such statements carelessly made by respected political leaders provoked me into conducting research into the distribution and balance of power and wealth in the republic of South Sudan. I encountered all kinds of obstacles besides getting funding that I had to abandon the data collection. However, from the informal conversations it is possible to glean the difficulties people hailing from small ethnic communities confront in finding opportunities in the government job market, government contract vendors, promotions in a bureaucracy that eschews meritocracy, qualifications, experience in favour of social and political relations.

The people of South Sudan are now faced with another atrophying experience that emanated from the surging ethnic nationalism of the large tribes drive by power and resources considerations not only at the national level but also at the state, county and payam levels. The Dinka and Nuer ethnic nationalism - the two demographically preponderant and politically violent nations whose perception of a state does not extend beyond the self in a country they have to share with the sixty-two nationalities is something that warrants serious consideration. The Dinka, particularly the Rek section of the Dinka in Warrap and Aweil states in Bahr el Ghazal, and the Nuer behave as if other peoples don't exist when it comes to resource sharing including state power.

The predicament of the small 'tribes' or nationalities is real; the Dinka and the Nuer have no tradition of statehood or institutions of governance that are impersonal. The chieftainships, which the colonial administration established among the Dinka and Nuer in the context of indirect rule didn't with time institutionalize as to become impersonal as other state instruments of power but remained personified linked to the person exercising that authority. Thus, Dinka or Nuer perception of the state remains an extension of this powerful individual at the top and every *'initiated'* male has the right to aspire to that status. This perception of power and authority becomes tricky in the state where there is clear demarcation between what is public or private. It becomes a source of serious tension when the leader dispenses public resources as if they were his personal property always preferring his close relatives to others.

Ethnic pluralism does not necessarily constitute grounds for conflict. However, it's the correlation of pluralism with other factors like unequal distribution of power and wealth that provides for potentially explosive admixtures (Prah, 1987). There have never been problems in South Sudan on account of 'large tribes' and 'small tribes' coexisting in close proximity to each other. The differentiation or categorization into 'large' and 'small' tribes, didn't arise nor was it a concern in a country of law and order. The small tribes collectively and disparaging called *fertit* by the British colonial authorities did not feel any threat to their existence posed by the neighbouring Dinka or Azande because the state was strong and powerful. The Sudanese state was powerful and, in many instances, intervened to prevent large scale ethnic wars. But the independence of South Sudan came along with a weak state in which certain ethnic communities have armed themselves becoming more powerful than the state security organs. The threat to the small tribes, therefore, springs from the weakness of the South Sudan state and the leadership of President Salva Kiir Mayardit that at times exercises partiality in favour of certain communities.

'Living among the giants' speaks to risk posed by state's abdication of its responsibility to protect its citizens particularly the weak one. The incursion of the pastoralists with their herds of cattle into the sedentary agrarian communities in Central and Eastern Equatoria without state intervention in spite of the murders of innocent peasants and destruction of their crops reflect the risks of living with giants in a weak state. On the other hand, the selective arming of some smaller tribes to challenge their larger neighbours amounts to the state's fragmentation of its citizens along ethnic lines.

The Chollo and their Padang Dinka neighbours never had a history of conflict between them over land or any other issue until suddenly conflict flared up in 1980 in the context of central government destabilization politics; Numeiri's policy of administrative decentralization and creation of Area Councils discussed somewhere in the book. The Padang Dinka agitation to push the Chollo people from the east to west bank of river Nile found support among some Jonglei SPLM leaders on account of nothing but ethnic solidarity[2]. This was a factor in the trouncing of all SPLM candidates in the Chollo constituencies in the 2010 midterms elections. The predicament of the 'small tribes' driven by factors of power, wealth and land in the context of a weak and failing state in South Sudan takes on different and complex dimensions. The segmentary nature of Nuer society pushed the migration of the eastern Nuer (Jikany) all the way from western Upper Nile into the east and into Ethiopia. This migration led to forceful displacement or assimilation of the Anywaa[3] Dinka and the Koma people who were the indigenous communities the Nuer found in the area in the middle of nineteenth century. The explosion of the Nuer population coupled with violent acquisition of agricultural and pastoral space placed enormous pressure on the Koma, who have become a negligible minority that they are scarcely visible at Upper Nile State level. But even with that configuration, Koma representation is dwindling that in three to five decades they may disappear. The fate of Koma is shared by many 'small tribes' cohabiting with even other 'small tribes' in different parts of South Sudan sharing the same payams, counties or states whereby they have to compete for political and other positions. It is possible that a group of 'small tribes'- sedentary agricultural communities, domicile together peacefully without incidences of violent conflict as in Raga and Wau in western Bahr el Ghazal nevertheless some are more included and visible in the political system than others, which could gradually and steadily trend towards permanent political exclusion and marginalization. We encounter the same situation in east bank Equatoria in Torit and Kapoeta districts where 'small tribes' have visibility difficulties. In a show of ethnic solidarity in East Equatoria State SPLM Congress, the Toposa went to their 'holy' rock to perform oath-taking to prevent any Toposa vote for leaders from other ethnic communities. The result was that the popular Otuho SPLM State chairman was trounced by a politically unknown Toposa. It demonstrates how social awareness without national political consciousness could be disastrous and could be categorized as negative in that it prevents a wider unity among the people who are equally poor, ignorant and culturally backward. The Jie, Toposa, Otuho, Didinga are all marginalized and barely visible at the national level yet will not unite in solidarity that could mutually strengthen them because they desire to be recognized and accepted as they are. The greed and selfishness of the political elite plays a role; they also use their own marginalization to marginalize and excluded other 'smaller tribes' who are cohabitants of the same locality. In Pibor Independent Administrative Area (PIAA) created ostensibly to protect the Murle from the Lou Nuer and Dinka Bor, the capricious Murle elite have found it convenient to also marginalized the Suri (Kachipo) in Boma and the Anywaa in Pochalla. It clear that ethnic multiplicity becomes problematic only when it correlates with factors of power and wealth and brings into play the notion of group's numerical strength to capture political power. In the same manner the Dinka or Nuer used the numerical strength to determine the leader, during the Eastern Equatoria State SPLM Convention in Torit in 2008, the Toposa exploiting their numerical strength over all other ethnic communities voted in block[4] to capture the SPLM leadership and hence the gubernatorial position in the state.

'Living among the giants' in this connection, the 'giants' don't necessarily connote only the Dinka or the Nuer. The 'giant' could have been any other small or medium numerical strength ethnic community. In Western Equatoria, the Moro elite supported the 32-state system because it gave them the Amadi state which to them broke the Azande hegemony and domination. But this didn't prevent the Moro elite in Amadi State from marginalizing and excluding the 'small tribes' like Morokodo or the Biele. The Nyiepo, a small sub tribe in Kaji-Keji county, identify themselves differently from the Kuku (majority) or the Bari with whom they share the same language, and are now agitating to have own administrative structure.

The driving forces in the 'small tribe' predicament are political exclusion, economic neglect and marginalization, and social discrimination. Language and religious persuasion are tools of social discrimination. These were the same forces that prompted the Southern Sudanese to separate from the Sudan. This situation therefore poses danger that some of the names particularly from western Bahr el Ghazal and eastern Equatoria may disappear sooner than later owing to physical and or cultural extinction on account of political exclusion, social discrimination, and economic marginalization.

The factors that would accelerate this extinction include the withdrawal of the South Sudan government from the provision of social services like education and health, and protection of life. Invariably, education was and remains the drivers of social mobility in South Suda as elsewhere in the world. It is a truism that visibility, whether individual or collective, of a people at the national, state, or local levels attributes to education and presence of school system up to secondary level in their territories. The withdrawal of the South Sudan government from provision of education in outlying areas far from the urban centres and leaving it to the vagaries of the NGOs or private sector is equivalent to condemning the 'small tribes' like the Tid or Tenet in Eastern

Equatoria or their equivalence in other areas of South Sudan to perpetual exclusion and marginalization. This is because, given their mode of production, social and cultural backwardness, they would prefer to continue living as pastoralist or honey gatherers in their natural habitat than venture into the unknown.

The political system, liberal multi-party democracy South Sudan adopted after independence operates to perpetuate the exclusion, the marginalization and more importantly the exploitation of the ignorance and cultural backwardness of many of these people. These factors play out when it comes to democratic representation in the legislative or administrative area councils. Undertaken without consideration of their numerical strengths large number of 'small tribes' were excluded from representative government and renders impossible their visibility at the national or state levels. The atavistic mannerism displayed in the context of the current social, economic, and political inequalities perpetuated by leaders of the so-called 'big tribes' in government defined and underscored the predicament of the 'small tribes' when South Sudan became an independent country.

That was not the case when the Sudan was one united country. The criteria the for leadership were completely different that at no point in time when a leader was there because he or she came from a large tribe. Luigi Adwok Bong, Clement Mboro, Ezbon Mundiri, Hilary Paul Logali and Gen. Joseph Lago did not hail from the 'big tribes' at one time provided leadership of Southern Sudan and yet they chosen by their southern constituencies. Ethnocentrism, ethnic chauvinism, and bigotry are a recent development. South Sudanese wouldn't have succeeded to win their independence if these negative social attitudes had clouded their struggle over the last six decades. These negative social attitudes not only pose a big threat for state formation and nation building processes in South Sudan, but they have also triggered a civil war. They are an existential threat to South Sudan's viability as a modern state and therefore must be combated

Had the debate about the "House of Nationalities – A space for preserving the diversity and unity of the people of South Sudan" as an idea been pursued in the context of the National Dialogue it would have been possible to chart a way out to avert the social, political, and cultural catastrophe for the 'small' tribes. There are about sixty-four nationalities in South Sudan. We underline *about* because some nationalities assumed earlier to be part of certain nationalities have stood up to be counted as sovereign. For instance, in Eastern Equatoria the *horiok* are all the small tribes Ifoto, Imatong, Dongotono, Lokoya, etc., who are linked to but not Otuho (Latuka) proper. Therefore, the exact number of nations, national groups or nationalities inhabiting South Sudan remains to be established, and their demographic weights established with precision in a population census especially that the civil war had caused heavy displacement and immigration. The way to combat ethnic chauvinism and bigotry is to raise the social awareness beyond the ethnicity, and beside changing the means by which the people live, whether they are pastoralists or sedentary agrarian communities. Ethnic chauvinism and bigotry are a function of ignorance and cultural backwardness, therefore, combating them must first address the underlying causes.

2. Power Configuration and Ethnic Relations in South Sudan

The greatest problem facing the people of South Sudan is the manner politics and economic have been organized. In many countries even in those where ethnicity and ethnic nationalism are still powerful factors in society, politics is organized to favour class, petty bourgeoisie class that unites all these ethnicities. In South Sudan the situation is different. Notwithstanding the reality that South Sudan is a product of twenty-one years war of national liberation spearheaded by SPLM/A, which united all the ethnic communities of South Sudan, nevertheless, its politics is organized on the basis of ethnic communities. It is so primitive and backward that this arrangement could only survive at the risk of profound suffering of the people. The long war of national liberation notwithstanding the dominant political elite remains culturally backward, politically unconscious, and perceives the state only in the context of extraction and plunder, and just like in the village relations are based on kinship. The current context of South Sudan echoed the manner the SPLM/A prosecuted the war of national liberation. Its leadership, instead of absorbing and transforming into revolutionary politics of nation building, exacerbated those ethnic and regional contradictions inherent in the Southern Region's politics It was permissible that at the beginning four out of five members of the SPLM/A High Command could have hailed from the Dinka nationality[5]. But that the leadership of the liberation movement remained narrow based could have been deliberate policy to entrench Dinka ethnic dominance. This played out in the training of the officer corps whereby the Dinka Bor had more than half the cadets training in the SPLA officer corps from Shield Four (1987) to Shield Nine (1997) on account of literacy advantage, while the bulk of the foot soldiers in the SPLA hailed from Bahr el Ghazal. This ethnic configuration in the SPLM/A had direct impact on ethnic relations and the distribution of power in South Sudan both during and after the war of national liberation. The return to the fold of the SPLM/A by Dr. Riek Machar and Dr. Lam Akol didn't change much in the ethnic alignment in the SPLM/A leadership hierarchy. Just before Dr. Garang introduced changes, the SPLM Leadership Council comprised Dinka (6), Nuer (2), Chollo (2), Bari (1), Luo (1), Lokoya (1), which weighed heavily in favour of the Dinka. However, following the tragic death of Dr. John Garang, President Salva Kiir Mayardit reversed the changes and placed the SPLM on ethnic and regional footings. This triggered the regional realignment of SPLM/A power in favour of Warrap and Aweil states in Bahr el Ghazal. Thus, political and economic power is now concentrated in Warrap particularly in Gogrial from where President Salva Kiir hails.

This configuration in which power and wealth concentrates in one area and poverty in the other areas is a recipe for serious future problems. It engenders uneven socioeconomic development of different regions of the Sudan as well as unequal power relations and the situation implodes at the weaker zones and could lead to dismemberment as it occurred in the case of the Sudan. The Warrap elite should understand that the vanity they now are displaying is generating deep fissures in South Sudan society and could result in bigger political problems for them sooner than later. No situation remains the same till posterity; things are bound to change.

ENDNOTES

1. There are no warrants of establishment for the two Padang Dinka counties; the warrant of establishment would entail a map, which would indicate the territory as of 1.1.1956 was Chollo not Padang territory. Nevertheless, the existence of these counties is maintained the situation of the civil war.

2. Madame Rebecca Nyandeng de Mabior and Cdr. Kuol Manyang Juuk went to the so-called Pigi County to campaign to Cdr. Gier Chuong Aluong under the false slogan that the Chollo were oppressing the Dinka people in Atar and therefore they should be assisted by the government of Southern Sudan.

3. The Nuer pushed the Anywaa on the Baro River very hard to the east that they are entirely Ethiopia citizens unlike the Ciro who still maintain strongholds in Akobo and Pochalla.

4. The process was enforced by 'oathing' performed by traditional priest that power belong to the Toposa and anybody against that would die to beat all Toposa voters into compliance.

5. The SPLM/A High Command comprised Dr. John Garang de Mabior, Chairman (Bor), Cdr. Kerubino Kuanyin Bol, deputy

Chairman (Gogrial), Cdr. Salva Kiir Mayardit (Gogrial) and Cdr. Arok Thon Arok (Bor) all hailing from the Dinka nationality, and Cdr. William Nyuon Bany, a Nuer (Fangak)

CHAPTER EIGHT

DID INDEPENDENCE COME TO SOUTH SUDAN A BIT TOO PREMATURELY?

It is human nature to reflect about the past, as Ustaz Bona Malual[1] in his autobiography put it succinctly that "No future without the Past". But reflect about the past should not just be for leisure but to enable discovery of mistakes and injustices with the view of rectifying them. In this way one learns not to repeat them otherwise it would be a meaningless exercise. In essence, the theme of this book, the problems of South Sudan is made up of many subtitles each discussed in its right. One of the subtitles was an interrogation, whether or not independence of South Sudan could have come a bit too prematurely. It isn't a rhetorical question but speaks to the current realities that depict the republic of South Sudan like a political toddler in its relations and transactions in the internal, regional and international domains. The question stems from deep sense of frustration, if not anger, with South Sudan's ruling elite as they display various degrees of rawness and political immaturity.

Independence was not the one-day event like the ceremony at Dr. John Garang Memorial Grounds that took place on 9th July 2011 to mark the independence of the young country in the world. No, independence of South Sudan was a process that spanned six decades, but the ruling elite turned out to be raw, uncivil, unprofessional or uncaring for the country and its people would suggest that no matter how long the struggle for independence took in terms of time and political resources, the South Sudan political elite would still remain inequivalent to the challenges of a modern state in terms of its governance, socioeconomic and cultural development of its people. No post-colonial sub-Sahara African country had the financial and economic resources South Sudan had it started off as a subnational entity in 2005, but today it is the poorest state in the continent depicting the manner a toddler plays even with the most valuable asset it owns. I am not thinking about time; it has been a long time, since 1947, when Southern Sudanese started struggling for independent statehood. My reflection revolves around the fact that this long struggle has not changed many Southern Sudanese that in less than three years after independence they were again destroying that state.

The UN Security Council's Resolution 1590 of 24th March 2005 leading to the formation of the United Nations Mission in the Sudan (UNMIS) to support the implementation of the CPA and to perform certain functions related to humanitarian assistance, protection and promotion of human rights, was an integral part of this independence preparations, which eventually led to the UN Security Council's Resolution 1996 of 8th July 2011 recognising the independence of the republic of South Sudan and the establishment of the United Nations Mission in South Sudan (UNMISS). In between the two dates laid what politically went wrong that the nascent state failed to transit from fragility to become a viable modern state with an accountable government.

The desire, will, and ability of the people to struggle determinedly are not the only determinants of independence to acquire international recognition and acceptability. There also ought to be other criteria in the international law vide which a people independence and sovereignty is granted and accepted in the community of nations. In this connection therefore, the ruling elite should at least demonstrate some degree of civility, capacity, and capability to govern; that is to say that there must be internal legitimacy gleaned from existence of functional institutions and instruments of public authority and accountable government, respect for human rights and the rule of law. However, sometimes, the existence of these conditions may not be sufficient to acquire international recognition and legitimacy; Puntland in Somalia and Western Saharawi Republic are cases in point notwithstanding the internal legitimacy their respective political systems enjoy.

The question of diplomatic recognition being dependent on internal or external legitimacy is not the point of my discussion.

It is rather how much prepared are the people for their independence which underpins this discussion. The assumption is that the preparation for independence – raising the flag and singing the national anthem, started with the war of national liberation suggesting that the longer the war lasted the more prepared for independence would be the people in terms of the institutions and instruments of governance, evolution of a national consciousness and unity among the people.

A prolonged interim period before the conduct of the referendum on self-determination wouldn't have impeded Garang's concept and vision of the New Sudan taking roots in South Sudan. On the contrary, a long interim period would have permitted the members of the SPLM/A to learn and internalize some important procedures in managing the state. The exercise of the inalienable right to self-determination would only have been a lesson for other Sudanese political leaders to learn the hard truth that people who ever felt the hegemony and domination of the larger sociocultural groups jeopardized their identity and culture. In this discussion, something strange lingers to suggest that if Southern Sudan were a part of Egypt, Kenya or Nigeria; countries which are friends of the United States of America and the West, and not parcel of a pariah state called the Sudan, it wouldn't have been easy for the people of South Sudan to win the right of self-determination. It would have been sabotaged like the cases of Puntland and Western Saharawi republic. This is to say that the people of southern Sudan were able to win the right to self-determination because it served some strategic interests of the American Administration otherwise, they could have ended up with Addis Ababa 1972 type agreement than the CPA. It was a case of time-respected adage that the enemy of your enemy is a friend. The arrogance of the Islamic fundamentalist regime paved the way for independence and birth of the republic of South Sudan. Perhaps, the international community assumed that South Sudanese are as rational as the rest of humanity when it comes to protecting or guarding their national interest. They were surprised.

Indeed, they should be surprised; anybody familiar with political struggle would be aware of the nitty-gritty in a political party or liberation movement. The SPLM/A undertook the struggle without doing periodic self-assessment and evaluation. If on a journey you don't look back, you won't know how far you have travelled. In the same vein, any political enterprise like a national liberation movement must engage in self-assessment or self-evaluation. It would help it know whether or not it's on the right track, or whether its membership and the entire people have internalized the message at the centre of the struggle. If the message at the centre of the struggle was independence that all and sunder would know its meaning, and the core values of being independent and sovereign.

In discussing the war of national liberation in its entirety it was clear that what plays out in South Sudan's inequivalence spring from the SPLM/A having failed to evolve into a genuine national liberation movement. It had enough time to address all the fundamental contradictions underpinning war together with those of accountable governance, social cohesion and national unity. Like many other southern Sudanese, I also campaigned for partition and independence of South Sudan but from the perspective that peace was better than unity, a slogan borrowed from the EPRDF, which in 1992 had to formally accept and recognize the independence of Eritrea instead of continuing the war of occupation. I haven't and won't change my position in respect of independence of South Sudan, only that I must admit that prosecuted within its political and ideological content the SPLM/A-led war of national liberation could have handed the people of South Sudan better results than the present content. The republic of South Sudan could have been conceived and delivered in bits while the war raged until all of it were liberated. Since this is a discussion in retrospect, nevertheless, it is worthwhile and necessary for the young generation of South Sudan leaders to acquaint themselves with the realities that resulted from cynical negligence that accompanied the war. It is now obvious that it was not liberation *per se* but power adventure. That independence may have come too prematurely emanates from the nature of the liberation era leaders and their fashion for primitive accumulation of wealth. South Sudan started off a rich country. By 2006, the subnational Government of Southern Sudan was receiving not less than US $700 million (seven hundred million dollars) in oil revenues per month that it left the collection of non-oil revenues, customs and other taxes estimated at US $500-600m (five to six hundred million dollars) to the individuals who pocketed them. I mentioned in my previous writings that the

CPA thrust the SPLM onto a unfamiliar terrain of managing a state, and most of the mistakes its leaders committed during the interim period, and after the independence stemmed from their ignorance and inexperience with government. This is proved by the way the leaders squandered the financial and economic resources they could have employed to redeem the promise of social and economic development they made to the people during the war.

It's testimony that the SPLM/A leaders ignored or rather were not conversant with the reality that liberation, and for that matter, the war of national liberation, was a school in which its leaders and cadres could have 'trained to govern'. The three weeks training session those leaders were dispatched to in South Africa wouldn't have been necessary at all. It was like paying back dearly for deliberately refusing to benefit from, or utilize the experienced and qualified former senior bureaucrats in the government of the Sudan. The 'trial and error' the SPLM/A leaders experimented during the war to avoid learning from others was a mere adventurous waste of time and human resources... And when the 'trial and error' failed to produce desired results, due to lack of theoretical understanding of issues, they recoiled back to their ethnic cocoons to find solutions. Ethnic solutions are exclusive in that they are not common or shared by everyone and therefore invariably contradict the principles of national inclusive approach. It was this absence of national inclusive approach to the building the state that underlies the social, economic, and political crisis in South Sudan.

As South Sudan sinks further into the abyss, one begins to understand the essence of a prolonged transition. Even now, looking back at the leaders' reluctance to implement the revitalized agreement, which they signed in September 2018, one feels the leaders' insensitivity and lack of political will to sacrifice in the higher interest of the people and the country. A longer interim period would have enabled the SPLM/A leaders, cadres, and combatants to transition from the mentality of war and destruction to mentality of peace and reconstruction; from outlaw mentality of a guerrilla army to a culture of civility and decency; from the militarism and culture of issuing command and orders to the culture of dialogue and building consensus and Southern Sudan could have emerged prepared for independence.

The condition that underpinned the establishment of the UNMISS wouldn't have obtained. While the government of the subnational entity was implementing the peace agreement, many parts of Southern Sudan started to witness such communal conflicts as never experienced during the war: between Lou Nuer and Murle, and between Murle and Dinka Bor in Jonglei or between the Aguok and Apuk or Rek and Luany-Jiang in Warrap or between the Mundari and Bari in Central Equatoria state, and the simmering conflict between the Chollo and Padang Dinka or between the Padang Dinka and the Maaban in Upper Nile. All these conflicts constituted the state of fragility under which South Sudan became independent prompting the UN Security Council resolution establishing UNMISS. The SPLM/A led GOSS failed completely to prevent the conflicts; it was easy to destroy than to build and having destroyed the administrative infrastructure without a functional alternative over the twenty-one years, the SPLM/A leaders had to put up with half-baked independence, sharing sovereignty eith UNMISS.

The tragic death of Dr. John Garang added another dimension to the obfuscation around the implementation of the CPA on the one hand, and the internal SPLM leadership scrabbles on the other hand. The SPLM and NCP spent the six-years interim period verbally bludgeoning each other in a tensely charged political environment of CPA implementation. The transition of leadership from Garang to Salva Kiir was abrupt and sudden that left many internal political hitches unresolved; these would pop up in form of personal quarrels that distracted focus and attention away from important national issues. In the absence of genuine collegial relations in the SPLM leadership, President Salva Kiir preoccupied himself with the processes in Southern Sudan leading only to the conduct of the referendum on self-determination. He paid less attention to state formation and nation building processes or provision of social services and economic development in the subnational entity.

This led to the failure to successfully implement the demobilization, disarmament and rehabilitation (DDR) programme provided for in the CPA to depoliticize and professionalize the SPLA, the police, prisons wardens, wildlife wardens and civil defence forces. Instead of implementing Garang's orders to restructure the SPLA, President Salva Kiir's reversed the order and absorbed the several militia groups into the SPLA exacerbating the confusion regarding such issues as the ranks; the militia groups came in with inflated ranks, and army discipline became a problem. Some elements of the militia groups who were formerly SPLA combatants but deserted in the context of the splits and splinterism came back as generals while their colleagues who remained in the movement were still first or second lieutenants. This rendered impossible the reorganization and professionalization of the SPLA.

It was particular importance in this transformation was the restructuring of the police to become consistent with democratic policing as provided for in the UN Security Council Resolution 1590. The importance of professional, efficient, and effective police service can't be overemphasized. Those SPLA officers transferred to the police force including those officers who formerly were graduates of the Police College in Khartoum had been militarized and forgotten their police functions. At the same time the SPLM leadership marginalized those army and police officers who worked for the NCP regime, most of them non-Dinka, supplanting them with SPLA officers and the mess began in the police force[2]. A situation which smacks of lawlessness at the government level occurred in Bor in 2007. That incident demonstrated that ethnic solidarity triumphed easily over allegiance to the state[3], would require more time and enlightenment to combat and align these ethnic sentiments to the national governance systems. This reinforces our argument in favour of prolonged transition to enable the evolution in society and in the liberation movement of strong patriotic sentiments to erase the narrow, chauvinistic ethnic ideology. Because it was short, the interim period ended before the internal political contradictions in the SPLM/A leadership had been resolved. The war triggered anger, bitterness, and the urge to vengeance remained raw within and between communities and the failure to implement the reconciliation and national healing entrenched those attitudes and sentiments. The SPLM unlike the NCP had no explanation or reason to ignore the process of reconciliation and national healing provided by the CPA and enshrined in both the Interim National Constitution 2005 as well as the Interim Constitution of Southern Sudan 2005. The reconciliation and national healing would easily dovetail with the people-to-people peace process initiated by the Wunlit Conference 1999, and indeed accelerated the transformation of the CPA from what it was a political compromise to peace, reconciliation, healing and social harmony in the communities.

One of the weakest points in the management of the war of national liberation, was the failure to establish a bureaucracy in the territories that came under its administration. Bureaucracy consisting of rules, guidelines, procedures, bookkeeping, record taking, and experienced professional workers, indeed a system, is the backbone of the state and the resistance to its establishment was closely linked to the resistance to subordinate the army to the political authority. As a result, the evolution of a professional, proficient, and diligent civil service based on meritocracy eluded the SPLM/A, and that had profound impact on state formation in the SPLM/A controlled areas. Ignoring this cardinal idea, the SPLM/A began to experiment with what called the Civil-Military Administration (CMA). This was nothing but senior SPLA officers, some of them very raw and ignorant, appointed to administer the civilians. The CMA was total disaster due to lack of separation between military and civil functions. This was then followed by the Civil Authority of the New Sudan (CANS) as another experiment with government. The SPLM/A leadership unfortunately had not drawn lessons from the failure of the CMA experiment. The underlying issue was the insubordination of the military to civil authority or subordination of the gun to politics. Unless, the civil administrators was a senior officer then his administration functioned without difficulties. But, generally seniority in the SPLA remained a stumbling block to a functional CANS.

The sticking point in the liberation movement was the lack of clear demarcation between what was military or what was civil. There were cases particularly in the pastoralist areas where some SPLA commanders on account of their military seniority usurped the functions of the traditional authorities and sat in community courts to settle customary cases; they did this with expressed intention to cope up for themselves resources in form of cattle. In some places they also usurped the functions of the CANS officers particularly in the domain of tax collection, rendering the civil authority system not only dysfunctional but also as an agency for corruption. This was the genesis of corruption in the liberation movement but which heightened later in the government of South Sudan; officers tasked with collecting government taxes and revenues ended up stealing public money with impunity. In most of these incidences, the leadership turned the other way in a deliberate policy of appeasement of recalcitrant and rebellious commanders. It was to maintain semblance of authority in the areas far away from the SPLA GH/Qs and where direct supervision was impossible.

The war ended while the confusion still raged between what was military or civil in the liberation movement, and the sudden death of Dr. Garang compounded it further. A system that could be counted as SPLM/A system had not been established and there was reference points to make. The SPLM Manifesto had been abandoned since 1994 and the SPLA Penal and Disciplinary Laws had been scrapped and thrown away. The formation of GOSS in the absence of a, established own bureaucratic system meant conforming to the Ingaz system already in place – a system of organized aggrandisement that resembled the practice in the SPLM/A administered areas, and many of the SPLM/A leaders, cadres, and combatants felt at ease with and intertwined with it, and corruption thrived. It was an environment where there was no difference between ignorance and lack of the system. Everyone assumed they were qualified for the position the occupied in the bureaucracy as directors, directors-general and even undersecretaries in the ministries mocking themselves as 'liberators' these functionally illiterate upstarts pushed the trained, qualified and experienced civil servants to the peripheries and the result was catastrophic. Discipline, meritocracy, diligence, and civil service culture collapsed and this affected government performance in service delivery and plans for socioeconomic development. The presence of ignorant and less experienced bureaucrats in the ministries were like gold mines for government contractors and their foreign collaborators. Instead of going-in for best practice in bidding, the highly over-priced government contracts paid upfront 100% without guarantees or collaterals were ditched out to friends, relatives and those who provided lucrative kickbacks. Many of these contracts were on a single-source mode that did not require diligence control by the ministry of justice and constitutional development.

When a country fails to fulfil its national, regional and international defence and security obligation it is automatically occupied by the United Nations. The Congo had been under UN occupation since 1960 and this did not prevent the regional coalition war to overthrow the regime of Mobutu Seke Seko. The presence of UNMISS has never presented political violence occurring either as a result of state or non-state actors meting it out to the people. The UPDF invaded South Sudan when it was looking for Joseph Kony or resist the Lou Nuer white army in 2013, the presence of UNMISS notwithstanding. Playing the role of a buffer state, this context is a threat to South Sudan's independence and sovereignty. The security breach in July 2022 in Mayom County in which the County Commissioner was assassinated and incinerated in his house together with his wife was awful, but the most obnoxious and indeed treacherous was the conspiracy hatched by Tut Gatluak with the authorities in Western Kordofan State in the Sudan to arrest and extradite the culprits to Mayom County H/Qs where they were summarily executed, and the ring leader incinerated in the presence of the state governor, Dr. Joseph Monytuil, not only that but the soldier who refused to shoot and the two men who shared the video of the execution were also executed. This can't be anything but the height of lawlessness that is pushing South Sudan to the edge.

Such incidences will not only encourage criminal activities but the state is in danger of becoming the main perpetuator of crime in the manner that some senior individuals are involved with the cartels in extraction and plunder of natural resources of the country. Soon, South Sudan might become a hub of regional and international terrorism; it won't be a wonder given that some of the rebels have no clear political or ideological agenda, incentivized by terrorist groups in the region or even far afield, they could easily transform into terrorist outfits for foreign agenda. The activities of the Islamic Call Groups in the neighbourhoods of Juba are suspect; a poverty-induced Islamic proselytization, which exploits the poverty and ignorance of the people to indoctrinate them with fundamentalist Islamic ideologies that would sooner than later pose danger to national security. The Shabab in the neighbouring Kenya began in the bourgeoning slums and were pushed to the edge of political violence by the regime.

Militarism in the SPLM/A was deliberately engineered as a means to entrench personal power of Dr. John Garang de Mabior. Over time, it became an impediment to introduction and inculcation of democracy and democratic principles in the governance of the national liberation movement. The SPLM has abandoned the democratic practice of electing leaders; the vacant positions in the Political Bureau and in the National Liberation Council, the two-deputy chairperson, the position of the secretary-general and his two deputies were filled by appointment even against the complaints from the members. This points to a possibility that President Salva Kiir may not countenance elections at the end of the extended transitional period.

There are more than fifty political parties in South Sudan, many of them are briefcase parties without the basic elements of political and legitimate existence. Only few of these parties could boast of multi-ethnic membership otherwise they would be family political outfits. This would include the SPLM, which drew its membership from the legacy of the war of national liberation. However, the SPLM has become only a shell without content, a name without a political or ideological meaning. It is only an agency for political rent; without employment opportunities it provides no one would be in the SPLM. As a result, it has attracted, pulled in, and absorbed anyone in South Sudan whose goal is personal aggrandizement in power and wealth. The notion of power-sharing in the revitalized agreement had triggered political opportunism in an unprecedented way leading to splits and splinterism in the parties and emergence of floating groups that created instability and confusion in these political outfits. These floating groups were political shifting sands that serve only short term individual economic interest but had long term negative impact on the political development of South Sudan. It created a psychology for quick fixes, short cuts and instantaneous profits at the expense of perseverance, sacrifice, and commitment to national agenda; why suffer if one could easily get to a desired objective was the motto of many of these people. It's a psychology that at the same time prevented the evolution of a national awareness to trump the personal interests or party allegiance and therefore blocked the emergence of a critical mass capable of independent political action to transform the oppressive reality in South Sudan.

South Sudan's rush to independence and sovereignty inadvertently entrenched and consolidated the culture of dependence on free external resources. This has become so generalized in a manner unprecedented across the different sociocultural formations. The peasants abandoned tilting the land and migrated to become squatters in the urban and peri-urban areas living in crowded relative's homes. This pushes these government employees to engage in corruption as a means to respond to sociocultural imperatives. It doesn't happen that government transforms into a charity, but what occurs in the central ministry of finance and economic planning is exactly like a charity, ditching huge sums of money to select few mostly from the same ethnic community armed with approval papers from government agencies. The ministerial docket has never shifted from Warrap since 2016 precisely to keep the cash flowing to members of the communities in the state. In fact, the community lobbies in the state would not permit appointment of the minister of finance and economic planning hailed from another region or state. It could result in a mayhem back home in Warrap state.

The situation in the towns like Juba was a bit better in terms of public services and public utilities when they established the subnational entity – GOSS, in 2005 but then things started to deteriorate that nothing in government functioned normally, rationally, and perfectly except when it serves one's personal interest. A culture of 'each for himself and God for all' engulfed and overwhelmed South Sudan both at the official and private levels subordinating the national and public interest to the self or one's ethnicity, clan or family. The concepts of patriotism, fraternity and justice or morality lost relevance even those officials who negotiated and signed government contracts did so after ensuring that the contractor has paid a fat kick back. In such a situation the contractor would have only a shoddy work to perform in order to gain a margin of profitability. Between the Ministry of Finance and the Central Bank a meticulous group emerged to extort money. In this connection confidentiality and secrecy in financial transaction had disappeared. It is dangerous to make huge withdrawal of cash because the banks have been infiltrated by criminal gangs. Many foreign business and NGOs have been robbed of huge sums of money; criminals trailed their official straight from the bank to their office. In a recent foiled robbery in the city centre the culprits were found to be members of the organized forces. The growing inequality in the distribution of wealth and delay in salaries pushes members of organized forces into this criminal business; it is much easier since they have their guns at their disposal. In view of the biting economic difficulties that pushes people to make ends meet, nobody with a mind would undertake duty professionally and diligently.

In fact, one is forced to ask about how in Juba people are surviving the uncontrolled market; a market and commodity prices driven by the price of US dollar. One wonders what makes a soldier, who has family but spends months in his job without receiving salary; how does he feed his family. It was not difficult to find out how the informal economy operates. The soldier has his gun; he won't allow himself and his family to starve therefore uses his gun to extort money from the poor unarmed civilians. Sometimes he rents his gun to criminals and in this manner compensate for delayed salaries. This same goes for those soldiers who cut trees and burnt charcoal and all other informal economic activities; suggesting that cash flow in this informal economy reaches all other people including women selling tea and food on the streets, shoes-shiners, war-washers, boda-boda drivers who ferry people to different destinations in the city. Juba is really a city of hustlers at every level whether we believe it or not. Those working in state institutions trade with the sensitive information under their custody that nothing again is secret in the corridors of power in South Sudan. Information leakers wield too much power of lobby that sometimes influence appointments or removal of governors and other constitutional office holders, and therefore receive huge sums of money as intermediaries. The victims of such a system are the unemployed intellectuals, former SPLA commanders, retired politicians; they have nothing to sell and therefore they try to hang on their relatives or waste away and die miserably. To many of those unfortunate ones, independence of South Sudan has no meaning if neither politics nor economics is functioning to be benefit of the citizenry.

That South Sudanese people find themselves at the mercy of a mediocre leadership can't be blamed on premature independence alone; it resulted from a combination of many factors, some of which we discussed in the previous chapters. South Sudan was an integral part of the Sudan and moreover had a successful self-governing subnational entity – the Southern Region, therefore, premature independence wouldn't count as a factor. It is the social and cultural backwardness of the dominant elite, and their primitive perception of the state that translate into the current chaos. The dominant elite has not transformed into petty bourgeoisie with refined mannerism, civil culture and respect for others' rights. Notwithstanding the affluence lifestyle it displays, this elitist class remains rural in thoughts and actions, and ignorant of urban etiquette, politics and economics.

This plays out in the decisions this class makes and actions they undertake; in their promotion of ethnicity and ethnic lobbies instead of democratic politics in this way they sabotage political conscious; in promoting imports of posh vehicles, manufactured, agricultural and food commodities that could have been produced locally, this class helped in capital flight from South Sudan; the competition and power struggle within this elitists promotes insecurity in the states and within communities prevents the people to engage in food production and this adds to their pauperization.

The process of democratization, which culminated in political independence of South Sudan, occurred before the people of South Sudan citizens of the samein their different sociocultural formations (ethnicities) had reached the level of social and economic development, and political awareness to accept themselves as citizens of the same country. When democracy precedes social and economic development of society but not its consequence, the equations and indicators are overturned and distorted. The determinants of power are no longer soft politics based on ownership and control of means of production but on primeval parameters of demography and physical strength. In this configuration the largest single ethnicity hegemonizes the state, captures the resources and its elements behave as though they were entitled to power and resources on account of their numerical superiority, and to the exclusion of other citizens; totalitarianism imperceptibly replaces democracy, the dominant political party, the SPLM, pretends to build political pluralism and puts in place liberal economic and free market policies to facilitate the extraction and plunder of the country's natural resources. Political pluralism in a socioeconomically underdeveloped and culturally backward environment like in South Sudan emerging from twenty-one years war of national liberation is a farce; political parties only become vehicles for political rent, and indeed this produced political patronage system and economic cronyism that has enabled the parasitic capitalist class to capriciously seize the wealth of the country.

It is ludicrous that the SPLM/A, after prosecuting a

revolutionary war of national liberation and winning political victory, notwithstanding the political compromise, reverses back to political pluralism in which it constructed a totalitarian dictatorship buttressed by ruthless and brutal national security apparatus that has shrunk the political and democratic space and prevents independent organization and action. I can vouch, Dr. John Garang unlike President Salva Kiir would have done it differently. Garang knew very well that South Sudan was a poor country but potentially rich in natural resources. As a poor country at the lower rungs of socioeconomic development what South Sudan needed was not a multiparty democracy but a decisive benevolent dictatorship to push the economy moving. Instead of going for political pluralism, I am sure Dr. John Garang would have gone for a benevolent dictatorial regime, and in line with his populist ideology would have constructed state institutions of accountable governance to promote social and economic development of South Sudan. Dr. Garang wouldn't have given sway to the parasitic capitalist class in the manner President Salva Kiir Mayardit had done to the disastrous disadvantage of the ordinary South Sudanese. The results of the two dictatorial regimes would have played out differently that different from the current context, Garang's dictatorship would have been something with a South Sudan -African nationalist streak.

1. What Should be Done to Rescue South Sudan

The present political context the people of South Sudan find themselves is something like from the pages of children fairy tales' books. Many regional and international friends of South Sudan find it hard and difficult to accept the turn of events following independence that transformed the political leaders into enemies of themselves, and in this fragmented their people into hostile camps; that there is a revitalized government of national unity (R-TGONU) comprising the incumbent transitional government of national unity (ITGONU), SPLM/A in Opposition, South Sudan Opposition Alliance and Other Political Parties comprising the Umbrella and National Alliance groups. This is a Coalition of Opposition Parties (COOP) in addition to the Hold-out Opposition groups in exile, who refused to sign the revitalized agreement on the resolution of the conflict in South Sudan. It is a political context in which those in government, R-TGONU, are only there because they are vice-presidents or occupy ministerial dockets, nothing more; while those in opposition are there because they are not in government not because they have something alternative to what is taking place in the country. These political groups are not engaged in any kind of political debate, consultative dialogue or consensus building although they are counting on the elections scheduled to be conducted in December 2024. President Salva Kiir asked the people to maintain peace as the country prepares for the papal official visit. Many ordinary South Sudan have tied their hope for peace in the country to the papal visit and the interdenominational prayers to work miracles. The visit of Pope Francis will definitely happen and pass, but South Sudan will still reel in uncertainty. The reason for this uncertainty is simple. The SPLM is no longer at the steering wheel as it was during the war of national liberation. Its leadership no longer feels for the people of South Sudan as he did during the struggle for liberation. The current crop of South Sudan political leaders are politically and ideologically bankrupt and therefore wouldn't attach any importance to the papal message about the suffering of their people. This is the negative impact of the several political and ideological shifts the movement's leadership beat in the course of the struggle; the emptiness the people are left with in the event of failure of historical dimension occurs that even the most ardent of revolutionaries feel there was no revolution again to defend. The people are intelligent and quick to learn; the sentiments with many people is that the SPLM/A, the concept and vision of New Sudan did on 30th July 2005 in the tragic helicopter crash. The political wheel shifted then from the multi-ethnic SPLM/A it was during the war to an ethnic – clan dynasty headed by first family and relatives' businesses facilitated by the NCP operative and cartels quite versed and experienced with the process of personal aggrandisement (*Tamkeen*). It is a political context that has considerably shrunk the political space, muzzled different political opinion, promoted corruption and impunity, and engaged in selective allotment of political and executive powers, and economic and financial resources to close business associates and relatives. It is a political context that rendered irrelevant the JCE, the once powerful ethnic lobby group, which helped destroy the SPLM power. It is a context of extreme inequality of power and wealth unprecedented in the history of South Sudan,

The question above about what must be done to extricate the people of South Sudan from this context requires deep thinking and clear ideological principles. What has transpired so far since the war began in 1983 until the eruption of the civil war in 2013 was a subversion of the revolution to transform South Sudan into a state whereby freedom, justice and fraternity reigned high in the consciousness of the people. This subversion took different forms; first the prosecution of the war of national liberation outside its political and ideological contents was the surest means of turning the liberation into its very opposite. The mobilization of the peasants and pastoralist organizing them into military units for fighting the war, but deny them political education and ideological training was to turned them into mere robots; programmed only to carry out orders and commands. This would explain how the privatization of the state in South Sudan and the current oppressive socioeconomic and political context could occur in the watch of more than three hundred thousand SPLA combatants, and no resistance or counter-action to stop it; Even the colonial-type professional armies would pull a putschist coup to overthrow the dictator.

The SPLM/A experiment, by virtue and character of its leadership, and the regional and international context in which it occurred, was bound not only to stagnate and compromise with the enemy, but also to create an oppressive dictatorship in the hands of a parasitic class quite averse to the social, economic and political interests of the masses. It was intended to pre-empt and completely subvert the evolution of the revolutionary forces in Southern Sudan. Posing as the revolutionary vanguard, the SPLM/A not only desensitised the people distorting their understanding of its core messages, but also prevented the revolutionary ideas taking roots in society; an equivalent of dampening and leaving the masses fragmented along ethnic and provincial lines.

Capitalism and capitalist development has not penetrated South Sudan and therefore its people still are living the stage of national democratic revolution; a stage through which colonial people remain on account of foreign occupation, domination, extraction and plunder of their natural resources in the service of the foreign power, leaving the people poor, ignorant and culturally backward. The people of South Sudan would exist this stage in the context of heightened social and economic development of the productive forces in the form of construction of physical infrastructure: highways and roads to connect the different parts of the country, tapping of hydroelectric power generation and transmission to different parts of the country, initiating industrial development, mechanization and commercialization of agriculture in all its different sectors of food and cash crops, and livestock, fisheries and others to contribute to food security of the people. This would enable a quantitative as well as qualitative leap towards social change.

However, social or revolutionary change occurs only at a nuance intersection marking the collapse of the current political order and the rising people's action to change the order. This would be where the level of social awareness and political consciousness merge into a revolutionary force to push away the decaying social order constructed by the parasitic capitalist class. South Sudan is yet, and indeed will take a long time, to reach that intersection point. This is because several factors, both intrinsic and extrinsic, conspire to block the rise of people's revolutionary consciousness. The neglect of social and economic development of the southern provinces of the Sudan over a long period of time prevented the emergence of a conscious working-class and a culture of political organization and struggle therein explaining why the struggle in the southern provinces for political and economic rights has always been violence and armed struggle.

But armed struggle in both cases produced an elitist militarist class that had little or no political obligation to the masses suggesting that armed struggle can't again become the model for bringing social change to South Sudan. Thus, discussing what must be done to transform the current context in South Sudan requires a shifting in the political thinking towards creation of a critical mass. This springs from the notion that real change comes from conscious action and this underpins the importance of the emergence of a conscious masses movement in the towns and cities capable of organized political action for change. The absence of an organized and unionized working class and the vagary of the informal economic sector had rendered difficult if not impossible to mobilize and agitate against the repressive totalitarian system in South Sudan. The masses of the people fragmented along ethnic and regional fault find it impossible to unify their struggle to serve a common purpose for change.

The rising levels of insecurity at the ethnic and clan levels in the states, the biting economic crisis that has completely eroded the purchasing power of the South Sudan Pound against the convertible currencies, the rising levels of inequality in society, the lumpen proletarianization of the urban dwellers, and the fractal politics among the elites that makes impossible political consultation and dialogue to achieve national consensus on many crisis issues are positive developments in that it will sooner than later will lead to the emergence of a critical mass of the deprived sections of the society to precipitate a revolutionary situation. This would be the only hope for rescuing South Sudan and to place it on correct social and economic developmental trajectory.

The lumpen proletarianization occurs as a result of growing inequality even within the parasitic class itself. The main source of money in South Sudan is the oil revenues. This lack of accountable governance of this sector led to wastage and hence decline in the resources available for rent. This meant that within the parasitic class differential treatment set in to generate inequality within the class and some have been pushed aside to become lumpens. With growing inequality whereby wealth accumulates on one side and poverty on the other side, a situation is bound to unfold that in South Sudan there would only be two tribes of the 'haves' and the 'haves not' albeit across ethnic contour lines. The stratification of South Sudan society on the basis of the 'haves' and the 'haves not' which are antagonistic would render tribalism and ethnic nationalism something of the past. For the first time since the sixties of the last century, South Sudan would witness the surge of South

Sudan nationalism and patriotism that trumps any tendency to ethnic chauvinism and bigotry.

It would be than that on the deathbed of tribalism or ethnicity shall rise the revolutionary South Sudanese patriotism defined by citizenship. However, this would by no means be simple or easy process. It will many-sided struggles of different dimensions and scopes. In the final analysis it would produce a leading revolutionary force from within the amalgam. Therefore, it would require the social and democratic forces interested in the transformation of the current oppressive situation to bring their act together in a spirit of readiness to sacrifice for the country and its people. The readiness to sacrifice shouldn't be construed as a call to arms to forcefully bring change. No, we don't mean that. The armed struggle was tried before, and was found to spur minimal or sometimes negative political development in the country. The armed struggle in South Sudan was a method vide which the petty bourgeoisie exploited the ignorance of the peasants to fight their wars for power.

There is a direct link between the repeated calls to arms and the current pathetic political situation in South Sudan. Wars prosecuted outside their ideological content devastate the peasantry and dampen their political consciousness and ends up producing an isolated elitist class. Situation of war prevents social and economic development because resources are diverted to war efforts and also blocks the evolution of a political culture of organization and action. The sacrifice meant here is the readiness to learn and conscientize with others and to arrive at the correct perception of the oppressive reality and how to transform it. Those who sacrifices for other people are individuals who have reach a certain level of political consciousness and ideological understanding of the oppressive reality. They indeed do engage in acts of sacrifice and solidarity with the victims of the oppressive regime. It is those people who understand the dynamics of oppression and exploitation engage in heroic struggle to free the society from totalitarianism. No one social political force could alone undertake this task. It requires the unity of all likeminded social and political forces; the social and revolutionary democrats, the communists, and other progressive forces to forge unity of purpose to enable them to build a political programme for this task. There is no other way that change could come to South Sudan except through the concerted efforts of all those who believe in freedom, justice, fraternity, and human dignity to rescue the people and the country from the most brutal regime our people have ever experienced.

In the process of transforming the oppressive reality, the people of South Sudan have to borrow a leaf from the experience accumulated by the Sudanese in the domains of political mobilisation, organization and mass action. It is a truism that successful revolution must be armed to protect its gains or prevent it being attacked or reversed/aborted by reactionary political forces. However, in this context, one of the most important tasks the revolutionary forces must undertake is to engage with and win over elements of the army, national security, police and other organised forces to the side of the revolution. In fact, many of them especially the low-ranking officers and soldiers are a section of the toiling masses and should be made to identify with them through political enlightenment. In this way, they will resist orders of the seniors to open fire on the demonstration and protestors against the totalitarian regime. This occurred in many places in the world like in Russia in October 1917, in the Sudan in October 1964 and the on-going standoff between the Sudanese masses and the remnants of the oppressive National Islamic Front regime. The success and victory of the Sudanese people must embolden the South Sudanese people to tread the same revolutionary path.

In summary, the republic of South Sudan has failed as a state. This failure was not consequent to premature independence but because of the mediocre leadership President Salva Kiir Mayardit provided in the seventeen years since August 2005, when his rise to power in straight succession to Dr. John Garang de Mabior. He was Garang's loyal deputy since 1992 but it was known that Salva Kiir was just nominal number two and therefore would only share by small proportion the responsibility for many of the decisions that came in the name of the SPLM/A leadership.

This introduces another dimension that places responsibility of failure of the SPLM/A as a national liberation project on the leadership of Dr. John Garang de Mabior. The SPLM/A leadership was not an institution; it was personified in Dr. John Garang as an individual. It was a leadership that provided no opportunity for his subordinate colleagues and lieutenants to learn and become leaders as well. In the previous pages we have equally debunked some false narratives related to this leadership to leave a naked reality that the so-called concept and vision of the 'new Sudan' was a falsehood whose objective was to ensnare the Nuba, the Funj and all the marginalized and politically excluded people of the Sudan into believing the lie and to enlist in the war. And they did it with dignity valour and honour. However, Dr. Garang's strategic political objective was not liberation or construction of the 'new' Sudan; for nothing would have prevented its creation in the areas the gallant SPLA combatants liberated in southern Sudan, Nuba Mountains, and southern Blue Nile. It was also not liberation or the democratic transformation of the Sudanese polity for that would have involved different political and ideological methodologies. Dr. Garang was interested only in power and leadership of Southern Sudan; This would be explained by the political and ideological shifts that the SPLM/A undertook in the years coinciding with the defeat of the Derg and the collapse of the Soviet Union. It proves that the SPLM/A was not a national liberation movement; it was just a power project and as a power project died together with its author.

In conclusion, the independence of South Sudan came at an appropriate and opportune time as the people would have wished. There shouldn't be regrets although the leadership under which the country became independent was inappropriate, weak, ignorant, negligent, not caring, a mere don't care, irresponsible, an ethnic chauvinist and bigot, etc. It has placed South Sudan in the rain shadow of socioeconomic development that most post-colonial sub-Sahara African passed through. Nevertheless, the context in which South Sudan situates provides opportunity for those who genuinely want to change this terrible reality of failure, and to build South Sudan into a vibrant modern multinational state.

ENDNOTES

1. Ustaz Bona Malual Madut remains one of the towering and indeed one of the most controversial leaders of Southern Sudan during the period discussed in chapter two. And although no longer active in the politics of South Sudan, he is one of the rational voices still alive

2. This included illegal promotion of relatives and friends until a non-police college graduate officer rose to become the Inspector General of Police.

3. The state director of police, a Brigadier hailing from Dinka Bor, on his own volition but ostensibly in vengeance ordered the murder in cold blood of six Murle men who were in the hospital receiving medical attention for different diseases. Instead of apprehending the brigadier, the governor, a fellow Bor, sent him on holiday in Renk and that was the end of the criminal case.

APPENDIX

Table 1. List of South Sudan Nationalities

01	Acholi	33	Lofit
02	Aja	34	Lugbwara
03	Anywaa	35	Lulubo
04	Avkaya	36	Luo (Jur Chol)
05	Bai	37	Maaban
06	Baka	38	Madi
07	Balanda (Bwor)	39	Mandari
08	Balanda (Bviri)	40	Makaraka
09	Banda	41	Moro
10	Bari	42	Morokodo
11	Beile (Jur Biel)	43	Mundu
12	Binga	44	Murle
13	Bongo	45	Näädh (Nuer)
14	Boya	46	Naka
15	Chollo (Shilluk)	47	Ndogo
16	Didinga	48	Ngungule
17	Dongotono	49	Nyangatom

18	Feroghe	50	Nyangwara
10	Gollo	51	Nyiepo
20	Hufra	52	Otuho (Latuka)
21	Imatong	53	Pari
22	Jieng (Dinka)	54	Pojulu
23	Jiye	55	Riel (Atwot)
24	Jur Man Angier	56	Shatt (Thuru)
25	Kakwa	57	Seri
26	Keliku	58	Suri (Kachipo)
27	Koma	59	Tenet
28	Kriesh	60	Tid
29	Kuku	61	Toposa
30	Lango	62	Uduk
31	Logir	63	Yulu
32	Lokoya	64	Zande

REFERENCES

Abel Alier (1990) *"Southern Sudan: Too Many Agreements Dishonoured."* Ithaca Oress, London

Abyei, Edward Lino (2017) *"Dr. John Garang de Mabior: The Man to Know."* Rafiki for Printing and Publishing. Juba.

Bona **Malual** (2022) *"No Future Without the Past – An Autobiography."* Analecta Publishing.

Churchill, Winston (1899) *"The River War – An Account of the Reconquest of the Sudan"* SkyHorse Publishing 2013.

Dambisa **Moyo** (2010) *"Dead Aid – Why Aid is not Working and How there is Another way for Africa"*. Penguin Books, London.

Edgar O'Ballance (1977) *"The Secret War in the Sudan 1955-1972."* Faber and Faber Limited, London,

Alex De Waal (2015) *"The real politics of the Horn of Africa: Money, War and the Business of Power."* Polity Press, Cambridge, UK.

Lagu, Joseph (2006) *"Sudan- Odyssey Through a State: From Ruin to Hope."* MOB Centre for Sudanese Studies, Omdurman Ahlia University, Omdurman, Sudan.

Garang, J Ukel (1961) *"The Dilemma of Southern Intelligentsia: Is it Justified?* Published by the Ministry of Southern Affairs, Khartoum, 1970.

Khalid, Mansour (2015) *"The Paradoxes of Two Sudans – The CPA and the Road to Partition."* Africa World Press

Khalid, Mansour (1985) *"Numeiry and the Revolution of Dismay".* Routledge. London

Khalid, Mansour (1990) *"The Government They Deserve – The role of Elite in Sudan's Political Evolution".* Routledge, Kegan Paul

Johnson, Hilde F (2016) *"South Sudan-The Untold Story: From Independence to Civil War"* I.B. Tauris, London

Hanssen, Halle Jørn (2017) *"Lives at Stake."* With Norwegian People's Aid in South Sudan during the Time of the Liberation Struggle. Skyline, Oslo

Nyaba, P. A. (1997) *"The Politics of Liberation in South Sudan: An Insider's View."* Fountain Publishers, Kampala.

Nyaba, P. A. (1999) *"The Chollo (Shilluk) Predicament- The Threat of Physical Extermination and Cultural extinction of a People."* In Laura N Beny and Sondra Hale (editors) Sudan's Killing Fields – Political Violence and Fragmentation. The Red Sea Press, Trenton, New Jersy, 2015, pp 79 – 98

Nyaba, P. A. (2014) *"South Sudan: The crisis of Infancy."* CASAS, Cape Town.

Nyaba, P. A (2018) *"The Curse of Elitism: South Sudan's failure to transition to statehood and nationhood"* in Amir Idris (editor) South Sudan Post-Independence Dilemmas. Routledge, New York, 2018, pp 19 – 37.

Nyaba, P. A (2019) *"South Sudan: Elites, Ethnicity, Endless Wars and the Stunted State."* Mkuki na Nyota Publishers, Dar es Salaam.

Nyaba, P. A. (2022) *"Up from the Village: An Autobiography."* Africa World Books, Melbourne

PaanLuel Wel (editor) *"The Genius of Dr. John Garang"* The essential writings and speeches of the late SPLM/A's leader, Dr. John Garang de Mabior. Vol. 1, 2015

PaanLuel Wel (editor) *"The Genius of Dr. John Garang"* The essential writings and speeches of the late SPLM/A's leaders, Dr. John Garang de Mabior. Vol. 2, 2015

Pete Dolack (2018) *"It's Not Over: Learning from the Socialist Experiment"*. Zero Books, New York

Bruce Bueno **De Mesquita** and Alastair **Smith** (2011) *"The Dictator's Handbook – Why Bad Behaviour is Almost Always Good Politics"*. Public Affairs, New York.

Seyoum **Mesfin & Abdeta** Dribssa Beyene (2018) *"The Practicalities of Living with Failed States."* Daedalus. The Journal of American Academy of Arts and Sciences, Vol. 147 (Winter) 2018, pp128 – 140.

Slatin Pasha Rudolf C (1895) *"Fire and Sword in the Sudan"* Personal Recollection of both fighting and serving the Mahdist during the later 19th Century. Leonaur @ Oakpast Ltd, 2013

Yash Tandon (2015) *"Trade is War: The West's war against the World"* O/R Books, New York

Lewis, David Levering (1987) *"The Race to Fashoda: European Colonialism in Africa."* Weidenfeld Nicolson.

Mao Tse-Tung (1971) *"Six Essays on Military Affairs"* Foreign Languages Press, Peking.

Prah, K. K. (1986) *"African Nationalism and the Origins of War in the Sudan."* Lesotho Law Journal. Vol.2, No.2.

Patrick **Chabal** & Jean-Pascal **Daloz** (1999) *"Africa Works Disorders as Political Instrument."* The International African Institute in association with James Currey, Oxford.

JF **Bayart**, S.D.K. **Ellis** & B **Hibou** (1999) *"The Criminalization of the State in Africa."* Africa Issues Series by Boydell and Brewer.

J **Millard Burr** (1995) *"Requiem for the Sudan: War, Drought and Disaster Relief on the Nile"* Routledge, London.

INDEX

Ababa 120-121, 129, 132, 188, 298, 384, 387
Abba 171
Abboud 21, 27, 30-1, 38, 91, 110
Abdall 38
Abdalla 21, 26, 30, 33, 38-9, 45, 60, 73, 77, 83, 120, 133, 178, 304
Abdel 8, 10, 35, 39, 72-8, 93-4, 338
Abdelrahaman 33, 171
Abdelrahman 8, 304
Abdeta 419, 485
Abdullahi 6

Abel Alier. 25, 99, 102-3, 107-110, 112-5, 117-9, 122-4, 126-7, 130, 132, 134, 138-143, 145-7, 152, 154-5, 157-8, 162, 172, 188, 190, 193, 196, 279, 394, 483
Abiy 398
Abiya 70
Abiye 420
Abobo 337
Abuja 42, 103
Abulgasim 109
Abur 171, 279
Abyei, Edward Lino. xii, xxx, 43, 56, 59, 92, 110, 182, 197,

199, 373, 483
Acholi 231, 366, 481
Acuil 123-124, 126-8
Adam 75, 94, 338
Addia 188
Addis 120-121, 129, 132, 298, 384, 387
Addis Ababa xxv, xxv, xxx, 23-4, 37-8, 40, 42, 49, 66, 99, 101-3, 107, 109, 119-122, 130-2, 134-5, 138, 140, 149-150, 187-8, 190-1, 193, 198, 218, 232-3, 239, 247, 259, 266, 321, 343, 377, 380, 384, 391, 399, 402, 451
Adhidhiang 429
Adigo 421
Advertently 10
Adwok xvi, 107, 440
Afghanistan 69, 280
Africa xix, xxi, xxi, xxx, 4, 12-5, 41, 50, 65, 89, 100, 162, 165, 180-1, 184, 186-8, 210, 234, 243, 247, 260, 284-5, 287, 307, 319, 356-7, 371-2, 403, 427, 453, 484-6
African xix, xxv, 16, 24, 30, 43, 55, 58, 72, 89, 130, 135, 156, 165-6, 173, 218, 241, 288, 301, 309, 322-3, 326, 344, 348, 352-4, 377-8, 383-4, 389, 448, 478, 486
Africans 166, 181, 198, 427
Agar 73, 75, 311-2, 375
Agencies 295
Aggrey 100, 131, 140, 157
Agroindustrial 162
Aguet 279
Aguok 160, 369, 454
Agwalek 65, 69, 365, 397, 430
Ahlia 484
Ahmed xxx, 32-3, 35, 40, 46, 70-1, 91, 280, 398-9, 402, 408, 420
Aja 481
Ajak 282, 338-9
Ajawin 332
Ajou 172
Akech 198
Akobo 141, 202, 279, 433, 444
Akok 133, 158, 208
Akoka 168, 426

Akol 94, 332, 334-5, 368-9, 397, 403, 405, 431, 443
Akumbek 131, 367
Akuot 133
Alas 256
Alastair 485
Aldo 172
Aleu 123-124, 126, 335
Alex 483
Alfred 279, 391
Ali 8, 10, 49, 54, 253
Aliab 8, 311
Alier 25, 99, 102, 107-110, 112-5, 117-9, 122-4, 126, 130, 132, 134, 140-3, 145-7, 152, 154-5, 157-8, 162, 172, 190, 193, 394, 483
Aliet 108
Aluong 444
Alur 94
Amadi 438
Ambrose 173, 369
America xvi, 188, 198, 243, 298, 311, 450
American 69, 189, 309, 367, 451, 485
Americas 427
Amhara 234
Amilcar xxx, 356
Amir 485
Amum ix, xii, 56, 58-9, 61, 92, 338, 362, 375, 378, 387, 390
Analecta 483
Angelina 392
Angelo 394
Angier 482
Ansar 8-9, 33, 99, 130, 178
Antonio 321
Anyanya 22, 199, 281, 298, 323
Anyidi 323-324
Anywaa 94, 153, 224, 438, 444, 481
Apadang 358
Apuk 160, 369, 454
Arab 4, 13, 15, 17, 19, 21, 23-4, 29, 51-2, 64, 71, 82-3, 91, 96, 98, 148, 165, 168, 176, 188, 199, 225, 243, 252, 320
Arabia 354
Arabian 93
Arabic 68, 222
Arabicisation 16, 91
Arabisation 30

Arabised 7
Arabization 21
Arabized 6-7, 10, 15-6, 78, 166
Arabs 172, 427
Arkoi 42, 73, 75
Arman 46
Arok 194, 207, 217, 256, 266, 334, 336, 445
Arol 173
Arop 172
Arts 485
Aru 159
Arusha 385-386
Ashigga 9, 12
Asia 188, 243, 319
Asmara xxx, 42, 232, 382
Assalaya 138
Assossa 240, 248
Atar 365, 426, 430-1, 444
Atbara 31, 72, 134
Atem 133
Athur 315
Ato 385
Atwot 311
Auditor 268
Australia 254, 293, 352

Authority xxx, 328, 371, 419, 458
Autobiography 483, 485
Avkaya 241, 481
Awad 72-73
Awan 392, 397
Aweil 8, 58, 160, 171, 173, 199, 256, 341, 350, 358, 362, 434, 443
Awet 420
Ayang 123-124, 126-7
Ayieny 335
Ayod 183, 336, 346, 365
Ayualnhom 205
Ayuel 289
Azande 152-154, 223, 240-1, 250, 310, 324, 397, 435, 438
Azania 323, 367
Azhari 20, 29, 96
Aziz 75, 94, 338
Baathist 98
Babiker 99
Bagadi 427
Baggara 252
Bagi 94
Bahir 402

Bahr xx, 92, 179, 224, 252, 305, 316, 342, 385, 431, 437
Bahr el Ghazal xi, xx, 13, 16, 22, 63, 80, 92, 101, 127, 129, 132, 144-5, 153-4, 160, 191, 218, 223, 228, 234, 244, 252, 256, 289-290, 293-4, 310-1, 324, 335, 341, 368, 373, 396, 425, 427, 433-4, 439, 443
Bai 481
Bailiet 389, 433
Baka 481
Bakasoro 397
Balanda 481
Balogun 341
Bana 193
Banda 481
Bany 171, 194, 205, 217, 284, 334, 336, 445
Bapiny 92
Bar 293
Barach 335
Bari 115, 118, 125, 153, 218, 366, 439, 443, 454, 481
Baro 444
Bashir 48, 54, 60, 69, 93, 102, 399
Bassiouni 316
Battalion 129, 182, 188, 190, 192, 196, 235, 278, 289, 361, 375
Battalions 235
Bayart, J.F. 366, 486
Beda 394
Bee 289
Beile 481
Beja 382
Belgian 324
Belgrade 108
Benjamin 107, 133, 158, 197, 208
Bentiu xx, 24, 116, 189, 199, 282, 288, 376
Beny, Laura N. 484
Bey 21, 26, 30, 38
Beyene, Abdeta Dribssa. 419, 485
Bichok 392
Biele 439
Bilpam 199, 201-2, 212, 217, 240, 244
Binga 481
Bishoftu 398

Blue xxi, 6, 10, 17-8, 41-3, 48-9, 89, 96, 103, 110, 165, 186, 232-4, 249, 278, 287, 373, 478

Bol 133, 158-9, 173, 193-4, 205, 208, 217, 219, 284, 334, 444

Boma 199, 205, 279, 438

Bona, Malual. 119, 124, 127, 152, 172, 228, 447, 479, 483

Bong 440

Bonga 200, 222, 240, 244

Books 483, 485-6

Bor vii, xi, xii, xxv, 24, 53, 80, 92-3, 115, 117-8, 125, 129, 133, 154, 159, 176, 182-4, 186, 188, 191-3, 195-6, 199, 223, 227, 231, 272, 277, 279, 284, 288, 324, 336, 351, 362, 366, 369, 376, 380, 438, 443, 454, 456, 479

Botswana 390

Boya 481

Boydell 486

Bradford 331

Bretton xiv, xxx, 105, 133, 260, 347-8, 356

British 3-5, 8-11, 37, 82, 86, 98-9, 250, 288, 435

Bruce 485

Budapest 116, 172

Bueno 485

Bul 60, 63-4, 93

Burhan 73-77, 93

Burr, J Millard. 20, 486

Bwor 94

Cabral xxx, 356

Cairo 15, 42, 45, 87

California 115

Cambridge 483

Canada xxv, 428

Canterbury vii, xii

Capt 279

Castro 36

Caught 150

Cdr xx, 92, 94, 200, 212, 217-9, 229, 238, 257, 266-7, 289-290, 295, 315, 332, 334-340, 391, 444-5

Census 165

Chabal, Patrick. 366, 486

Chaban 109

Chad 78, 93

Chagour xii

Chama 386
Chan 173, 369
Charles 124
Chatim 124
Che 199, 242, 297
Checkpoint 281
Cheeseman 282
Chevron 115-116, 184, 189
Children 302
China 221, 419
Chinese 36, 298, 330, 355
Chol 219, 279
Chollo xi, xii, xxx, 7, 65, 80, 94, 227, 281, 292, 307, 335, 346, 365-6, 426, 428-433, 436, 443-4, 454, 481, 484
Christian 11, 133, 279, 335
Christians 155
Chukudum 209, 295
Chuol 133
Chuong 444
Churchill, Winston. 483
Chwogo 281
Ciec 153, 311
Ciro 444
Cirrillo 397
Clement 152, 157, 440

Col 99, 194-7, 205, 207, 214, 227, 234, 237, 247, 252, 279, 322
Collin 42
Comboni 367
Congo 24, 66, 94, 104, 231, 241, 243, 282, 288, 324, 349, 397, 460
Congolese 305
Corps 16, 19, 29-30, 96, 135
Criminalization 486
Crisis 217, 336, 351
Cuba 221, 317, 349
Cuban 36, 282, 300
Cubans 300
Currey 486
Cyril 386, 418
Daedalus 419, 485
Daglo 72-74, 76-8, 84, 93
Dahab 73, 173
Dak 81, 124-5, 365, 392
Daloz, Jean-Pascal. 366, 486
Dam 380
Dambisa, Moyo. 483
Dan 92
Danagalla 166
Daniel 25, 125, 219, 281, 420

Danish 281
Dar xxi, 17-8, 42, 46, 88, 93, 103, 165, 181, 284, 382, 385, 485
David 316-317, 486
De Waal 483
Debray 170, 180, 271
Debri 108
Democracy 259
Denay xii
Deng vii, 34, 94, 172, 177-8, 203, 282, 335, 338-9, 362-3, 369, 391-2, 419
Derg xxi, 41, 200-1, 204, 210, 233-4, 238-9, 246, 248, 252, 280, 285, 302, 478
Desalegn 70, 386, 398, 420
Desertification 419
Dhieu 75
Dhol 123-124, 126-8, 219
Dhurgon 374
Diaspora xxv, 238
Didinga 289, 331, 438, 481
Dimma 240, 244, 248
Dinka xi, xii, 52, 65, 84-5, 89, 115, 117-9, 121, 123, 125, 127, 130, 135, 148-151, 153-4, 156, 160-1, 167, 172, 179, 190, 203, 220, 222-5, 227, 229-231, 252, 260, 277, 281, 307, 312, 317, 326, 340, 346, 358, 366, 369, 375, 389, 424, 426-436, 438, 442-5, 454, 479
Dirdiery 71, 384, 399
Disciplinary 200, 459
Dok 63
Dolack, Pete. 485
Dolieb 227
Dongotono 441, 481
Doup 392
Dribssa 419, 485
Dro 172
Dubai 352
Duk 365
Dungu 241
Durham 428
East 4, 15, 64, 98, 127, 153, 162, 344, 353-4, 356, 367, 372, 389, 427, 437
Eastern xii, xxi, 42, 93, 123, 152-3, 165, 199, 232, 304, 360, 382, 436, 438-9, 441
Ebony 355

Economic 347
Edgar 483
Edward 182-183, 195, 197, 483
Egypt 4-5, 9-12, 14, 24, 98, 166, 288, 380, 390, 450
Egyptian 4, 9-11, 90, 97-8
Egyptians 8, 10
Eighteen 107
El-Obeid 72
Elia 421
Ellis, S.D.K. 366, 486
Elven 317
Emmanuel 171, 279
Eng 25, 123-5, 127-8, 152, 172
England 428
English 17, 36, 180, 428
Equality 75
Equatoria xi, xii, xxx, 13, 16, 19, 22, 29-30, 92-3, 96, 101, 114, 119, 121, 123, 127, 129, 132, 135, 144-5, 152-4, 172, 179, 190-1, 223-4, 234, 240-2, 244, 254, 289, 304, 310, 316, 324, 329, 331, 355, 360, 366, 373, 392, 396-7,
417, 425, 436-441, 454
Equatorian 114, 179, 190, 223
Equatorians 122, 222, 326, 362
Ernesto 242
Ethnic 220, 230, 357, 375, 435, 441-2, 453
Ethnicity xxi, xxv, 154, 485
Ethur 94
Europe 254, 311
European 5, 12, 14, 48, 309, 382, 427, 486
Europeans 355
Everybody 329
Extermination 484
Ezbon 99, 131, 140, 157, 440
Faber 483
Fadhil 10
Falsification 187, 196
Fangak 346, 365, 430-1, 433
Farouk 99
Fashoda 7, 80, 292, 326, 365, 426, 429, 432
Fatah 72-78, 93
Feroghe 482
Festus 390, 402, 408
Fidel 36

Fifthly 336
Formative 187
Fourthly 336
Francis vii, vii, 152, 194, 363, 428, 469
French 7
Fula 262, 328
Fulla 162
Funj xxv, xxx, 15, 17, 30, 43, 89-91, 166-7, 176, 181, 253-4, 326, 478
Fur xxi, 9, 15, 17-8, 42, 46, 88, 93, 103, 165-6, 284
Furi 181, 382
Gaafar xxv, 23-4, 73, 95, 97, 100, 102, 105, 110, 117, 119-121, 129-130, 140, 149, 191
Gaajak 194, 202
Gaajok 202
Gadeang 66
Gaderef 281
Gadhafi 237
Gahouth 238
Gai vii, 94, 133, 202, 204, 362-3, 391-2
Gambella 171, 239, 433

Garang, J Ukel. vii, xii, xvi, xvi, xix, xx, xxi, xxi, 29, 35, 40, 43-5, 49-50, 53-5, 84-5, 91, 102, 177, 182-3, 186, 193-200, 202-7, 210, 212, 214-7, 224-5, 227-9, 233, 235, 238, 247, 252-3, 256, 260, 264-7, 269-272, 283-4, 288, 298-9, 303, 308-9, 322, 325, 328, 331-341, 361, 372, 374, 393, 407, 415, 443-4, 448, 455, 459, 461, 468, 477-8, 483-5
Gatkuoth 141, 172
Gatluak 60-61, 63-4, 67-8, 75, 362, 364, 404-6, 421, 431, 460
Gatwech 69, 364-5, 430-2
Gawaar 429
Ge 430
Genesis 288
George 131, 197, 315, 323, 367
German 173, 367
Germans 428
Germany 367
Gezira 37, 171

Ghazal xx, 92, 153, 179, 224, 252, 305, 316, 342, 362, 431, 437
Giap 240, 298
Gibril 73, 75
Gier 444
Gismalla 119, 141
God 464
Gogrial 153, 159-160, 341, 369, 433, 443
Gollo 482
Gordon 131, 201, 219
Gosh 60
Greek 315
Guevara 199, 242, 297
Guffa 110
Gulf 348, 354
Guma 110
Guterres 321
Haag 92
Hague 56, 76
Haile 37, 70, 99-100, 129, 239, 247, 252, 280, 322, 398, 420
Hale, Sondra. 484
Halfawiyieen 166
Halle 484
Hamdalla 99
Hamdan 72-75, 78
Hamdok 73-75, 77
Hanssen, Halle Jørn. 484
Hassan xxx, 27, 38-9, 45-6, 71, 83, 91, 120, 178, 304, 399, 402
Heglig 55, 57
Hercules 126
Hibou, B. 366, 486
Hilary 107, 118, 440
Hilde 484
Hilu 94, 338
Hobbes xxx
Hol 375
Hon 152, 208, 387
Hufra 482
Hungary 116, 172
Hussien 94
Ibid 173
Ibn 72-73
Ibrahim 21, 27, 30, 38, 45, 55, 91, 110
Idris, Amir. 485
Ifoto 441
Igga ix, xii, 94, 351, 362
Ignorance 85

Imam 33, 171-2
Imama 155
Imatong 441, 482
Implementable 388
Infancy xxi, 484
Ingaz 50, 73, 153, 233, 235, 321, 459
Insecure 387
Intibaha 54
Intifada 236
Introductory 283
Iraq 98, 368
Isaih 241
Isiash 240
Islam 13, 82, 93, 96, 190
Islamist 21, 260
Islamization 21-22, 30, 91
Ismael 17, 398
Ismail 13, 18, 21, 29, 71
Israeli 243
Itang 201-202, 217, 235, 248, 280, 299, 336-7
Ithaca 483
Jaden 100, 131, 140, 157
Jakaya 386
James ix, xii, 25, 94, 123-5, 127-8, 152, 172, 346, 351, 362, 486
Jamus 235-236
Jarad 236
Jebel 396
Jekau 202, 237-8
Jerry 77, 111
Jersy 484
Jie 438
Jieng 84, 159, 230-1, 275, 389, 429, 431, 482
Jikany 65, 153, 376, 380
Jinubieen 158
Jiye 482
John vii, xii, xvi, xvi, xix, xx, xxi, xxi, 40, 43-4, 49, 53, 84-5, 91, 102, 182-3, 186, 193-9, 204-7, 212-4, 216-7, 224, 227-9, 233, 235, 247, 252-3, 256, 264, 266, 269-272, 274, 283-4, 288, 298, 303, 308, 322, 332-4, 336, 338, 340-1, 361, 372, 393, 407, 415, 443-4, 448, 455, 461, 468, 477, 483, 485

Johnson, Hilde F. 69, 364-5, 430-1, 484

Jonglei xii, 66, 80, 109-110, 122, 125, 155, 184, 223, 304, 351, 360, 365-6, 397, 425, 432, 436, 454

Joseph 24-25, 29, 35, 69, 93, 99, 101-2, 107-8, 111-5, 119, 122-8, 130, 133-4, 140-3, 145, 147-9, 152, 155, 158, 172-3, 188, 190, 198, 204-5, 223, 233, 397, 440, 460-1, 484

Joshua 368

Juba vii, vii, xi, xvi, 1-5, 15-6, 20, 22, 24, 32, 45, 55, 58, 60, 68, 74, 77, 80-1, 86-7, 106-110, 114-5, 117-8, 121, 125-6, 128-9, 137, 139, 141, 145, 151, 179, 183-5, 190-3, 195, 220, 222, 257-8, 281-2, 288, 304, 310, 320, 327, 330-1, 345-6, 363-5, 368-9, 375-6, 384, 387, 391-2, 395-400, 403, 406-8, 419, 421, 427-9, 431, 461, 464-5, 483

Jur 335, 427, 482

Justin 172

Juuk 257, 362, 444

Kabashi 241

Kaguta 399, 402

Kakwa 153, 482

Kampala 168, 173, 232, 343, 354-5, 387, 484

Kapoeta 162, 289, 305, 316, 328, 331, 355, 437

Kapur 105

Karl 82

Karzai 280

Kassala 72, 134

Katire 329-330

Kazuk 236

Kegan 484

Keliku 482

Ken 281

Kenya 12, 24-5, 41, 94, 168, 231, 247-8, 254, 263, 283, 285, 287-8, 290, 294, 304-5, 313, 316, 344, 349, 352, 372, 376-7, 418, 450, 461

Kenyan xii, 252, 306, 314, 325, 382, 386

Kenyetta 386, 390

Kerrari 7

Kerubino 192-194, 200, 205, 207, 217-9, 238, 256, 266, 284, 334, 336, 444
Khalid, Mansour. 23, 484
Khalifa 7
Khalil 21, 26, 38, 73
Khaliq 35
Khartoum vii, xix, 1-3, 24, 31-2, 37, 39, 43, 45, 48, 59, 63, 66, 68, 70, 72, 74, 77-8, 93, 100, 107-8, 110, 112, 116, 119, 126, 128, 132-4, 137, 144-5, 150-1, 155-6, 165, 172, 178, 182-5, 189-191, 195, 260, 320, 327, 331, 334, 364, 399, 402-3, 406, 420, 456, 484
Khatimiya 8-9, 33, 99, 178
Khor xii
Kiir vii, ix, x, xii, xii, xx, xxi, xxx, 44-8, 55-6, 59-64, 66-70, 74, 76-7, 79, 81, 84-6, 92-4, 161, 194, 200, 207, 212, 217, 220, 229-230, 256, 260-2, 266-8, 272, 274-5, 284, 295, 321, 326, 332-7, 339-342, 344-7, 349, 353, 357, 361, 363, 365, 367-9, 374-5, 378, 382-394, 396-7, 399, 402-7, 410, 416-421, 430-2, 435, 443, 445, 455, 462, 468-9, 477
Kikwete 386-387
Kinyetti 329
Koang 219
Koat 25, 124-5, 219
Kodok xi, 80-1
Koma 437, 482
Kongor 93, 227
Kony 69-70, 93, 460
Koor 369, 397, 431
Kordofan xxi, 17, 42-3, 48-9, 103, 460
Koreas 367
Koryom 237
Kosti 24, 31, 116-7, 189
Kriesh 482
Kuai 99
Kuanyin 192-194, 205, 217, 219, 266, 284, 334, 336, 444
Kuch 369
Kujur 396
Kuku xii, 231, 439, 482
Kuol 257, 362, 420, 444

Kur 7
Kurmuk 110, 337
Kwanai 131, 323, 367
Kwongo 81, 365
Laak 429
Lado 2-3, 200, 213, 323-4, 326
Lago 25, 233, 440
Lagu, Joseph. 24, 38, 99, 101-2, 111-5, 119, 122-3, 126, 130, 132-4, 138, 140-3, 145, 147-9, 152, 155, 157-8, 172-3, 188, 190, 198, 484
Lam 332, 334-5, 368-9, 397, 403, 405, 443
Lancaster xxv
Lango 482
Latin 188, 243
Laura 484
Law 293, 486
Lawrence 25, 153
Lazaro 377, 408
Leonaur 485
Lesotho 486
Lewis, David Levering. 486
Liberation v, xxi, xxv, xxi, xxx, 23, 37, 41-2, 75, 93, 99, 175, 180-1, 199, 209-210, 220, 238, 245, 259, 268, 279, 300, 367, 419, 462, 484
Libya 98, 260
Libyan 98, 300
Lifeline xxx, 248, 283, 302, 305, 316
Limestone 162
Lino 182, 195, 197, 483
Litmus 65
Lofi 481
Logali 107, 118, 440
Logir 482
Lokichogio 248, 313
Lokoya 441, 443, 482
Lokurnyang 200, 213
London 37, 483-4, 486
Lou xii, 8, 65-6, 202, 277, 376, 380, 438, 454, 460
Loya 229
Luach 231, 375
Lual 133
Lugbwara 481
Luigi 107, 440
Lulubo 481
Luo 94, 443, 481
Maaban 153, 366, 454, 481

Mabior vii, x, xvi, xix, xx, xxi, 43-4, 91, 94, 182-3, 194-5, 197, 199, 205, 212, 217, 224, 233, 271, 283-4, 333, 338, 363, 375, 403, 415, 444, 461, 477, 485

Mach 107, 118

Machar vii, ix, x, xii, 56, 59-61, 63-4, 66, 69, 74, 80-1, 84, 92, 94, 220, 227, 331-2, 334-5, 346, 362-5, 368-9, 374-8, 380-3, 385, 387, 389-392, 396-8, 400, 403-7, 410, 416, 418-9, 430-1, 443

Madi 231, 366, 481

Madut 173, 228, 369, 479

Mahathir 18

Mahdi 8, 45, 178, 308

Mahdist 6-7, 485

Mahdists 7

Mahdiya 5-6, 86

Mahgoub 32-33, 35

Mahommed 97

Mairum 350

Maiwut 202

Majesty 81

Majier 133, 204-5

Makaraka 424, 481

Makuac xii

Malaath 205

Malakal xi, 24, 32, 65, 81, 126, 258, 281, 288, 304, 328, 330, 351, 376, 380

Malath 133

Malaysia 18-19, 82

Mali 78, 93

Malik 73

Malong 392, 397

Malual 119, 124, 127, 152, 172, 228, 236, 238, 479, 483

Mama vii

Mandari 481

Mangalla 138

Manime 60, 362

Mansour 23, 484

Manyang 257, 362, 420, 444

Manyiel 289-290

Manyo 80, 365, 429, 432

Mao 233, 249, 297, 300, 486

Mapinduzi 386

Marchand 7

Marginalizing 329

Mariam 70, 239, 247, 252, 322, 386, 398, 420

Maridi 349
Marshall xxv, 23, 38, 129
Marx 28, 82
Marxism 36
Marxist xxx, 26, 89, 211
Masalit 166
Mathok 75
Matip xx, 60, 267, 282, 339
Matthew 92, 123-4, 126-8, 158, 171
Matthews 25, 125, 153, 219
Matthysen 281
Maulana 117, 143, 394
Mauritania 78
Mayardit vii, ix, xx, xxi, 44, 47, 55, 61, 92, 194, 200, 212, 217, 229-230, 266, 272, 274-5, 284, 295, 321, 332-3, 335, 337, 339-340, 346, 353, 367, 374, 393, 402-3, 435, 443, 445, 468, 477
Mayen 131, 201
Mayom 91, 460-1
Maz 10
Mbeki 55
Mbili 141
Mboro 152, 157, 440

Medani 72, 134
Mediation 371
Melut 80, 138, 168
Memoria xvi
Menawi 73
Mengistu 41, 234, 236, 239, 247, 252, 264, 322-3
Mesfin, Seyoum. 376, 385, 408, 419-420, 485
Mesquita 485
Militarization 215
Military 10, 27-8, 30, 32, 72-3, 77, 219, 222, 458, 486
Millard 486
Minami 60
Mini 73
Mirror 107
Mkuki 485
Moammar 237
Mobutu 460
Mogae 390, 402, 408
Mohammed xxv, 3, 23-4, 32-3, 45, 49, 54-5, 71-5, 78, 93, 95, 105, 109, 121, 130, 140, 149, 191, 198, 253, 399, 408
Monytuil 92, 461
Moro 152-153, 241, 438, 481

Morokodo 439, 481
Mortat 131, 201
Moyo 483
Muller 281
Mundari 125, 454
Mundiri 99, 131, 140, 157, 440
Mundu 241, 481
Murahalieen 92
Murle xii, 277, 279, 366-7, 433, 438, 454, 479, 481
Museveni 66, 69-70, 355, 383, 386-7, 399, 402
Music 325
Muslim 10, 15, 27, 33, 37, 52, 82, 96, 120, 133
Muslims 13, 15, 144, 189
Mustafa 54
Myopia 83
Nahof 72-73
Nairobi vii, 41, 66, 168, 248, 282, 290, 294, 343, 354, 376, 382
Naka 481
Nasir 91, 93, 125, 202, 217, 219-220, 254, 292, 303, 305, 315, 336, 369, 372, 380, 418

Nasserites 34, 98
Nationalism 220, 486
Nationalities vi, 225, 441, 481
Ndogo 481
Ngachigak 200
Ngachiluk 200
Ngok 89, 366, 375
Ngok Dinka xxx
Ngor 194
Ngungule 481
Nhial xx, 34, 60, 177-8, 203, 267, 335, 339, 369
Nic 282
Nicaragua 259
Nicolson 486
Niger 78
Nigeria 87, 103, 341
Nigerian 341
Nigers 93
Nile xx, xxi, xxx, xxx, 6, 8, 10, 12-3, 16-8, 20, 22, 41-3, 48-9, 64, 89, 92-3, 96, 101, 103, 107, 110, 115, 122-3, 125, 127, 129, 145, 153-4, 165, 171, 184, 186, 190-1, 193, 228, 231-2, 234, 243, 248-9, 278, 287, 304-6, 316-7, 324,

326, 331, 351, 358, 362, 364, 368, 373, 376, 389, 397, 407, 417-8, 427, 429-433, 436-7, 454, 478
Nille 119
Nilotic 311
Nilotics 81, 324
Nimule 162, 256, 304
Nobody 253
Noma xxi
Nonetheless 137
Norway 48
Norwegian 311, 378, 484
Notwithstanding 54, 374, 442, 466
Nuba xxv, xxx, 6, 10, 17-8, 30, 41, 43, 89-91, 94-5, 165-7, 176, 181, 186, 232-4, 249, 253-4, 278, 287, 326, 373, 478
Nubawi 171
Nubians 7, 10, 144
Nuer xi, xii, xx, 60, 63-6, 68, 80, 85, 93, 153-4, 172, 201-2, 222-4, 226-7, 267, 277, 281, 307, 311, 339-340, 346, 362, 365, 369, 375-6, 428-430, 432-4, 436-8, 443-5, 454, 460
Nuers 93, 369, 375, 400, 428, 431-2
Numeiri xxv, 23-4, 34, 37-8, 42, 95, 97-100, 102-3, 105-7, 109-110, 112, 114, 117, 119-121, 123-4, 126, 128-132, 134, 137, 140, 142, 144-5, 149-151, 155-6, 172, 189-190, 193, 196, 237, 263
Numeri 191, 193
Nuqud 45, 55
Nur 99
Nyaba, P. A. xvi, 484-5
Nyandeng vii, x, 61, 94, 363, 375, 378, 403, 444
Nyangatom 481
Nyangwara 153, 482
Nyarweng 375, 429
Nyidhok 7
Nyiepo 439, 482
Nyilek 171
Nyota 485
Nyuon 171, 194, 200, 205, 207, 217, 266, 284, 334, 336, 445
Nzara 20, 162, 171, 330

Oakpast 485
Obama 392
Obang 124-125
Obeid 31, 134
Obote 233
Obur 123-124, 126-8, 158
Oduho 107-108, 133, 204-5, 223
Ojway 124-125
Okiech x, xii, 56, 338
Olony 430-431
Omdurman 1, 171, 484
Omer xxx, 46-7, 54, 56, 64, 66, 69, 71-2, 74, 91, 93, 102, 399, 402
Oress 483
Osama 69
Oslo 484
Osman 40, 49, 54, 253
Othwonh 124-125
Otor 131
Otto 367
Otuho 153, 224, 433, 437-8, 441, 482
Oweci xi
Oxford 486
Oyay 282, 338-9

Padang 231, 346, 389, 426, 430-2, 436, 444, 454
Padiet 81, 124-5, 365
Pagak 391
Palestinian 82
Panyagor 315
Panyikango 65, 417, 426
Parasitic 259, 357
Pari 94, 224, 482
Paris 116, 172
Pasha 485
Patrick 486
Paul 107, 118, 240-1, 392, 397, 440, 484
Paulino xx, 267, 282, 339
Paweny 231
Peking 486
Penal 459
Pete 485
Peter xvi, 141, 172, 279, 281
Petros 419
Pibor xii, 183, 192, 277, 304, 366, 438
Pigi 444
Poalino 60
Pochalla 304, 337, 438, 444
Pojulu 153, 482

Polity 483
Portuguese 428
Powel 42
Prah, K. K.. 486
Preliminary 1, 175
Pretoria 387
Prof 218
Puntland 449-450
Quan 18
Quran 150
Rafi 483
Raga 437
Rahad 212, 248
Rahaman 8, 39
Ramaphosa 386, 418
Rasas 119, 124, 141
Rath 7, 81, 365
Rebecca vii, x, 61, 94, 363, 375, 378, 403, 444
Reconquest 483
Reech 173, 369
Regis 170, 180, 271
Rehabilitation 290, 292
Rek 153, 161, 358, 366, 434, 454
Renaissance 380
Renk 80, 168, 389, 479
Reno 263
Requiem 20, 272
Resurrection 162
Revitalization xxx, 66, 70, 396, 398, 401, 409
Revitalized vi, 362, 402
Riek vii, ix, x, xii, 55, 59-61, 63-4, 66, 69, 74, 80-1, 84, 92, 94, 220, 227, 331-2, 334-5, 346, 362-5, 368-9, 374-8, 380-3, 385, 387, 389-392, 396-9, 403-7, 410, 416, 418-9, 430-1, 443
Riel 482
Riiny 173, 369
Robotization 251
Rolf 141
Rome 36
Rt 126
Ruben 107, 118
Rudolf 485
Rumbek vii, 22, 34, 53, 159, 178, 209, 282, 311-2, 336-7, 369, 433
Russia 477
Russian 352
Rut 429

Ruweng 277, 366-7
Rwanda 358, 428
Sadeq 193
Sadiq 33, 38, 40-1, 45, 178, 304, 308
Saharawi 449-450
Salaam 485
Salah 60
Salihieen 108
Salva vii, ix, x, xii, xx, xxi, xxx, xxx, 43-8, 55-6, 59-64, 66-70, 74, 76-7, 79, 81, 84-6, 92-4, 161, 194, 200, 207, 212, 217, 220, 229-231, 256, 260-2, 266-8, 272, 274-5, 284, 295, 321, 332-7, 339-347, 349, 351, 353, 357, 360-3, 365, 367-9, 374-5, 378, 382-394, 396-7, 399, 402-7, 410-1, 416-421, 430-2, 435, 443, 445, 455, 462, 468-9, 477
Salvation 397
Samson 143
Samuel 133, 159, 173, 202, 241
Sandinistas 259
Saudi 93, 354
Sayed 13, 46, 177-8
Sayyed 33-34, 178, 304
Schouten 281
Scotland vii, xii
Secession 100
Secretariat 275, 395
Seke 460
Seko 460
Selassie 37, 99-100, 129
Sellasie 280
Sennar 138
Seri 482
Seyoum 376, 385, 408, 419-420, 485
Shaabia 238
Shabab 418, 461
Sharief 116
Shatt 94, 482
Shilluk 17, 81, 153, 222, 224, 229, 231, 365, 369
Siamese 51, 91
Sidney 343
Simon 69, 364-5, 430-2
Singapore 18-19, 82
Sirr 32
Slatin, Pasha Rudolf C. 485
Smith, Alastair. 485

Sobat 304
Socioeconomic 347
Solomon 419
Somalia xxv, 284, 379, 418, 449
Somalis 355
Sondra 484
Southerners 21, 158
Soviet xxi, 36, 323, 478
Spanish 428
Stephen 219
Suda 439
Sudan v, vi, vii, vii, ix, x, xi, xii, xii, xiv, xv, xvi, xvi, xvi, xix, xx, xxi, xxi, xxi, xxi, xxv, xxv, xxv, xxv, xxi, xxx, xxx, xxx, xxx, xxx, xxx, xxx, 1-35, 37-62, 64-72, 74-80, 82-93, 95-109, 112, 114-7, 119-122, 126-7, 129-139, 141-152, 154-6, 158, 160-173, 175-189, 191-3, 197-9, 201-3, 206, 210, 212-3, 216-8, 220-5, 227-233, 235, 237-240, 242, 244-9, 251-4, 257-264, 267-9, 271-4, 277-9, 281, 283-308, 311, 313-6, 319-327, 332-4, 337-341, 343-8, 350-363, 365-9, 371-380, 382-395, 397-403, 405, 407-412, 414-421, 423-437, 439-444, 447-455, 457-8, 460-479, 481, 483-6
Sudanese vii, vii, xxi, xxi, xxi, xxv, xxv, xxv, xxi, xxx, xxx, 1-17, 19-20, 22-9, 31-2, 34-5, 37, 39-44, 46-8, 50, 52-4, 61-2, 66-7, 71, 74-5, 77-8, 81-6, 88-91, 95-8, 103-6, 108, 116-7, 120, 122, 130, 133-5, 138-9, 141-7, 155, 158, 165-6, 168-9, 173, 175-181, 183, 186-190, 195-9, 202, 206-7, 211-2, 215, 218, 225, 231-3, 235-6, 246, 248, 253-4, 272, 278, 284-5, 288, 290-2, 298, 303-5, 309, 314, 317, 323-5, 351, 356, 373, 384, 388, 398-9, 419, 425, 428, 435, 439, 441, 448, 450-2, 466, 468, 475-8, 484
Sudanization 28
Sudans 2-3, 484
Sudd 394

Sue 323-324
Suez 5
Sumbeiweyo 377, 408
Sunday 22, 30, 91
Suri 279, 438, 482
Swaka 397
Swar 73, 173
Synopsis 95
Syria 98
Taban vii, 94, 362-3, 391-2, 419
Tah 49, 54, 253
Taliban 69, 280
Tambura 25, 123-5, 127-8, 152, 172, 349
Tandon 353, 355, 486
Tanzania 94, 344, 386
Tauris 484
Temitope 341
Teny 376, 392
Terikeka 115, 361
Thabo 55
Thao 56, 92
Thiik 173, 369
Thirdly 104, 195, 336, 432
Thomases 177
Thon 194, 217, 256, 266, 334, 336, 445
Thubo 69, 364-5, 431
Tid 439, 482
Tigray 41, 181, 234, 237, 247, 259, 279, 284
Tigrayan 182
Timsah 85, 235
Tokar 281
Tom 77, 110
Tonga 365, 417, 430
Tonj 159, 178, 328, 369, 433
Toposa xii, 153, 307, 433, 437-8, 444, 482
Torit vii, 16-7, 19-20, 22, 29, 105, 135, 279, 289, 304-5, 437-8
Trajan xxi
Trenton 484
Tribalism 135, 149, 156, 159
Tripartite 293, 303
Tripoli 37
Troika 94, 402
Tuhami 116
Turabi 27, 178
Turkiya 5-8, 12
Tut xii, 60-1, 63-4, 67-8, 74-5, 133, 202, 362, 364, 369,

404-6, 421, 431, 460
Twic xii, 228, 366
Uduk 482
Uganda xvi, 1, 24-5, 66-7, 70-1, 93-4, 104, 148, 168, 173, 231, 233, 254, 263, 282, 285, 288, 294, 304-5, 316, 324, 344, 349, 352, 355-6, 372, 377, 379, 386, 402, 418
Ugandan 66, 69, 305, 314, 386
Ugandans 305
Uhuru 386, 390
Ukel 35, 484
Ulang 315
Umma 9, 12, 21, 26, 29, 32-3, 40, 45, 96, 134, 171, 178
Unionist 12, 29
Unity xx, 46, 80, 121, 123, 172, 282, 351, 362, 366, 376, 398, 419
Unmaking 115
Untold 484
Usman 33
Ustaz 49, 54, 228, 253, 447, 479
Vatican vii, 363

Vice 351
Vide 293
Vietnam 221, 367
Vietnamese 36, 298
Violence 484
Wad 171
Wahid 75
Wai ix
Wais 71, 398
Wajo 152
Wani xii, 94, 346, 351, 362
Wanji 218
Warille 107
Warrap xii, 63-4, 80, 85, 93, 160, 340-1, 350, 358, 360, 366, 397, 434, 443-4, 454, 463
Watajwok 32
Wau xi, 32, 81, 126, 141, 198, 241, 258, 279, 288, 310, 330, 427, 437
Waweru 317
Weidenfeld 486
Wel 485
West 93, 138, 367, 418, 450
Westminster 30
William 34, 133, 171, 177-8,

193-4, 200, 203, 205, 207, 217, 238, 263, 266, 284, 334, 336, 445
Winston 483
Wol 25, 75, 133, 153
Women 98, 294
Wunlit 457
Yac 172
Yam 105
Yambio vii, 240-1, 249-250, 310, 349
Yash Tandon. 353, 355, 486
Yasir 46
Yassir 46-47
Yei xx, 92, 217, 220, 266, 328, 334, 336, 349
Yemen xxv, 93, 260
Yoweri 66, 69, 386, 399, 402
Yu 18
Yugoslavia 108, 361
Yugoslavs 108
Yulu 482
Zaghawa 166
Zaire 241
Zambia 282
Zande 433, 482
Zedong 249, 297, 300
Ziet 108
Zimbabwe 12, 260, 282

www.ingramcontent.com/pod-product-compliance
Lightning Source LLC
Chambersburg PA
CBHW031358290426
44110CB00011B/199